Anthropology as an Aid to Moral Science

ANTONIO ROSMINI

ANTHROPOLOGY AS AN AID TO MORAL SCIENCE

Translated by
DENIS CLEARY
and
TERENCE WATSON

ROSMINI HOUSE
DURHAM

Rosmini House, Woodbine Road
Durham DH1 5DR, U.K.

Translated from
Antropologia in Servizio della Scienza Morale
Critical edition, Stresa 1981

Cover photo: Adam and Eve,
from a 13th century fresco in the church of
St. John at the Latin Gate, Rome.

Typeset by Rosmini House
Printed by Courier International Ltd.

ISBN 0 9513211 4 5

Note

Square brackets [ ] indicate an editor's note or addition.

[. . .] indicates an omission from the text.

References to this and other works of Rosmini are given by paragraph number unless otherwise stated.

Abbreviations used for Rosmini's quoted works are:

AMS: *Anthropology as an Aid to Moral Science*
PE: *Principles of Ethics*
OT: *The Origin of Thought*
CE: *Certainty*

Foreword

The aim of this foreword is to indicate the place of Rosmini's *Anthropology* in his moral system, to describe schematically the work itself, and to indicate its present importance and usefulness.

Rosmini in his *New Essay on the Origin of Ideas*[1] had elaborated a theory of knowledge dependent upon the innate light of being as a foundation of his philosophical work. This light, an essential constitutive of human intelligence, is not a subjective ingredient of knowledge, but an objective element of thought characterised by qualities superior to the finite being, to whom it is conceded. It illuminates subjective human feeling, which it makes intellectually perceivable.

On this basis, Rosmini founded his theory of moral science which he developed in four works dealing respectively with the principles of ethics, the philosophical history of the development of systems of morality, the human being as subject of morality, and the application of the principles to the actions of this subject.

In *Principles of Ethics*[2] Rosmini examines the nature of good, of natural law, intrinsic evil, obligation, and of the will as an essential component of every moral act. In his *Storia comparativa e critica dei sistemi morali*[3] he shows clearly the sources on which he had drawn in propounding his own teaching. This he evaluates and clarifies in the light of the deficiencies or excesses inherent to moral systems prior to his time. Finally, he draws the ultimate conclusions of moral science in *Conscience*[4] by showing how the principles of ethics are to be applied reflectively by individuals to their own actions.

Still lacking, however, is any systematic examination of the nature of the subjects of morality, that is, human beings who, possessed of the light of intelligence and quickened by feeling, have to govern

(1) *Nuovo Saggio sull'origine delle idee*, Rome 1830. The second volume of this work has been translated under the title, *The Origin of Thought*, Durham 1989 (2nd edition).

(2) *Principi della scienza morale*, Intra 1867. Translated as *Principles of Ethics*, Durham 1989 (2nd edition).

(3) Critical edition, Stresa 1991.

(4) *Trattato della coscienza morale*, Milan 1844. Translated as *Conscience*, Durham 1989.

reason and instinct with their will according to the dictates of the moral law impressed upon their nature. This gap is filled by Rosmini's *Anthropology as an Aid to Moral Science*: 'In *Principles of Ethics* I presented the theory of moral law and obligation. But the theory has to be applied, and we must be careful not to err in its application . . . we have to know intimately the subject . . . to which the theory is applied. Hence the necessity for . . . an anthropology which provides us with knowledge of human nature relative to morality'(1).

This anthropology is concerned with the whole human being in its essence and in all the activities which have their root in that essence, and solely in that essence (Rosmini is not concerned here with human beings as subjects of any action of God's grace which would raise them to a supernatural level). He simply observes what nature has to offer, and reflects upon that. From the beginning, his observations enable him to define the human being clearly, if not briefly, in a way that foreshadows the complete account of human nature that he intends to give in developing his study.

The human being is 'an animal subject endowed with the intuition of indeterminate, ideal being and with the perception of its own corporeal, fundamental feeling, and operating in accordance with animality and intelligence' (23). On the basis of this definition Rosmini is able to order his work by examining in turn the constitutive elements of human nature — the corporeal term, the feeling principle, the fundamental corporeal feeling, instinct, intelligence, ideal being, will, reason — and of person, the high point of human existence. He does this under three main headings: animality, spirituality and the human subject.

In dealing with the animal part of the human being, Rosmini first distinguishes between the passive and active faculties that lie at the basis of feeling and instinct before showing how feeling and instinct act together within animality to provide the animal subject with all that it needs for preservation and generation. Of particular importance here is Rosmini's insistence that the corporeal term cannot be understood without reference to an immaterial principle, the *anima* (soul), and his conviction that instinct, the reaction of this principle, cannot be discussed in material terms alone. The well-being of the animal will depend on the harmony or discord produced in feeling by the differing capacities of the life instinct and the sensuous instinct. Illness, for example, will be the result of the disharmony produced by the prevalence of the sensuous instinct over the life instinct.

It is important to note that Rosmini's conclusions in this section of his work are not the result of speculation. They depend upon his own and others' observation, and the use of principles necessary to provide an explanation of these observations. He also makes use of scientific discoveries in so far as they provide an additional source of observation. Consequently, his conclusions, especially those concerned with the nature of feeling and of the body, with the activity of instinct and the fundamental causes of animal well-being, are not only valid today but would, if rightly used, throw a good deal of light on matters, such as the nature of digestion and of death, that remain a mystery .

But the human being is not only an animal. Careful examination and observation (a pre-requisite for Rosmini in all his work) reveal the existence of something more in human beings than in mere animals. Intellect and reason on the one hand, and will and freedom on the other, are respectively the active and passive faculties that constitute the human spirit. *Intellect* as the power that intuits ideal being is a presupposition of *reason* which applies the idea of being to feelings, and provides human beings with the functions of abstraction and reflection.

The active powers of *will* and *freedom* receive very extensive treatment, as we would expect in an anthropology intended as an aid to moral science. The human act, the willed act, the moral act, the act of choice, the free act and the intellective act are all analysed at length with particular attention being paid to freedom.

The liberty possessed by us as developed human beings is exercised when we are placed in the position of having to choose between an objective good (which is good in itself, and known as such intellectually) and a subjective good (that by which the subject is attracted irrespective of the place in the order of being of that subjective good). As a result of the choice we make, we find ourselves exercising morally or immorally the supreme human activity that enhances or degrades us as persons. This activity differs in moral quality from that produced by other individual faculties in the human being each of which if permitted acts unilaterally and of its own accord.

The final section of the work is devoted to a synthetic view of the human subject. Making use of his detailed analysis of the individual elements constituting the human subject, Rosmini is able finally to offer a definition of *person* in general and of the human person in particular. Every person is 'an intellective subject in so far as it contains a supreme active principle', that is, an independent and incommunicable principle. Perhaps the most important words of this definition are 'in so far as'. They indicate the essential element of person, the substantial relationship which, as substantial, provides the intelligent subject with that supreme act constituting the subject as independent and incommunicable. '"Person" cannot mean simply either a *substance* or a *relationship*. It must mean a *substantial relationship*, that is, a relationship found in the *intrinsic order of being* of a substance' (833, ftn. 395). When these constitutive, ontological elements of person are found in the human subject, we have arrived at the concept of human person.

The supreme, active principle in the human subject is the will, first as intellectually instinctive reaction in the undeveloped being, and then as free reaction in the growing person. The ontological relationship between this supreme activity and the individual powers of human nature is such that nature, when freely activated, is to be subject to the objective power and dominion of the will. When this is not the case, and the will allows itself to be dominated simply by the acts of nature, immorality rules in the human person.

It is clear that for Rosmini 'person', as the fount of moral, human action, is the foundation of all right in human relationships because its very own worth is drawn from that which ultimately forms the human, intellective subject. 'This moral excellence and superiority by right, which elevates the human person above the whole of nature, must have the same source as all morality and right. This source is the light of reason, the source of right and of moral good and evil' (848).

Thus we return to the starting point: the light of reason, the idea of being, superior to human nature yet forming the inmost core of that nature, and now seen to be the spark of divinity shared by the human spirit. It is this light which makes persons ends, not means, and provides the foundation for immensely important conclusions relative to daily existence.

But before we deal with present-day matters touching directly upon the human person as such, it will be necessary to indicate underlying problems which, although greatly neglected today, are treated by Rosmini as essential prerequisites to serious meditation upon the sacred reality of person. Briefly we may say that Rosmini in his *Anthropology* stimulates thought at several different levels of perennial interest and at points of immediate, vital importance for us today.

First, he offers a thorough examination of the problem of materialism, and concludes that body can neither be understood without soul, nor confused with soul. His conclusion is not, however, rooted in some *a priori* necessity demanding the distinct existence of body and soul. Rather, he takes his stand on observation and then goes on to deduce reflectively the essential elements required to make the facts of observation intelligible.

The same method, which is constant throughout the work, enables him to deal at length, and very satisfactorily, with the difference between what he calls the subjective and extrasubjective elements in feeling. All feeling springing from the union between one's own body and soul is subjective; feeling dependent upon the perception of bodies other than one's own is extrasubjective. This very important distinction opens the way to further clarifications about the nature of body and soul within the animal sphere.

Second, Rosmini's work on instinct provides ground for dealing with the problem of apparent intelligence in animals. In particular, he examines the nature of the unity of feeling and instinct in the animal. This part of his work, taken in conjunction with the elaboration of the distinction between subjective and extrasubjective within the ambit of feeling, is the most original and helpful in the section of the book on animality. And although Rosmini makes extensive use of the scientific knowledge of his own time, it will easily be seen that such knowledge provides what we may call an atmosphere consonant with his conclusions rather than substantiation of them. In other words, his philosophical results are clarified, not proved by the scientific knowledge available in the first half of the nineteenth century. At the same time, it is evident that the philosophical conclusions themselves are often indications for the path to be taken in the progress of scientific knowledge. If there is indeed an immaterial element effective in the constitution of the animal, it is impossible for medicine to restrict research into the elimination of pain and illness to the chemical composition of the body, just as work on psychological problems would be deficient if it took no account of chemistry and related sciences in tackling these problems.

Third, in the section of the *Anthropology* on spirituality Rosmini lays the foundations for a sure grasp of the essential difference and comprehensive unity between animal soul and intelligent, willing spirit. In this part of the work, he is not dealing with spirituality in any religious sense, but simply with the spirit, that part of human beings which distinguishes them from what is animal. Here finally, at the apex of human existence, he deals with will and freedom, and their relationship with morality, the aim of the entire work. In the last analysis, only our voluntary acceptance of things as we know them through our direct knowledge enables us to embrace interiorly and freely all that is. Morality is not an imposition upon human subjects, but the willed perfection and completion of the human subject that enables these subjects to acquiesce in the unlimited dignity for which their intellectual nature provides the essential repository.

It should now be possible to comprehend the usefulness of Rosmini's work in today's world. Above all, we find ourselves in need of a suitable basis for the development of our understanding of the nature of human rights. Are they simply something granted by positive law, or public opinion, or are they innate in individuals? If they are innate, what is their source? Is it the simple existence of the human being, so easily swept away? Or the presence within human beings of something which provides them with inviolable dignity even when they, as babes in the womb, as children, as handicapped mentally or physically, are physically and mentally defenceless? And in the end, are human rights simply a bundle of privileges to be respected in some way according to circumstances, or the growth from a single seed of a single inviolable right which is to be respected in its essence despite occasional, inevitable limitations of parts of its exercise? The basis for answers to these questions is provided in this *Anthropology*.

DENIS CLEARY
TERENCE WATSON

Durham,
January, 1992.

Contents

BOOK 2
ANIMALITY

SECTION ONE
THE PASSIVE ANIMAL FACULTIES

SECTION TWO

THE ACTIVE ANIMAL FACULTIES OR INSTINCT

BOOK 3
SPIRITUALITY

SECTION ONE
THE *PASSIVE* FACULTIES OF HUMAN UNDERSTANDING

SECTION TWO

THE *ACTIVE* FACULTIES OF HUMAN UNDERSTANDING

BOOK 4
THE HUMAN SUBJECT

Dedication

This *Anthropology*, newly corrected and improved, is dedicated to the Royal Academy of Sciences of Turin as a sign of gratitude for my election to membership, and to draw the attention of its members to the psychological and physiological investigations which form the object of the study and are so important for the progress of the science of the human being, and for the good of humanity. I hope that the complex nature of these investigations and the difficulty of establishing them on a firm foundation will allow you, my illustrious colleagues of the Academy, to forgive the imperfections of the work, and enable me to gain your co-operation in perfecting it. If the book should seem worthy of your study, science will have gained simply from the judgment you bring to it, and I will be your debtor.

A. Rosmini

Stresa, 27th July 1846

Introduction

1. In *Principles of Ethics* I presented the theory of moral law and obligation.[1] But the theory has to be applied, and we must be very careful not to err in its application. Consequently, we have to know intimately the subject, the human being, to which the theory is applied. Hence the necessity for prefacing *applied morality* and the *science of applying the supreme law*[2] with an *anthropology* which provides us with knowledge of human nature relative to morality. My intention in writing this book is to propose such an anthropology as an aid to moral science.

2. Obviously, it must not be thought that everything can be said about the human being in this study, even in a general sense. 'This little world', as the ancient writers called it, is not so quickly dismissed. Indeed, even the little we know about ourselves is sufficient to form not one but many sciences. There are innumerable disciplines which have human beings as their object. Considered from the point of view of bodily health, the human being is the object of medical science; considered as founder and member of civil society, the human being is the

[1] The *obligating force* is the formal part of laws. I have shown that the first law of all obliges in itself and is itself the obligating force. It is therefore the *form* of all other laws. Cf. *Storia comparativa e critica de' sistemi intorno al principio della morale*.

[2] I distinguish *applied morality* from the *science of the application*. The latter is 'the ordered complex of the rules according to which the supreme law (*the moral principle*) must be applied'. The former (applied morality) is the result of the application, and is a body of particular duties and responsibilities. Thus the science which teaches the way to apply the moral principle is a kind of *moral logic*. Cf. the *Preface* to the works on morality [*PE*].

object of political sciences. Psychology concerns the human soul and its powers; pedagogy, eudaimonology, ethics and many other studies consider human beings relative to their needs, inclinations, means of progress, their ceaselessly changing acts and states, the fruits of their labour, the laws to which they are subject, and the relationships that bind them to all beings, to all points of the universe, and even to what is infinite. And while anthropology in general is limited to considering the *nature* of this being that is so fascinated by itself, the present work limits the study still further. In *moral anthropology*, as we call it, we consider the human being solely from the moral point of view.

3. We note, however, that moral perfection is the unique point to which all human energy and every human faculty is naturally directed. Morality is the summit from which to view the human being; it is the panorama which in some sense embraces all partial views, and subjects them to itself. Everything concerning human beings touches upon morality, which extends to every relationship, watches over everything, and subjects everything to its judgment, by applying to everything an order, measure and character. Because of this extent of moral anthropology I have obviously not exhausted the argument in this book, but I will have done enough if I have succeeded in outlining its borders and indicating simply the principal paths to follow in this vast subject.[3]

4. Another preliminary reflection is called for. When we ask about the moral state of humanity we are dealing with a matter of fact; we are observing human beings and describing them as they are. So too when we ask about the necessary aids by which

[3] In spite of this, some may find we have devoted too much time to a particular topic, for instance to the *animality* of the human being. This is true, but perhaps I can be excused if the reader reflects that the section could have been shortened if a *psychology* had been written to which I could have referred. As long as the different sciences are not arranged in order, I often have to speak at length about something not strictly belonging to the subject, although I should be able to presuppose such matter, and refer to it. The same can be said about the two *postulates* with which I begin this *Anthropology*; they are equally necessary for all philosophical sciences, and ought to be discussed in the part of *logic* which deals with *method*. But until the reader can be referred to an already existent *logic*, we have to use and justify those postulates. We cannot leave the reader to invent or imagine what we are not saying.

human beings can render themselves good. This further question of *moral anthropology* deals with a complex, real question, not with something purely abstract. We cannot omit anything necessary for the complete development of human good, and consequently cannot restrict ourselves solely to what is purely rational and ignore the great historical, moral facts of the human race.

Clearly, therefore, *moral anthropology*, considered in its entirety, cannot be classified among those sciences which limit themselves to a quality abstracted from a total complex, as pure mathematics does when it reasons about quantity as conceived solely in the mind by virtue of abstraction, although such quantity does not exist in reality. All abstract sciences are commendable in that they prepare us, although remotely, for practical conclusions. But as long as they are treated in isolation they have no effective use; in order to insert these sciences into the order of realities, all the omitted qualities of the case must be included. Thus, a surveyor wishing to apply his theories either to building a bridge, to moving a large mass, or pumping water, must first identify and assemble all the data about the real bodies on which he intends to work. These facts are neglected in general, abstract theory. In my opinion, this explains why abstract sciences are studied by so few: they do not directly arouse the interest and universal study of human beings. In the last analysis, human beings seek what is of real, practical use, and only when they have obtained it do they feel they have complete, effective knowledge.

A public administrator, for example, urgently required to make a piece of land productive or to establish some industry or trade, cannot be satisfied with a general theory of economy. He has to apply the economic rules, and obtain the most detailed information about the local climate, soil, population, customs, prejudices, and level of skills available, that is, he needs practical information. Nature is not aroused to action by abstract ideas; it must be dealt with effectively and its forces acted upon. This cannot be done unless positive knowledge with its applications and modifications is added to the general theories. Thus, sciences like *moral anthropology*, that have a complex object, and aim at complete, finite knowledge, cannot and must not limit themselves solely to details obtained by pure speculation.

[4]

They must make use of every opportunity to enrich themselves through reason or history.

It would be strange, or even ridiculous, if someone, intending to produce a certain effect, used method as a pretext for rejecting the means necessary for the effect. Yet many writers fall into this curious error. They claim that the most important things concerning human beings, namely, how to be virtuous and happy, must be deduced *a priori* by reason. To do this, they use an unreal rationalism which never descends to the level of human needs. They intend to teach us how to become happy and good, but they also claim to speak only according to the natural light of reason, and to prescind entirely from the fact of divine revelation and the consequent positive relationships that the human being has with God. They do not deny revelation itself; they simply think that good philosophical method is offended by mentioning it. Thus, instead of offering suitable nourishment to the hungry human race, they insist upon a solemn disputation about the plate on which the food is served. They deny human beings sustenance simply because the dish is silver rather than the porcelain or other substance they would prefer. Consequently, these teachers of virtue and happiness never go further than halfway. Because an isolated, abstract part of an art is insufficient to obtain the end proposed by the art itself, they never succeed in teaching the human race to obtain what it longs for, or what they promise, namely, a virtuous and happy life.

A similar situation would be that of a person who gives orders to a commander attacking a fort, and instructs him in the art of assault simply by quoting a few general principles about lines of defence, earthworks, mines and so on, making him believe that attention to details through inspection of the real parts of the fortress and its defences is useless. These details, it is claimed, are foreign to the rigorous method followed by science. The commander might say: 'Your method is good, but do not claim that it alone will overrun this fortress; it will overrun only the fortress you have created in your mind. I am faced with the enemy; I have to manoeuvre on the terrain you can see and against a real fortified stronghold. To your fine theories you must add very accurate details about the construction of the fortress, and about the people and artillery defending it. In applying your rules to my case, you must pay careful attention to all the circumstances

[4]

which you are neglecting because you are not in command. You conquer fortresses in the classroom; you fight only with words.'

5. The commander's position is that of every human being relative to happiness and goodness. All human beings have a supreme need to attain real satisfaction, and an absolute duty to be good. It is the real, concrete human being, not some philosophical abstraction, who must be good and happy. We must not, therefore, be surprised to see that the only discipline which attracts, and always has attracted, the attention of the human race, is full knowledge of the means by which human nature obtains its moral end effectively.

The human race differs greatly from the small section of mortals who call themselves learned. People such as these, accustomed to a solitary life of study, deceive themselves when they declare that the only thing they consider important are certain formulas of abstract knowledge and method they think they possess. Meanwhile, because the light, unnourishing fare of abstractions does not satisfy, the human race can look only to religion, especially positive religion, for what is real and complete. For the human race, wisdom today as in the past is only that knowledge which teaches (and shows it can teach) the whole truth and has never been taught apart from religion.

6. The great thinkers of the past agreed with this feeling proper to the human race. They consistently used the word *wisdom* for the body of teachings which responded most eminently to the highest needs and purposes of humanity. These teachings included traditions and theories, historical facts and rational principles, beliefs and proofs, divine revelations and human reasons. Cicero says: 'Philosophy is the science of human and divine things.'[4] Wisdom, of which philosophy is merely the love and study, is defined by Plato as 'a perfect union of justice and holiness with prudence, by which humans become like God'.[5] Aristotle states that the philosopher's occupation is 'to speculate about everything, because no one will consider what the philosopher does not consider'.[6] Such was the elevated thought, the UNITY and TOTALITY with which the early thinkers considered

[4] *De Off.*, bk. 2, 2 [5].

[5] Cf. *Theaetetus.*

[6] *Metaph.*, bk. 4, c. 2.

human cognitions. They thought and wrote for people as people, and were not drawn from the real needs of human nature to chase after curious, unrelated speculations.

7. In a word, the *truly wise* did not teach for the sake of teaching, nor restrict themselves to the limits of *arbitrary method* and thus forget the only true, effective purpose of knowledge.

However, while I defend the need for a complete, effective knowledge, and praise the early thinkers for having constantly kept such a need before their eyes, I do not deny the great merit of modern writers who have sought to introduce distinction — the mother of light — into different parts of knowledge. I criticise only the action of those who, not content to distinguish, divide up the different parts of human knowledge, even the most insignificant, and sift them like chaff. I also criticise the action of those who, after dividing knowledge into so many parts, choose the parts which suit their taste, condemning the remainder as useless because unsuited to their palate, and opposing its use. By such intolerable harshness and boldness, they dismember human genius and set themselves up as distributors and judges of its dead remains! Analysis, distinction and light should continue but exclusion be avoided; arbitrary methods should be rejected, for they suppress the more important part of knowledge and retard rather than advance civilisation.

We must work to unite the advantages of both modern and older methods, retaining the methodical distinctions which clarify cognitions so well, without losing the bonds which draw them together into a beautiful, wonderfully ordered whole. We must not neglect the abstract part of knowledge which is the warp, nor the concrete part which is, as it were, the weft and draws a teaching to its final act where alone it is appropriate for helping us and bringing us the real good we need [*App.*, no. 1]. To accomplish all this, I see no better way than that which I have always endeavoured to follow in philosophical matters, namely, to place the pure, abstract part of knowledge first, followed by the concrete, particular part.

8. I intend, therefore, to follow the same procedure in this *moral anthropology*, which requires me to consider the human being as *author* and *subject* of moral actions and of the good and evil resulting from those actions. I have to discuss the present moral conditions of human nature and the variety of human,

moral states; I have to speak about the means and impulses by which human nature passes from one state to another. It is clear, therefore, that I must deduce the necessary, relevant points of the argument from both rational and historical sources, and that my work divides naturally into two parts which, although different, cannot be separated, just as the limbs of a human being differ from one another without being separated from the body.

Human, moral states and means result partly from human nature itself and partly from positive relationships with the Creator. The first are known by observation of the internal and external facts of human nature, which to some extent can be carried out with our natural light. The second must necessarily be obtained from what tradition teaches. Hence, in any anthropology there must be a *rational* part and a *positive* part in conformity with the two orders to which human beings belong. *Nature* is one of these orders; and the moral conditions deriving from it form the first part of the book. But because, according to the Christian system, human beings belong also to a supernatural order, of *grace*, the moral conditions which flow to us from this higher order are the subject of the second part.

9. This book contains only the first of the two parts; the second and principal part will be deferred to a more suitable time. This first part, an aid to *natural ethics*, is the foundation for the part which will follow (God willing). It deals with the *imputation* of human actions, a subject which causes much difficulty relative to the theory of human freedom and of the *connection between the different parts* of the human being, especially the connection between the physical part and the wonderful faculty of free action with which the Creator has endowed us.

10. However, before beginning, I must state the two postulates required not only by our subject but generally by any subject whatsoever, for they contain the conditions that alone make discussion possible.

Postulates

POSTULATE 1

BEING IS KNOWN OF ITSELF

To understand the justification for this postulate, we have to consider that *being* is what is first known. All other knowledge always presupposes knowledge of being. It is obvious that if we did not know what existence was, we could not think any thing at all, nor could we reason, since every object of our thought is an entity, a real or possible being.

If being is *what is known first*, it is not made known to us by means of any other mental conception. If it were, this mental conception would be prior to that of being, which would therefore no longer be the first but a second, derived conception.

If being is known of itself, we cannot expect it to be defined. We have to grant that it is known prior to any reasoning whatsoever. Our postulate therefore is justified.[7]

COROLLARIES

11. I. If this postulate is accepted and presupposed in all human reasoning, it must preface not only this *Anthropology* but every system of human knowledge.

12. II. The whole system of human knowledge presupposes *being* as known (*Coroll. I*); being therefore contains the property and nature of *light* of the mind, or of idea.[8]

13. III. If being is in itself light or idea (*Coroll. II*), it constitutes the essence or form of knowledge. It is therefore the seat of the *evidence* to which, in order to be perfect, every demonstration of knowledge must be reduced as to its final term.

[7] This teaching, which makes *being* the *point of departure* of human knowledge, would not seem new if people knew the riches they possessed. Many wise men at least glimpsed this truth and included it in their writings throughout the ages. Eight centuries ago, Avicenna, in his commentary on the 'Metaphysics' of Aristotle, declared that it was impossible to give a definition of *being*, or of what is *necessary* and *possible*, or of the other elementary ideas of being. We must therefore uphold these truths, if we do not wish to be continually looking for the *principle of knowledge*. As long as we do not firmly posit this principle, scientific knowledge cannot exist.

[8] Being as light of the mind is properly called *ideal being*, or simply *idea*. We also call it *idea of being* or *possible being*. These terms, however, involve some mental relationship over and above pure, ideal being. Cf. *OT*, 540–557.

POSTULATE 2

EXPERIENCE OF THE *FEELING* UNDER DISCUSSION MUST BE GRANTED

14. This postulate also can be easily seen.

Being is known in itself; in order, therefore, for *feeling* to be made known to a mind, the spirit must refer feeling to being, the form of all cognitions. But feeling cannot be referred to being by someone who does not have feeling; having and experiencing feeling is the same. A feeling therefore cannot be *known* by anyone who has no experience of it. Thus, experience of the feeling under discussion must be presupposed in both interlocutors. Otherwise, one could not talk about it, and the other could not understand.

This truth explains why words can never make a person born blind understand colours, nor a deaf person sounds. *Feeling*, therefore, must be accepted as a postulate and incapable of definition.[9]

Comment

15. The core of every argument is in fact reduced ultimately to feelings, because by *feelings* we understand what belongs to internal as well as external sensitivity. Hence feeling, in its more

[9] If we examine all the definitions claimed for *sensation*, we discover that either they consist in the description of the external circumstances accompanying the formation of the sensation, in which case the definition applies not to the sensation, strictly speaking, but to what accompanies it, or words are simply substituted for other words which at most indicate the sensation for anyone who knows it but not for someone who has not experienced it; or finally they are false definitions.

Richerand defines *sensitivity* as 'the faculty of the living organs which, on contact with another body, enables them to *experience* a more or less intense impression which changes the order of their movements by hastening or slowing, suspending or exciting the movements'.

If we consider simply the word 'experience' in the definition, either it means 'feel' or it means nothing. If it means 'feel', the supposition is that I know what 'to feel' is, and if I know that, the definition is of no use; it does nothing but substitute the word 'experience' for the word 'feel'. But nobody can understand 'experience' unless 'feel' is substituted for it. The definition therefore only substitutes a meaningless for a clear word!

general sense, constitutes the *matter* of human knowledge, just as *ideal being* constitutes the *form*.

COROLLARIES

16. I. *Feeling* and the *idea of being* are the two basic elements of all human knowledge. Every *definition* and every *demonstration* must be referred to and terminate in these two elements.

17. II. Every time the definition or demonstration of a thing reaches a point where its only undefined terms are the two elements known *per se*, *being* and *feeling*, the definition is reduced to its final stage of clarity and evidence. In order, therefore, to make a given definition finally clear, it is necessary to define accurately any word in it that is *per se unknown*, that is, all the words not expressing *existence* or *feeling* or anything contained in these two first known things.[10]

Each definition must be taken singly and each word in it examined and defined until only those definitions finally remain which are composed of no other terms than indefinable *being* and *feeling*.

18. As an example of this rule of method, I shall define the word 'body'.

FIRST DEFINITION

'Body is an extended, tactile, odorous, coloured, etc. substance.'

Besides the word *is*, which is known *per se* and needs no definition, the following words are present in the definition: 1. substance, 2. extended, 3. tactile, 4. odorous, coloured, etc. They must be considered as unknown, and their value found by means of definitions. Let us substitute for them their definitions which we shall call

SECOND DEFINITIONS

1st. *Substance* is the act by which an essence *subsists*.

2nd. *Extension* is the mode and the term of what we therefore call material feeling.

[10] For the content of the *idea of being*, see *OT*, 558–628, where the idea is shown to embrace the supreme *principles* of reasoning and *pure ideas*. The only explanation of such idealities within the idea of being depends upon a demonstration by analysis that they are in effect contained in ideal being.

3rd. *Tactility* is the cause of the sensations of touch, a particular form of material feeling.

4th. *Odorous, coloured, etc.* means *being the cause* of those sensations which are known as particular forms of material feeling.

Let us examine what remains unknown in these new formulas. In the first definition the unknowns are the *act by which* essence *subsists* and *essence* itself. In the second, nothing is unknown because we are dealing with feeling and its mode; the definition is composed of elements which admit of no definition. Because extension is included in touch, sight, etc., all that is required is to explain the matter in other words so that the definition is clear to anyone who knows the language in which it is given and has experienced these feelings of touch, sight, etc. In the third definition only the word 'cause' needs defining, because the rest of the definition is feeling. The same applies to the fourth definition. Three things therefore remain to be determined and defined in order that these second definitions be perfectly clear: 1. the act of subsistence; 2. essence; 3. cause. And the values we must substitute for these unknowns will be

THIRD DEFINITIONS

1st. The *act of subsistence* is the first, immanent act of being.

2nd. *Essence* is determinate being in so far as it is known in the idea, and does not act.

3rd. *Cause* is a subsistent entity which has for the term of its act another entity.

There is nothing unknown in these definitions. If we carefully examine the words composing them, we see they express simply being, or the action of being, or the mode or determination of being and of its action. The meaning of each of them is contained in *being*, and properly speaking they need no further definition; all we need do is *observe* and find them immediately in the idea of being. We must all be capable of doing this for ourselves, and of ourselves cannot be taught to do it, although we can be helped by a certain stimulus and direction coming from a teacher, whose words and example can serve as a guide for our faculty of observation.

Now, if we substitute the meanings given in these third definitions for the 1st., 3rd. and 4th. of the second definitions, they become second definitions:

[18]

1st. Substance is determinate being in its first, immanent act.

3rd. Tactile being means being acting in such a way that touch sensations are the term of the action.

4th. Odorous, coloured being, etc. means being acting in such a way that odorous, coloured sensations of this kind are the term of the action.

And if we use these definitions together with no. 2 of the second definitions, we can form a definition of body in which all the words or terms express nothing more than known elements, that is, *existence* and *feeling*, or their appurtenances. This is demonstrated by the following definition, which admittedly is cumbersome but nevertheless logically exact:

'Body is a determinate being in its first, immanent act (substance), having a common mode with material feeling (extension) and acting on us in such a way that the term of its action is felt extension and sensations called tactile, odorous, etc.'

Comment 1

19. Whatever is present in a *definition* is also present in a *demonstration*. To become evident, every demonstration must proceed by means of definitions and a combination of all the terms to the point that an opponent is forced to deny either *being* or *feeling*, and is thus unable to escape the force of the argument. Reasoning is valid up to this point, and an opponent always has the right to ask to be led to it, but not beyond it. As soon as the question concerns the *idea* of *existence* or concerns *feeling*, the dispute is at an end. The participants can only enter into themselves and meditate in silence, persuading themselves of the truth, which is no longer hidden from them if they wish to see it.

It is a mistake, therefore, to think that written works and discussion can bring agreement among people without the cooperation of their good will. Both truth and mendacity are deeply rooted in the human heart, which cannot be reached by external demonstration, verbal bombardment, or skills in human knowledge. The human word terminates with an appeal to our deepest sense, the awareness we each have of being and feelings. Pursuing a demonstration to this final term helps in a wonderful way all those who seek the truth in good faith. And far from claiming to have accomplished anything further with my writings, I would think I had obtained all I could hope for if I succeeded solely in clarifying and demonstrating the supreme truths by their reduction to the first elements of knowledge.

Comment 2

20. In order to see the relationship between the two elements of human reasoning known *per se*, we must note that, as we have said:

1st. being is the *formal* principle of reasoning, feeling the *material* principle;

2nd. being is the principle in the *order of ideas*, feeling in the *order of reality*;

3rd. being rules and constitutes *intellective nature*, feeling constitutes *animal nature*;

4th. *being* constitutes the *objectivity* of perceptions, *feeling* their *subjectivity*.

In these two elements, therefore, we have the 'seminal reasons', to use an expression of St. Augustine, of all natures and of all the entities composing the universe.

THE METHOD FOLLOWED IN THIS WORK

21. The name of this book is *Anthropology as an Aid to Moral Science*, that is, discussion of the human being or human nature considered from the point of view of morality. Hence, because the *human being* is the subject of the work, it will be useful to begin by accurately defining 'human being'. This will allow us to analyse the concept, note all its parts, and finally reunite them in order to throw new light on the initial definition of human being.

Following this method, we begin with the whole and then arrive at the parts. It is an *analytical* method, which consists in analysing the whole, that is, separating it into parts.[11] We then retrace our steps, going from the parts to the whole, *synthesizing*, that is, making a unity of the separate parts. The method we intend to follow in our argument can therefore be appropriately called analytical-synthetical.

[11] It is an error to give the name *synthetical* to that which begins with the whole and moves to the parts, and to call the opposite process *analytical*. In the method I am proposing, the *synthesis* (the whole) is given by nature, and is therefore not the object of the method. An *analytical method* presupposes a *synthesis* because only a complex whole can be divided by analysis (αναλυειν), but it is contrary to reason to give the name 'synthesis', which precedes the method, to the method itself. The name of the method must be taken from the *procedure* used in the method, not from the object of the method. The procedure of a method which divides a whole is a procedure of *division*. Only this kind of method therefore can be called analytical.

Book 1

THE HUMAN BEING

DEFINITIONS

22. The first definition: the *human being* is an intellective and volitive animal subject.

23. The second definition: the *human being* is an animal subject endowed with the intuition of indeterminate-ideal being and with the perception of its own corporeal fundamental feeling, and operating in accordance with animality and intelligence.

1

COMMENTS ON THE MOST CELEBRATED DEFINITIONS OF HUMAN BEING

24. Two of the best known definitions of human being have come down to us from antiquity. One, attributed to Plato and recently sustained by de Bonald, says: 'The human being is an intelligence aided by organs.'

25. The other definition is found in Aristotle and amongst the Scholastics: 'The human being is a rational animal.'

26. Bonald's comments in favour of the first definition are more than sufficient to eliminate the strange definitions of human being proposed by our modern materialists, but they do nothing to free his own definition from the defect already pointed out by Plato's most famous pupil. That is, if we say that 'the human being is an intelligence aided by organs', we leave undetermined the connection between organs and intelligence. But without this connection, there would be no human being. An angel, for example, furnished with a body which served him as a kind of instrument without his informing it, would not be a human being, although the definition in question would apply very well to such an angel.[12]

27. The aristotelian definition, accepted by the Scholastics in general, certainly has its advantages but, it seems, can scarcely be freed from the following defects. 1. The simple words 'rational animal' express the *intelligent* but not the *volitive* part

[12] Fr. Gioachino Ventura clearly shows the limitation of this definition in his *De Methodo Philosophandi*.

of this animal, although both parts are elements in the essence of human being and differ greatly from each other. The *intellective* part entails a kind of receptivity, the *volitive* part a kind of activity. The human being is not only something inert and receptive; his very nature is founded principally in his own activity.

28. It is true that the *volitive* part of the human being actually originates as a consequence of his *intellective* element, but there is no proof that this happens necessarily and that the opposite involves absurdity. If there is such a proof it could be defended only with great difficulty, as far as I can see, on the ground that the concept of will is included in that of intellect, and vice-versa, so that the two elements functioned as terms of a relationship. In this case it would be logically repugnant to think of a being that simply received light without its being moved to act in accordance with that light. But as far as I can see such logical repugnance cannot be demonstrated.

The will, therefore, which is the active part of the human being must be noted and expressed in the definition. Later we shall see that this active part of the human being is properly speaking the seat of human personality (cf. 832–837).

29. 2. Again, it seems more appropriate to call the human being an *intellective* rather than a *rational animal* because the *intellect* precedes *reason* and provides the principle of human reasoning. The proper act of reason is to pass mentally from one thing to another, an impossible transition for reason unless it first receives something. As St. Thomas says, it is our intellect that first intuits what is given to us: 'Every rational, discursive act depends upon the intuition of principles. This intuition pertains to the intellect.'[13]

Reason, therefore, is not properly speaking the first human power, but originates from the intellect, as a brook from a spring, when the intellect associates itself with the animality that furnishes the matter of knowledge. After asserting that the human being is an animal, it would be better therefore to place intellect rather than reason in the definition.

30. Others, however, have made a much more serious mistake by extending the definition of human being to matters beyond the basic, inborn elements of human nature, to effects and derivations of what is inborn. *Sociability* provides us with one

[13] *S.T.*, I, q. 79.

example of this. Romagnosi, who saw that human beings differ from brutes by reason of sociability, erred in thinking that sociability must, therefore, be inserted into the definition of human being. Sociability as a difference dividing humans from animals is not entitled to a place in the definition of human being because only basic differences arising from basic elements, not secondary differences, are to be found in such a definition. And it is clear that sociability originates in human beings as a necessary effect of their possession of intellect, reason and will. It does not form anything of itself, as though it were not already seminally present in the intellective and volitive faculties that must without doubt be expressed in the definition. Otherwise, there would be no end to what might be included in the definition of human being. Every degree of human development would have to be expressed in it because each differentiates humans from brute animals. Even the famous definition, attributed to Plato, that the human being is a 'laughing animal', would not be out of place because laughter is indeed a specific human difference. Nevertheless, laughter depends upon the intelligence and affective power with which we apprehend mentally the unexpected *quirk* which produces a feeling expressed in laughter.

31. 3. A third defect in the aristotelian definition is no less serious.[14] Stating simply 'the human being is a rational animal' could give the impression that the *subject* were an animal and nothing more, and that *rationality* were simply a property, faculty or attribute of this animal. In this case, reason would form part of the *human* subject only in the same way as the faculties or qualities which are not the subject, but spring forth as the subject's first acts. The subject must in fact be conceivable as distinct from its faculties or qualities in such a way that it remains after the latter have been mentally abstracted from it. But this needs clarifying.

32. There are two orders: the order of things and the order of

[14] The Scholastics defined the human being as a *rational* rather than an *intellective* animal because they saw that the quality *rational* distinguished the human being from angelic intelligences as well as from brute beasts. Angels *understand*, but they do not *reason*. Despite my preference, therefore, for *intellective* rather than *rational* in the definition of human being given above, *rational* has its merits, and we shall make good use of it elsewhere.

ideas. In the *order of things* some are so connected with others that they cannot subsist without them. In the *order of ideas* also, there are connections and dependencies between ideal things in such a way that one cannot be conceived without another. But the connections and dependencies between things are not the same in both the order of things and the order of ideas. Consequently, certain things cannot subsist without others although the mind can conceive these things separately. Let us apply this to our argument.

A given subject cannot subsist without its faculties and particular powers. This is valid in the order of *things*. But in the order of *ideas*, the same thing can be conceived as subsistent, that is, can be thought of as a being, without its having to be thought with its faculties and particular powers. This mental function is what we call *abstraction*. On the other hand, it is impossible, even through abstraction, to think the subject while abstracting from an element that forms and constitutes the subject itself. If I omit what is essential to the subject, I lose the idea of the subject entirely. In other words, it becomes something else in my mind.

33. We affirm, therefore, that the *intellective* element has to form part of the *human subject* in such a way that without this part I can no longer think the human being, even through abstraction. Without the intellect, the subject of human understanding no longer remains.

Considering the form of the definition, 'a rational animal', in this light, we see that the word 'animal' expresses all that pertains to the *subject*. The animal is the subject that reasons, while rationality becomes an operation and faculty (although essential) of the animal (subject). No *reasoning principle* is present in the human being; it is the *animal principle* that reasons. It would seem therefore that this definition does not faithfully express the nature of humanity because it does not show the true connection between *animality* and *intelligence*, that is, between the feeling principle and the reasoning principle.[15]

[15] The Scholastics' acceptance of this aristotelian definition of human being caused great trouble when they tried to prove that the intellective soul must be the form of human nature. If the subject, *human being*, was animal and nothing more, it became necessary to prove that the intellective soul was the

2

COMMENTS ON THE TWO DEFINITIONS OF HUMAN BEING PROPOSED BY US

34. We shall now examine our own definitions.

Article 1.
The first definition of the human being

It is clear that by defining the human being as 'an intellective and volitive animal subject', we have avoided the three difficulties mentioned above. In this definition:

1st. Both the *passive* and the *active* parts of human nature, which we have called *intellective* and *volitive*, are expressed.

2nd. The primitive faculty of the understanding is indicated by calling the human being *intellective*, not *rational*.

3rd. The human being is first said to be 'a subject'. Three conditions are then added to this subject: 'animality, intelligence and will'. In this way these qualities have the same relationship to the 'subject'; none is more privileged than another. In other words, the *principle* which forms human unity is posited as distinct from animality, intelligence and will, but common to them all. The subject which feels as an animal is also that which understands and wills as intelligent and volitive.

35. Any supposition which sustained the contrary would involve logical repugnance and manifest absurdity. It is impossible for an animal to be that which understands, just as it is impossible for the principle constituting animality to possess intelligence.

form of the *body*. This difficulty is apparent in the extremely subtle arguments of St. Thomas in *S.T.*, I, q. 76, art. 1, where he endeavours to show how the soul can be the form of the human being (and we may note that *form of the body* and *form of the human being* are phrases used promiscuously in this article). In the end, after a great number of subtle distinctions, St. Thomas himself concludes: 'The intellective soul is indeed the *form of the body* according to its essence, but not according to its *act of understanding*; understanding is the kind of act which is done entirely without the instrumentality of a bodily organ' (*ibid.*).

Such an assertion would presuppose confusion between two things which are separate of their very nature. When I say 'animal', I say 'a principle which feels materially, and moves from place to place in accordance with these sensations'; when I say 'intellective being', I say 'a principle which conceives in an immaterial way, and wills without moving from place to place'. These properties are contraries. With the first, I know and define *animal*; with the second I know and define *intellective being*. If the animal were to understand, it would to that extent cease to be an animal. To say that an animal reasons is the same, strictly speaking, as attributing *reasoning* to the *sense-principle*. But with such an attribution I either destroy reason by reducing it to material feeling, or I destroy *material feeling* by maintaining that the animal principle (which is always understood as a principle of material feeling) is a principle of immaterial feeling, that is, of reasoning. In the former case, I have not attributed rationality to the animal, but only the animality[16] already possessed by the animal; in the latter, I have not attributed one of the two principles (sense-principle and rational principle) to the other, but by destroying the first I have retained the rational principle just as it was. In a word, when I say 'rational animal', I must understand one of two things: either 1. that the feeling principle, as feeling principle, reasons, which is as absurd as saying that the principle of vision, which perceives colours, is that which perceives sounds, smells and tastes, or as saying that the non-intelligent principle (the animal) understands; or 2. that the principle which feels, also reasons, not in so far as it feels or is the proximate principle of feeling but in so far as it is referred to and rooted in a common principle of feeling and reasoning. In such a case, this common principle of feeling and reasoning would be a third principle, not a principle rather of one than of the other of these two functions. It would be a principle uniting both functions in itself. Hence it would no longer be true to say that 'the animal reasons'. We would say that this third principle feels and moves itself as an animal, and at the same time reasons. Clearly the expression 'rational animal' is not altogether exact, precisely because in saying 'animal' I say 'a principle which feels' and is called 'animal' only in so far as it feels but does not reason.

[16] *Aristotelian sensism* is evident here. Aristotle's definition of human being is dependent upon it.

36. A favourable interpretation could be given to the common phrase 'rational animal' if, after finding that the *human* subject were as much animal as intellective, we were to maintain equally 'the subject who understands is an animal' and 'an animal is that which understands'. Granted the fully perfect unity of the subject, which is both animal and intellective, the two ways of speaking could be true. Unfortunately, such an interpretation is excluded by Aristotle wherever he endeavours to prove that 'rational animal' should be used instead of 'animal, intellective being'.[17] Nevertheless, we wanted to draw attention to this possible interpretation so that the reader might understand the meaning of such phrases as 'intellective animal' and 'rational animal' when we use them, as we often do. They are in part true, although they are not sufficient to constitute an exact definition of the human being.

Article 2.
The second definition of the human being.

37. I added another definition to that just examined, and called the human being 'an animal subject endowed with the intuition of indeterminate-ideal being and with the perception of corporeal-fundamental feeling, and acting in accordance with the animality and intelligence it possesses'. This second definition is more explicit than the first.

The former could be criticised for the reason which led the Scholastics to call the human being *rational* rather than *intellective*. By saying 'rational', the human being is characterised differently from beasts, which have feeling but no reason, and from angels, which have intellect but no reason. Hence St. Thomas

[17] It will not be out of place to note that although the expression 'rational animal' applied to the human being is tainted with the materialism of which Aristotle was sometimes accused (and from which it is difficult to absolve him altogether), such an accusation cannot be levelled at the Catholic schools which resisted every kind of materialism. The worst that can be said of them is that in taking Aristotle as their guide they accepted certain of his philosophically in exact expressions which they could not correct and justify without great subtlety and ingenuity.

affirms with great precision that human beings are *rational natures*, and angels *intellective natures*.[18]

38. It would be possible to maintain that, in the first definition we have given, the human being is sufficiently distinguished from angels by his perceived animality, and from brute beasts by intelligence. On the other hand, in calling angels *intellective* natures, they are not assigned a difference truly distinguishing them from human beings. The word *intellective* does not exclude *reasoning*, and is applicable to angels and human beings.

39. Nevertheless it cannot be denied that the word 'intellective' in the first definition requires some explanation. In the second, however, all is made clear by substituting the words 'endowed with the intuition of indeterminate-ideal being and with the perception of corporeal fundamental feeling, and acting in accordance with the animality and intelligence it possesses' in place of the attributes 'intellective and volitive'. The expanded definition illustrates the specific difference between human and every other intellect.

It is of course true that the nature of any intellect whatsoever consists in the intuition of ideal being, but the characteristic note of the human intellect, as we showed in *The Origin of Thought*,[19] is the intuition of indeterminate-ideal being and the perception of its own corporeal fundamental feeling[20] alone. This initial conception of being and first perception forms the foundation of human intelligence and human *species* and distinguishes human beings from all separate intelligences that can be conceived mentally (that is, from angels).

40. This highly imperfect intuition of being shows why creative wisdom connected animality to human intelligence, the lowest grade of intelligence. Animality is given to the human being as a means of partially completing the human vision of, and share in, being, as we showed in *The Origin of Thought*. Feeling furnishes the intelligent subject with a fundamental perception and adds many determinations to being as naturally intuited by human subjects.

[18] *S.T.*, I, q. 58, art. 3.

[19] Cf. 481–482, 486–487.

[20] The theory behind this perception will be examined in our work on psychology.

41. But intelligences which by nature already possess various operations and perceptions in an order higher than that of animality have no need of this means. Ancient writers correctly characterised and described the human being when they maintained that 'the human being occupies the lowest position in the order of intelligences'.[21]

42. By adding to the definition the words 'acting in accordance with its animality and intelligence', the degrees and modes of human action are indicated. First place is given to *reason* as the operative principle which joins and binds intellect and feeling in itself by means of perception. In this way, the chief powers of human nature, which are rooted in the unity of the subject, are sufficiently expressed in the definition.

3

THE DIVISION OF OUR STUDY

43. Having established the definition of human being, we must now *analyse* it according to the method we have described. The *human being*, which we already know synthetically in the definition, has to be dismembered and divided into its various elements.

44. The definition itself indicates three quite distinct elements: 1. the *animal* part; 2. the *spiritual* part, as we shall call the complex of intellectual and volitive powers; 3. and what we may call the middle part, which joins the first two parts in itself and makes an individual, a *subject*, of the human being.

These three parts give rise to the areas of study comprising this *Anthropology*. In the first section, we consider the *animal* part of the human being; in the second, the *spiritual* part; and finally, in the third section, the human *subject*, the principle which, uniting the first two parts in a marvellous way, becomes as it were their thalamus.

[21] St. Thomas, following in the footsteps of Aristotle, had already observed that knowing something in a universal sense without determinations is more imperfect than knowing the same thing with its determinations and in its particular aspects (*S.T.*, I, q. 85, art. 3).

Book 2

ANIMALITY

DEFINITIONS

I

45. We call *animate* 'the extended, immediate term of a sense-principle'.

II

Animal is 'an individual being, materially feeling and instinctive, organically formed and with organic-excitatory movements'.

III

Animal *life* is 'the unceasing production of corporeal and material feeling'.

IV

Life as attributed to the sense-principle, that is, to the soul, is 'the corporeal or material principle itself'.

V

Life as attributed to the body is 'the act with which the body, acting in the soul, produces unceasingly in the soul the corporeal or material feeling'.

VI

Life as attributed to the anatomical body is 'the unceasing reproduction of all the extrasubjective phenomena which in parallel with the material feeling precede, accompany and follow it'.

VII

Life in general is 'the act of a substantial feeling'.

46. As we begin to study the human being relative to the *animality* he has in common with brute beasts, we have to remember that our aim is not a complete treatise of animal nature, but an

endeavour to clarify our notion of animal relative to animal *activity*, and to show that the animal's various operations can all be reduced, without call for intelligence and will, to an efficacious sense-principle. Our conclusions about animal activity should enable us to consider the same kind of actions in the human being, where they are found along with, and in relation to, the intellective principle and free will.

47. This difficult, mysterious study of the way in which brute beasts are determined towards action, and do in fact act, depends for light on an exposition of the nature of *feeling*, from which animal *instinct* and activity originate.

48. We shall first turn our attention, therefore, to the *passive faculties* of the animal, and then to the *active faculties* which flow from them. In this way, our study of animal nature will have two parts, the first dealing with *feeling* and the second with *instinct*. We do in fact reduce all passive animal powers to the feeling-power and all active animal powers to instinct, and this explains why, in our definition of animal as 'a feeling, instinctive being', we think we have indicated all possible animal powers.

49. We shall see later how animal *desire* and *instinct* are rooted in the *feeling-power*; and as a consequence we shall also see how the feeling-power properly constitutes radical animal essence. For the moment, we begin by showing the error of those who aim to place the definition of animal in something other than the feeling power.

SECTION ONE

THE PASSIVE ANIMAL FACULTIES

50. Everything that can be said about animal *feeling* falls under two principal headings, that of *fundamental feeling*, which constitutes the essence of animal, and that of acquired, *accidental feelings*, which are modifications of the fundamental feeling.[22]

51. The accidental feelings are of two kinds, *figured* and *non-figured*. *External sensations* and *images* belong to the first group. This whole section on animal feeling, if rigorously divided, would therefore follow this pattern:

1. The fundamental feeling.
2. The modifications of the fundamental feeling.
   - a) Non-figured feelings.
   - b) Figured feelings:
     - i) sensations
     - ii) images.

52. However, if the various parts were discussed as completely separate from one another, it would be necessary eventually to draw them together in order to indicate their mutual relationships and dependencies. Consequently, we think it better to relate them as we go along, if this proves more convenient, especially as the order of ideas seems sufficiently outlined in the schema set out above. Our only division will be that of the chapter headings that follow.

1

A FALSE DEFINITION OF ANIMAL

53. The sounder naturalists, such as Linnaeus and Buffon,

[22] What we have to say in this book about the fundamental feeling and its modifications can be considered as a continuation of the same subject in *OT* [692–748].

have no doubt that the essential characteristic of animal is found in *feeling*.

54. Some less noted authors seem to have doubted this.[23] Their arguments, however, indicate a total absence of logical rules in their method of defining things, and a clear tendency to materialism, where materialism is not in fact openly professed. I can understand that it is possible to abuse the word *animal* by making it mean anything one wishes, but the fault lies then with the person who so uses it. If it is going to be taken in an arbitrary sense, different from ordinary usage, the reader should at least be warned. He can then avoid mere questions of words.[24] To say, as some naturalists do, that not all animals show traces of sensation means presupposing either that sensation plays no part in the meaning of the word *animal*, or that its role is accidental. If it were essential, these authors could not maintain that the beings they are examining and in which they find no trace of sensation are animals.

If these beings are called 'animals', would it not be better to employ ordinary usage which indicates that people think feeling is present in such beings? If then it is found that these beings have no feeling, they cease to be classified as animals, and take their place with vegetables or something else. What we must not do is to force on the word *animal* a meaning it does not possess in order to maintain certain beings in a single non-applicable species. In fact, of course, such a species would no longer be a single, but multiple species if it were composed of such different things as beings with feeling and beings without feeling.[25] Asking 'What is an animal?' is a very different question from asking 'Do

[23] Cabanis considered life as feeling, but then used the word *feeling* to describe what a body does in responding with certain exterior effects to the action of stimuli. This is not *feeling* as Linnaeus, Buffon and ordinary people use the word.

[24] Crusca's dictionary defines *animal* very well as 'that which has a feeling soul'.

[25] It is sad to see how many confused ideas are present in Gioia's book, *Esercizio Logico*. He maintains, for example, that some brute beasts lack sensibility, while others are endowed with intelligence! Our young people will derive only imperfect and imprecise ideas from such sloppiness, although their education should at the right time provide them with more accurate, trustworthy notions of things.

[54]

these beings belong to the class "animal" or not?' Ordinary people can easily be deceived in answering the second question without making any mistake about the correct answer to the first.

55. If we examine the origin of the word, it is clear that animal comes from *anima* [soul], and means that which has a soul. Now I do not believe that anyone today holds Aristotle's theory about the vegetable soul, a hypothesis that enabled him to eliminate all difficulty encountered in explaining the growth of plants. Under cover of a word he disguised his ignorance of the special causes of this marvellous event in nature. Leaving aside, therefore, this old philosophical red-herring, which was never accepted by the man in the street, we have to say that the word *anima* [soul] was taken from the word for air (ανεμος) which appears to move of its own accord, and was applied to the sense-principle as the principle of spontaneous movement. Why should we suppose the existence of a soul in bodies if everything happened within them as a result of external, violent movements which are sufficiently explained by physical and chemical forces or by any forces in physical nature? The name 'anima' [soul] must have been chosen in order to indicate something quite different from the possibilities of activity inherent in material forces. What it indicates is *sensation*, the only phenomenon of nature so different from physical movement as to bear no likeness or proximity to it, although sensation has another kind of relationship with movement, which we shall touch upon later.[26]

2

THE ESSENTIAL DIFFERENCE BETWEEN THE FEELING PRINCIPLE AND THE BODY

56. We have to be clear about our need for a word other than 'body' to indicate the principle of the phenomena of sensation. We can understand this need by noting the different and even opposite characteristics of the two series of phenomena of

[26] Giacopo Sacchi was right, I think, when he opposed Brown's analogy between *animals* and *plants* on the ground that the two kinds of beings were essentially different, and that life could not be predicated univocally of both.

which we are speaking, that is, the external phenomena of bodies, and the internal phenomena of sensation. When these differences have been established, the distinction and even opposition of their separate principles, which have rightly been called *body* and *soul*, will be apparent.

This kind of explanation brings in its wake the special advantage of providing my argument with a foundation totally independent of the way in which words are used. In showing the existence in nature of two quite distinct series of phenomena, the consequent necessity of indicating their two distinct principles will require the use of two separate names. If the words *body* and *soul* are then denied me, it will still be necessary to substitute two other words in their place, which is perfectly satisfactory provided there is agreement about the matter in itself. However, once the necessity of two names has been established, there should be no difficulty even in the choice of words, and I am sure that I will be permitted the word *body* to indicate the principle of purely material phenomena, and *soul* to indicate the principle of sensation.

57. The nub of the problem lies in observing the difference between material phenomena and the phenomena of sensation. Let us imagine, then, that we have in front of us a human being, or any animal whatsoever, affected by various sensations. And to make the matter clearer, let us imagine that these sensations are of extreme violence. We perceive this animal with our senses, each of which plays its part in receiving the sensations the animal produces in us. But amongst all the sensations of sight, touch and so on that we have received, there is no trace of the extraordinary pleasure or violent pain that we suppose to be present within the animal. Its pleasure or pain will, of course, have produced contractions and alterations in different parts of its body, and these serve as a sure sign of the pain or pleasure it experiences. In the case of a human being, change of facial colour, wide-open eyes, gritting of the teeth, uncontrolled rigidity or flexibility of the body, and other effects of intense pain, even when not accompanied by groans and screams, show us what the other is suffering. We are not asking, however, if we know another's pain through the effects the suffering produces in the state and shape of his body. We are asking whether we perceive the pain itself or simply the effects of the pain when we see and touch him. Do we see, touch, hear, smell or taste his suffering with our own senses?

We must answer 'No' unhesitatingly. Our sense-organs experience bodies only in so far as bodies are coloured, hard, impenetrable, sonorous, odiferous, tasteful or possess similar feelable qualities which are very different from the other person's pain. The pain, in other words, is not a body.

If I still doubt whether the pain is a body, I can go on to ask myself what colour, shape, hardness, weight, movement, smell or taste it manifests. The question shows immediately how absurd it is to suppose that the pain is a body, or possesses the qualities proper to bodies. And yet, if the pain were perceived by us with our sense-organs, it would have to possess feelable qualities of one kind or another.

This kind of argument is easy to follow, and each one can conclude for himself: 1. that neither the *pain* nor the *pleasure* experienced by another person falls under our senses — it is impossible to imagine that another's pain is a body, that is, a being capable of stimulating our sense-organs; 2. that we knew the other was suffering not because we perceived the pain with our senses, but because we perceived the effects produced by the pain and apparent on his body (change of colour, and so on). We made a rapid calculation and reasoned from the signs to what was signified, that is, from the effects to the cause and concluded that the person was in great pain because his body showed phenomena normally associated with suffering.

58. There is no doubt that the body of the suffering person, which changes externally, and the sensation of his pain are two totally different things. The body falls under my senses, and produces sensations in me; his pain does not fall under my senses, but remains in him alone. The body that falls under my senses is the term of my senses; the pain of someone else is not and cannot be the term of my sense-activity. The pain does not pass outside the *subject* in which it is found. Of its nature, therefore, it is appropriately called *subjective* because it is simply an entirely internal modification or experience of the subject itself. Shape, on the contrary, and the other feelable qualities of the perceived body can be called *extrasubjective* in so far as they are adapted and offered to my sensory faculties as their term while remaining external to them and to me, the perceiving subject. Each of these things (pain and feelable quality) is inconfusible with the other: the term of my sense-organ is not the sensation

itself, and the sensation is not the term and cause of the feelable quality. The term, the cause of sensations (the body) is essentially different from 'myself', that is, from the subject, and even opposed to it. The body does in fact act on 'myself', and hence is active with regard to 'myself', while 'myself' is passive relative to the feelable body. Sensation, on the contrary, appertains to 'myself', exists in 'myself' as perceiving, is a new state of 'myself' and a mode in which 'myself' (that is, the subject) is found to exist.

59. Two opposite kinds of things are felt by us, therefore, which we can call if we wish two series of totally dissimilar phenomena: the phenomena which appear in the body, the external term and cause of sensations, and those pertaining to the subject and remaining within the subject, that is, the sensations themselves. The first series makes us perceive a foreign *activity* upon ourselves, the second a kind of *passivity* in ourselves. And the two series cannot be confused with one another, just as we cannot confuse what is *sensiferous* with what is *sensitive*.

60. But if this is obvious, it is also obvious that such distinct and opposite series of phenomena must depend upon opposite principles. It is clearly necessary for us to admit the existence both of a principle that operates and of a principle that suffers; of a principle proper to that which falls under the senses and of a principle proper to that which constitutes the sensory subject under which the first principle falls; an extrasubjective agent and a feeling subject; in other words, a *body* and a *soul*, inanimate beings and animals.

Whatever name is applied to these principles, they remain the two great classes of things into which the phenomena composing the universe are divided. They can never be reduced to a single principle.

3

LIFE AS A QUALITY OF THE LIVING BODY AND AS A QUALITY OF THE FEELING SOUL

61. Summing up, we may say that there are two entirely different series of phenomena. In one case, phenomena have a

relationship with something different by nature from the feeling subject. We call these phenomena 'extrasubjective'. In the other case, phenomena do not exceed the bounds of the feeling subject, in which they are totally contained. We call such phenomena 'subjective'. The first group of phenomena constitute the *sensiferous qualities* of bodies, and are the cause of sensations; the second constitute the *sensations themselves*.[27]

The two series suppose and require two principles on which they depend: the *sensiferous principle* which prompts sensation, but does not feel; and the *feeling principle*, which feels but does not prompt sensation.

We contrasted these principles by considering them in an animal or a human being under the influence of great pain. The body of this human being, with the alterations in shape caused by the pain, falls under our senses and stimulates them to feel. It pertains therefore to the *sensiferous principle*. The pain by which the person is tormented does not fall under our senses, does not stimulate them, and does not provide us with new sensations. It pertains to the other person's *feeling principle* and is totally contained in the being of whom the pain is an act or a state.

In naming these two principles differently, as we must, we followed normal usage and called the first *body* and the second *soul*, 'anima'. The principle of the *animal* is found in this *anima*. 'Animal' is 'that which has a soul'.

62. This shows clearly that even the merely *feeling* soul is not a body. It is another nature, furnished with properties entirely different from those of the body. We can also see that the body alone, without some other, different principle, could not form the animal. Taken by itself, the body is essentially extrasubjective matter. The animal, on the other hand, supposes an internal subjective principle, that is, a subject.[28]

[27] In *OT*, 640–646, where we distinguished *feelable qualities* from *sensations*, we used the phrase *feelable qualities* instead of the more correct *sensiferous qualities* in order to avoid unnecessary scientific neologisms. But now that we have to deal *ex professo* with *animality* and analyse sensations more closely, we are forced to distinguish what is *feelable* from what is *sensiferous*. Our need for such a word to provide clear, distinct ideas will be seen to be justified as the work proceeds.

[28] Cf. *OT*, 989–995, for an extremely simple, but irrefutable confutation of materialism deduced from the two essentially distinct series of extrasubjective

63. We cannot, therefore, accept the definition of soul given by Aristotle, even if it is restricted to the definition of a merely feeling soul. This famous definition, later accepted by the Scholastics, spoke of the soul as 'an act of an organic body'.[29] If the soul were nothing more than an act of the body, it would not be distinct from the body except to the extent that the act of something is distinct from the thing to which the act pertains. In other words, it would in the last analysis be simply a mode of being of the thing itself. But this is wholly unsatisfactory. The soul is not a mode of being of the body, but something different from the body and, moreover, of an opposite nature. While the body is merely the stimulating or excitatory principle of sensation, the soul is that which feels and possesses sensation in itself, and through the sensation establishes itself in a certain state.

64. We can say, however, that the soul brings the organic body to an act which it did not have previously. In this sense we can call it, as St. Thomas says so clearly, 'the first principle of life',[30] but never, I think, the act itself of a body. It is sufficient to compare a dead with a living body to see that an organic body is given an altogether new act by the soul (the corpse is immobile and corrupt, the living body is constantly in motion, and incorrupt; colour, smell, mien, flexibility and everything perceivable differs from one to the other; the living body possesses an act absent from the dead body), but I would call this *animation*, never *soul*.[31]

65. The matter will be seen more clearly if we re-examine the distinction between our two series of extrasubjective and

and subjective phenomena. The historical origin of materialism is also accounted for in this way. The two series of phenomena are continually united, as we can see from the example of someone in pain. The sufferer manifests himself to us as an extrasubjective principle although in himself he is an altogether subjective principle in which take place phenomena of pain that cannot be observed externally. But it is very easy to confuse the two series and meld them, persuading oneself that all these phenomena are of the same nature. This is the essence of materialism, a system based upon defective observation.

29 *De Anim.*, bk. 3 (text. 4 and 5). 'The soul is the act of a physical, organic body having life in potency'.

30 *S.T.*, I, q. 75, 1.

31 The Platonists were right therefore to distinguish *animation* from *soul* whatever their blunders in other matters.

subjective phenomena which constitute the unchangeable difference between the feeling soul and the body.

To which of the two series do those phenomena belong which, in the living body, enable me to distinguish it so easily from a corpse? They fall under my external senses. I know the distinguishable characteristics of a living body through the sensations it produces in me. My eyes see its colours and movements; my hands feel its diffused, vital heat, the flexibility of the flesh, and the beat of the heart and the pulse; my ears take in its articulate and inarticulate sounds; and further observation reveals that it eats and carries out the other animal functions required to keep it alive. All this I understand by means of the many sensations coming to me from that body.

Passing then from the signs to what is signified, I judge that this body is alive and possesses an act unknown to bodies that are not alive. In other words, the living body has singular qualities and powers which are absent from pure, simple matter. I call the complex of these powers, or rather of these phenomena which I encounter in the body, *life* of the body. Nevertheless, because I receive all these signs from the action that the living body exercises on my sense-organs, these signs belong to extra-subjective, not subjective phenomena. They are phenomena coming from a principle outside me, that is, from outside the feeling subject. Such a principle is not a *feeling* power, but a *sensiferous* or stimulating power present in the body acting upon me. I judge that the *animation* of this body has brought about an alteration in its *sensiferous* power because it arouses sensations in me that cannot be caused by what I call inanimate body; I judge that the sensiferous power of that body has been modified by its reception of a new act which I call *life of the body*; but I do not judge consequently that the *life of the body* is the soul, which is a principle of phenomena wholly opposed to sensi-ferous phenomena, that is, of subjective phenomena. Aristotle's confusion between *life* of the body and the *soul* that produces life had its origin here, and gave rise to a definition of soul ('act of the organic body') which is applicable only to the life of the body.

66. I foresee an objection to what has been said, but the difficulty will in fact help to throw more light on the matter. It will be objected that I have supposed the animation of the body to

be known only through external, feelable signs by which the person who receives the sensations of sight, touch and sound that living bodies normally give concludes that the body is alive. But, the objection runs, the proof of the life of the body originates in what occurs in the living being itself rather than in what takes place in the external experience proper to the senses of others when applied to the living being. One who is alive, knows he is alive, and has no need of external signs to reassure him of life. He alone possesses certain proof of his life; signs that are merely external may easily be deceptive.

I agree. But these signs can be deceptive precisely because they do not permit us to experience the life in question, but only allow us to argue to our conclusion about it. When however we feel that we are alive, we perceive subjective life itself; we have no need to deduce it from signs. We cannot therefore be deceived. But the living being perceives its own life by the sensations or feelings that it receives internally from its own body, and it is here that we need to pay attention to the distinction between the two series of phenomena that we have indicated. Even in the sensations or feelings that a living being experiences in itself independently from external bodies, we have to distinguish the *sensations* themselves felt by that feeling subject from the *agent* which stimulates them in it.

We can take the matter further by considering the case of one who feels life from within and, if we wish, feels simultaneously that he carries out all his vital functions without having to appeal to his eyes or touch or other powers of external feeling. First, we can concentrate our attention solely on the feelings he experiences in himself, and ignore the agent which stimulates these feelings. In this case, we are dealing with phenomena that all take place in the *feeling* principle; sensations or feelings can only be referred to a feeling principle, outside of which we cannot imagine they exist. But that which feels is what we have called the *subject* of sensations. We are concerned, therefore, only with subjective phenomena. Second, we can go beyond the sensations by recognising that they are *passive* phenomena which modify or constitute the state of the being that feels, and conclude that the feeling subject must be stimulated by another principle exterior to itself whose effect is to produce the feelings in the subject. In this case, we have discovered and recognised

[66]

actions done in the subject by some other agent. These *actions*, which cannot be confused with the *sensations* they produce, are the second kind of phenomena which we have called 'extrasubjective', and have referred to a principle totally extraneous to the feeling subject, although it acts in this subject. Once again, therefore, we are faced with the two principles, subjective and extrasubjective, that we have already distinguished.

Each of the two series of phenomena within the feeling of the living person can now be compared with the external phenomena which, through the different sensiferous properties found in a living body, allow us to know it is alive. Without doubt we find that the extrasubjective series is more like this third series of external phenomena. As we have seen, the qualities we find in a living body through our external senses are not the *sensations* themselves, but actions that excite our *sensations*.

Let us now grant that the living being feels its life by means of internal sensations. This feeling of life is either considered to consist in the sensations themselves or in the action or impulse that the living being receives from something different from itself (which is called *body*). In the former case, we are dealing with the *life of the subject that feels* because the sensations come to fulfilment in this subject and remain within it. In the other case, we can rightly speak of the *life of the body*, which does not consist in sensations as the life of the spirit does, but is marked by the nature and characteristics of the life found in the living body when such life is examined with the external senses. This life does not consist in feeling, but in arousing feeling, and can be defined as an aptitude or 'power to act in the feeling subject, and cause in it experiences we call feelings'. In this way the *agent*, which we rightly call *body*, always remains distinct from the *subject*, rightly called *soul*, in which it acts.

67. This gives rise to an important corollary. Through lack of analysis, naturalists are unaware that they take the word *life* in two very different meanings. The resultant confusion is fertile ground for much mistaken teaching. To say 'the subject is alive' and 'the body is alive' is to affirm different realities. The life of the feeling subject consists entirely in sensations; the life of the sensiferous body consists only in certain movements and functions that are the term or cause of sensations but are not themselves sensations.

The same happens with many words that take on different meanings through application to different objects. *Health*, for example, is applied to the *animal* and to medicine, but in very different senses. When we speak of a *healthy* animal, we mean that it is healthy in itself; when we call medicine *healthy*, we mean that it produces health, not that it has states of health and sickness.[32] Affirming that a body has life means that it possesses a power capable of causing a determined system of sensations in a feeling subject which either observes the body from without, or experiences its action from within. A body without this power is said to be dead.[33]

68. There is no doubt that this power has two different kinds of effects all of which, however, are equally subjective. The first kind are those which it causes in a subject that observes the living body from without; the second, those which it causes in the subject that experiences the action of the body from within, that is in itself. The first effects are only *signs*, as we said (cf. 66), from which we reason that a body is alive. We note in the body certain effects of life which are reduced to certain systems of sensations stimulated in us, the observers. The second effects, that is, the internal actions that the living body produces in the feeling subject which as it were inhabits the body are not simply signs of life; the complex or rather the operative power of these effects constitutes *the very life of the animate body*. The first effects are revealed

32 Philosophers must simultaneously adhere faithfully to the common use of words, and make every effort to distinguish the unique, *proper* use of a word from its *derived*, multiple uses. Separating the different meanings of words is often extremely difficult, if not impossible, and gives rise to errors in those who want to employ semantics as a means of discovering the basic opinions of mankind. We can know the true opinion of common sense only through the proper meaning of the word we are studying. — The principal object of dictionaries is first to establish and illustrate the *proper* meaning of each word, and then to indicate its derivations according to their proximity to the proper meaning. But this principle has not yet been employed in the composition of dictionaries.

33 Bichat's definition of life merits attention only as an example of the ignorance of logic often found in famous modern writers on medicine. He says: 'Life is the union of functions which resist death' (p. 1, art. 1). To understand this definition, we need to know the meaning of death. But what is death if not the cessation of life? Life, according to this author, is therefore the union of the functions which withstand the cessation of life!

and noted through *external observation*; the second are revealed only through experience and *internal observation*.

69. These considerations help us to evaluate correctly the common definitions of life offered by naturalists. We now see that these definitions indicate only a complex of signs enabling us to know where life exists. In fact, naturalists normally define the life of the body only through those effects which fall under external observation (which are only signs of life), not through the experience caused by the body to the feeling subject that inhabits it (where the life of the body is properly to be found).

70. The value of this observation can be seen if we consider the two following definitions of life.

According to B. Cuvier:

> Life is a more or less rapid and complicated vortex of molecules which, remaining constant relative to their initial number, take on different appearances. The individual molecules come and go in the vortex in such a way that form is more necessary to the living body than matter.[34]

Ranzani describes life as follows:

> In bodies commonly called living, we *observe* an uninterrupted, visceral movement under attack by certain external agents which tend to alter and destroy it, but supported by other internal and external agents which attempt to sustain it. We also *see* that living bodies, as we call them, generate beings like themselves which grow by means of the introduction of nutritive materials into the basic substance (a feature unknown to other bodies). We also have frequent opportunity of *examining* the internal structure of living bodies and *noting* their organs, that is, the channels through which fluid matter runs. Pores are found in non-living bodies also, but although liquid can be put into these pores, they do not form true channels for the fluids, which do not become part of those bodies and serve to destroy rather than conserve them.[35]

[34] *Le règne animal distribué d'après son organisation*, Introduct.

[35] Readers who wish to test the truth of our observation by applying it to the principal definitions of life given by the best authors will find a collection of these in L. Martini's *Fisiologia*, less. 33. The definitions include those of Stahl, De-Sauvages, Boerhaave, Hoffmann, Gaubio, Leroy, Gregory, Cullen, Vrignauld, Goodwing, Kant, Baumes, Erhard, Caldani, Dumas, Crevisano, Schmidt, Gallini, Girtanner, Chaptal, Humboldt, Sementini, Lamark, Virey,

71. A glance at these and similar definitions and descriptions of the life of bodies is sufficient to show that they refer only to extrasubjective phenomena, and are based on external observation of the living body. They do not truly define life, therefore, but are simply collections of external signs which enable the presence or absence of life to be argued. And it should be carefully noted that I am not referring to *life* as applied to the soul, but to *life* in so far as it can be applied to the body. As we said, *life*, even taken in the sense applied to the body, does not consist in phenomena supplied to us by external observation (these phenomena are only effects and signs of life), but consists solely in phenomena which, although they may be extrasubjective, are supplied by internal experience and observation. Life consists in the power the body has, or rather in the act with which the body acts on the subject that inhabits the body to produce the multiple feeling predicated of life.[36]

4

CLASSIFICATION OF NATURAL BEINGS

72. We have said:

1st. There are two series of *phenomena* in nature: those which *produce* sensations, and can therefore be called sensiferous, and those that *are* the sensations themselves. The former have *body* or matter as their principle, and are *extrasubjective* because they arise and terminate outside the feeling subject. The latter have *soul* as their principle, and are *subjective* because they arise and terminate in the feeling subject.

2nd. Investigation reveals two different states of the body as

Richerand, Hufeland, Darwin, Cuvier, Morgan, Cabanis, Bichat, Adelon, Moion, Sprengel, Brown, and of Martini himself.

36 Paolo Ruffini, the celebrated Modanese doctor, noted with his usual perspicacity that the word *life* was misused by modern naturalists. He wrote about their habit of changing the meaning of the word: 'It is impossible to reach an exact definition of life, incapable of leading to error, as long as life is considered too generically or taken univocally (as modern philosophers tend to do) in the case of vegetable, brute and human life.'

principle of the extrasubjective phenomena. In the first state the body is said to be *alive*, in the second, *dead*. In both states the body remains the principle of extrasubjective phenomena alone, but the phenomena differ according to the living or dead state of the body. These different kinds of phenomena determine whether we say the body is alive or dead.

3rd. The first kind of extrasubjective phenomena, by which we affirm a body is alive, is further divided into the two classes of *externally* and *internally observable* phenomena. Internal observation can be carried out only on our own body, and it is precisely for this reason that we call it our own body.

73. 4th. If we restrict the phenomena which indicate a living body to those which fall under our external observation, we find that they are simply external effects and signs, from which we argue that the body is alive. On the other hand, if the phenomena indicating a body is alive belong to our own internal experience (for example, when we feel ourselves to be alive by means of internal pleasures and pains), such phenomena are not merely effects of the life of the body but actions carried out by the living body directly upon the feeling principle. Hence:

5th. If we judge solely by external signs that a body is alive or dead, we can sometimes be mistaken, as in the case of apparent death, especially from asphyxia. If we know through internal experience that a body is alive, we cannot err, because we feel the living body's action directly, and not simply the effects or signs of the action.

74. 6th. The definitions of life given by naturalists are simply a collection of external signs by which we can know or conjecture that a body is alive. These definitions do not contain the proper notion of bodily life, because this notion is found only 'in the body's power to act constantly and directly on the soul, producing what is commonly called the feeling of life'.

7th. Consequently, we can say that *life* always refers to sensation, and properly speaking, resides in the *soul* where alone sensation is present. Nevertheless, if life means the union of a body with a feeling soul, life is also attributed to the body. In a word, we call life *feeling* or *the term and proximate cause of feeling*.

75. These precise notions allow us to form a rule for dividing natural beings. The indisputable foundation of the first division of natural beings must be, on the one hand, those beings which

lack feeling and give no sign of feeling, and on the other, beings which have feeling and manifest the phenomena of feeling. The former do not indicate a truly subjective, internal existence, but the latter do. The two most general categories or classes of natural beings, therefore, are:

I Class. Extrasubjective beings lacking feeling.

II Class. Subjective beings with feeling.

76. From this we can draw another corollary. When we wish to assign different natural objects to these two general classes, we have to note their internal and external structure and organisation, their forces and relative properties, and finally their functions, because all these observed qualities constitute different systems of extrasubjective phenomena. But we must not take them as the basis of the first, fundamental classification except in their relationship with the feeling they signify and of which they give some degree of probability. This probability or certainty allows us to place them in one of the two classes indicated.

77. Classical writers on natural sciences have always proceeded in this way. In recent times, only a few, influenced by materialism and the accompanying decay of dialectic, have deviated from this important canon of natural science. Consequently, they have not gone beyond the external phenomena, considering such phenomena in themselves and not as an indication of internal sensation.

If Linnaeus, Pallas and other naturalists have placed amongst animals certain productions that Tournefort has placed amongst vegetables, they have done so because they thought they had observed signs of sensitivity. They did not stop at considering the organisation and other external characteristics in themselves, but considered them as signs of internal, subjective phenomena.

78. However, a more thorough examination could reveal that the signs from which Linnaeus and others believed they could deduce the presence of sensitivity, did not demonstrate the existence of feeling with sufficient certainty. In this case, the classification of those natural objects would have to be left in doubt. Spallanzani himself raised doubts of this kind about some natural beings. He says:

> Could not the effects which seem to indicate feeling in certain animals be simply the result of a merely mechanical force. If we start with the monkey and descend through the

different levels of animals, we see that the organs which indicate feeling always become either less in number or harder to identify, so that eventually, in the case of polyps and sea nettles, we judge their feeling by the movements of their contractions and dilations, their capture of prey, and their ingestion, etc. But such a judgment is not really sound because many other kinds of movement resemble these, for instance, a wasp cannot use its sting without detaching the sting from its abdomen; a frog's heart beats for a long time after its removal from the body, and intestines separated from the lower stomach and cut in pieces continue to undulate. If we do not doubt that the movements of the sting, heart and intestines depend on the force of irritability, why cannot the movements of polyps and sea nettles depend on similar causes, especially as these animals indicate pronounced irritability?

The following considerations support these doubts:

A polyp[37] does not hunt its prey, nor search for it with its tentacles.[38] When a foreign body touches the tentacles, they seize it and carry it to the mouth; the polyp swallows the object whatever it is. If the object is digestible, the polyp feeds off it, but if the object has remained intact for some time in the alimentary canal, the polyp rejects it whole. We must not look for feeling in this series of actions, nor in the movements of the leaves of the *dionea musipola* which, when touched by a fly or other insect, closes by crisscrossing its spines or edges like the teeth of a mousetrap. It is true that movements such as these cannot be attributed to feeling because polyps often swallow indifferently their own tentacles together with their prey, but the tentacles, being indigestible, exit later from their stomach like many other bodies.

79. It may be suggested that the phenomena exhibited by zoophytes and similar beings of doubtful nature cannot be reduced to the phenomena of the vegetable kingdom, but this is not sufficient reason for allocating them to the animal kingdom. The *irritability* of zoophytes could be a property entirely of its own and therefore constitute a new kingdom, neither animal nor vegetable.[39] If this were so, the kingdom would be simply a

[37] A tiny, sightless, gelatinous animal found on rocks.

[38] Long thread-like arms that move in all directions.

[39] The movements observable when the sensitive *mimosa pudica* is touched are not attributed to irritability because the movements are simply

[79]

subdivision of the large class of extrasubjective beings from which the class of animals or subjective beings would always remain distinct. Thus, wherever the existence of *irritable* but *non-feeling* beings were identified, the class of extrasubjective beings in nature would be divided into three, not two kingdoms, as follows:

I. Inorganic minerals.

II. Vegetables, the first kind of organic beings.

III. 'Irritable' natures, the second kind of organic beings.

80. This simple suggestion does not seem entirely baseless. Certainly, *irritability* and *contractility* do not need to be accompanied by apparent *sensitivity* in order to exist, because the organs of sensitivity differ greatly from the organs of irritability. Irritability continues in the body even when all feeling has ceased, and some argue that it is present in the human body up to two or three hours after death. A frog's heart continues its contractions for thirty hours after extraction from the body; carp, eels and colubers, when cut into pieces, twist and turn for some hours after the severance of the nerves to the brain. Bacon says he personally saw the heart of an executed man which had been torn from the body and thrown into a fire, jump several times half a metre into the air and then lesser heights for a period of seven or eight minutes. Finally, where irritability is greater in an animal, sensitivity seems less: for instance, in cold-blooded animals whose bodies exhibit great irritability and little sensitivity, while warm-blooded animals seem to have greater sensitivity and less irritablility.[40] Because it can be satisfactorily

the leaves bending back on themselves at the point of articulation. Nor do the branches and leaves become shorter or extend themselves rapidly several times, which is typical of the phenomenon of irritability. It was thought that something similar to this phenomenon had been observed in the male fern of Dodoneus. Swammerdam observed that, when the husks are fully ripe, the dried, rigid funiculus suddenly extends in a straight line dividing itself into two half spheres and shooting the seeds forcefully into the air. But such phenomena are simply the action of elasticity. The same can be said about similar phenomena observed in other plants.

40 We should note (as has already been observed) that, prescinding from the contractility or irritability of these bodies, their other properties indicate a closer proximity to the species of less perfect rather than more perfect vegetables. Thus some zoophytes were mistaken for algae or other cryptogams and not classified as plants with a more perfect organisation.

demonstrated, therefore, that irritability and contractility[41] do not definitely indicate feeling in a body, why could they not be the distinguishing mark of a separate kingdom of beings?[42]

5

THE CHAIN OF BEINGS

81. I would like to indicate an erroneous consequence of the naturalists' attempt to define life. For them, life lies in certain external qualities of bodies (which, however, are often only uncertain signs of life — life is an internal power). They believe that a continual gradation can be found in the beings of nature, without any intervening gap.

It is clear that once the subjective element is ignored, only the extrasubjective characteristics remain as a basis for classifying natural beings. These characteristics do indeed exhibit a kind of finely graduated scale. As long as we consider corporeal beings solely in their external, sensible appearance, we notice only variation in colour, shape and movement, a combination of colour, shape and movement according to certain laws, and their being ordered in systems or functions. These variations can constitute only accidental differences, never an essential difference of

[41] Undoubtedly, the phenomenon of elasticity has some analogy with animal contractility. Elasticity is due apparently to a displacement of the elements constituting the *elastic molecules* which, however, do not exceed their mutual sphere of attraction. Thus, if they are moved by force, they return to their natural position, determined by their centre of gravity, as soon as the violence disturbing them ceases. But before coming to rest, they oscillate as a result of the impulse they have received. Is it not possible that a similar displacement and replacement of elements takes place in *contractile molecules*, thus producing the repeated contractions of the fibre? Is it possible to know the mobility of the elements of contractile molecules, the laws of their mutual attraction, and the weightless agents that are simultaneously involved in producing the phenomenon without any apparent need of animal action?

[42] Brown considered that *irritability* and *sensitivity* both depended on *excitability*. Dr. Marzari refuted this system when he observed that these two properties, because of their great difference, cannot be confused nor reduced to a single principle.

[81]

genus and species. Accidental differences can be arbitrarily classified, even according to a gradation not observable by our senses.

But the case is quite the opposite if in addition to considering natural beings in their extrasubjective existence, we also note in them subjective existence. Immediately we discover two essences that are so different, so contrary (as are a *sensation* and what I call the *sensiferous quality*, which produces the sensation), that they admit of no dividing grades, nor of any passage from one to another. The distance between feeling and non-feeling is one of essence, not of grade, just as the distance between what is active and what is passive, between cause and effect, is a distance of essence and not of grade.

82. Some naturalists, therefore, observing that the higher and more perfect organisation of some plants resembles that of some of the more imperfect animals, thought they had found the two links in a chain that joined plants to animals. But they did not notice that in comparing the organisation of animals and plants, they were comparing only something external to an animal (its sensible organisation), not the animal itself;[43] animality, which is internal and not subject to external observation, entirely escaped their attention. Even if the gradation of animals is ascertained through what they *exhibit* externally, the immense leap (if we can call it that) from feeling to non-feeling, that is, in what they *are*, always remains [*App.*, no. 2].

83. These observations are true even granted the hypothesis which claims that everything is animate. Such a hypothesis can be conceived only by distinguishing the feeling soul from its body, an insensitive or non-feeling term which is simply felt. This immense difference remains to separate that which feels from that which does not feel, in other words, to separate the soul from the body. Hence, even in this hypothesis, the classification of natural beings into those that give signs of feeling and those that do not, remains true.

43 St. Thomas says: '"Animal" is that which has a feeling nature' (*S.T.*, I, q. 3, art. 5).

6

THE DISTINCTION BETWEEN ORGANIC LIFE AND ANIMAL LIFE MADE BY SOME PHYSIOLOGISTS

84. Naturalists must apply themselves, therefore, to determining which signs definitely indicate *sensation* and which do not. Only this criterion will allow us to classify experimentally as animal or non-animal the different beings produced by nature.

85. In the meantime it seems certain as a result of what we have noted that neither the force of *contractility* or irritability alone, nor elasticity, extensibility, swelling and similar forces in which some scientists think they have observed what resembles spontaneous movement, can be claimed as a definite sign of sensitivity. Thus, without more definite signs of feeling, a body should not be classified among animals simply because it indicates these forces.

86. Some may wish to apply the name 'life' to these kinds of *mobility*, although we cannot presume that sensation accompanies it. But that is their business; I do not want to discuss words. It is sufficient if we understand that the kind of life we predicate of any *organism* whatsoever that is capable of moving itself according to certain laws or under certain stimuli, is far removed from, and of an entirely different nature to, the life present in *feeling*. This life is subjective, independent of any external observation and located totally in a principle that feels, manifesting itself solely in its external effects.

87. Moreover the ideas of physiologists concerning animality and life are extremely confused, for the reason, I believe, that they take little account of psychological studies.[44]

Bichat, at the beginning of his work on life and death, distinguishes two lives, *organic* and *animal*. He says: 'One of these lives is common to vegetables and animals simultaneously, while the other is the special heritage of animals.'[45] It is clear that life

[44] It is a fact that materialism, although rejected today by all sciences, is still entrenched in medicine. Psychological and philosophical studies should be part of medical science.

[45] P. 1, art. 1, §1.

common to vegetables can never consist in *feeling*, since vegetables as such do not have feeling. Because this author considers life solely in its phenomena and external effects, he considers it in organs and movements, without grasping its internal, subjective and essential characteristic. This characteristic is *feeling*, which cannot be observed under the microscope or cut with a knife. Consequently, he attributes *sensitivity* to both organic life (such as vegetables) and animal life. He combines true sensitivity with visible, palpable characteristics without being aware that sensitivity is neither seen nor touched, nor subject to external experience in the way that corporeal qualities are.

88. He says: 'In organic life, sensitivity is the faculty of receiving an impression, but in animal life it is the faculty of receiving an impression and transmitting it to a common centre.'[46] In these definitions we see two sensitivities indicating impressions and movements. But impressions and movements are external things. The principal thing, the core, that is, *feeling*, which alone constitutes sensitivity, is missing. In fact, the most insensitive object, whether soft or hard, can receive an *impression*, which, depending on the thing's composition, will propagate itself to a material centre by vibrations or some means of movement. But if the thing has no sense-capacity, no feeling of any kind is aroused in it; neither the impression nor communication to a centre constitute sensitivity. Sensitivity is something essentially different from all such external phenomena.

89. Bichat adds: 'The stomach is sensitive to the presence of food and the heart to blood. — The amount of sensibility in the excretory channels is analogous to that of the fluids flowing through them but disproportionate to that of other fluids to which it does not allow entry.'[47]

These words clearly indicate what led him and many other physiologists into error. They noticed that the stomach, heart and excretory orifices perform their functions in the presence respectively of food, blood and certain fluids, but not in the presence of other fluids. They concluded that all these parts have their own *sensitivity*. But this is a misuse of words, and I cannot really think that these scientists mean true sensations;

[46] P. 1, art. 7, §3.

[47] P. 1, art. 7, §3 and 4.

they must mean movements similar to those seen in beings that have feeling. These beings flee what causes them pain or distress, seeking out what gives pleasant sensations.[48] The word *sensitivity* is grossly misused if such effects and organic sensitivity are interpreted by these scientists simply as a kind of affinity or attraction which enables the parts to unite with certain bodies but not with others. If, however, they mean a real *sensitivity*, we can only repeat that this is inadmissible if there are no clear indications of the presence of feeling. Although the effects noted are not sufficient proof of feeling, movement away from what is unpleasant to what is pleasant can manifest some capacity, as it were, to choose and discern, because movement could be referred to a cause entirely lacking in sense, for example, to a particular kind of molecular attraction, or to animal magnetism, or any other unknown cause which up to the present these physiologists understand as material. It may be claimed that the orifices of the milk channels, for example, have real feeling solely because we observe that the open orifices in the intestines attract the chyle alone and reject all other fluids mixed with it. It is not my intention to discuss the value of this hypothesis (which would require us to explain all phenomena of chemical affinity by means of feeling in the smallest particles). The question is: why should this kind of sensitivity be called organic, not *animal* like every other feeling? If real feeling can exist without real animality, we need to know how this is possible.

90. In other places, the author under discussion (and nearly all modern writers on physiology) seems to deny any feeling to organic sensitivity, positing feeling as the distinguishing characteristic of animals: 'All the phenomena of digestion, circulation, secretion, respiration, absorption, nutrition, etc. belong to this organic sensitivity . . . It is common to plants and animals: zoophytes have it equally with the most perfectly

[48] Bichat tries to distinguish his *organic sensitivity* from *contractility*, but this puts him in the embarrassing position of having to explain organic sensitivity by some hidden, entirely hypothetical cause which contracts the organ by means of an *impression*. He says: 'All the authors maintain that *irritability* indicates simultaneously a sensation aroused in an organ on contact with a body, and the contraction of the organ as it reacts on the body itself' (P. 1, art. 7, §5).

organised quadrupeds. *Sensations*' (we should note this) '*and perception* derive from it, as do the pain and pleasure which modify it . . . Furthermore, this sensitivity cannot be considered as an attribute of vegetables, to which it does not belong.'[49]

Accordingly every sensation and perception, pleasure and pain pertains to animal sensitivity, while organic sensitivity is simply *sensitivity* that feels nothing, like the sensitivity of a vegetable!

After our author (and a large number of physiologists with him) has thus described these supposed animal and organic sensitivities, he compares them and finds no essential difference between them. The only difference, he claims, is one of degree: animal sensitivity is merely a greater quantity of organic sensitivity! This statement may appear unbelievable to a thinking person, but it is found in the authors we are discussing. Bichat says:

> At first, these two kinds of animal and organic sensitivity present a notable difference, but their nature seems to be essentially the same; probably, one is only the *maximum* range of the other, the same force presenting itself more or less with different characteristics.[50]

The sensitivity proper to vegetables, therefore, which according to Bichat have neither sensations nor pleasure nor pain, is the sensitivity proper to animals, varying only in quantity. Such an absurdity is the inevitable conclusion of considering in *sensitivity* only the external *impression* and the movements sensitivity produces. Feeling, which alone appertains to sensitivity, is lost to view. The *impression*, the movements it causes, the systems of these movements (called functions), all fall equally under *external observation*, and therefore belong to the same species; their visible differences are simply accidental, variations of quantity and degree, but not of essence. I repeat, however, that sensitivity is not present in external things visible to the eye; sensitivity is something completely hidden, invisible, and situated solely in the feeling subject, not in any piece of matter.

91. The inaccuracy of the physiologists' language will become clearer if we consider the proofs Bichat uses to establish that

49 P. 1, art. 7, §3.

50 *Ibid.*

organic and animal sensitivity differ only in degree. All of his proofs are drawn from the observation that certain parts of the body which seem without sensitivity exhibit a feeling of pain when subject to determined stimuli. He concludes: 'It is evident that the difference established earlier in the sense-faculty concerns the various modifications of which the nature is susceptible, not the nature itself, which is the same throughout. This faculty is common to all the organs penetrated by it, because none of them can be said to lack feeling'; consequently, 'the sensitivity, distributed in a certain quantity in one organ, is animal, but in a lesser quantity is organic.'[51]

First, we must differentiate between a question of physiology and a question of logic and psychology, because only the latter concerns us in this study. Physiology asks 'which parts of the human body have feeling, and under what conditions do they give us a sensation to which we do not advert'. This question of fact is not our concern here; we are happy to let the physiologists dispute whether the nerves alone or other parts have feeling [*App.*, no. 3].

Bichat says that the 'organic sensitivity' he is discussing is in fact animal sensitivity, but in a lesser quantity. We want to know if this lesser quantity or, if preferred, least quantity, of animal sensitivity has any *feeling* at all. It would seem it has, because he says: 'The sensitivity is changing all the time from animal to organic and vice versa according to the increase or diminution of its intension.' But if this is true, how can he say that animal sensitivity is suddenly extinguished at the moment of violent death, while organic sensitivity persists for an unspecified time? His proof is: 'The lymphatics continue to absorb, the muscles still feel the point of a pin, nails and hair grow and feel the fluids they draw from the skin, etc.'[52] But when animal sensitivity has been annihilated by death, are we dealing with real *feeling* or with the function of organs entirely devoid of feeling? If even the least quantity of feeling is present, should we not say that the animal is still alive, or at least that living animality remains? And if feeling is no longer present but only contractility, tonicity, elasticity, affinity and other forces that are considered entirely

51 *Ibid.*

52 *Ibid.*

devoid of feeling and continue their functions for a period of time, how can we say that this organic force, whatever it is, differs only in degree and quantity from the animal sensitivity now said to be annihilated? In other words, although there are degrees of lesser or greater movement in one direction or another, the difference between feeling and not feeling is in no way a matter of degree. Granted that for some time after death we can find functions in vegetables and animal bodies that resemble the functions of an animate body, the difference between life and death, between vegetable and animal, is not a matter of degree.

7

THE FEELING PRINCIPLE IS UNEXTENDED

92. What has been said shows once more how serious a mistake it is to confuse the *sensiferous* principle, which causes sensation but does not itself feel, with the *feeling* principle, which feels but does not cause feeling. In other words, it is a mistake to confuse *body* with *soul*.

We are forced to conclude that life resides properly speaking in the *feeling* principle although the *sensiferous* principle, if considered as acting directly and constantly on the *feeling* principle, is called *animate* or *living body*, and if considered as acting only indirectly on the feeling principle, that is, modifying the animate body, is called *brute body*. Nevertheless in both cases the *sensiferous principle* simply remains what it is, and feels nothing. The *life* attributed to it does not have the same meaning as that attributed to the feeling principle, the proper seat of life. In the sensiferous principle, which is alive only in the sense that medicine is said to be healthy, we simply find a cause that stimulates feeling.

93. Having distinguished the two principles and the two series of phenomena so that one cannot be confused with the other, the philosopher now has to concentrate more explicitly on the relationship between these two principles and two series of phenomena.

In this and the following chapters, I want to offer only a few thoughts on this relationship to draw attention to the importance of such investigations. I shall begin by pointing to the opposing aspects in the relationship between these two principles, and show that the body, the principle of extrasubjective phenomena, is essentially extended, while the soul, the feeling principle and principle of subjective phenomena, is essentially unextended.

Article 1.
First demonstration of the simplicity of the feeling principle

§1. Demonstration

94. I take any body whatsoever as the object of my thought, and I ask myself what is its characteristic, essential property. Without doubt, the body that I conceive mentally (and I can speak only about my own mental conceptions, not of anything else) has the following essential, characteristic property: every single part is outside every other part. And the same can be said about every other body. I conclude therefore: 'Body is an entity whose essence is such that every part, great or small, which can be thought in it, is outside every other part'.

95. Having established this essential property of body, I now wish to see if it is possible, or impossible and contradictory, for the body to be the feeling principle. The core of the difficulty can be expressed as follows. Let us suppose that feeling adheres to a body as a property of the body. In this case, all the parts I assign in the given body will possess feeling. However, each part in the body is essentially outside every other part. Because each part has its own boundaries, therefore, our supposition necessarily requires that the feeling adhering to these parts likewise remains within these boundaries and limited to the individual parts of the body. Consequently, the feeling of one part will be outside the feeling of all the other parts. If this were the case, the feeling would make up not a single feeling principle, but as many principles as there are assignable parts in the body. Moreover, each of these feeling principles would feel

only its own part without extending to the other parts because, as we said, each part to which a feeling principle adheres is outside all the other parts.

Now it is also certain that the parts thought and noted in a body can be divided indefinitely, and that each of the tiny assignable sections which make up the whole body is always outside every other. The feeling of each of the minute sections, therefore, will be outside the feeling of all the others. But however small we imagine a part to be, it can always be mentally divided into still smaller sections. Thus we can go on assigning feeling principles without ever arriving at the last feeling principle. Finally, we can choose between two suppositions: either the minute parts remain extended, and therefore with parts always allocated outside one another; or (and this supposition is absurd as we have shown)[53] the minute extended parts finally come to be changed through constant division into simple points. In the second case, feeling would adhere to simple points and would never be suitable for feeling that which is extended; in the first case, the true seat of feeling would never be discovered and the final consequence would be that of the second case. Because the minute sections would continue to be extended, with each of their assignable parts outside every other, the feeling adhering to each point could never emerge from that point (a point never exceeds itself) and therefore would not be suitable for feeling what is extended.

96. This argument provides the evidence for a very beautiful, unassailable truth: 'That which is extended cannot feel what is extended.' What is extended always has its parts outside each other — one part is not extended inside another. If one part feels, its feeling would, therefore, be outside the feeling of the other parts, and any feeling with an assignable point in the part would be outside the feeling of all the other points.

97. It is clear that extension, as an essential property of body, makes the body different in its essential properties from the essential properties of feeling, which cannot be found in what is extended but only in a completely simple subject to which the whole of what is extended is simultaneously present. There is, I

[53] *OT*, 871.

think, no answer to this demonstration of the simplicity of the feeling principle, if the demonstration is understood correctly.

§2. *Corollary 1.* On forming a correct concept of the simplicity of the feeling soul

98. An important corollary dependent upon this demonstration concerns the correct concept we should form of the simplicity of the feeling soul. We should never imagine the soul as a mathematical point (as some do). If the soul were a mathematical point, the feeling proper to this point could never go outside the point (for the reason we have stated) and would not be suitable for feeling anything extended.

99. Moreover, a mathematical point is only a *mental being* which we form by abstraction. It never exists in nature or of itself. As the extremity of a line, it cannot be separated from the line. If it were separated it would simply form another line, however small, but never a point. The concept of a point is not that of any real being, but of a simple relationship, that is, of the term of linear extension. Those who take a mathematical point as an example of the simplicity of the soul set out on a path that leads them away from the right understanding of the feeling principle.

100. We have to be on our guard against seeking the nature of this feeling principle through images and in abstractions taken from matter. We need to be satisfied with observing the feeling principle in itself and in its proper phenomena without adding anything extraneous to the principle. If we do this, we can convince ourselves, notwithstanding the wonder we experience, of the existence in nature of a being different from material beings, and naturally distinct from them. This being has no likeness whatsoever to matter, although it can be related actively and passively with matter. Penetrating thinkers soon find their wonder directed at a new object, and begin to notice that it is more difficult to explain the existence of matter than that of an immaterial principle possessing a mode of being altogether different from material being.

§3. *Corollary 2.* The seat of the soul in the body

101. Another very important corollary from what we have said concerns the proper seat of the soul in the body. If the soul is neither extended nor simply a mathematical point, where is it to be found?

As long as the soul is regarded as a point, it is natural to ask about its location. A point always has a situation relative to matter, and this place can be mathematically determined through three planes or three lines in different planes. But if the soul is not a point, does the question about the place of the soul in the body have any meaning?

102. As soon as we have formed a correct concept of the simplicity of the soul, it becomes clear that the question has no meaning in itself. After the appearance of philosophy, however, the problem occupied and divided astute minds for many centuries. No compromise could be reached on an answer because in fact the question permitted no answer. Descartes decided that the soul was to be found in the pineal gland; Lancisi, De la Peyronie, Teichmeyer placed it in the corpus callosum. Digby, not having found it in the corpus callosum, decided that its dwelling was the septum lucidum. After a vain search here, Drelincourt settled for the cerebellum, Willis for the corpora striata, Le-Cat for the meninges and Vieussens for the marrow part of the brain called the centrum ovale. Others located it, and go on locating it, wherever they please. But such learned discussions and work, the fruit of an unclear idea and a confused concept of the soul, are useless despite the multiple theories, systems and stupendous libraries constructed upon them.

103. Once the notion proper to the *simplicity* of the soul has been adequately clarified, great theories vanish like smoke. Once we realise that the soul is not extended, and is not a mathematical point, it is easy to conclude that it does not occupy space, and is not to be found in one place rather than another. We do indeed discover traces and effects of its action in different parts of the body, but the soul itself is not found in any large or small part of the body, nor in the body as a whole, nor in any point. Its mode of being cannot be compared, proportioned or likened to anything material, or to any property of matter. As we said, it possesses only a *relationship* of activity and passivity to matter, which is nothing more than a *relationship of feeling*.

Article 2.
Second demonstration of the simplicity of the feeling principle

§1. Demonstration

104. We need to demonstrate the same truth in another way. This proof also starts from facts.

It is very easy to see that many parts of the human body used immediately and obviously in the service of sensations are duplicated, while those which support organic life are single. The stomach, heart, intestines, spleen, liver, and so on, form unique working parts in the body; the eyes, ears, nostrils[54] are duplicated, and the nerves receiving the impressions — the optic, acoustic, taste and olfactory systems — are distributed in symmetrical pairs. In the case of the exterior senses, therefore, each person has a twofold impression through his two eyes, ears and so on. Moreover, each *impression* taken on its own has a corresponding *sensation*. If I close one eye, the other gives me a complete sensation; if I block one ear, I receive all the sound from the other, and so on. When I use both eyes or ears together, however, a single sensation corresponds to the two impressions. My two eyes do not provide me with two sight-objects: my two ears make me hear the single flute that is playing, not two. This is a fact, and with this as my basis I reason as follows.

105. Suppositions about the fusion in the brain[55] of the two

54 'Although a single membrane receives taste impressions, the membrane itself is divided in two by a line separating two perfectly similar segments' (Bichat, *Ricerche fisiologiche* etc., p. 1, art. 2, §1).

55 Woolaston offered the ingenious hypothesis that each optic nerve is divided to form immediately half of both retinas. Consequently the images outside the optic axis would come half from one eye and half from the other. There are serious difficulties against this hypothesis, as physics shows, but what concerns us here is the undoubted fact that when the two eyes are fixed on something directly in front of them, one part of the impression they receive corresponds to the middle part of the image which is equal for both eyes, although the person receiving the impressions sees a single scene, not a twofold scene. In Woolaston's hypothesis, therefore, the spirit through its own simplicity would have to compose a single image from four, rather than

impressions received, for example, in the optic nerves are not confirmed by anatomical findings which show rather that the brain itself is divided into two distinct parts.[56] This is not, of course, a decisive argument. The conjunction between each pair of corresponding nerves could yet be found, or could be present in nature without its being found. But there are other effective reasons for excluding it. If in fact the two optic nerves were united at some point, how could the two eyes see different images simultaneously, as sometimes happens? In such a case, the same small bundle of nerves in which the two optic nerves united would be affected differently by either optic nerve. The result would be a single, in-between movement which would be neither the one image nor the other, but a confused sensation made up of both.

106. Moreover, an obvious proof that the two nerves cannot unite to form one is given by the following reasoning.

The action of light on the two small, end-surfaces of the optic nerves is not uniform unless the object seen possesses a uniform shape and colour. The action varies with the variations presented by the shape and colour of the seen object. If it were possible to distinguish physical points or tiny surfaces in the two surfaces formed by the iris, then the light, in accordance with the tint that has to be aroused in the sensation, would make a different impression in each tiny surface or section. The image or total sensation aroused is lined and varied according to the various actions of the light, and results from the complex action of the light on all the tiny parts or sections of the terminal surface of the optic nerve. Hence every varying point of colour or tint in the image or sensation corresponds to a point in the extremity of the optic nerve affected variously by the light.

We can now conceive mentally either that the optic nerve is formed of a tiny cable of minute nerve-threads, each of which is

two images. Hence the difficulty remains.

[56] 'Amongst all the organs, the brain by which we receive so many impressions is especially noteworthy because of the regular shape of its parts. These are exactly equal on both sides as we can see in the thalami of the optical nerves, and so on. The dissimilar parts are themselves divided symmetrically by a median line of which there are obvious traces in the corpus callosum, the arch with three pillars, the annular protuberance, and so on' (Bichat, *Ricerche fisiologiche*, etc., p.1, art. 2, §1).

responsible for transporting to the brain the impression made upon it by a little ray of light (and this seems certain); or that, in place of these nerve-threads, the optic nerve transmits every differing point of impression through distinct movements. In this case, the nerve itself is moved differently along the length of each of its sections as though it were made up of many, very subtle, smaller nerves, each with its own movement. In both hypotheses, I maintain it is easy to prove the impossibility of the optic nerves terminating in a single, united nerve which gives rise to a single image.

If a single nerve hypothesis were possible, the phenomenon could only be explained by admitting that two corresponding filaments of the optic nerves come together and continue as a single filament, just as the nerve which receives the two filaments would continue as a single nerve. Otherwise, if the filament of one optic nerve attached itself to a filament of the central nerve and the filament of the other optic nerve attached itself to another filament, the corresponding impressions and sensations would have to be two, not one. But granted that every nerve filament of one eye which transmits a point of the impression (corresponding to a point of the image or sensation) is united to the same point of the central nerve as the corresponding nerve filament of the other eye, the unity of the image could no longer be explained, because such a unity could come about only if there were a unity of impression in the central nerve. But this unity would require that the filament of the nerve of one eye which carries the impression, for example, of a tiny red square, should bring this impression of red to the point in which the corresponding filament of the other eye brings an equal impression. If the red square were brought to the central nerve not by the corresponding filament, but by another joining the central nerve in a different point, there would be two, not one, red squares in the central nerve. If the corresponding filament brought to the central nerve the impression of a blue square, two impressions would be concentrated in the same point of the central nerve, one corresponding to the red and one to the blue sensation. The result would be an in-between sensation in which the image would be confused or made up of alternating and varying colours. The object viewed by both eyes would be coloured differently from the same object seen with one eye.

[106]

In order that the two corresponding filaments may transmit the same impression, they would have to be touched at their extremities by an equal action of light. This, however, is precisely what does not happen, as we can easily notice by observing how light coming from the same object strikes the two eyes. It does not strike the two eyes in such a way as to make an impression with the same rays on the same extremities of the optic nerve, nor does it strike the eyes from the same angle, especially if the eyes are turned to look at something to one side. If this object has a white spot, we still see it as a single spot with both eyes although the light moving from that spot does not fall exactly upon the same place in the retina of both eyes, nor affect the same nerve filaments which are supposed to unite in a single point of the central nerve. On the contrary, it strikes the filaments that join the central nerve in different places. According to such a hypothesis the white spot should be duplicated because a twofold impression has been brought to the supposed central nerve that receives the two optic nerves.

Unless I am mistaken, this is an irrefutable, convincing proof that even if the two optic nerves did join to form a single nerve, the unity of sensation corresponding to equal impressions in the two eyes would still not be explained.

The same proof can be strengthened if we note the optical law according to which two impressions present a single object to our feeling. 'When two optic axes terminate in a single point, this point is seen as something simple, not double.' The direction of the optical axes depends upon the terminal plane of the optic nerve against the light. The compenetration of the two impressions, therefore, does not arise because the extremities of the nerves are affected, but from the angle at which the light falls upon these extremities. It would be of no help if the nerves were joined at some point in the brain. Everything depends upon the position of the plane which the nerves present to the light at their extremities.

107. G. B. Venturi affirms that there would be grounds for believing in the union of the impressions of the two eyes in the same part of the brain if it were true, as some have maintained, that a green sensation resulted from blue rays being made to fall on one eye and yellow rays on another. Venturi himself does not give credence to the union because he has never managed to

reproduce the green phenomenon.[57] But even if green were reproduced, such a phenomenon would not provide sufficient proof for accepting the union of the two impressions: the unification of the image does not arise from intermingling of colours, but from identification of space.

My own opinion is that even if the supposed phenomenon were verified, it would serve to confirm the separation of the two optic nerves rather than their union in a single nerve. If I look with one eye at a patch of blue and with the other at a patch of yellow, it is certain that my yellow and blue sensations are distinct as long as the optical axes remain parallel. This alone is sufficient to prove that the two optic nerves do not form a single nerve in which the impressions are centred in the same space. But whenever I have crossed my eyes, I have always seen one colour on top of another, while both become lighter and as it were transparent. This proves that the image is not unified through the conjunction of the optic nerves, but through the identical space to which the soul refers the two images. This space is the proper term of the feeling principle, and hence internal, relative to the soul. I have also observed that I could render colours more or less strong or weak at will by looking more steadily with one or other eye. Looking equally steadily with both eyes, however, I found the colours taking on a paler hue and fading into one another. All this shows that their union does not come about materially in a common nerve.

108. The union of the two nerves in a single nerve cannot be granted therefore, or if it is granted it does not help to concentrate the impressions. Truly distinct *impressions* remain in the body, and a single *sensation* in the soul which, in this case, is like the single sound from a single bell rung by two people. Such a sound is obviously a phenomenon that does not occur in the body, although the impressions that go to producing it do occur there. If this phenomenon adhered to the bodily impressions without being distinct from them, it would be twofold as they are twofold. It is therefore distinct and separate from the bodily impressions and pertains to another principle bereft of bodily multiplicity. This principle is called the *soul*.

[57] *Riflessioni sulla conoscenza dello spazio che noi possiamo cavar dall'udito*, inserted in his *Indagine fisica sui colori*, Modena, 1801.

§2. An objection resolved

109. I realise that this demonstration, although it appears very convincing to me, will cause difficulties to some readers. I hope that the following reflections will resolve their problems.

First, we have to eliminate the idea, held by some, that two *sensations* as well as two *impressions* of every object we see are truly in our eyes. It would seem, according to this objection, that the two sensations appear as one because of touch, which certifies that only one object is actually seen. Our judgment, the objection continues, habitually goes beyond the twofold sensation to the simple tactile object to which it refers the two sensations of the eyes.

110. A careful examination of the facts presents the following reasons for not accepting this explanation.

1st. While the objection is applicable to the eyes, it cannot be applied to the ears because the sound-sensation is not referred to the sonorous body in the way that colour is referred to the tactile body.

111. 2nd. If we did in fact have two sensations, it would be impossible not to be aware of them, at least through determined, concentrated effort. Sensations remain in us, whatever our habitual judgments. There never will be a case in which sensations, especially ocular sensations, which are very noticeable, will disappear completely from our attention in virtue of some habitual judgment we have made. This becomes even more marked when we consider that the judgment made about the unity of the object is different from that made about sensations. If the sensations were two, and the tactile object one, we would pronounce two judgments, one of which would affirm the two sensations, and the other a single object indicated by the two sensations.

Let us consider a simple fact which will show us without doubt that we could not avoid observing the two sensations if they were present in us. Sometimes our eyes become distorted if, for instance, we bring a small irregular object very close to them. In this case two sensations are indeed present. Moreover we are immediately aware of them and of what appears to be two objects. But with hand and judgment we correct the mistake, and conclude that they are one. The same thing happens in other cases where our judgment corrects the error to which our feeling-power would lead us. If we stand at the end of a long drive of cypresses, for example, we judge that the trees are all more or less of the same size. This judgment, however, does not destroy or even change the actual sensation we have of the trees, nor does it prevent us from becoming aware of the sensations. We are still capable of telling ourselves that we see the last cypresses in the drive as much smaller than the first. Our habitual judgment does not prevent us from noticing the sensations although they have been emended, as we say, by the judgments themselves.

112. 3rd. If naturally we had two sensations in our eyes and corrected this error through habit, it should be possible to discover the twofold sensation in babies. A habit as strong as this, which enables us to judge the opposite of what sensations show us and would lead us to nullify a sensation (this is what is implied), can be formed only gradually. There is no experience of this in babies, however.

113. 4th. Moreover, we need to consider that the sensation received by a person with both eyes open and motionless (we speak only about sight because many of the things said about this sense can be applied to other senses)[58] is a single sensation made up of three sections. In other words, the whole luminous orbit seen by the two eyes can be divided into three parts: 1st. the right part, not seen by the left eye; 2nd. the left part, not seen by the right eye; 3rd. the middle part, seen by both eyes. The two impressions produce a single sensation only in the middle part where they become identical. Despite the different view of these three parts of the visual orbit when seen by one or two eyes, the orbit itself presents a uniform, continuous and therefore single sensation where no lines of separation can be found. Consideration of this phenomenon enables us to conclude

[58] According to G. B. Venturi's experiments, sound is heard in the direction of the acoustic axis. This proves that the two impressions on the ears cannot be turned into one in the brain. The sensation of the single sound is truly composed of two sensations each of which is capable of being heard separately, as Venturi himself observes. Cf. *Riflessioni sulla conoscenza dello spazio che noi possiamo ricavare dall'udito*, in his *Indagine fisica sui colori*, Modena, 1801.

that the habitual judgment could not simplify the sensation, if this were a double sensation, because it would simplify the total sensations received by the eyes, not just a part of them. The fact is, however, that one part of the sensation of each eye remains separate, and the other part coalesces. There must therefore be a difference not only in the judgment passed on the same sensation but also in the nature itself of the sensation. Consequently, the middle part of the visual orbit has indeed two impressions in the eyes, to which corresponds, however, a single sensation in the soul. On the other hand, the extreme parts of the orbit have two impressions to which correspond two sensations in the soul. These sensations are in continuity with the sensation of the middle part in such a way that we see a single visual screen without divisions. This is possible because the space of the screen, which adheres to the soul, is one.

114. 5th. Finally, the matter can be reduced to a rigorous demonstration. It is clear that when we see a single body, e.g. an orange, with both eyes, the orange as seen proffers a single space, a single round disc. If there are two sensations they have only the single disc as their term because what we feel is certainly reduced to that disc. If, however, the same disc is the term of both sensations, the sensations can only be one sensation because every sensation essentially possesses extension. The single extension, however, is not that of the real body because the real body is outside our eyes and soul. Nor can the extension be that of the impressions of light upon the retina because they would then be two. The soul, therefore, has a single space in which, under certain conditions and dependent upon certain laws, it arouses a single sensation on occasion of the twofold impression it receives in the optic nerves. The soul could not do this if it were not simple.

§3. The law governing the fact which has been adduced as a proof of the simplicity of the soul

115. We now have to indicate the reason why the sensation corresponding to the two impressions of symmetrical organs

is single in certain cases but duplicated in others. The law states: 'Everything seen by the soul by both eyes is a surface plane with a position given by nature,[59] that is, a felt plane. If the two impressions occupy different parts of this plane, the soul has two sensations dependent upon different extensions and sometimes different colours; if the two impressions occupy the same parts of the felt plane, the soul has only one sensation relative to extension, although the impressions may be separated from one another in external (tactile) space. If the colours in the same space are different, the soul sees them mixed and, as it were, transparent' (cf. 107).

116. To understand this stupendous law, 1. we have to set aside the common opinion that sight of itself sees distances. It sees distances only in the way that distances are seen on walls painted with scenes in perspective. Perspective drawing presents distances to the imagination, not to sight. The eye, therefore, sees only a plane painted in different colours. 2. We have to notice the difference between touch and sight sensations. The former are curved surfaces because their locality is the surface itself of our body which varies in curvature. To these sensations are added the traces of motion that remain, dependent upon certain laws, in our feeling. Sight sensation on the contrary is always a perfectly flat surface in a position given by nature. Because touch sensations are distributed in different planes, they can be felt separately from one another; but relative to the eye, impressions made in different planes give sensations in a single plane. On the other hand, two impressions are often mixed because they appear on the same part of this given plane.

117. Sensations therefore which come from two impressions made on different planes identify when they fall on the same points of the plane destined by nature for sensation.[60] This

[59] The position of the plane of visual sensation is an evident argument for the wisdom of the author of nature. This position is exactly what is needed in order that the eye may help us to distinguish distances according to the laws of perspective.

[60] Note, however, that it is not necessary for the two impressions to occupy the same parts of each retina in such a way that the same point of the impression falls upon the same point of the retina. It is sufficient for the planes of the impressions to form whatever angle is necessary for the sensations to be aroused at the same points of the optic plane.

identification of sensation is not the result of a lack of a feelable effect in the soul corresponding to the impression made on each eye. On the contrary, it is certain that a sensation corresponds in the soul to each optic impression; as we said, a single impression is sufficient to produce an entire, distinct sensation. But the law consists in this: the two effects, the two sensations, when brought into the soul by the two impressions in accordance with the condition we have described, are *identical* just as the sound of a bell rung by two arms rather than one is identical. And this explains why the identical sensation resulting from the two impressions which correspond to the same points on the feelable plane is somewhat more vivid when produced by two impressions rather than one — just as a bell has a louder ring when pulled with two arms.

118. Granted this law, the contrary is also true. That is: 'If sensations correspond in different parts of the feelable plane (in what I call the *optic plane*) to the two impressions, they do not identify but remain separate.'

119. This explains 1. how the total sensation, received when both our eyes are open and motionless, is composed of the three parts we have indicated, but in such a way that only the middle part of the two sensations is identical. This happens because the impressions received by the two eyes from coloured bodies do not strike the same parts of the optic plane except in the middle where alone the sensations are identical; 2. how by distorting an eye we can sometimes have two clear sensations of a single object. This happens because the impressions received by the two eyes correspond to sensations in different parts of the plane of sensation, that is, the optic plane, so that these sensations cannot identify.

120. Finally, I note that the difference of the impression, considered relative to the sensation corresponding to it, is due to 1. either the difference of position in respect of the constitutive parts of the visual orbit or the difference of the size of the visual orbit; or 2, if the respective position of the parts of the visual orbit is equal, to the different power and perfection of the optic nerve.

121. If only the respective position of the parts and the size of the visual orbit is unequal, two clear, distinct images can be received. These are in fact the two extreme parts of the visual orbit, each

of which is seen by one eye alone because the visual orbit of each eye extends further on one side than the visual orbit of the other eye. And these images are not confused. The same happens to animals which use single, independent eyes. Finally, when one eye is moved, the objects are duplicated because they change their position in the visual orbit and in the optic plane, and are seen as clear and distinct. In this last case, it sometimes happens that we say we see badly although our defective sight does not, properly speaking, reside in the sensations but in the error of judgment to which we are drawn by the sensations when we maintain that the object is twofold, not single. Such sensations are not defective or muddled as sensations, but as signs serving as a basis for judgment.[61]

122. If the light causing the image varies in force or precision, either because one organ is weaker than another or because one eye is looking through a lens, we then see the same image with one eye as with the other, but coloured differently. In this case, the confusion arising in the feeling subject renders the single sensation defective. We must note, however, that if one image is larger than another, as happens when a lens is used for one eye, the image is seen clearly from the point where its greater extension exceeds the bounds of the smaller extension; the smaller image, the nucleus as it were, while vividly coloured, is less distinct in its coloured sections[62]

61 Another law may be stated thus: 'The impression is equal, that is, strikes the same points of the optic plane, when the two optical axes go to the same point.' The reason behind this law is that the luminous points from which the coloured rays start (each point is the vertex of the angle made by the optical axes) have their own distribution which is maintained by the rays as they move to the eye. If their respective position is disturbed (if, for instance, the ray going to one eye passes through one or more media, while the ray going to the other eye passes freely), the images are multiplied. The same happens if the rays are broken up by means of mirrors located at various angles, as in an kaleidoscope.

62 According to the observations of Buffon and others, what is called a false *ear* arises principally from the inequality of the two acoustic organs. The two sound impressions are not perfectly equal and give rise to slightly differing sensations in the soul. The same phenomenon has been observed regarding other sensations. 'If a cold inflames one nostril,' says Bichat, 'and both nostrils remain open, the sense of smell is confused. It becomes distinct if the affected nostril is closed. A polyp on one side of the pituary gland weakens

§4. The law governing the fact used to prove the simplicity of the soul furnishes further demonstrations of the same truth

123. We can now deduce a new proof of the simplicity of the feeling principle from its capacity to make one sensation from *several* sensations, even when they are varied. This would be impossible if the feeling principle were not one and simple. A few experiments will help to elucidate this.

Let us imagine that we are looking at a huge blue area without variation in colour. In our hypothesis, the colour fills our total visual field, but we view it with one eye weaker than the other, or with one eye strengthened by the use of a lens. As a result, one eye sees the blue less vividly than the other. If, however, we open both eyes together, the soul has a single sensation in which it sees the more vivid blue because, in forming a single sensation from the two it receives, the soul must have the brighter colour in the total sensation. If a colour of a certain tint is superimposed on another of the same tint, the colour and the tint remain the same; but if a colour in a strong tint is superimposed upon the same colour in a weaker tint, the brighter colour prevails. This shows that the soul, by integrating what it feels, produces for itself a single total sensation, and that confused sight results only when the many colours, varying in distribution, do not strike the same lines of sight.

the efficiency of the nostril so that harmony between the two organs is defective and gives rise, as in the previous case, to confusion in the perception of smells.

'We can say the same about taste. Here too it often happens that we notice one side only of the tongue affected by paralysis or spasms. It would seem, therefore, that a middle line sometimes separates one feeling part from another which still retains its own sensitivity. If this takes place when infection has reached a high level, there is nothing to prevent us believing that it happens at a lower level. In a word, one side maintains perfectly its power of perceiving tastes, while the other has a lesser sense of taste. In this case, taste becomes irregular and confused as a result of two unequal sensations which, although induced by the same object, cannot induce a precise, exact perception. As a result, certain bodies, whose taste is doubtful, are the cause of pleasing sensations in some people, and of painful sensations in many others' (*Ricerche fisiologiche*, etc., p. 1, art. 2, §1).

§5. Continuation

124. Another experiment will show how the soul makes one sensation from two, relative to the *extension* of the sensation (the previous experiment demonstrated the unifying power of the soul relative to the *brightness* of the colour or light we see). Let us imagine that we are looking at two trees in line, but standing slightly to the right of them so that when we close our right eye, we see the right edge of the nearer trunk just making contact with the left edge of the more distant trunk. The union of the two trunks appears as a single continual sensation of bark and trunk without any intervening gap.

If we now close the left and open the right eye, without changing position, we see the two trees with a space intervening between them. This occurs because the right eye, seeing the outline of the first tree from a different angle, separates the trees and restores each of them to its original size. The sensations given by the two eyes separately, therefore, differ notably, and their objects are distributed in different fields of sight.

How does the soul join these sensations in such a way that no confusion arises between them? What total sensation do we have if we keep both eyes open? If the soul simply joins the two sensations, it will duplicate the objects. If it superimposes one upon the other, it will confuse the sensations and once more duplicate the objects: if one eye sees an area as large as the two trunks together, and the other eye sees two separate trunks, each smaller than the double-trunk sensation and with a gap between them, the two sensations when superimposed ought to present one plane composed first of the two trunks united (the sensation from the left eye), then of what remains of the empty section, and finally of the other trunk (the sensation from the right eye). But the soul does not do this. Instead it retains the entire sensation of the right eye and, preserving the disposition of the parts given by this eye, uses the sensation of the left eye only to make the coloured area brighter.

This is explained by what we have already said: the two trees are perceived equally by the two eyes but retained by the soul without being duplicated. One eye, however, perceives in addition a gap between the trees and contributes this to the rest of the sensation so that the trees are at some distance from one another. This proves that the sensation itself of each tree is not tied to a place (this must be noted carefully), but exists in itself. In other words, the relationship of place between the things we see is given only by the sensation and therefore by the optic plane (cf. 118) with which the soul is furnished.[63]

125. Let us try a third experiment. In the previous example, we saw the two contiguous tree trunks in a single sensation, seen by one eye; then we saw them apart, with a space between them, as a result of their being seen by the other eye. This time we shall see the opposite: two sensations at a distance from one another will form a single sensation by the exclusion of the gap between them.

Let us take a small disc of any colour. We first place the extended palm of our hand sideways on between our two eyes to separate one eye from the other, and then bring the disc close enough to touch, or nearly touch the outer edge of the palm. One eye will see one part of the disc, the other eye the other part. The gap in between will be covered by the hand. Each eye, therefore, sees a part of the disc, without the parts being contiguous — they are divided by the thickness of the hand. If we now cross our eyes so that the lines of sight meet, the two visible parts come together and produce a single sensation which, however, is oval, not round: the two parts of the circle have united perfectly, top and bottom. The philosophical explanation of this phenomenon is to be found in the law already presented (cf. 115–118);[64] we need take the matter no further here. Observing the phenomenon will be sufficient.

63 A good example of the way in which the soul joins two images into one is provided by the illusion produced by Wheatstone's *stereoscope*. Wheatstone observed that projecting a cube on the retina of each eye, when the cube is very near the eyes, produces impressions so different that it is almost impossible to recognise them as images of the same object. Nevertheless the result is a single cube because the two images are made one by the soul. If these two images are seen in appropriate positions, the illusion we have mentioned takes place: that is, we see a single solid cube produced in this case by the *stereoscope*. The explanation must lie in the nature of the optic plane, the immediate term of the feeling soul.

64 If we restrict our examination of the eye to what we know about the direction of the optical axes, we can prove the existence of the law according

126. It is clear, therefore, that these composite phenomena could not take place if the soul, which produces one sensation out of two, were not perfectly one and simple. *Identification* and *composition* of sensation by the soul are facts which cannot be explained in any way unless we accept the soul as perfectly simple. These facts offer irrefutable proofs of the simplicity of the soul.

§6. Further development of the proofs offered in this article

127. Finally, I cannot conclude this chapter without drawing attention to another observation about the phenomenon of a double impression with a single sensation. The observation will be of considerable assistance not only by confirming the simplicity of the feeling principle, but also in explaining further the phenomenon under discussion, and forming a correct concept of the simplicity of the soul.

Let us imagine that the composition of the impression received in one eye (corresponding to the optic sensation) is the same as that received in the other, that is, equally divided so that every point struck by a colour and tint of light is at an equal distance from other points in each impression. In this case, when we close one eye, the other will have as a total sensation a coloured picture in which all the colours and their gradations will be distributed in the same proportions. For example, if the picture contains the image of a tree, a column and a human being, these three objects will have the same respective positions whichever eye they are seen by. The same may be said about the lesser divisions making up the tree, the column, the human being and the entire field of the coloured picture or screen formed by the sensation in each eye.

We can now make two suppositions. First, that the feeling principle is simple and totally devoid of parts and extension; second, that the feeling principle is extended. What would be the result of each of these suppositions?

to which the phenomenon occurs, but we cannot explain it.

If the feeling principle which receives an equal sensation from each eye is simple, it follows necessarily that the two visual sensations, occupying an equal position (in the optic plane), identify as one. The opposite could happen only if the feeling principle were extended. I am persuaded of this by the following argument.

If it ever happened that the two equal impressions made by the light in the two optic nerves aroused two sensations in the soul (which we take as synonymous with the feeling principle), the soul would see simultaneously two coloured orbits or screens in each of which it would see a tree, a column, a human being, and so on for all the objects and parts in the two screens which constitute the two sensations. As a result, there would be a space between the two trees, columns and human beings (in visual sensation objects are distinguished from one another only by being seen in different places; if one were seen in the same place and point as the other, it would already be identified with and absorbed by the other). But the distance between the duplicated objects could be determined only by the distance intervening between the two orbits in which the sensations appeared to the soul. What principle would determine the separation or mutual exclusion of these two orbits? What principle could establish their continuity or the gap between them? If one object is contiguous to the other, so that the two together form a single double-sized orbit providing a visual sensation with double width, we have to say that this phenomenon exists in the soul itself, that is, where the sensation is situated.

The visual sensation, we must carefully note, is in the soul. If therefore the two sensations in the soul, as well as the two impressions in the material organs, are distinct, there must be something in the soul holding the sensations apart in such a way that one visual orbit is in one part of the soul, and the other in another. But in this case, the soul has parts, which is against our supposition.

The argument is even clearer if two orbits appear in the soul divided by a gap. In this case, the interval, which is not furnished by either of the orbits, must be posited by the soul. That is, there must be in the soul which receives the impressions the interval with which the soul sees the separated impressions.

But the argument is equally strong whether the interval

[127]

between the orbits is large, or small or non-existent. If the soul were to see the two visual orbits, there would never be a satisfactory explanation why these should appear separated from or contiguous to one another (one will always be outside the other wherever they are) except the very nature of the soul which would place the two orbits where they are rather than elsewhere. In other words, it would receive one orbit in one part of itself, and the other in another.

This is the conclusion we would have to reach if we supposed that the soul were something material. It is clear that if the soul were only the internal extremity of the nerves, the distance of the extremities in which the sensation arose would determine the separation of one sensation from the other. The same conclusion would prevail if the soul received the two impressions in two separate particles of itself. These particles or molecules would be outside one another, and consequently the sensations in each of them would be outside one another. The respective distance between the particles would also determine the respective distance of the sensations. But even in this hypothesis, which would explain how the two visual sensations remained double, there would be two insurmountable obstacles: 1. the unity of the feeling principle (because the molecule which felt one sensation would not be the molecule which felt the other sensation); 2. the impossibility of either of the particles feeling the distance or separation between each other (because they would be outside one another, and outside the distance separating them).

Our argument may now be simplified as follows: the visual orbit, in order to appear double in the soul, would have to present the soul with a space at least twice the size of each orbit. But this double space is found in neither orbit. In this case, the soul has to posit it of itself and receive the sensations in different parts if the sensations are to remain separate. If the soul has no parts, however, it is clear that the two sensations aroused in it, in the same point as it were, must compenetrate one another.

128. It will be objected that in each visual sensation the soul can distinguish and separate individual parts without our having to infer that the soul itself has parts. Equally the two sensations can appear distinct to the soul without our needing to posit parts in the soul.

But the cases are different, not analogous, and we have to

distinguish between two quite opposite questions: 'How does the simple soul feel the extension which is given it in sensation?' and 'How does the soul feel an extension which is not given by sensation?'

All doubt about the first question is removed by demonstrating, as we have done, that what is extended can never be perceived and felt by what is extended. What is extended can be felt only by what is simple. The demonstration does not resolve entirely the mystery of what takes place in this particular case, and we shall have to speak about this at length. However, it is sufficient to convince us that there is nothing absurd in supposing that what is simple feels and perceives what is extended, although it would be absurd to suppose that what is extended would feel what is extended (cf. 94–96).

The other question 'How does the soul feel an extension which is not given it by sensation?' admits of only one answer. The soul itself not only feels and perceives *what is extended* but feels and perceives it *as extended*. In other words, the mode itself of perceiving and feeling what is extended is subject to the laws of extension or (and this amounts to the same thing) the act of the feeling soul is the act of an extended being.[65]

129. Careful consideration shows that the extension accompanying visual sensations is provided by the visual sensations themselves; the extension necessary to divide and separate them is not. It is not easy to understand what I want to say, but it can be grasped if thought about attentively. The picture which I see is one thing; where I locate this picture is another. Although the same picture is transmitted to me by both eyes, the eyes never indicate to the soul the space in which it has to locate the two pictures. Each eye accomplishes its function by giving the soul its picture; each picture exists in itself, not in any place, and has

65 It will be objected that if the sensations of the two visual orbits adhere to the two optic nerves as other sensations do, the soul would be able to see them according to the distance between the optic nerves in which they are aroused. This is a mistake. We must remember that we are talking about *visual* not *tactile* sensations. The eye feels only something making an impression on the retina; it cannot therefore feel whatever exists between one optic nerve and the other. The distance between the optic nerves cannot be part of the visual orbits, nor separate them; that distance is not seen, and has no part in what is presented to the soul by the visual sensations.

no relationship with the other picture. When the soul receives a picture from one eye, and an equal picture from the other, the soul itself has to locate them according to its own nature. If it is simple, it will not provide any place for them, nor locate them anywhere, but retain them simply as they are given to it. In this case, they will identify with one another as the soul sees the same space in each equal sensation (the *place* in which the two sensations would have to be located would be a space or extension added by the soul because the local relationship of the two whole sensations is found neither in one nor the other, but only in the subject which perceives them both). The soul, therefore, feels the sensations outside place, in themselves alone. It retains, that is, sees the space they have in themselves, but does not locate this space in another space. As a result the two spaces, not located in different places, become of necessity one single space.

Article 3.
Third demonstration of the simplicity of the feeling principle

130. As we have already noted, philosophers were led into many errors about sensation through paying almost exclusive attention to the phenomena of sight, the properties of which they adapted to all other senses. Another, perhaps greater source of error was the incapacity of the majority of philosophers to distinguish between the two series of phenomena that we have noted.

As a result, they confused subjective with extrasubjective phenomena (cf. 84–91), and failed to see the wonder present in the origin of sensation, although they thought they had found the explanation of such a stupendous phenomenon. The following is one example of the way they conceived the arousal of visual sensations. 'Light depicts tiny images on the retina of the eye, which is only the optic nerve itself spread over an extremely soft, white film of skin and therefore capable of receiving all the various tints presented by colours. These little images, depicted with such delicacy on the nerve-membrane, are transmitted through the optic nerve to the brain where the soul receives and feels them.' This is well put, but how do these philosophers know that light depicts the tiny images on the retina of the eye? They appeal to observation, and refer to the state of the eye when it is removed from the cranium of an animal immediately after the animal's death.

If we take away the covering from the retina, they say, and then point the eye like a lens towards a well-lit object, with the pupil turned towards the object and the reverse side towards ourselves, we will see the back of the stripped retina reproduce faithfully, but inverted, the tiny image of the object.

It is impossible to be satisfied with such a badly applied experiment. It is undeniable today (and was well-known to antiquity)[66] that secondary corporeal qualities, such as colours, do not adhere to bodies as they appear to, but are merely sensations belonging to the subject which perceives with the senses the action of bodies.

The image which I see in the eye of the dead animal is, therefore, quite different from the visual sensation of the image, and cannot explain sight in a living being. Even if I could see into the retina of a living being, I would not see colours truly existing in that retina. These would be only my own sensation, which is in me. In the retina I am looking at, there is only a force causing my perceived colours, but not an image made up of variously distributed colours, variously distributed sensations. This observation alone is sufficient to destroy the explanation attempted by the philosophers we have referred to: it totally refutes the possibility that light depicts something in the retina that can be transmitted to the brain. Granted the presence of colour, granted some image, sensation is already present, and there would be no further need of any kind of mechanism or

66 Protagoras was one of the classical authorities who saw the truth clearly, although he misused it. His arguments are set out by Plato (*Theaetetus*) in the words of Socrates who maintains that colour is found neither in bodies nor in the eye, but originates through movement, stimulated by bodies in the eye of the spectator. 'As we have seen, what we perceive has a certain correlationship with the senses. The eye, which is constantly moving, generates a white colour in accord with what is like it. And so a stick or stone, or anything that appears white — or heavy or hot — to us, is nothing *per se*. Rather, all things and every change comes about as one succeeds another through movement. It is impossible to think that what acts or what suffers passively is of itself something unique or fixed, etc.' (cf. *OT*, 878–905).

[130]

transfer to explain the origin of sensation in such a case. But the fact is that the tiny image supposed to be visible in the retina of some other person is not that which he actually sees. He sees something totally different, for example, an immense scene terminated by a horizon of hills or sea. The image visible in his eye is only a tiny circular patch, scarcely a hair's breadth in diameter. If I could see in the living being the image depicted on his retina, I would see only a speck of black where he sees an entire world. My sensation, therefore, is not his. My sensation is the tiny image that I see, but he does not. His sensation is what his own soul sees. If we wish to discover the origin of sight sensation, therefore, we have to abandon altogether the simplistic arguments of the philosophers we have mentioned.

But if it is not true that light carries the colours on to the retina as an artist puts colours on a canvas[67] (and no educated person can disagree with this today), the phenomenon of colour-sensation still remains intact and unexplained. Our question 'How is sensation aroused in the soul?' still has to be faced.

131. The force of the question will be felt more strongly if we try to discover what the action of light actually does in the iris. Granted that it does not put colours there (the colours are the sensation which arises as a result of the action of the light, and are not therefore the action itself), we can only think of tiny impacts and displacements that the light induces in the optic nerves either through mechanical impulse, or chemical affinity, or some organic law.

It is also certain that there is an obvious analogy between the

[67] It is true that I also have said that the retina is designed or painted by light (Cf. *OT*, 907–922, where such expressions are used frequently), but I employ these common ways of speaking only when there is no fear that the reader will be misled. I do it for brevity. I will say, for example: 'Let us imagine the white or yellow patch in the pupil', meaning that a white or yellow sensation corresponds in the soul with this impression. It would take too long to repeat everything constantly. Finally, I sometimes speak of the image in the retina, or of the colours scattered over and pitted upon the retina. Here I am not indicating the impression seen in the retina by others, but the visual sensation that, according to my opinion, is truly returned to the pupil immediately by the soul which, however, does not advert to its location as a result of the sensation until it can refer the sensation to external bodies through the use of touch.

auricular and visual sensiferous phenomena. Sound is produced in the soul only if the means — the air, say — that strikes our acoustic nerve does so repeatedly, causing tremors of a certain frequency. The deepest sound that can be heard by human ears is produced by a frequency of thirty-two air waves per second from the oscillations of the sonorous body; the highest range of sound requires oscillations and waves to the marvellous number of 16,284 per second. Between these two extreme numbers, we have the number of waves necessary to arouse intermediate sounds. It is clear, therefore, that the movements caused by such action of the air in the acoustic nerve are only vibrations of certain frequencies. A certain degree of frequency and speed is necessary in these vibrations which move the acoustic nerve if the soul is to respond with a sound-sensation. No sound will be occasioned in the soul if the frequency and speed of the air waves is insufficient to cause less than thirty-two tremors per second in the nerve.

The following is a probable explanation, as far as I can judge, of the way in which similar movements are required in the optic nerves in order to arouse colour sensation. The mechanism needed can, I think, be conceived like this.

Imagine that the optic nerve, as I said before, is divided into innumerable, very thin threads, each of which terminates in the retina. The tiny nerve heads, packed together on the external surface of the retina,[68] are struck by rays of light falling upon them. These rays are like the fingers of a piano player striking the keys.[69] The nerve ends move in and out constantly with the

[68] The retina is effectively a cellular net in the meshes of which are distributed the substance of the optic nerve. Darwin submitted the retina of a bull to the action of liquid potash and found that the nerve-part dissolved, leaving only the cellular net.

[69] There is, however, a difference to be noted between the tiny heads of the optic nerves and the keyboard of the piano. When a piano-key is struck, only one note is heard. But every tiny optic nerve would give any visual colour and tint sensations if it were activated and moved in the appropriate manner. This seems far more probable than supposing that there are different kinds of fibres in the eye for different colours if we consider: 1. *The phenomenon of imaginary colours.* If we look for a time at something white, and then place ourselves in darkness, the white sensation does not disappear immediately from the eye. It first changes into yellow, then red, then indigo, then blue, then green, until it finally fades away. This transformation of a white sensation into various successive colours offered G. B. Venturi an exemplary

speed and frequency communicated to them by the pressure of the ceaselessly repeated blows of luminous fluid which surges forward in high-velocity waves. The tiny nerves (or the fluid they contain), which are endowed with elasticity or contractility (or any specific mobility suitable to them), produce tremors and oscillations in varying rhythmic, harmonious movements. This variation in the tremors and oscillations in each nerve would produce a specific colour or tint in the soul, according to the hidden laws governing such a marvellous occurrence. The speed, number and size of the oscillations is, however, something that we do not wish to consider at the moment.

Whatever may be thought of this hypothesis, the irrefutable truth is that the light falling on the retina does not posit colours there — as we normally think it does — but only excites movements in the same way as the air, pressing wavelike upon the acoustic nerve, does not put sound in the ear, but simply sets the nerves in motion. When the nerves move in accordance with specific stimuli, then colour and sound sensations corresponding to that movement are felt in the soul. The same may be said of other species of sensation. We have to conclude, therefore, that the *sensiferous* phenomenon which takes place in our body and precedes the sensation is reduced to *movements* of a certain speed and frequency. The *feeling* phenomenon, that is, the sensation, takes place in the soul as a result of these movements in certain parts of the body.

132. It is now easy to see 1. that the *movements* aroused in our

argument for concluding that different colours do not spring from different orders of fibres, but depend upon different movements of the same fibre (*Indagine fisica sui colori*, Modena, 1801, c. 5). 2. *The analogy between imaginary colours and imaginary sounds.* As a sound dies away in the ear, it changes into a sound harmonising with its predecessor. Does the ear also have different fibres on which sounds depend? Such fibres would presuppose different stimuli, but until now no way has been found of separating the soniferous liquid into seven species, as has been done with light, despite Mairan's ingenious hypothesis to this effect (in his *Teoria del suono*, 1737). Perhaps we could more reasonably say that the speed of the oscillations decreases according to a certain law, and that this is the cause of the imaginary sounds and colours? 3. *The discovery that every colour becomes white when it is highly concentrated.* This fact should perhaps be ascertained more definitely by new and more varied experiments.

nerves are not the *sensations* themselves; 2. that the sensations cannot be connected with a single movement of these nerves.

In fact, if the sensations were the movements themselves, or adhered to the movements, the movements would feel themselves. As a result anyone who sees, would see and feel a trembling or oscillating sensation, and sound would reveal the number of oscillations by which it was produced. But this is absurd. Moreover, as the movement begins and gradually increases, sensation should be present, however delicate the movement, and increase and spread in accordance with the increase of the movement. This does not happen. Sensation only appears when the movement attains a certain speed, and vanishes totally. Again, a distinct sound is not dependent on the force with which the air strikes the ear. For example, oscillations produced with a frequency of 64 per second give us the sound of the first octave. But whatever the force present in such a frequency, the tone of the sensation will remain the same, despite the change in the strength of the sound. The sound varies in degree, but the tone does not. Sound sensation, therefore, is not produced by any one of the oscillations taken on its own but by many of them together.

133. The oscillations are many. On which of them does the single sensation depend? If on none of them in particular, it must depend upon all of them together. If so, the sensation must be simple, despite the multiplicity of the oscillations that pass through space. This also proves that the sensation is outside space; it cannot be located at any point in the lines followed by the oscillatory movement. The sensation does not have its seat in any point, but is aroused along with or after the spread of the whole movement. It remains outside all the points through which the movement passes.

It would be easy to carry on with this explanation, and compare movement and sensation under many other aspects. Many other arguments could be brought forward from other kinds of sensation to show that sensation is quite separate from the extension, succession and multiplicity of movement. But what we have said so far is sufficient to make perfectly clear that the feeling principle can only be simple and one.

Article 4.
Fourth demonstration of the simplicity of the feeling principle

134. Finally, an equally clear proof of the simplicity of the feeling principle is given by its *identity* in many sensations.

The same principle that hears sounds, hears many sounds simultaneously, and together with sounds has many sensations of sight, smell, taste, touch, hunger, thirst, and so on. This is certainly the case in the more perfect animals in whom, moreover, many sensations join to produce a universal feeling, different for each animal, which pervades and dominates the entire nervous system of the animal. We shall, however, speak more of this elsewhere. Meanwhile, it is clear that only a simple principle can draw together so many sensations and make itself the subject of them all. If the subject of the sensations were divided into two corporeal particles, even of the smallest dimensions, or as mathematical points if you wish, each point could feel only its own sensation, and not that of the other point. Hence, the *identity* of the feeling principle in many sensations clearly proves its perfect immateriality and simplicity.[70]

8

THE LAWS GOVERNING THE RELATIONSHIP BETWEEN THE *FEELING PRINCIPLE* AND THE *SENSIFEROUS PRINCIPLE*

Article 1.
Popular ideas of the body are unreliable

135. We shall now investigate in greater depth the nature of the

[70] A fifth demonstration of the simplicity of the feeling principle can be drawn from properties of tactile and visual sensations, which extend only on the surface, as we shall see (cf. 177). But all the phenomena of animal life constitute proofs of the same truth.

feeling principle, *soul*, and its relationship with the sensiferous principle, *body*. But before doing so, we must dismiss any popular ideas we may have formed about body and soul, and mistrust the different ways people speak about material and spiritual substances. Our task is to investigate how the ideas of body and soul originate and take form in our minds, how reliable these ideas are, and whether imagination adds anything to them. Imagination easily invents, or adds so much to our thoughts that they lose their pristine simplicity. As I have said, we must, by divesting our thoughts of the phantasy that clothes them, keep them in their naked simplicity.

136. Only observation and analysis can perform this task. We have to observe and analyse carefully the *feelings* we are aware of and see what ideas of the soul and body we can draw from them. If our opinions and persuasions about the body and soul do not have for their foundation and origin the feelings we experience, we must regard these thoughts as inventions of the imagination, and exclude them entirely from knowledge, like all false ideas.

137. The feelings we are speaking about must be put in order through observation, that is, we must distinguish our first, independent feelings from those which we observe to be dependent. Only after such a carefully ordered observation, can we safely commence the analysis.

Article 2.
Our body is first known through the fundamental corporeal feeling

138. Our first, immediately observable feeling is our *fundamental* feeling, as we have called it. Its existence has been shown and described in *The Origin of Thought*, to which we refer the reader.[71] We said that human beings have an intellective-fundamental feeling, different from the corporeal-fundamental feeling, although the subject of both is a single human being.

[71] Cf. 693 ss. Physiologists have recognised the existence of this fundamental feeling, calling it in Greek κοιναισθησις, *universal feeling*.

Here we are not concerned with the intellective but solely with the animal part, common to both humans and animals.

139. In order to form a clear idea of the corporeal-fundamental feeling we have to strip it of every other feeling or sensation. We have to close our eyes and remove, first of all, every sensation of light, then all the sensations of our external senses, and finally all the partial feelings aroused in our body by individual stimuli. When all these external and partial feelings have been completely removed, the animal, in my opinion, still subsists with the feeling I have called *corporeal-fundamental feeling*, or feeling of life. We then come to know that this feeling is entirely uniform and simple: it has no shape because shape is given us by the exterior senses; it is not coloured because colour is supplied solely by our eyes. Having neither shape nor colour, it cannot have any surrounding limits that situate it in space.

140. We can in fact reflect on this first feeling, but without the experience of other sensations we could never extract from it our present ideas and concepts of the body. However, it would offer us sufficient ground to understand that two active principles are united in us, namely, that we feel, and that this feeling comes to us from the action of something different from ourselves, which, however, can be defined only as the proximate cause of our vital feeling.

141. If we wanted to give a name to the activity taking place directly within us and chose the word *body*, we could be sure that no one would understand us. The reason is very clear: the only meaning we can give the word is 'proximate cause of the unique feeling we experience', a feeling which is, as it were, dumb, deaf, blind and empty. Everyone else, however, would be using the word to indicate the cause of their innumerable vivid, changing, moving, individual, extended, coloured sensations. For others, the word would indicate not only the cause of the sensations but also the subject of many of them, because they would take the sensations to be sensible qualities of the cause.

142. We can now ask who uses the word 'body' more correctly: those in our hypothesis who are blind and deaf, bereft of every particular sensation, but able to reflect, or the many others who, enriched by the innumerable, attractive sensations of their particular organs, begin to philosophise?[72]

[72] I say 'others who begin to philosophise' because if we did not reflect on

143. The question is not as strange as it first appears. There is no doubt that those who have only the fundamental feeling as the source of their ideas will know only that 'body' is an active principle generating the simple feeling. Others will be able to draw upon many different feelings furnishing them with a great deal of knowledge about the principle which causes those feelings. But their possession of such abundant material does not ensure that they can legitimately deduce any wealth of knowledge from it. It is far easier to arrive by reflection at a single, simple conclusion than to work through many sources of information.

People equipped with many different sensations can no doubt form innumerable opinions and convictions about bodies, and think, write and talk about them at length. But those we have in mind, whose total knowledge is limited to a single, stated proposition to which nothing can be added, may well have greater understanding of body than those whose quantity of knowledge is far more extensive. In a word, our simple-minded persons could provide the word 'body' with ideas more accurate and precise than those furnished by the learned.

144. Before we can logically accept that popular ideas about the nature and properties of the body, formed from acquired sensations, are genuine and free of all error, we have to presume: 1. that external, acquired sensations indicate the nature of the body more accurately than the fundamental feeling; 2. that in deducing knowledge about bodies from acquired sensations, only the faculty of *reason* is used, not *persuasion*. *Persuasion*, aided by *imagination*, continually fabricates *opinions* that are completely arbitrary.

145. Unfortunately for the mass of people, these two suppositions cannot be easily proved. We cannot easily show: 1. that corporeal nature is more acurately indicated by what we feel and experience in acquired sensations than by our experience of the fundamental feeling; 2. that when people in general suddenly begin to reflect, they refrain from using their imagination to fabricate notions of bodies from external, partial sensations, and use reason instead of their capacity for blindly believing in

our sensations at all, we could not say that external bodies are their subject. In fact we could say nothing even to ourselves about our sensations, and our actions would be governed by sensible appearances.

arbitrarily formed opinions. The difficulty of demonstrating these two points is immense, and indeed a more balanced reflection demonstrates precisely the contrary of the two suppositions.

146. Serious reflection on the second supposition reveals that in general people prefer not to suspend their judgment; if they cannot bring their judgments to a strict logical conclusion, they rush to any conclusion, using the faculty we call *persuasion*. This faculty consists in forming an opinion to which full credence is given, although the opinion lacks logical foundations. Popular philosophical ideas about nature and the properties of bodies have been formed this way.[73]

147. The inaccuracy of the first supposition is also easily demonstrated. We need only note that acquired sensations are subsequent to the fundamental feeling; they are in fact simply a partial modification of the feeling. Hence, it is clear that when we know our body through feelings (which are effects of the body's action), the first action carried out on our soul by this principle called 'body' is the most constant, universal action, which alone can make us know the nature of the body. Partial variations of this universal, constant action of the body help us greatly in knowing the laws which govern that first action wherein all other actions are virtually contained. But the variations alone, without their first original action, make us know the body only partially, and certainly not without error.[74]

148. Even granted the corporeal fundamental feeling, it will be said that we cannot observe *extension* in it, and therefore cannot say it makes us know our body, of which extension is an essential property. The objection, however, clearly concerns extension based on the concept obtained from external sensations. Our task is to ascertain whether there is another concept of extension in addition to that obtained from external sensations, or

[73] All this has been demonstrated in *OT*, 692 ss. where the theory of bodies is discussed. One of the errors found in common opinions about bodies, and now acknowledged by all philosophical schools, is the confusion between *sensations* and the *qualities* of external bodies. However, many errors found amongst the masses can be excused if we bear in mind what I said in *Certainty*, 1302–1306, about popular errors.

[74] For the relationship between acquired sensations and the fundamental feeling, see *OT*, 705, 706, where I have shown that acquired sensations are only modifications of the permanent, universal feeling.

whether, more accurately, extension is already felt in the fundamental feeling, although without the qualities provided by external sensations. We must also decide if these qualities are genuine or simply illusions supplied by the impatient human spirit. This is often the case with the ideas of corporeal qualities formed by people generally.

149. I am convinced that the same extension is felt in the fundamental feeling as in the external sensations, but without the phenomenal qualities (which are not entirely true and valid), although the external sensations lead us to believe that extension possesses these qualities. Extension felt in this way I call *fundamental* or *internal extension*. I admit that it is difficult to form an accurate concept of it, because people generally cannot conceive any real extension except by means of shape, colours, and limits. But if serious thinkers turn their attention to the extension obtained from all our feelings and then set aside everything supplied by external sense, they will be able to form the concept of the extension I am speaking of. All the qualities supplied by external sense can be reduced to limits, colours, and the possibility of motion, that is, the possibility of variations in the colours. When we remove these qualities, we do not eliminate extension. The foundation and subject, as it were, of the limits and colours remains (even if it seems undefinable) [*App.*, no. 4].

150. We must, therefore, be very cautious about accepting all the notions popularly formed about corporeal nature. Thinkers and those who seek the truth must subject such notions to the most exacting critique and separate out everything that does not strictly belong to extension. Otherwise our ideas will be formed from a figment of our imagination, as so often happens. In order to subject all popular ideas of the body and its qualities to rigorous investigation, we need to see whether they have been formed directly or as the arbitary product of our imagination.

Article 3.
The second kind of corporeal feelings: those without shaped extension

151. We must return to our hypothetical subjects who although

unable to use their external senses, can think and reason about their internal fundamental feeling.

These sentient subjects could now be affected by two kinds of successive sensations: 1. extremely intense feelings of pleasure and pain where the feelings present no shape, limits or colour; 2. sensations or feelings, such as touch and sight, which present shape, limits and colours. In our example, the subjects have only (corporeal) sensations of the first kind, without shape, boundaries and colours. A question immediately comes to mind: 'Are these shapeless and colourless sensations which we receive, referred to some part of our body?' The question itself is sufficient indication that we have not entirely rid ourselves of popular, common opinions about the body, and are as yet incapable of conceiving the state of a human being who has only the corporeal fundamental feeling and sensations devoid of shape and colour. To ask if such a being would refer sensations of pleasure and pain to some part of his body presupposes that for him his body already has distinct parts. But his body, relative to himself, cannot have distinct parts, because the parts cannot be perceived without his perceiving the limits distinguishing them and making them parts of the whole. Such a being, however, has never perceived nor felt the limits in any way, nor the shapes formed by the limits.

152. If the pleasant or painful sensations are corporeal, as we have supposed, they can be caused only by changes taking place in our subjects' bodies, that is, by movements of their nerves stimulated in some way.

But this kind of language, too, shows that popular ideas of bodies are still present as an obstacle to understanding the argument, which cannot be grasped until such ideas are completely banished. By insisting that pleasant or painful sensations can be caused by nerve changes, and so on, we have presupposed knowledge of nerves in our body, and of their power when stimulated to generate sensations by their movement. Moreover, we have accepted these things as though they had been proved with certainty, despite setting out with the deliberate intention of testing them and not admitting them as valid in our argument until they had been proved true. We wanted to avoid introducing unproven current opinion into our work lest we construct a system based on deceptive and erroneous preconceptions.

If we say that the shapeless, colourless sensations (hypothetically granted to the feeling subject) are the effects of movement stimulated in certain feeling parts of our body, we have begun to describe the body according to ideas provided by the external senses, especially the eyes and hands. Anatomy is founded on sensations of this kind, and our argument now begins by presupposing, as legitimate and certain, tenets of popular philosophy about the body for which we no longer require proof. We presuppose that the phenomena given by our eyes and hands constitute the objective reality and truth of things. We also presuppose that the only ideas we have of the body are those I call *visual* and *tactile*. In a word, when we say *body* we mean the visible, tactile body. This would be true if the only way of knowing the body were by means of the eyes and hands. But there is, as we have shown, another more basic way which precedes all others, even if it presents no shapes or colours. Our question, based on serious reflection and without preconceptions, has to be posed as follows: 'Do those who have only the fundamental feeling refer the shapeless and colourless sensations they receive to some part of their visible, tactile body?'

It must be carefully noted that here we are not asking simply about the body of these hypothetical subjects, but about their visible, tactile body, the phenomenal body which manifests itself to us by the sensations of sight and touch. This phenomenal body, however, does not exist for those who are supposed to be without the sensations of sight and touch. To ask if they refer the pain or pleasure they feel to some part of their tactile or visible body or of their body shaped in a more general way, is to ask about something foreign to their state. On the other hand, refusing to allow the question simply leaves undecided whether the phenomenal body of sight and touch (the object of anatomy) is real or illusory.

153. We can therefore never refer any pleasure that we experience to any part of our shaped body, if such pleasure does not present shaped space to our feeling principle and we have not yet felt and perceived our body as a shaped object with parts. Such a body does not yet exist for us. On the other hand, extension is certainly present in corporeal sensations, which are only simple modifications of the fundamental feeling. This extension, which I have called *internal* (cf. 149) is completely shapeless

and devoid of parts, like the extension itself of the fundamental feeling.

Article 4.
The third kind of corporeal feelings: those with shaped extension

§1. In order to know shaped extension, we need to perceive limits to extension

154. We must now consider carefully how the sentient subject begins to feel any shaped extension.

First of all, we should note that corporeal extension is shaped only by the limits surrounding it on all sides. Consequently, the perception of any shape implies the perception of the limits enclosing a space.

155. Indeed, very careful observation reveals the great difference between feeling and perceiving *a limited space*, and feeling and perceiving *the limits* enclosing the space. If this distinction is not borne in mind, what I wish to say cannot be understood.

I have said we cannot feel or perceive shape without feeling the limits that form it. This is what happens when touch and sight perceive shape: our hand and eyes perceive only the limits of the objects, that is, their surfaces. Conversely, while the extension in which the fundamental feeling terminates, along with the other internal feelings that modify the fundamental feeling without presenting shape, is undoubtedly limited, its limits are not felt. Thus, although the felt extension is limited, it lacks shape, having no felt limits.

§2. In order to perceive the limits of a body, we must perceive something beyond the body

156. What we have just said is important and requires further comment.

In order to feel the limits of my own body, I have to feel something beyond my body, something terminating my body, for the clear reason that no thing is its own limit.

157. If I consider the outline of my body, the limit is a line that follows the body's different curves and angles. But I cannot mentally conceive a line without conceiving simultaneously a space on either side of the line, for example, a convex space on one side and a concave space on the other. Without this condition, the line cannot be conceived at all. Thus, if the line is my body, the space on the other side of the line will be either empty or full but always different from my body. I cannot feel and perceive the line terminating my body unless I simultaneously perceive something beyond and outside my body.

158. Now the the same is true if, instead of considering the line-limit of my body, I consider the limit extended as a surface. I can conceive a surface only if I perceive it as a plane cutting a solid space in half, that is, I need to perceive the two parts of the solid divided by, and lying on either side of, the surface. I cannot perceive the surface of my body unless I perceive it as a division between the space occupied by my body and the space outside my body. I have to conclude therefore that I could never feel and perceive the surface limits of my body unless I felt and perceived the external space limiting it.

§3. Shape is not perceived in the fundamental feeling

159. The preceding observation demonstrates clearly why there can be no shape in the fundamental feeling, although the feeling is limited in itself.

The fundamental feeling, like the body felt by it, is limited, but presents no shape; it seems as formless and indeterminate as black night. It feels only the body, nothing more; and because it feels no other space outside the body, it does not feel the limits of the body that give it shape. The same is true of all feelings which have no shape: they feel no space outside the body which constitutes their limits.

§4. The principle for establishing which feelings are shaped and which are not

160. An important corollary of the preceding observation gives us a firm principle for determining the feelings in which, while feeling corporeal extension, we feel no shape: 'Whenever a feeling is diffused in a given extension of our body but tells us nothing more about the extension or about anything limiting the extension, the feeling has no shape in space.' Thus, pain in a sensitive part of our body produces a shapeless sensation, if the pain is due to an internal alteration or movement of the parts and not to an external stimulus. The same is true if the stimulus gives no surface sensation limiting the solid space in which the pain is diffused.[75]

§5. Space felt in the fundamental feeling is solid

161. We see therefore that the space felt in the fundamental feeling, and all undefined space, is *solid*, having the three distinct dimensions of length, height and breadth. Contrariwise, the space perceived by shaped feelings is *surface* space, because the sensations of external touch and of sight present only a surface-extended feeling terminated by lines.

§6. The space felt in shaped feelings is only surface extension

162. We must not think that external touch also perceives solid

[75] When Condillac speaks about the odours he supposes to be in the nostrils of his statue, he sometimes says that 'the soul might consider itself to be all the different odours it sensed' (p. 58); other times he says that the soul might think 'it has the odours within itself'. The statements are clearly contradictory, because if the soul believes it has the odours within itself, it cannot believe it is the odours. Neither of the statements is true. When the soul first has an odour, it neither distinguishes *itself* from the odour, nor confuses *itself* with the odour. It has not yet discovered itself. Its activity is only in the odour; it is completely ohlivious of itself. Hence, it cannot judge the relationship of identity or difference that the odour has with it.

spaces, even if we form some concept of solids by means of touch and sight, and by means of the imagination.

163. We grant, of course, that solids, considered as the subject of geometry and anatomy, are mentally conceived by the help of touch and sight, and also of the imagination. But it is no less true that the perceptions proper to these two senses never go beyond a surface, and that we know only the surfaces of solids perceived in this way.

164. No one can deny that the concept of something solid is determined by surfaces, but it is difficult to explain how these felt surfaces present a solid. Clearly surfaces can circumscribe a solid only if they have a given situation in space, with such a relationship between them that they enclose and limit a portion of solid space in every direction. In order, therefore, to perceive solids through touch and sight, that is, by means of surfaces, which are the immediate, proper term of these senses, it is not sufficient that the surfaces be perceived; their relative situation must also be perceived. For this to happen, we need somehow to feel the same solid space in which the surfaces extend, especially in the case of a line or felt surface which supposes that we feel what is on either side of the surface (cf. 156–158). This first difficulty is eased by the theory of the fundamental feeling: solid space, whose limits must be the surfaces felt by touch and sight, is precisely where, as we have said, the fundamental feeling is extended (cf. 161). This fact itself is a proof of the existence of the fundamental feeling, for without this feeling we could not explain how touch and sight enable us to conceive solids.

165. But because of its many variations and the laws governing it, the fact still needs further explanation. For example, if the solid space which is the term of our fundamental feeling is no more than the space occupied by our material body, how can we feel the respective position of the surfaces of exterior bodies? The solid space of these bodies is foreign to us and therefore cannot be a term of our fundamental feeling. It may be suggested that if we know the position in space of the surfaces of our own body, we must also conceive the space beyond these surfaces because, as we have already explained, a surface cannot be felt if we have no feeling at all of what is outside it (cf. 156–158). This solution, however, only increases the difficulty. The supposition that the fundamental space is only that of our body

may indeed allow us to think we have explained how we perceive at least the surfaces of our own body, but if the solid space of the fundamental feeling is no more than that of our body, the very perception of the position of the surfaces of our body obviously becomes impossible. It is clear, therefore, that in order to be capable of knowing the position in space of the surfaces of our body, we have to admit that simple unlimited space, as well as the space of our body, is the term of our fundamental feeling, and that this is true even though our sense-organs occupy a limited space, and material sensations arise in, and are limited to the organs.

166. There is still greater need to presuppose this if we are to explain how touch can inform us of the solidity of external bodies, when their surfaces are perceived solely by means of touch. I fully agree that when we hold a ball in our hand, we are aware of a solid sphere. We experience a concave sensation in the internal surface of our hand to which must correspond a similar, convex surface in the body. But the problem is how to identify the space that our spirit had to perceive so that it could have this awareness. If touch indicates the concave surface of our hand, it must also indicate the convex surface of the ball. But both surfaces are only limits of solid space. Our spirit therefore cannot be aware of the concave form assumed by the palm of our hand or of the convex form of the ball unless we suppose the spirit to have in some way the feeling of the solid space limited by these surfaces. Furthermore our spirit feels both the solid space occupied by our hand and the solid space occupied by the ball. But with one difference: together with the feeling of the solid space occupied by our hand, our spirit also has the *feeling of the felt, living matter of our hand*. The latter feeling is not present in the portion of solid space occupied by the ball. This presents us with a very important corollary: 'No part of space can be perceived unless we presuppose the feeling of all space,' or: 'We cannot feel limited space unless we feel unlimited space.'

167. What makes it difficult for us to be convinced of this is the immense difference between the surface sensation of touch and the fundamental feeling of space. The former is vivid, actual, transitory; the latter is habitual, immanent, uniform and simply does not stimulate or attract our reflection. Thus the illusion

easily arises that the only feelings that exist are those of actual, partial sensations, whereas these merely indicate the limits bounding the universal feeling.

168. However, other arguments demonstrate the necessity of presupposing in the human soul both a basic feeling of unlimited space and a material feeling of one's own feelable body which occupies only a little part of that space. If we consider, for example, the phenomenon of movement, especially active movement by which the animal transports its body from one place to another, we find that such a phenomenon is impossible unless we presuppose that human beings, in addition to feeling the space occupied by their own body, also feel space not occupied by their body. If we did not feel the latter, we would be unable to transport our body from the place it occupies to a space it does not occupy.

169. The laws governing the phenomena of sight offer us an even more effective proof of the argument. Let us suppose that the sensation of sight considered in itself presents phenomenally a simple surface plane that can never be used to form a solid. Let us also suppose that the solids perceived by sight are formed by means of an unknown, habitual judgment or association of sensations. In this supposition, the luminous points of the optic sensation would be referred to the corresponding points of the sensation of touch and movement in such a way that the sensation of sight would act as a sign to the soul for noting the solid forms and distances perceived by touch and movement.[76] If this were all that was involved, the difficulty would concern touch alone, and once we had explained how touch perceives solids, we would have explained everything. We would need no other argument to demonstrate the fundamental feeling of unlimited space.

But my argument is drawn from the laws of perspective governing external objects, which I have already discussed (cf. 115–129). One of these laws, the basis of many others, states that when the optic axes meet at a fixed external point, the soul sees one point, although the sensations are two because we have two eyes. The law is determined by straight lines drawn in the space outside our body. The laws of optics therefore do not depend on the portion of space occupied by our body, but on external,

[76] *OT*, 906–921.

unlimited space, as the whole science of optics demonstrates. This science establishes the laws of vision; it does not investigate what happens inside the eyes or the brain but simply indicates lines beginning from the eye and continuing to a luminous body, as if the eye itself projected the visual rays and struck the object seen at a distance (as the ancient thinkers believed).[77]

This error of the ancient thinkers was natural and fully excusable, because in effect the phenomena of sight respond perfectly to the hypothesis that the act of vision is a projection of visual rays to the object. But the fact is that rays emanating from the eyes do not exist. We cannot doubt that the eyes receive impressions like all the other external sense-organs, that the impressions are two, because the eyes are two, and that the impressions do not physically unite.

How, therefore, can the sensations of the eyes be subject to the laws of external space if this space itself is not part of our fundamental feeling? When both our eyes are fixed on a distant point, the point is outside and distant from our eyes. The very energy required for focusing both eyes on the point demonstrates that we see one point only with both eyes, although the eyes are two and receive two sensations. Thus the space where we locate the fixed point is a plane in unlimited space. This plane and its position, however, must be given by nature, as we have said (cf. 115–116); sensation alone as experienced by our eyes cannot give it, because this kind of sensation, in its physical reality, is double, and adheres to the retina. If, for example, we fix our eyes on a relatively close object, we notice that we have to turn the two planes of the retinas so that the apex of the angle formed by the verticals striking the retinas is the fixed object. This explanation of how both retinas can thus see the same object would obviously be impossible if external space were not considered as part of the fundamental feeling which enables the action of the retinas to be determined by the laws of this external space. Consequently, space, relative to the actual, partial and transitory sensation of sight, is said to be *external*, but relative to the fundamental feeling, is truly *internal*.

170. When we gaze steadily at some distant object, we are conscious of directing our sense-activity to a point outside us, and

[77] Cf. St. Augustine, *De Genesi ad Litt.*, 1, 31.

outside our material feeling (which would be impossible if the point were not within the sphere of our activity or fundamental feeling). We can also act on the external point by using other faculties: for example, we could throw a stone and, if our human nature were perfect, hit the target infallibly. We are told that sight sensation gives only a sign of the object and that the sign is used as a norm for the locomotive force needed to determine the direction and energy of the throw. Although this is possible, it does not explain the phenomenon sufficiently, for the following reasons.

1st. If the sign is different from the object, we see the sign but not, properly speaking, the object. If, however, we saw both the object and the sign, we would see — contrary to fact — two things, the sign in us and the object outside us; and the original difficulty returns. If we see only the sign, it must be situated somewhere, otherwise we could not direct our aim. We see it, therefore, either in our body or outside our body. It cannot be in our body, first, because we never say we see external objects in our body, and second, because the sign could not indicate the external spot to aim at; rather it would indicate our body as our target. If the sign of the object appears outside our body, as the laws of optics show, we still have the original difficulty. Seeing the sign in external space without seeing the object contributes nothing to solving the problem.

2nd. To introduce an habitual judgment by which we refer the sight sensation to the external object supplied by touch and movement does not, on careful examination, explain the matter satisfactorily. First, it is difficult to understand how touch sensation, which is not present and must be supplied by the imagination, can prevail over sight which is present. This requires an extraordinary illusion by which touch changes the place of the object, making it appear where it is not. Second, we would have to compare the actual sight sensation with the imaginary sensation of touch and the feeling of movement associated with touch. In this comparison, we could not be unaware that the imaginary sensation prevails over and subjects the sight sensation to its own laws, granted the laws of vision. Third, touch alone knows the distance of objects, which are not felt unless they touch the body. Consequently, we have only the feeling and intensity of actual movement for measuring the distance of an object from us by means of the time required to reach the

[170]

object. But the movement by which we transport our body from one place to another in unlimited space cannot be explained without the feeling of unlimited space (cf. 168). Fourth, the feeling of the active movement of our body is unable to give us the precise measure of the distance of a body we see; we also need the help of the visual sensation in which objects grow smaller in proportion to the distance. This gradation of the distance of different bodies indicated by their sizes helps us to know the relative distance of many bodies but does not help us to know the absolute distance of a body close at hand. If we want to throw the stone accurately, we need to know the absolute, not the comparative, distance. Fifth, if our feeling of the active movement necessary for reaching a body is not in fact seconded by sight (which helps us to know only comparative distances of objects), it cannot in any way give us the measure of the absolute distance of the object, unless we in fact move towards it and touch it. Sight, therefore, which actually guides the thrower's arm, needs some other means to know distances independently of actual movement.

3rd. Finally, I agree that the association of sight with touch and with the feeling of movement produces in us an habitual criterion which helps us to measure the absolute distance of objects. But this association would be inexplicable and impossible, if the object were not actually seen in a point of unlimited space. If the eye saw only one object, not many, without any association of touch and movement, it would not know the distance of the object, because it would have no other felt object with which to make the comparison. Equally, if it did see the two objects whose distance is to be measured, but did not feel them in two points of unlimited space, no comparison could be made at all. This is true whether the objects are felt by sight alone or by different senses such as sight and touch joined with the feeling of movement.

These reasons demonstrate rigorously that the phenomena of the perception of surfaces are inexplicable unless we first grant solid, uniform, unlimited space in the feeling of the soul.

171. We can see how mistaken Emmanuel Kant was when he said that space was the form of the external sense (if we understand *form* as he understood it). I admit that in introducing his 'form', he saw better than others the difficulty of explaining the

phenomena of external sensitivity, and I can accept his indirect confession of the need to find some principle, then unknown to philosophers, which would explain the phenomena. I must, however, indicate two serious errors in his theory.

1st. His arbitrary form is insufficient. This 'form' is only a law or natural disposition which obliges the spirit to clothe its external sensations with space. If this were to take place, sensations would have to come first in order to be clothed with space, and be followed by the space needed to clothe them. But the opposite is true: no external sensation exists unless it is in space. Moreover, the spirit would create space on the occasion of sensations. But because we have no proof of this, such an affirmation is arbitrary. In fact, consciousness tells us the contrary: our soul does not create space; space is given to and imposed on the soul.

2nd. If space were a creation of the soul, it would be only a modification of the soul, not something in itself. Consequently even bodies would be subjective illusions, since they need space to exist.

172. These difficulties can be entirely avoided if we posit pure, unlimited space as the term of the fundamental feeling. The first difficulty disappears because in this case sensations truly exist in space. The second loses all validity if our own theory is correctly understood. The term of our feeling does not change its nature whether it is given to us on the occasion of an accidental, transitory sensation, or at the beginning of our existence by the Creator himself. In both cases it retains its nature as term of our feeling. And if it has the nature of term, it is really distinct from the feeling principle which is the subject. Hence, it is not a modification of the subject. It is something extrasubjective, not subjective, and when applied to the thinking human being is *non-self*, which cannot in any way be confused with its opposite, *self*.

173. What we said at the beginning, therefore, remains true: solid space, which comes to be circumscribed by the surface sensations of sight[78] and touch, is given by nature and not by

[78] We said that the position of the surface plane of visual sensations has been wisely determined by the author of nature (cf. 115). But we must also note that although all visible points are depicted in the surface plane, they are referred to this plane according to the laws of vision. These laws state that an object of our vision is always situated at the apex of the angle made by the optic axes. The distance of the apex corresponds to the distance of the

these sense-organs, which only limit space, enveloping it in surfaces, and therefore presuppose it as already given to the spirit.

Touch, for example, makes us feel the whole surface of a sphere or the six surfaces terminating a cube. But it never enters a cube or sphere; only our imagination does this, creating an 'inside'. The imagination is supported and strengthened by the mutability of the shape of the two solids; the sphere can be divided into two hemispheres, the cube can be cut in any direction. This gives rise to the illusion that we touch and see the inside of the sphere and cube, when in fact we see only fresh surfaces as a result of cutting the two bodies in half and changing their shape and location. Even if both bodies were smashed into smithereens, we would still neither see nor touch the inside, because every tiny bit of them would itself be a new body, offering only surfaces to our touch and eye. Our touch and sight would never penetrate what is solid because what is solid is not the term of these senses; they always see and touch surfaces, which can be infinitely changed. This mutability, aided by the imagination, leads us to believe, as I have said, that solids themselves are felt with our hands and seen with our eyes.

object. But in the pure, isolated sensation of the eye, the seeing subject finds nothing that marks the distance of an object. Hence, the sensation always has the form of a surface plane, like a screen stretched out, as it were, before our eye, but a screen suspended nowhere because there is nowhere to hang it; for the eye, it is the whole of space. Moreover, the screen could be changed into another nearer to the eye without the visual sensation undergoing any alteration if the objects appeared on the nearer screen with the correct relationship of vision, as Wheatstone's experiments demonstrate. Consequently, relative to pure eye sensation, the distance of the screen is indifferent, precisely because the screen, relative to the sensation, has neither distance nor location. But the case is not the same relative to the unlimited space which is the term of the fundamental feeling. If the visual sensation is compared with this space, it corresponds equally to all the planes (provided they are parallel) into which the space can be divided. Thus, we can say that the sensation of a disc seen by the eye corresponds in solid space to a cylinder that stretches to infinity. Hence, if an object seen at a distance grows in size as it approaches the eye, the growth becomes a sign to the eye that the object is approaching. Afterwards, touch and movement can verify the existence of the solid space that adheres to the fundamental feeling.

[173]

174. Solidity, therefore, is given by nature but without limits. Only that part is limited in which what is felt corporeally is extended.

§7. The incorrect method used by Locke and his followers to form the idea of substance

175. We can now see how a serious error arose in *sensist* philosophy, whose only idea of substance is that formed from bodies. This idea of bodies, however, is only the common, popular idea formed from external, shaped sensations. The sensists observed that shaped sensations presented only sensations of surfaces to the soul, and nothing solid beyond the surfaces. They concluded that corporeal substance, which is thought to support the surface, is entirely unknown, and consequently that all substances are unknown.[79]

176. But such a conclusion is hasty and false. We must distinguish different substances and not reduce the concept of substance in general to the concept of the particular substance of bodies. Moreover there is a first, fundamental way of feeling and

[79] The truth of this observation can be verified by reading chapter 23, bk. 2, of John Locke's *Human Understanding*. We see clearly how 1. he draws the idea of substance in general from the particular substance of bodies; 2. considers bodies as an amalgam of tactile and visible qualities; and therefore, 3. infers that the substance of bodies, and even substance in general, always remains entirely unknown to us. The following extract will suffice for those without time to read the whole chapter: 'So that if any one will examine himself concerning his notion of pure substance in general' (we note how he speaks here of substance in general, not simply of the substance of bodies), 'he will find he has no other idea of it at all, but only a supposition of he knows not what support of such qualities, which are capable of producing simple ideas in us; which qualities are commonly called accidents. If any one should be asked, what is the subject wherein colour or weight inheres, he would have nothing to say, but the solid extended parts' (here Locke is speaking of the particular substance of a visible, tactile body, not of substance in general): 'and if he were demanded what is it that that solidity and extension adhere in, he would not be in a much better case than the Indian beforementioned, who, saying that the world was supported by a great elephant, was asked what the elephant rested on; to which his answer was, a great tortoise. But being again pressed to know what gave support to the broad-backed tortoise, replied, something, he knew not what.'

perceiving space and solid bodies. I fully agree that the senses of touch and sight cannot in any way give us the idea of corporeal substance, which presupposes something solid and not mere surfaces. But if we reduce the concept of body to the aggregate of the qualities given us by these surface senses, we will never be able to form a positive concept of body as substance, nor even of surfaces enclosing a space. The concepts of solid space, corporeal substance and substance in general are not deduced from touch and sight.

§8. Sensations extended in surfaces offer a new proof of the simplicity of the feeling principle

177. Not only sensists but philosophers in general have, it seems, given no more than passing attention to what I call 'surface sensations', which deserve the closest consideration. Indeed they offer a new and clear proof of the simplicity of the feeling principle.

What is extended in surfaces and devoid of thickness of any kind cannot be a body, because extension in the three dimensions of length, breadth and depth is essential to body. It is only the mind that by abstraction separates the dimensions; in reality they are inseparable and indivisible. If those who feel were to feel the three dimensions, they could never have sensations in the form of pure surfaces because the felt surface would have to be really separated from the dimension of depth, a separation which contradicts our concept of bodies. Surface sensations, therefore, are essentially incorporeal; they are phenomena that take place only in an entirely incorporeal, simple principle.

No one can doubt that touch and sight sensations are limited to surfaces and do not penetrate the bodies we see and touch, even those with the most delicate of surfaces (cf. 173). But we can be misled into believing the opposite either by the transparency of the body, when we seem to see the colour below the surface, or by touching a soft body, when we seem to feel a harder body below. But even these sensations are only surface sensations, although they lead us to make a judgment about the bodies below the surfaces. We reason to these bodies from the quality of their combined effect. The effect itself, however, is never more than a surface sensation.

§9. The soul does not refer sensations to different parts of the body; the parts are revealed to the soul by means of the position and shape of the sensations

178. It may be suggested that these sensations are of only apparent surfaces, and that the soul, although it feels in the brain, refers its feeling to the extremities where its body is touched. But we have shown that it is gratuitous and contrary to fact to say that the soul feels in the brain.[80] This is a common mistake of physiologists, who confuse impression with sensation. They see that there is no sensation unless the disturbance of the nerve reaches the brain, and conclude that the brain feels. But nothing could be more gratuitous, because the only thing we can infer from this fact is that the propagation of the movement to the brain is a necessary condition of sensation. Such a fact, however, is not sufficient to determine the place where the sensation must be felt, a place that can be known only from its own factual existence.

179. Moreover, saying that the soul *refers* its feeling to the extremity where it is touched unnecessarily introduces a mysterious action. To say *refer* is both obscure and contradictory because the soul cannot refer a sensation that it does not have. But if it already has the sensation, the sensation must either be referred somewhere, in which case we have two sensations, or the soul must send the sensation somewhere, in which case we would be aware of its passage because as a sensation it must make itself felt at every point of its movement. Such an action, therefore, is neither real nor tenable as an explanation of how the soul or brain transmits and refers sensation to different parts of the body.

We have to say that the feeling of the soul is a simple fact, which either does or does not exist. If it exists, we must analyse it. If we find space in it, we must accept space as one of the

[80] *OT*, 732–734.

feeling's properties and modes. We must not arbitrarily presuppose that the space we notice in sensation, whatever it is, is something different from sensation, or requires another action of the soul to explain it. Such a procedure would truly be a false use of hypothesis. If there are sensations which make the soul feel surfaces, these surfaces must be part of the sensations themselves. We do not need to suppose that the soul produces them there by referring the sensations to certain parts of the body.

180. These errors and the apparent clarity with which they are expressed deceive many superficial thinkers. The errors originate, as we have said, when we accept as proven some opinions about bodies which, lacking proof, are the product of our imagination. Indeed, the very statement 'the soul refers sensations to certain parts of its body' implies that such a soul has a body endowed with shape and parts. But the contrary is true: the soul does not have a body endowed with shape and parts. It feels the body in this way only after receiving the surface sensations we are discussing.

Sensations of touch and sight cannot be referred by the soul to the phenomenal, anatomical body, which does not yet exist for it. The anatomical body begins to exist for the soul by means of touch, sight and shaped sensations in general. These sensations have within themselves a space extended in surfaces, and these surfaces are the origin of every form and shape, and of the many variations in form and shape caused by the continual change in surfaces. Thus the anatomist, when he has observed all the external surfaces of the human body, can go on to cut away the outer skin and discover another surface. He can then cut this away and so on, penetrating further into the body, but never seeing or touching anything other than another surface. The only knowledge he can obtain about this kind of body, no matter how perfect his instrument, is simply an aggregate of infinitely varying surface sensations which constitute the indefinitely variable limits of the anatomical body.

The anatomical body, therefore, exists for the soul only as an aggregate of its surface sensations which wonderfully delineate the body for it. We cannot accept that this phenomenal, anatomical body surrounding the soul exists prior to shaped sensations, so that the soul can place sensations in different parts of it. On the contrary, the different parts are, for the soul, the parts themselves of sensations, and the extension of the anatomical body is identical with the extension of the sensations of the soul. The soul, therefore, does not create extension and location for its sensations. The sensations are, from the outset, in extension and naturally located there.[81]

Article 5.
The laws of relationship between the fundamental feeling and the second and third kind of feelings

§1. These laws show the wisdom of the Creator

181. The soul, therefore, by means of shaped sensations, perceives shapes first and foremost as limits of the body already felt by the fundamental feeling. The only shapes it feels are its own.

The wisdom of the Creator established the wonderful harmony between acquired, incidental feelings and the first, fundamental feeling. Shapeless feelings were to be simple alterations and modifications of the fundamental feeling, not completely new feelings. Shaped feelings were to reveal forms and shapes serving as boundaries and limits to the fundamental feeling which they would better delineate and define, and were to possess other relationships determined by the purposes they were to serve; they were not to be independent of the fundamental feeling or of one another. We must now carefully examine and reflect on this harmony and law of relationship which the Creator has established between the fundamental feeling and incidental feelings.

[81] It seems that sensation gives space to the soul because sensation, by limiting space, makes the limited space more vivid and therefore observable. Furthermore, the parts of a total sensation have a position in the sensation like objects seen in a mirror. But the same total sensation presupposes unlimited space devoid of material feeling.

§2. Shaped feelings, the third kind of feelings,present surfaces which, relative to each other andto the fundamental feeling, have a constant, harmonious position

182. Let us suppose that a human being has only the fundamental feeling. If this person were touched successively over the whole surface of his body by a small object, a piece of metal for example, he would successively experience many surface-extended sensations situated at the extremity of his corporeal-fundamental feeling. The sensations would present (by means of the faculty of sense-retention) shapes which, relative to each other and to his fundamental feeling, are distributed according to a definite order. Relative to each other, they are so positioned that they constitute a continuous surface-covering in all directions, that is, a surface enclosing a solid. The shape they assume is precisely what we call the human body. However, relative to the fundamental feeling, the sensations define the limits in such a way that the feeling subject feels that his corporeal-fundamental feeling receives a previously unknown determination which now circumscribes him in a portion of space.

183. It may be objected that this is not surprising because, evidently, when the body is touched in all its extremities, the sensations must take place there, and thus be contiguous, while encompassing and determining the fundamental feeling. But this only repeats popular ideas of the body and fails to recognise that my suggestion of a piece of metal tracing the surface of the body entailed the use of everyday language in order to make myself understood. Our feeling subject, however, is ignorant of metals or surfaces; he simply feels himself as a feeling subject modified by something different from himself and acting upon him. He must wonder (if he thinks at all) at the harmony between the modifications he experiences, and must say to himself: 'These feelings are not the result of chance, but of great wisdom. The unknown agent acts upon me according to a constant law of harmony and balance.'

As a result of these harmonious modifications of the fundamental feeling, the sentient subject 1. perceives the *shape* of the space occupied by his fundamental feeling; 2. invents the words *shape*, *space* or extension, *surface* and *body*; 3. perceives a surface-extended agent, which he calls *metal*; 4. perceives the motion of an agent which gives rise to partial sensations contiguous to each other.

Reflection on his feelings will certainly lead him to express himself in this way. For example, he will say that a piece of metal has moved over all the extremities of his body. Despite the fact, however, that he has distinguished, named and expressed different ideas, his initial wonder caused by the conformity and union of so many sensations need not be extinguished. The phenomena remain subject to the same wonderful laws, and their author still exists. Coining words like *metal* and *body*, does not mean I know what metal or body is. I have simply noted and described the apparent mechanism of an action, not the real forces involved in it, nor the wise principle legislating for them. In a word, I have not found a *sufficient reason* for the relative position of so many different feelings.[82]

184. Through force of habit we look at what nature presents, but forget its wonderful teaching power. There seems no reason to ask ourselves why things are done in one way rather than another. We see them as they are, and that is sufficient. In this case, the shape of our bodies is formed by a complex of feelings produced by sensations of touch. The sensations are collocated in such a way that relative to each other and to the fundamental feeling they describe the limits of the fundamental feeling. We do not ask ourselves why this is so because there is no apparent, intrinsic reason for it, as I shall explain.

Let us suppose that the piece of metal touches the whole surface of my arm. No intrinsic reason requires that I have a circular sensation or, more correctly, that I have a complex of sensations which, granted I retain them all, trace a circle for my

82 It is clear that if the various shaped and non-shaped feelings experienced by a feeling principle were all isolated from each other, we could not form with them the notion of a fixed, determined entity, like the popular notion of body. To acquire this notion and the persuasion that *bodies* subsist, and therefore to be able to name them, the union of the surfaces or forms that we feel must clothe and limit a solid extension in every direction; otherwise we would have only independent surfaces. This distribution of the sensations of surfaces is particularly necessary for forming the concept of our own body; the surface-covering must enclose the fundamental feeling entirely, and thus constitute a living solid.

sense-faculty. There is no reason why different modifications of my fundamental feeling could not arouse in my feeling principle a straight, rather than a curved, sensation, or a flat surface rather than a curved one. This possibility becomes obvious when we consider that the law which locates sensation at the extremity of the fundamental feeling applies solely to touch; the other senses have their own laws, and amongst these we must carefully consider the law that applies to the space perceived by the sense of sight.

If we consider only what this sense has in common with touch, the position of the visual sensation must be in the retina of the eye and occupy the various, tiny planes in which the different points of the retina can be moved. But if we consider sight as a special sense, its sensations, in common with touch, are spread over a surface. Visual surfaces, however, do not take their relative positions according to the law determining the position of tactile surfaces. Unlike tactile surfaces, which appear at the limits of the fundamental feeling where the stimuli are applied, visual surfaces do not appear in the planes determined by the nerve extremities which end in the retina of the eye. They are subject to quite a different law. If they followed the law of touch, each eye, when looking at a luminous object, would see a little surface in a different plane, because the rays from an object, striking the nerve extremities of the eyes looking directly at the object, fall upon two surfaces which are not in the same plane but inclined at an angle to each other. This angle varies according to the distance of the object, and therefore according to the acute or obtuse angle formed by the optic axes. If the visual surface adhered to our body, as a tactile surface does, it would necessarily divide into several surfaces whose location would depend on whether our gaze were fixed on a single, close or distant point, or on two different points. However, both eyes show only one visual surface, perfectly flat and determined by its own special law (cf. 115, 169).

185. According to what we have said, this law consists 1. in all the objects being seen in a flat surface whose position is given by nature; 2. in the alignment of the optical axes which determines the way the external objects are carried on to this surface of given position: if the axes are parallel, each luminous object in which they terminate is felt individually on the visual surface. If

the axes intersect to form an angle, the object situated at the apex of the angle appears on the visual surface as a single object. But how can this apex, whose distance varies, influence the eyes, if it is outside the eyes? And in such a way that the feelable object situated at the apex appears as a single object to the soul in the visual screen of given position? It is impossible for light rays, passing from an object and striking the retina of each eye, to undergo a refraction after striking the retina according to certain laws of refraction which would determine that the rays, or the movements initiated by the rays, are carried on to the same internal screen and in the same place.

Neither the visual surface in its position given by nature, nor the way in which the sensations of both eyes are initiated and distributed in the surface, can explain first how a single object becomes two objects, and then how two objects merge into a single sensation, and finally how a single sensation corresponds to two impressions made by the light on the eyes. The only explanation is that the surface has a relationship with external space and that, as a necessary condition of this relationship, space is present in feeling (cf. 164, 172).

It is clear, therefore, that this visual wall, a wall of the soul, as it were, is a surface located by the Author of nature in pure space. The process he employs differs radically from that used to locate the walls or tactile surfaces at the extremity of the fundamental feeling. But the law by which tactile sensations are arranged in surfaces to form the boundary of our body is no less extraordinary than the law that requires visual sensations to be placed in a flat, uniform surface within pure space.[83] The two laws are equally admirable.

§3. An animal *faculty of sensuous retention* is necessary in order to explain the connection between the three kinds of corporeal feelings

186. We continue to consider how sensations are composed.

[83] The flat surface of sight, however, has a certain intrinsic relationship with the total feeling of our body. The relationship makes us aware that the visual surface is in front of us, not behind us, nor anywhere else.

First, in the case of sensations of touch, we note at once that when the piece of metal in our example moves over the whole surface of the body, the sensations it produces are successive, not simultaneous. Consequently the sensations alone cannot give us the limits of our fundamental feeling; they need a retentive faculty in the soul, which either unites successive sensations or at least extracts a single message from many. The continuity of position of the sensations, therefore, is not determined by the soul but is inherent in the sensations themselves, whose mode of existence is not only extension but also a position relative to each other in solid space.

§4. When surface sensations give shape to the extension of the fundamental feeling, the extension becomes the origin of the idea of bodies other than our own and their measure. It also gives rise to the popular idea of body

187. When examining the sensation produced by the piece of metal passing over our skin, we have to distinguish very carefully between the sensation itself, which consists wholly in a modification of the fundamental feeling (enabling the feeling subject to feel only a partial mode of this feeling), and the perception of the external agent (which we later call 'a piece of metal'). However, the sensation of our body and the perception of the external body have quantity and extension in common. For example, if we have two simultaneous sensations, we deduce that the agents must also be two, that is, that two pieces are touching our skin. If the extension of each of the two felt surfaces is a square centimetre, we say that each piece of metal has an extension of one square centimetre.

188. We must also take into account the *passivity* proper to sensation, and the *activity* proper to an external agent: an agent is not perceived unless its activity is felt in our passivity.

189. Moreover, we associate with the external agent what in reality belongs to our feeling. We say, for example, the metal is cold, although 'cold' is not a property of the metal, but simply our sensation. The same is true of all the secondary properties of bodies. This kind of confusion gives rise to popular error,

although we can allow bodies their secondary properties in order not to introduce unnecessary difficulties into our argument. We shall therefore call bodies enveloped by secondary qualities *ordinary bodies*. If they are also animal bodies, we shall continue to call them *anatomical bodies*.

190. Nevertheless, we must be careful to maintain the distinction between the modification of the fundamental feeling, which is properly called *sensation*, and the *perception* of an external agent, which consists entirely in the disturbance experienced in the modification of our fundamental feeling, where the modifying energy, alien to the feeling subject, is clearly evident.

We have called sensations *subjective phenomena*, and perceptions of external agents *extrasubjective phenomena* whether the external agents are considered in their genuine qualities or as ordinary bodies.

§5. The constant position of *shaped* feelings together with movement and the faculty of sensuous retention gives us the perception of indefinitely large sizes

191. We must now see how by means of touch the soul perceives an extension greater than that presented by the limits of the soul's fundamental feeling.

I say 'perceives' although 'perception' is not altogether correct. We accept unlimited space as the constant term of the fundamental feeling, and find that as such it does possess indeed the nature of 'term' of feeling. Space, however, does not begin to be perceived properly speaking (that is, to be distinguished as foreign to the feeling subject) except in the perception of bodies and as modes of bodies. It was under this aspect that we considered space in *The Origin of Thought*.

192. We said that a space larger than that occupied by our body can be perceived only by means of the sense of movement. As long as we imagine the feeling subject at rest, it could never, even if touched by foreign bodies, be touched in an extension greater than that presented by the limits of its fundamental feeling. Hence, such sensations could never make it feel a greater

extension. In order to supply for this limitation of the fundamental feeling, the wisdom of the Creator endowed the feeling subject with movement. But movement is a phenomenon that does not attract particular attention; it is so ordinary and natural that we give no thought to it. Nevertheless, careful reflection reveals how extraordinary it is.

193. I shall confine myself solely to the action of touch. Let us suppose that our feeling subject places his extended hand on the edge of a table and follows the edge with a continuous motion to the opposite edge. It is certain that his moving hand cannot have a sensation extending beyond his hand. The only way his hand can feel an extension greater than itself is by feeling successive sensations, each the size of the extension of his hand. But this is not sufficient, because it could be merely the same sensation repeated. Indeed, if his hand remains motionless and is touched successively many times, the extension it feels will be no greater than that presented by the hand on contact with external agents. Moreover, the feeling principle, in addition to feeling many successive sensations in the surface where its fundamental feeling terminates, would have to know in some way that the surface-extended agent which first touched it (in our case, the part of the table touched by the palm of the hand) is not the second agent, not the part of the table touched by the hand when it moved. The feeling principle would also need to know that these two agents, and all the successive agents, are continuous and form a single surface extension.

The soul comes to know all this by means of a wonderful law which governs the modification of its feeling act. According to this law the soul can change both the space it occupies and the partial limits of its corporeal fundamental feeling: this is motion. In fact the movement of the hand is only 'a change of place of the limits of the corporeal fundamental feeling', and such a change presupposes the solid space given to the soul by nature. The change also requires *sensuous retention* of the limits of the preceding space. But even the union of the preceding and following limits by *sensuous retention* would be insufficient to constitute a continuous space for the soul if the change from one limit to another took place by leaps and bounds, so that, for example, the feeling of my arm when moved from pointing east to pointing south would not be extended in the quadrant between the two points. There is no contradiction in conceiving the possibility that feeling is subject to such a law. But if this were so, the soul would never feel a surface greater than that presented by its own limbs, while each felt surface would be separate and totally independent. Thus, if the surfaces were equal, they would be confused in the soul, identified like the sensations of the two eyes, and distinguishable only by their inequality.

194. For the feeling principle to present a surface greater than that given by the limits of the fundamental feeling, 1. the limits of the corporeal fundamental feeling must be variable, that is, they must circumscribe another portion of space (space is the term of the fundamental feeling); 2. the variability of the limits must be subject to the law of continuity, so that the new limits of the corporeal fundamental feeling are in a position of continuity with the preceding limits; 3. the change of limits and the law of continuity must be feelable, that is, within a space felt by nature (if the corporeal fundamental feeling, which has changed shape and limits, did not feel the change or the manner of the change, it could never inform the soul, as we know it does, of the extension which exceeds the limits of the body); 4. the soul must retain the limits it first felt and unite them in space (which is the term of feeling) with limits felt afterwards; otherwise, the soul could never form for itself the large extension of the table under discusion. We call this faculty of the soul *sensuous retention*.[84] According to its capacity for sensuous retention, the feeling subject, granted movement, can perceive how much a corporeal extension exceeds its own body.

195. We have already explained how sight, using signs of extraordinary precision and detail, wonderfully helps touch to indicate a variety of objects (cf. 169).[85] There is nothing more wonderful than the harmony of these two senses. Sight sensations have no similarity whatsoever to touch sensations, and visual objects are essentially different from tactile objects. Nevertheless, although the objects differ in size and in everything else, we accept them as identical simply by the analogy

84 This is a function of the animal *unitive force*, as we shall see later.

85 *OT*, 907–922.

of their forms and the amazing correspondence of shape that exists between the sensations of sight and touch. The illusion originates in the fact that the size of the objects given by each of the two senses does not have a *common measure*: tactile objects are measured by touch, which is unable to measure visual objects; and visual objects are measured by the eyes, which cannot measure tactile size by comparing it with the size of its own objects. Thus the difference of size remains unknown to our feeling; it is revealed only by intelligence after careful reflection.[86]

196. Sight sensations, however, offer further assistance for perceiving an extension greater than that of our own body. Despite its tiny size, visual sensation corresponds not only to a single sensation of touch, but to the innumerable touch sensations produced as a result of great movement. Moreover, the eyes enlarge their sensation both with the movement of the fundamental feeling and when they are kept fixed on a scene which changes before them, provided the scene is varied and not entirely uniform.[87]

86 To understand better what I am saying, let us suppose that the nerve membrane, sensitive to light, instead of being extended solely in the middle of the pupil, extends over the whole of our body, covering it entirely. Only in this case could we compare the absolute size of the sensation received in the retina with the size of our whole body, because the whole body would be sensitive to the same stimulus of light. On the other hand, if optic sensitivity is restricted to the pupil, the whole visual world is restricted to the pupil while, relative to this way of feeling, the rest of the body would apparently be non-existent. It is impossible, therefore, to compare the size of the retina with the size of our body, which is not felt, or to know the difference between the two.

87 I do not deny, however, that something similar can happen in touch, provided the uniformity in the sensations is not interrupted. For example, if a perfectly smooth rod is drawn across a part of my arm, I cannot know the length of the rod. The sensation is constantly equal, and therefore I cannot be certain whether the same agent is acting all the time or the agent is continually different. On the other hand, if the rod has a jagged surface, I successively feel new sensations and am able to note the direction in which they are moving; I can form for myself, although with great difficulty, a single perception of the multiple sensations. Even if the rod had only one or two irregularities, these would distort my skin and thus indicate an agent moving continuously across my arm. In this case and in similar experiments, I would not deny that the length of the rod could be perceived, at least in a general way.

Article 6.
The laws of the relationship between feelings and our real body perceived extrasubjectively

§1. The same surface-extension that forms the seat of shaped feelings presents a foreign agent to our fundamental feeling. This wonderful law makes us perceive: 1. that our body and foreign bodies possess the same corporeal nature; 2. that our body perceived subjectively and extrasubjectively is identical in its entity

197. We have seen how the feeling subject comes to know 1. the limits of the fundamental feeling and the size of the space occupied by this feeling; 2. the spaces and external bodies that limit the fundamental feeling (as a result of the shapes presented by touch and sight).

We must, however, always keep in mind the difference between the perception of external bodies and the perception of our own. The perception of external bodies was explained by the extrasubjective agents' modifying the fundamental feeling; the perception of our own body was explained by the subjective modification of the fundamental feeling. The two explanations are so different that if we perceived our body only subjectively, it would be impossible to believe that it was of the same nature as external agents. We would have called it simply 'fundamental feeling', or at most 'extension of the fundamental feeling', but never 'body'. But we saw that this being, although passive to external agents, is active in its own turn. It becomes an external agent itself, maintaining identical size and shape in both active and passive states. We cannot doubt, for example, that our hand, which we feel subjectively, makes itself felt extrasubjectively: it can be touched and seen like any other thing devoid of subjective feeling. When we touch our hand, an extended agent is felt in exactly the same surface that forms the limit of our fundamental feeling. We can easily demonstrate this by placing one hand on the other, when each naturally becomes an agent and recipient. The surface of one hand in which a feeling is aroused is the same surface acting on, and arousing a feeling in, the other hand.[88]

Our body, therefore, has the same active energy and the same laws of extension as any other body, and is rightly called 'body' in common with all external bodies. However, it has something else: the space it occupies is the exact space of the fundamental feeling and its modifications.

198. The fundamental feeling is of course passive, and therefore the opposite of the agent which produces it. Nevertheless, because it occupies the same space and dimensions as the body, it melds with the body, which we then call sentient and living.[89]

§2. Our real, extrasubjective body and ordinary, anatomical, extrasubjective body. Physical reciprocity between the soul and the real, subjective body

199. We must carefully distinguish the two ways of considering our body. They constitute two series of facts which have only extension in common, and presuppose two beings, as it were, in the same extension.

Our investigation into the relationship between the two beings or series of facts must ignore theory and *a priori* conceptions, and be guided solely by attentive observation. Our aim is to deduce the harmonious laws that unite the two kinds of phenomena, subjective and extrasubjective, which may in some way be seen as parallel, although they cannot be considered united as cause and effect; this is excluded even by the anomalies present in their parallelism.

200. For the sake of clarity in touching upon the law of the relationship between the two series of phenomena, and their parallelism and its anomalies, I call our body 'extrasubjective body' in so far as we know it as an external agent, that is, in the

[88] To avoid any equivocation, the words 'agent' and 'recipient' must here be understood solely in relationship to the sensations. If I see a *living* body cut by a knife, the body, relative to myself who see, is as much an agent as the knife, but, relative to the living body that receives the impression of the knife, the knife is the agent and the body the recipient.

[89] *OT*, 842–844.

extrasubjective way we know all foreign bodies. I call 'subjective body' the extension we feel subjectively, as presented to our soul in our feelings. However, I also consider the *subjective* and *extrasubjective body* as two entities having the same limits and, generally speaking, the same extension.

201. I must point out immediately that the extrasubjective body is either real, or is phenomenal, popular and anatomical.

Our *real* extrasubjective body is known by us simply as an energy which modifies our soul, giving it extended sensations (as a sensiferous principle) and modifying the other energies capable of modifying our soul.

The *popular* or anatomical extrasubjective body is the same energy considered in its indirect, not its direct, action on our soul, and clothed with the so-called secondary qualities of colour, smell, etc. The body, considered as directly acting on our soul, cannot be an object of anatomy or of our exterior senses, and is known only in a direct way by the feeling it produces.

202. Following our argument, we say that such energy can be considered clothed with secondary qualities not because the qualities are part of the energy but because some element causing them must be present in the energy. Thus, when we speak of a white body, we do not intend to attribute whiteness, which is a sensation, to the body. We are attributing a power which, granted certain conditions, produces whiteness in us. Whiteness is understood as the sign of the power of this quality, whatever it may be.

203. The relationship to be investigated, therefore, is that between *our ordinary, anatomical, extrasubjective body* and the *subjective body* or, more accurately, between the extension of the anatomical body and the subjective extension in which feeling terminates. This relationship is at the core of our investigation and the subject of all the great controversies.

204. The relationship, however, between the corporeal feeling and the body acting directly on the soul is simple and unique, without any possible anomaly in its parallelism. Feeling itself makes known the agent causing the feeling, so that the body, by the very fact of this action, becomes the cause of the feeling.

This observation has led me to ascertain, without doubt as far as I can see, reciprocity between soul and body.[90]

If, however, instead of considering the body in its essential act, where its nature is given in the very fact itself, we turn our attention to the *ordinary, anatomical, extrasubjective* body, the case is quite different. Our task now is to investigate the law of the relationship which unites this body to the extension of the corporeal feeling, that is, to the subjective body.

Article 7.
The laws governing the relationship between the subjective body and our ordinary, extrasubjective body

§1. A common error: to every change in the ordinary body there corresponds a change of feeling in the same place

205. The human mind, impatient and desirous of reaching immediate conclusions, always prefers to guess about nature rather than observe it. Thus, in the question we have proposed, our first thought is that the law of the connection between the extension of the *ordinary or anatomical extrasubjective body* (the only body our mind usually considers) and the extension of the *corporeal feeling* simply states that 'to every change in the extension of the ordinary, extrasubjective body there corresponds a feeling in the same place'.

206. A person who makes this kind of judgment has already progressed beyond the first stage, despite his mistake. In the first stage anyone could have confused the impression or change in the ordinary, extrasubjective body with the feeling accompanying it — the childish error, one might say, of materialists. But the person who has made some progress distinguishes the impression or change taking place in the anatomical body from the

[90] I do not think, however, that it is possible to argue from the extension of the fundamental feeling to the extension of the body, which acts directly on the soul. For this reason, in *The Origin of Thought*, I demonstrated the extension of the body by deducing it solely from the action of external bodies on our body. Cf. *OT*, 842–871.

subsequent sensation, although he believes that 'feeling is always joined with identity of place to the impression or change in the anatomical body'.

207. Now, because the absolute motion of our body is in itself totally unfeelable,[91] the question is reduced to examining whether this opinion is true in the case of the relative motion of the parts composing our body.

§2. Haller's experiments on sensitive, irritable parts should have disproved the error, but the error remains

208. The man in the street does not doubt the truth of the opinion we are examining. Hence, granted this common error which springs from excessive generalisation, Haller's discovery was considered of great importance. He demonstrated that a corresponding feeling was not always present in the place where parts of the body were touched and moved; only the nerves were the proper seat of feeling. Such a discovery was contrary to the opinion that sensation must accompany every change of place in the parts of the anatomical body.

209. Despite Haller, the error was maintained not only by people in general but also by the most learned naturalists, although the latter limited it to the nerves. The well-known anatomist, Felice Fontana, firmly held that a sensation took place where a nerve was touched. 'Feeling,' he said, 'is a quality of the nerves and cannot exist where there are no nerves. We can have clear ideas about what we are trying to understand, only if we realise that extension, weight, and impenetrability of bodies (qualities proper to bodies) cannot be found separate from bodies themselves.'[92] Such words presuppose as certain that 'feeling is a quality inherent in bodies'. But the bodies mentioned are only *ordinary bodies*, which do not feel, but cause feeling, although only indirectly and as acquired feeling. Popular opinions of this kind are maintained with great facility even by those who, like

[91] Cf. *OT*, 806.

[92] Letter to Prof. Scarpa, 8th September 1801.

Felice Fontana, firmly aim to be guided in everything by accurate, logical observation.

§3. The error or misconception is refuted by the facts

210. It is important therefore to demonstrate the falsity of the claim that to every movement produced in a part of the ordinary, anatomical body there corresponds a new feeling in the same part and place. Nor is it true that the extension with which feeling is endowed is modified in a way fully parallel with, and corresponding to the modification of the ordinary, anatomical body. To show this, we begin with an observation on the very phenomenon used to support the popular misconception we refute. For example, when a sharp point is applied as a stimulus to the external surface of our body, we feel pain at the spot where the point is applied. From this we generally conclude that the feeling happens in the part of the body which has been modified and touched. We also consider the conclusion applicable to all parts of the body (or at least those considered to have feeling) and to every kind of stimuli.

211. But if we consider this phenomenon of external touch carefully, the opposite of what we think proves to be the case. Everybody accepts that there is no evident sensation unless the movement of a nerve touched at its extremity reaches the brain. If a finger is pricked, the movement does not remain there alone, but is communicated along the arm to the brain. Now, if the opinion we are refuting were true, we should feel the pain not only in the finger but in the whole nerve as it is moved and modified throughout the length of the arm to the brain. But this does not happen. Thus, the modification of the anatomical body and the new feeling it arouses in the soul are different things. Although both present an extension, they do not present the same extension; nor is the extension modified according to the same laws. In the example given, the extension of the modification of the nerve follows a line stretching from the finger to the brain, but the feeling is concentrated in a point, at the extremity of the finger.[93]

[93] We must note carefully the disharmony we are discussing between the

212. We should not be surprised, therefore, at the phenomenon presented by those who have had an arm or leg amputated: they sometimes claim to feel pain in the extremities of the limb, which they have lost.[94] Such a fact would indeed be a source of wonder if it were true that the affected part of the anatomical body corresponded at every point to the location of the feeling. But we cannot say this, and if we wanted to say it, we would first have to identify it by a very attentive observation rather than imagine it or argue to it *a priori*. Hence, we believe that the laws of the relationship between these two kinds of location demand deep, careful study.

213. There is in fact no difficulty in indicating similar phenomena, in which the location of the feeling corresponds not to the movements of the parts but to the external surface of the body. Diseases are a good example: it is not uncommon in the

subjective and extrasubjective body. When I say 'the pain I feel in a finger' I am speaking about the subjective body. When I say 'the impression made by a point pricking my finger and the movement it produces to the brain', I am speaking about the extrasubjective body. But what is this extrasubjective body and extension which we wish to translate, as it were, into a subjective body and extension? Note how I perceive the point, the impression and the movement of the whole nerve to the brain. I perceive them by touch and sight: by touch, by actually touching them or imagining they can be touched; by sight, by actually seeing them or imagining they can be seen. Now, if I touched or imagined I touched with parts of my body the point, wound and whole length of the nerve up to the brain, I would trace a line on the surface of my body which would have the same length as the nerve; a sensation would correspond to the whole line where the surface of my body was touched. If we say that the impression and movement of the extrasubjective body has the same length as the nerve from the finger to the brain, we are saying that the impression and movement is the cause of a subjective feeling of equal length. In order to express in precise philosophical language the relationship between the anatomical, extrasubjective body and the subjective body, we would have to say that the following law applies in our example: 'If a living body is modified by touch, which produces in the person perceiving the modification a subjective, extended feeling whose length is the distance from the finger to the brain, a sensation having the extension of a physical point located in the finger is aroused in the subject of the modified body.' The same reasoning would also apply to sight.

[94] This is another fact concerning the relationship between corporeal sensitivity and the unlimited space given in the fundamental feeling (cf. 191–194). Note that the painful sensation cannot be referred by habit to the place of the amputated fingers. Cf. *OT*, 761, 762.

case of fevers of the nerves for internal parts to be inflamed while the extremities are cold.[95] Sometimes the whole surface of the body is seized by cold, as in the case of the fever which antiquity called *algida*.[96] At other times a feeling of warmth covers the whole external surface, while the sick person feels cold internally. In these cases where the feeling of warmth and cold is situated in the skin, we cannot believe that the movement of the nerves preceding the cold in the anatomical body is restricted only to the skin. The body of the sick person is not touched externally by anything hot or cold, which might warm or cool it. The feeling of cold and warmth located in the skin comes from internal movements of the nerves. But these movements are not felt, at least not with a cold or warm sensation located solely in the surface extension.[97] Sometimes the cold in the skin is the effect of the internal action of poisons, like the sap of the *cinchona* or the poison of a rattlesnake bite. We have to conclude therefore that the divine Author of the human race has in his wisdom established the following law: 'corporeal feeling (given certain circumstances) is principally referred to the surfaces of the body'. By this wonderful law human beings are able to perceive, as I have said, shaped spaces which are necessary for the development of their understanding and for daily life.

95 Coldness of the skin is shown also by external signs, such as paleness, dryness, wrinkling, goose-flesh, loss of feeling, etc.

96 The earlier thinkers had also observed the phenomenon of the feeling of cold diffused only on the surface. Celsus distinguishes between 'cold' and 'fright': 'I speak of "cold" when the extremities of the limbs are frozen; of "fright" when the whole body trembles' (Bk. 3, c. 3).

97 The distinction between the subjective and the extrasubjective way of perceiving the body is further strengthened by reflecting on the phenomenon sometimes experienced by sick people, who complain of feeling cold, although their body-heat, according to the reading on a thermometer or even felt by hand, is normal, or even higher than normal. The same can be said about feeling hot. The difference of opinion arises because the sick perceive their body subjectively, but anyone touching them perceives it extrasubjectively.

§4. The remarkable law by which the surfaces of the body are the special seat of feelings

214. It used to be thought that the vital principle resided at the centre of the animal. For a long time this opinion prevented physiologists from devoting to the surfaces of the body all the attention that modern thinkers have given.

215. Professor Santarelli called these surfaces 'organic levers of life'[98] — an extraordinarily apposite phrase, I think. In one of his writings he enumerates the different classes of sensations, and says: 'All these sensations take place where the nerves begin, that is, in both the external and internal *surfaces* of every cavity and vessel. The movement of the nerves therefore begins at these apexes, from which it spreads to all the parts, giving rise to the harmony and accord which is health.'[99]

[98] Among the studies carried out recently on the membranes present externally in the surface of the body, those of Donné are important. He observed that the skin secretes an *acid* fluid, while the mucous membranes inside the body from the mouth to the anus secrete an *alkaline* fluid. He thought the explanation could be electrical currents between both membranes acting like the two poles of Volta's battery. Donné presented these findings to the Academy of Science of Paris (cf. no. 38 of the Journal of the *Institut*, 1834). Matteucci, in an article in the *Biblioth. Univ.* (August, 1834), accepted these facts, but did not agree that the acid and alkaline substances, separated from each other by the body's internal and external surfaces, were the cause of electrical currents. He thought they were the effects of these currents, principally because the acidity and alkalinity remained after death, while the electrical currents ceased. They therefore seemed to be an effect of life. We see how all these studies must contribute to discovering the laws of the relationship between feeling and the ordinary, extrasubjective body, but the relationship can be one only of parallelism, never of cause and effect, as I shall explain.

[99] Prof. Santarelli's findings are presented in the *Giornale Accadico*, vol. 54, Jan., Feb. and March, 1832. However, the professor, despite such an important observation, does not show himself completely free of the misconception we are refuting. 'Consciousness,' he had said a little earlier, 'makes us attribute sensation to the organ where it arises' (no. 36). The proposition is not exact. In the first place, sensation does not arise when the movement of the nerve begins. Granted all the movement necessary for arousing sensation, it arises immediately, locating itself appropriately, according to certain hidden laws which must be deduced, as I have said, by observation. In the second place, we refer the feeling to the surface even when the movement of the nerve does not begin at the surface, as in the case of cold skin produced by fever or fright.

§5. The distinction between extension and the position of feelings

216. The intestinal canal can be considered as a continuation of the skin. The covering of the larynx, trachea and bronchial tubes is also considered to have the same texture. If the different kinds of sensations we experience along this passageway are not shaped, as is the case with those referred to the skin, we must bear in mind that the precise position of the sensations situated in the cutaneous surface depends largely on two conditions which cannot be present relative to the internal surface of the intestinal canal. The conditions are: 1. the use of sight, which is a sense eminently adapted for outlining or shaping things and an incredible aid for perceiving the positions, relative to the whole body, of the external stimulus arousing the sensation and of the sensation joined to the stimulus; 2. the use of movement, especially of the hands, with which we can touch successively all the parts of the external surface of our body, become fully acquainted with our body in a practical way, and are thus able to note precisely the position of sensations. Noting the position of sensations means knowing the place where they are situated relative to all the other parts of our body. In order to be able to state where we feel, we have to perceive all the parts of our body. And the only parts we can feel totally are the external surfaces, precisely because they are all perceived together by our eyes, and by our touch which can be applied to all the parts successively.

217. Thus there is a difference between a sensation with its real seat in a determined place and limb, and our *adverting* and telling ourselves where we feel respectively these different parts of our body. We can feel in a part without knowing which part, because we lack this awareness. For example, if we had never seen or touched the surface of our body, and had as our first sensation the prick of a needle in our arm, we would certainly feel in the spot where we had been pricked. But we would not be able to know, advert to, or state to ourselves the distance of the sensation from our head, feet or hands, etc., because we would not yet have perceived the size, shape and respective position of these parts. I have already pointed out that if we sit for a long time in

darkness without moving, we lose awareness of the way we have disposed our hands and feet, so that we cannot say how they are folded relative to each other. A friend of mine was once sitting in church next to an old man who had the habit of crossing one leg over the other. On this occasion the man made a mistake and crossed his leg over the knee of my friend, who made no move. Only when it was time to leave, did the old man become aware of what he had done.

§6. The difference between the *absolute position* of feelings and their *position relative* to the parts of the body

218. When speaking about the position of sensations, we have to distinguish two very different cases. The first, *absolute* position, is inherent to all sensations that have position. The second, *relative* position, is not inherent to individual sensations but deduced from the relationship of place between many sensations. This deduction is carried out by mental *advertence* rather than feeling.

The relative position of sensations is known only by experiencing all the parts of our body. This experience, which helps us determine the relationship between the subjective feeling and our body perceived extrasubjectively, is due particularly to the two senses of touch and sight, as I have said.

219. The *absolute* position of sensations (and its relationship with the position of movements produced in the anatomical, extrasubjective body) offers many phenomena that would need careful study, in addition to those I have already mentioned. Here I shall mention only a few in the hope that others will be encouraged to consider the matter more deeply.

Cold, by obstructing the functions of the stomach, can sometimes cause convulsions in people subject to such attacks. The convulsive movements can be preceded by exceptional cold in the neck, but the cold certainly has its origin in the stomach, even if the place of the sensation is the lower part of the head. Pains in the head are common with gastric fevers. The stimulus therefore is very often in the stomach nerves, but the sensation phenomenon reveals itself in the brain. Hunger, when felt, produces an intense sensation only in the cardiac, although all abdominal parts involved in digestion are affected. The explanation could be a possible nerve communication between the cardiac and the brain, but even so the communication is not felt. My observation, therefore, that the place of sensation is different from that of movement, remains valid. Bichat says:

> When a large area of the pleura or lungs is inflamed, the resulting pain is very often concentrated only at one point. Many times a pain, limited to some point of the head, stomach or elsewhere, coincides with a widely diffused infection in a part quite different from the one we indicate. Hence, we must never consider the place to which we refer the feeling as a certain indication of the place of the infection, but solely as a sign that it must be nearby.[100]

220. Physiologists unhesitatingly posit the nerves as the seat of feeling. They then find it inexplicable that certain, apparently nerveless parts of the body seem, under certain conditions, to have feeling. Ligaments irritated by an acid or a concentrated alkali or by some instrument do not give any feeling, but when scratched or torn cause intense pain. Cartilages and serious membranes, which appear insensitive in their natural state, cause very sharp pain when inflamed — I have already mentioned the painful caruncle of Professor Scarpa (cf. 91). Fontana suggested that these apparent pains in parts devoid of nerves could be explained either by the communication of movement to the neighbouring nerves or by the disturbance of the fluid which he thought filled the basic nerve canals and which he believed he had undoubtedly seen under very powerful microscopes. But it would be difficult to believe that the fluid disturbed by the nerves had feeling independently of the transmission of its movement to the brain because the movement could not conceivably propagate itself outside the vessels.[101] In the other case the movement communicated to the nerve would explain the

[100] *Ricerche fisiologiche intorno alla vita e alla morte*, pt. 1, art. 6, §4. We would do well to investigate carefully whether the places where the pain manifests itself are not the *extremities* of some complex or organ.

[101] For this to be possible, we would have to suppose that the fluid issuing from the nerve canals finds other natural vessels suitable for constructing a continuation of the canals.

origin of the pain, but not how the seat of the pain is outside the nerve.

221. Dumas sought to explain the phenomenon by saying that the nerves possessed the property of *radiating* the feeling and extending it to the parts devoid of nerves. Many have used the expression after him. This, however, would be a case not of radiating the feeling but of projecting it over a great distance, because in fact where there are nerves, there is no feeling, and contrarily, where there are no nerves, there is feeling. Is it not preferable to say that subjective feeling is not inherent to any part of an extrasubjective body but may occupy different places at various times, according to laws which must be deduced by patient observation? It would be impossible to find, in the modifications and movements of the anatomical body, any identity between place and extraordinary sensations such as those of the auras of a person subject to epileptic fits.

222. We must also distinguish the *position* of certain sensations from the *extension* with which they are endowed. For example, sight sensation has extension but no position in its phenomenal part (cf. 173). A coloured surface is perceived, but, as we have already indicated, the soul does not assign any place to the surface, nor refer it to any part of its own body. In fact, if the soul referred sensations of light to the retina, the objects would undoubtedly be double because referred to the two retinas. Because the sensations are not referred to any part of the body, the surfaces can be identified in space, and the objects of sight transported outside us, making the coloured surface of the eye like a stage, whose scenery depicts the objects of touch.

§7. The phenomenal part of those sensations in which we find neither *position* nor *extension*

223. Finally, there are feelings entirely devoid of *position* and *extension*; smell, sound, colour and taste are evidently of this kind.

224. I do not doubt that these sensations in so far as they possess something in common with touch have a position in our body. However, the quantity of the tiny sensations from which

they result, and the inequality of the impact of a stream of particles on the nerve endings, prevent them from presenting a clearly defined extension.[102] Thus, if the light is too strong for our eyes, or disease has made our sense of sound (or sense of smell, in the case of women after childbirth) extremely acute, an unpleasant sensation is associated with the unextended, phenomenal sensation. This unpleasant sensation has position by being referred to the place of the affected organ, which then acts like the general sense of touch.

225. Consequently we must distinguish: the *quality*, *extension* and *position* of sensations.

226. The *quality* of sensations requires different conditions from those necessary for their *extension*. Relative to the anatomical body, the *quality* varies according to 1. the varying construction of the organs, 2. their healthy or diseased state,[103] 3. the degree of natural vitality, and 4. the accidental stimuli activating the vitality in different ways.[104]

[102] These sensations give us two kinds of different phenomena: 1. those which I call the phenomenal part, and 2. those which the sensations have in common with touch. This arises from the two laws of shaped and non-shaped sensitivity. As we have seen, the principle of the law of shaped sensitivity is that 'surfaces affected by a stimulus give shaped sensations'.

[103] Relative to this, changes due to disease manifest extraordinary phenomena that should be carefully assembled and studied. Phenomena like this would throw much light on the theory of sensitivity. We have an example in a man subject to convulsions. When he was in a convulsion, he did not hear sounds directed to his ear, but did hear when the sound waves struck his epigastrium and the vicinity of the apex of his heart. Cf. *Bulletino di scienze mediche*, published in Bologna, Year 4, vol. 6, facc. 131 ss., September and October, 1832.

[104] I do not mean natural stimuli, which are conditions rather than accidental increase of the vitality of the organs. Such stimuli belong to natural vitality, which is the third kind of causes I have listed. This vitality, however, also has its own levels, which are largely dependent on natural stimuli. Thus the blood is the natural stimulant of the brain, and the quantity of vital excitement of this main organ depends on the amount of such a stimulus. The stimuli I am speaking about, therefore, are accidental and foreign, like food and alcoholic beverages, etc. For example, the experiments carried out by Davy at the Royal Institute of Bristol with nitric acid and nitrogen gas, demonstrate that a person breathing the gas manifests phenomena similar to those of the early stage of drunkenness: objects become very clear, hearing acquires an extraordinary sensitivity, muscular strength increases, with an accompanying

§8. The laws of the relationship between our subjective body and the ordinary body do not and cannot indicate a connection of cause and effect

227. I conclude these comments on the laws of the relationship between the changes in our anatomical extrasubjective body and those in our subjective body by noting that this relationship can never consist in a *connection* of cause and effect. It consists solely in concomitance or parallelism, in two accompanying series of phenomena, as it were, without either being the cause of the other. What I have said about the ordinary, anatomical, extrasubjective body clearly indicates that the phenomena of this body cannot be the cause of the subjective phenomena. The extrasubjective body does not present us with what it really is, but only with the effects of an agent on us, effects which depend in great part on the nature of the subjective body and our soul. Hence the cause of both series of phenomena must be sought in an unknown principle, that is, the real body, the *sensiferous* principle, which truly acts in our soul, producing the subjective phenomena and subjective body, and then modifying this subjective body. With this new action or impact on the subjective body the sensiferous principle produces the extrasubjective phenomena and the ordinary body. Because these phenomena are so vivid, distinct, limited, shaped and constant, they generate an overriding, almost invincible persuasion in us that together they constitute the only corporeal reality.

228. We can easily understand, therefore, why the interaction of the soul with the body fruitlessly exercised the greatest minds, and was ultimately considered inexplicable.[105]

tendency to move about, laugh, etc.

105 St. Augustine himself was desperate to find a solution to the problem. He writes: 'The way in which spirits adhere to bodies and become animals is extraordinary. We humans cannot understand it, and we ourselves are composed in the same way' (*De Civ. Dei*, 21, 10). It must be carefully noted here that we do not claim to have explained the interaction between soul and body, but only to have demonstrated that philosophers ask the question out of context. This makes any solution not only difficult but impossible and absurd. On the other hand, once the real nature of the problem is known, the matter is reduced to the action of two beings. This mutual action is explained in exactly the same way as all the other facts of the universe consisting in mutual actions.

Only the ordinary, extrasubjective body was considered. Consequently, the cause of the subjective phenomena was sought where it could not be found. The truth is that the ordinary, extrasubjective body is not and cannot be the cause of the subjective phenomena or feelings.

§9. Corollary on craniology and phrenology

229. As a corollary of this teaching, we may affirm that the principle posited by Gall, Spurzheim and other *phrenologists*, 'certain forms of the brain correspond to certain dispositions of the soul', cannot be accused of materialism or rejected *a priori*.

Experience alone must identify the laws of the relationship between the forms of the anatomical body, the feelings and the dispositions of the spirit. But whatever these laws may be, they will never constitute a connection of cause and effect. Such a union is seen to be impossible and absurd as soon as we ask 'what in reality are the brain, fissures and protuberances'. The question cannot be answered unless we acknowledge that they 'are simply effects and phenomena produced in our touch and sight (or in our imagination which reproduces similar sensations) which do indeed suppose an unknown agent. But it is absurd and even childish to put our faith in them by changing the phenomena into absolute reality and entity'. The materialists' error consists precisely in their belief that the two series of subjective and extrasubjective phenomena are cause and effect. Materialists are not satisfied with the fact, which presents the phenomena as concurrent, or with serious reflection, which tells us that their only possible connection depends upon parallelism and nothing more.[106]

[106] The *facts* adduced by *phrenologists* must be separated from the *arguments* and systems they use. Unfortunately their systems are very often affected by materialism, because they give so much importance to the study of matter and very little to the study of spirit. Logic was not their chosen discipline, and consequently they have not hesitated to disseminate absurd conclusions in every direction. Examples of their false reasoning, which is not worth the trouble of correcting, can be seen even in the most recent writers, for example, Broussais and others. But we accept facts gratefully whatever their source. If

9

HOW THE FEELABLE PRINCIPLE IS DISTINGUISHED FROM THE FEELING AND SENSIFEROUS PRINCIPLES

Article 1.
How an unextended principle can feel an extended principle

230. The argument outlined in the preceding chapter would require much greater development than we can give it in a work devoted to moral anthropology. What we have to say here will simply continue and clarify the matters already dealt with. We begin by making an observation about the nature of bodily or material feeling.

If we consider the general notion of feeling, we find that it does not include the concept of *extension*. And it is certain that there are feelings which do not furnish the spirit with anything extended.

231. But we are also aware that we experience sensations or feelings that of themselves furnish us with some extension, and others that provide us with at least some location. These we have called *corporeal feelings*.[107] We saw that this extension is found in the corporeal fundamental feeling and its modifications, especially in those arising from touch and sight. But we also saw that the feeling principle[108] is totally unextended. We first ask, therefore, how that which is extended can be contained in what is unextended.

232. This question has its source, however, in a material way of conceiving the *inextension* of the feeling principle.

In the case of two bodies, the more extended of the two certainly cannot be contained in the less extended. In the same way, if the inextension of the feeling principle were that of a

they have been verified, they are common property, bringing greater light, and confirming the truth, the sole object of our work and love.

[107] The only source of our concept of *extension* is feeling. Cf. *OT*, 820–839. This is an irrefutable proof that extension is found in feeling itself.

[108] We sometimes call this 'the *feeling* principle' and sometimes 'the *sentient* principle'. They differ only in so far as the sentient principle is the feeling principle considered in act.

mathematical point, in the normal understanding of mathematical point, we would be dealing with an impossibility: there is no extension in a mathematical point. But such a way of conceiving one thing's existence in another is altogether material and false when applied to our present case. We have to consider carefully that the relationship between the *feeling principle* and *extension* is not a relationship of size, according to which two extended things are measured with one another. It is a relationship of *sensility*, which means that the extended, besides being an extended element, has (relative to the feeling principle) *feelable entity*. In other words, it is an entity superior to that of *extension* and, as such, simple in itself and altogether different from and foreign to extension. The soul receives extension in itself according to this *feelable beingness*. That which feels receives what is extended as feelable; what is unextended does not receive as extended what is extended.

233. I realise that this will be a difficult, if not impossible notion for all those who depend upon matter alone for their concepts, and cannot understand how things can have other than a material mode. But such persons should begin by distrusting the exclusive, restricted concepts drawn from matter which they have arbitrarily generalised. They have to persuade themselves that their material way of perceiving things does not adequately explain the entity of things. It is subjective, relative, limited, phenomenal and — let us be clear about this — highly misleading for those who want to be misled.

Article 2.
How what is *feelable* is distinguished from the *feeling* and the *sensiferous* principles

234. It remains that two irrefutable facts have to be taken into account, whether one understands or not my way of stating how the feeling principle feels what is extended. They are:

1st. that in its own nature the feeling principle is without the slightest likeness to the nature of extension. Hence its description as 'unextended';

2nd. that extension is presented in what we have called corporeal feeling.

And here we must stop to meditate on these two facts. They show that the analysis of corporeal feeling furnishes two very different elements: 1. the unextended *feeling* element; 2. the *felt* element, endowed with extension, which can be called *feelable* in so far as it is capable of being felt.[109]

What is the difference, therefore, between what is *feelable*, what *feels* and what we have called *sensiferous*?

What is *feelable* is the opposite of the *feeling* principle, as we have said. It is therefore distinct from that which feels, although it has its seat in the feeling principle. But that which is feelable is no less distinct from the *sensiferous* principle. This principle provides sensations only as an agent stimulating feelings in the feeling principle.

235. In itself, therefore, the *sensiferous principle* is present in feeling only through its action; for the rest, it is outside feeling. What is *feelable*, however, is an element of feeling itself, as we have also seen.

Besides the feeling principle, or soul, therefore, there are two things distinct from it and from one another: the force that causes feeling without contributing its own proper entity to the formation of feeling, and the force which is an element in already formed feeling.

Article 3.
Justifying common sense in some of its apparent errors about body

236. These two things give rise to the different notions people have about *body* and *matter*, which can however be interpreted correctly.

In the first place, it is not wrong for common sense to judge that what is *feelable* is totally different from the soul: that which is extended and feelable is not the soul, which is simply the sentient principle.

237. In the second place, common sense does not err in judging

109 The difference between what is *felt* and what is *feelable* is the same as that between the *sentient* and the *sensitive* principles: that is, they differ as act and potency differ in the same being.

the *sensiferous* principle as the *substance* of body and something unknown. Although the sensiferous principle acts in the feeling, it does not become, with its own entity, an element in the feeling. Its *entity* is not therefore perceived in itself by us.

If we go on to reflect that this substance which produces feeling in the soul could not do so without bringing its action to bear on the soul, we will easily see how common sense is right in seeing a body (the corporeal substance) present where common sense feels what is *feelable*. In fact, corporeal substance acts in this situation. Finally, if we note that a body must be in act where something *feelable* is present, we realise how common sense attributes what is *feelable* to body as a *quality* of the body. The effect of bodily action is taken as the nearest indication we have of the qualities hidden in a body itself.

Article 4.
Philosophers have misinterpreted certain opinions of common sense about bodies

238. Common sense wisdom has not found worthy interpreters amongst philosophers. Those who badly misunderstood common sense and rebelled against it took refuge in *idealism*, which should more truly be called *sensism*, because its proponents, so-called *idealists*, reduced external bodies not to ideas (which these 'idealists' did not understand), but to sensations.[110]

239. Reid stood out against this error, but was no less disloyal to common sense when he maintained: 'People attribute two very different meanings to the words "colour", "taste", and so on. One meaning expresses the sensation, the other a body perceived as alien to the sensation.' But it is impossible to show that the *feelable qualities*, which are indeed comprised in feeling, are not attributed by ordinary people to bodies.[111]

110 It is well-known that Berkeley's idealism is founded on the definition of body as 'a complex of sensations'.

111 Many very penetrating ideas have been proposed in Italy ('lazy, slow old Italy', as they say, yet hopeful of revival), without their receiving the attention they merit. The same ideas, when regurgitated by writers of other nations, were sometimes acclaimed as discoveries and the foundation of systems. As

Article 5.
The Scholastics' interpretation of common sense opinions

240. The teaching of the Schools,[112] especially as it is explained in various places by St. Thomas, harmonises far more easily with common sense, which it takes as its master. In fact, our interpretation of the word 'body', which depends upon the analysis of both sensation and common sense opinion, is in perfect agreement with Aquinas' assertion that it is more fitting to say 'The body is in the soul' than 'The soul is in the body'. The body does indeed act in the soul by revealing itself there and positing in the soul *that which is feelable* as one of the elements of sensation. To say 'What is feelable is a mode of the soul itself', is to speak materially, unreasonably and absurdly. The soul, as feeling principle, can feel itself only as a feeling entity. In that which is feelable the soul feels nothing, not even the act of feeling; it simply feels the term of this act.

241. The same teaching harmonises with St. Thomas' other affirmation: 'That which feels and that which is felt "unite" in the act of feeling'; and 'That which is feelable in act is feeling itself [*sensus*] in act.'[113] This can only mean that the feeling act *terminates* in the act of *that which is feelable*.[114]

a contribution to some future history of philosophy in Italy, allow me to note that 'feeling', which attracted such attention when proposed by the Scottish school in their endeavour to eliminate *ideas* as intermediaries between things and ourselves, is very similar to, if not identical with, the concept suggested by Niccolò Cantarini in Italy three centuries ago. In his book, *Della perfezion delle cose*, Cantarini set out to destroy systematically the 'intellective species' of Aristotle. Cf. *De Perfectione Rerum*, bk. 6, c. 6, Venice, 1576.

112 The teaching of the Schools means the teaching of Aristotle understood and modified by the Schools.

113 'In operations present in the acting subject, the object identified as term of the action is in the agent itself as the operation in act. Hence in bk. 3 of *De Anima*, what is feelable in act is a feeling in act.' (*S.T.*, 1, q. 14, art. 2).

114 'The feeling act is that which is feelable in act. Not in the sense that the power of feeling is itself a likeness in the feeling of the feelable thing, but because together they make one being, as act and potency do.' (*S.T.*, 1, q. 55, art. 1, ad 2). Note carefully that in this Scholastic theory the *feelable species*, or the *image of what is feelable* (which is also called simply the 'feelable') was not the *substance* of body, but the term of the act of body.

Article 6.
Refutation of the sensists' prejudice that one being cannot in-exist in another

242. We have to affirm unambiguously therefore that although the extended, feelable element is in the soul, it is nevertheless essentially distinguished from the soul. A most important corollary, which we must not overlook, follows from this truth.

Note that the distinction and opposition between these two elements (the unextended feeling element and the extended feelable element), together with their in-existence, are unavoidable data dependent upon simple observation of feeling. Only an hypothesis intended to eliminate feeling itself would abolish these relationships. In other words, in order to destroy these observed data we would have to invent an *hypothesis* which would enable us to believe that the two elements, although distinguished in our observation, were in fact one single thing, that is, the single, identical soul. Now although it is true that the hypothesis can be shown to be absurd, we have no need to show its absurdity. We live in a century in which the only scientific method worth considering is that recognised by Galileo, a method principally aimed at firmly establishing observed facts. Any hypothesis whose avowed aim is to destroy undeniable facts is out of place. Such a mistake in method, which is concomitant with any attempt to annihilate the clear distinction between the elements uncovered by us in feeling, would be sufficient to exclude opposition based upon it.

243. But the corollary we wish to draw from the quality called feeling is this: fact and careful observation of fact show undeniably that 'two beings can exist, one within the other (with their activity), and form a third without destroying one another, without mixing with one another, and without being confused'. This is an ontological truth of the greatest relevance, directly opposed to the sensists' common prejudice that 'one thing cannot exist in another', at least not without confusion and admixture between them. Such a conclusion springs from the sensists' observation that impenetrability prevents one body's existing in another (cf. 232), and from their usual headlong rush to a universal conclusion from a particular premise. Even Leibniz, a

truly great man, was subject to this prejudice, on the basis of which he decreed the impossibility of interchangeable activity between his monads. However, the truth we have indicated stands as a renewed confirmation of our teaching on ideas, a teaching which ordinary people find difficult to understand principally because they cannot see how '*being* can be present in our spirit and not be confused with our spirit itself'.[115]

244. It is difficult to exaggerate the errors springing from this ontological prejudice, or the evils which accompany these errors. The prejudice itself has become the foundation of a popular philosophy that has ruined science through *sensism*, and morality through *hedonism*.[116] This philosophy is thus summarised by one of its principal exponents:

> Just as it is absolutely impossible for a person to go *outside* himself[117] and feel outside himself, so it is absolutely impossible for him to act except from self-love. Virtue can only be self-love expressed outwardly[118] in such a way that the common pressure for exclusive, individual interests is forgotten.[119]

The fallacy contained in this passage depends entirely on the gratuitous, false supposition: 'Within us there is nothing

[115] Cf. my *Rinnovamento della filosofia*, bk. 3, c. 47.

[116] The teaching on pleasure.

[117] I have already noted that this phrase is proper to bodies in their relationship to one another. It cannot be applied, except *metaphorically* (I sometimes use it in this way), to spirits in relationship to one another or in their relationship to bodies. *Body* is not properly speaking *outside* the spirit, but *different* from, although in, the spirit.

[118] How can human beings express self-love *outside themselves* if it is *absolutely impossible for them to go outside themselves*?

[119] Romagnosi, *Note all'articolo 'Progressi e sviluppi della Filosofia e delle scienze metafisiche dal principiare del XIX secolo'*, in the *Indicatore Lombardo*, t. 1, 4th series, pp. 36 ss. This quotation from Romagnosi gives us some idea of the so-called *experimental* method which gives its name to the school. The *experiments* they bring forward are reduced to: 'It is impossible for a person to get outside himself, it is impossible for a person to act other than for self-love, etc.' Are these *experiments*, or are they absolute, dogmatic opinions? These authors introduce experiments and facts in the prefaces to their books, but then abandon them to fill the rest of their volumes with strings of axioms and general opinions proclaiming what is possible or impossible for nature. Nature herself never gets a hearing, but she goes on producing her facts nonetheless.

different from us.' If it were true that there could be, and were, nothing in ourselves except *ourselves*, it would be in some way legitimate to conclude that we could love only ourselves.[120] In fact, we would have no object other than ourselves. If, however, we find through analysis that an entity *different* from ourselves, which is not and cannot be confused with us, has its place in us (by means of the action it exercises, or its immediate manifestation), the conclusion 'Self-love is the only possible effect' is totally mistaken. There is indeed something for us to love other than ourselves.

Article 7.
Agreement between this chapter and the preceding chapter

245. One difficulty remains to be solved. According to what I have said in this chapter, common ideas about bodies have apparently been justified; in the preceding chapter, however, they seem to have been condemned.

I answer that although the first ideas we form of bodies are correct, our first *reflections* upon these correct ideas are mistaken. These reflections, however, are more appropriate to beginners in philosophy than to people in general. And sensists never pass beyond the stage of beginners. This is why I said that common sense finds unfaithful interpreters amongst philosophers.

246. These mistakes consist:

1st. in forgetting the body perceived subjectively, and reflecting solely upon the body perceived extrasubjectively; this imperfect reflection helps to compound imperfect concepts which then give rise to errors;

[120] 'In some way' because strictly speaking even love of ourselves would be impossible if in us there were nothing different from us. Love always presupposes the twofold presence of subject and object, loving principle and loved term. But 'ME, the object' is not '*I*, the subject'. For '*I*, the subject' to become 'ME the object', I have to conceive myself *intellectively*, that is, as a being. There must be present in me, therefore, the essence of being (an element different from me) in order that I may conceive myself mentally and so become an object of my own love.

2nd. in attributing to a body other than our own the *felt* element of our feeling, which is an effect of the action of our own subjective body on our soul;

3rd. in the conviction that we perceive distant bodies without need of the unlimited space given by nature to our fundamental feeling, and solely by relying on the phenomena of sight that serve as signs of unlimited space, or on the images that depend upon movement (in this case, it would be the eye that leads us to believe that we touch coloured things although our eye, restricted to its own limits, could only enable us to believe that the visual image of the hand which touches something takes the place of the visual image of the body it touches — sight cannot tell us that the hand touches, and that the body is truly touched);

4th. in applying to the soul the concept we have formed of the body conceived extrasubjectively, and describing the soul through principles and arguments that can express, as we have said, nothing more than bodies perceived extrasubjectively.

10

MATTER

247. *Body* and *matter* are normally taken as interchangeable words, and I have often used them in this way. Nevertheless, ancient authors distinguished their meaning, and I think that ideas could be clarified and made more distinct if the words regained their proper meaning. In this chapter, therefore, I will attempt to make clear and distinguish the concepts contained in the words *body* and *matter*.

If the feeling principle had constant, uniform and unchangeable feelings furnished with extension, it would certainly perceive a *body*. But would it be in a condition to affirm to itself that it perceived a *material body*? The answer to this question depends upon the concept, *materiality*, which we must now examine.

248. When we consider the reality of feeling, it is easy to see that the *feeling principle*, although it receives, also posits an act of its own, the act of receiving. There is no doubt that it is not

inactive. This act of the feeling principle expands in extension, that is, in what is felt. But how is it modified?

In the first place, the soul can develop different grades of activity and, given certain conditions, can in various ways separate its capacity for feeling from the act of feeling. It could possibly separate this capacity from stimulation altogether or, through an efficacious act of the will, could further the capacity in its feeling. Such a modification of feeling through the influence of the soul is a first change in feeling.

249. Observation, too, shows that the act of feeling can be modified not only by the activity of the feeling soul, but also by what is felt, because what is felt can in fact be withdrawn from, or submitted to a given feeling principle. In this case, however, the act of feeling is not modified directly. It remains what it was although its term is removed, or added, or changed[121] in the way that a scene changes before our open eyes (the act of sight remains unchanged but the eyes see changing pictures).

This takes place continually in our corporeal feelings which vary from one moment to the next not because of change on the part of what feels, but because of change on the part of what is felt. As a result, the extension and shape of our corporeal fundamental feeling changes without our knowledge and against our will. In addition the quality and intensity of feeling changes. What was pleasant becomes painful or less pleasing, and we begin to feel in new ways as previous feelings cease. Colour, taste, and aural phenomena, together with many other modes of feeling, are stimulated in us, although we are not conscious of any increase or decrease in the activity applied to our act of feeling. Without any direct change in this act, we find it modified continually through change in its terms. We are not, therefore, in command of these terms of our feeling. A principle different from ourselves exists which like a magician produces all kinds of surprises on the stage of our feeling. But there is more.

250. Not only are we incapable of dominating the things we feel, which sometimes vanish when we want them to remain and arrive when we least desire them; we realise also that the wonderful production of many associated feelings springs from a single, identical principle. For example, when we feel the pain

[121] Cf. *OT*, 705–706.

caused by a thorn, we see the thorn under our nail and take hold of it to remove it. The pain-, sight- and touch-feeling together indicate the presence of a single agent producing three very distinct feelings which harmonise only in so far as they are diffused in a unity of space, and cease within a unity of time when we realise that the thorn has been removed.

251. When the various agents have been distinguished from feelings in this way, the agents themselves reveal certain laws about themselves all of which are based on a fundamental dictum: 'One agent cannot take the place of another without removing it.' These are laws which we infer from the feelings resulting from the action of many individual agents. Such laws are independent of the act of feeling and of ourselves as feeling beings, and produce terms and stimuli of feelings irrespective of our own desires.

252. We are, therefore, passive in regard to our feelings and their changes. Moreover, the agents which render us passive are completely out of our control. They show their independence by the disturbance they exert on us as they change the place and quality of our feelings, and by the way in which they change place amongst themselves according to certain inflexible laws over which our will has no power whatsoever. This agent, which does not directly modify us, that is, our act of feeling, changes and modifies the extended terms of our feeling according to definite laws. And this agent is called *matter*.

253. The concept of *body* contains therefore: 1. a principle acting in us as feeling beings, and 2. an extension which is the term of the feeling caused in us by that action. The concept of *matter*, however, contains in addition a force that: 1. by disturbing corporeal extension, the term of our feeling, limits, shapes and modifies it according to certain laws, and produces movements within it; and 2. independently of ourselves as feeling principle, exercises the disturbing action on the extension we feel.

254. Comparing the properties of *body* and *matter*, we see that *corporeal feeling* does not require amongst its elements any principle extraneous to feeling. *Material feeling*, however, does require and presuppose an active principle extraneous to feeling. This principle extraneous to corporeal feeling is itself felt only through the *disturbance* it exerts on the term of corporeal feeling; it is not felt as an *element* of feeling itself. If it did contribute

as an element constituting feeling, it would be necessary to seek another principle capable of modifying this element, and so on *ad infinitum*. We have to stop, therefore, at a principle which, without itself forming part of feeling, changes the corporeal thing felt in a feeling. This agent, at work in the extended term of corporeal feeling, is called *matter*.

255. And our body is said to be *material* because in it, that is, in the extended term of our feeling, an action is revealed according to which one part of the corporeal extension acts upon another according to certain laws and independently of any intervention by us.

256. We may now re-state as follows what we have said in the preceding chapters.

1st. Only what is *feelable* suffices to make us perceive *body*.

2nd. To make us perceive matter, we also need what is *sensiferous*. This makes us experience a disturbance which is not exercised directly on ourselves as feeling beings, but on what is *felt*, the term of our feeling.

3rd. The force that changes what is felt, by removing it from the act of feeling according to determined laws, provides us with the concept of some brute thing called *matter* which does not enter our feeling, and is independent of our understanding and will.

257. We have to be careful not to confuse the notion of matter in general with the notion of the *matter of feeling*, which we considered in *The Origin of Thought*.[122] Moreover, a kind of *matter* and *form* can be distinguished in the fundamental feeling. The act of feeling is the formal part of that feeling; what is felt can be called its material element in so far as it is the term — an active and necessary term — of the act of feeling. This *matter of feeling*, however, is not related to the *matter* of *body* about which we have spoken in this chapter. The word *matter* expresses a relative concept which, therefore, is variable in accordance with any variation in the term of the relationship.

[122] *OT*, 1005–1019.

11

THE INTIMATE UNION BETWEEN THAT WHICH FEELS AND THAT WHICH IS FEELABLE

258. From what has been said it is clear that corporeal feeling requires *what is feelable* as one of its essential elements. At the same time, it has no absolute need of a *material* principle in so far as such a principle is distinguished from what is feelable and exists as an independent force modifying the feelable without acting directly in *that which feels*.

259. This also explains why we form the concept of *matter* not simply as something distinct from feeling, but also as some hidden and completely unintelligible substance. If the agent modifying the *feelable* element, but not acting directly on the feeling principle, were non-existent, we would never attain our present idea of *matter* (even if we were to grant that what is feelable — or better, *what is felt* — underwent modifications from our own energy).

260. An analysis of feeling itself will serve to reassure anyone who may find difficulties with the assertion: 'Corporeal feeling can exist only if what is feelable exists, and therefore only if extension (the mode of what is feelable) also exists.'

Let us imagine a feeling deprived of its extended term. Nothing remains when it feels no space of any sort. Corporeal feeling is annihilated without a large or small space in which to expand; it would be inconceivable, a feeling of nothingness. For instance, we have a pain, in some part of our body. If we make this part smaller, the sphere of pain also becomes smaller. The only doubt which could arise is about the possibility of the pain's being concentrated in a mathematical point. Several arguments can be employed, however, to show that such a hypothesis is contradictory and inconceivable.

261. First, the mathematical point does not actually exist in nature, where only solids have a place. Points and lines are the products of abstraction, and nothing more.[123] But if pain is

[123] It is true that *surface* phenomena exist in nature, as we have seen, but not

corporeal it must issue from a painful area of our body, and a part of a body can never be a mathematical point.

Secondly, the nature of a point as a simple relationship and as nothing in itself excludes the possibility of focusing material pain in a mathematical point. But this focusing is excluded by the nature itself of the body which we know only through sense and which, as we have shown, is the result of extended elements, not unextended points.[124]

Thirdly, the nature of sensation itself enables us to demonstrate that it is impossible for corporeal pain to be centred in a point. The phrase 'to feel pain concentrated in a mathematical point' can only mean that I feel the mathematical point by means of the pain I experience in it. But a mathematical point cannot be felt nor its place assigned except through the relationships of the point with solid extension; that is, it cannot be located and felt except as the term of three lines. A point not determined by any line, distance, or relationship with solid extension can neither be imagined nor exist.

Let us consider the same thing in the case of extrasubjective perception and imagine that we see or touch a point. This point must be in a place and be determined by its place. A point without a place, or without some extension in which it may exist, is an absurdity, is nothing. In fact a point can be felt in sensation only if the extension surrounding it, to which it refers, is felt along with it. The point exists in and through the extension as a limit exists in and through the limited thing to which it appertains, or as a place depends upon adjacent spaces. It is impossible for a corporeal sensation to be restricted to a single mathematical point and not expand into the extension surrounding such a point. If indeed a point could be felt, it could be felt only along with the other extension surrounding it, in which it is assigned a place and located (cf. 160–172).

If therefore we could subtract every extended term from the sensation of which we are speaking, the sensation would be annihilated.

bodies extended only in a surface plane.

[124] Cf. *OT*, 846 ss.

12

CLARIFICATION OF THE DEFINITION OF LIFE

262. We are now in a position to clarify our definition of *animal life* as 'an unceasing production of material and corporeal feeling'.

We have seen that feeling is produced unceasingly by the union of two elements, that is, of that which feels, the feeling principle, with that which is felt, the term of feeling. These two elements — that which feels and the felt, principle and term of feeling — although distinct from one another and in a relationship of opposites to one another, cannot be really divided and separated without the destruction of both. If we presuppose a complete lack of what is felt, we can no longer conceive the continuing existence of a feeling principle which, if it feels nothing, is nothing. Every feeling principle ceases because feeling, once one of its two essential elements is removed, has vanished.

263. We might prefer to imagine that something remained after the elimination of feeling. This 'something' could perhaps be conceived mentally as an *object*, but never as a *subject*. It would be capable of becoming the term of my thought, but in itself feel nothing and be nothing. In other words, it would be purely imaginary and totally alien to feeling. It would not be found by analysing feeling itself, and hence could only be a substitute for the feeling principle of which we are speaking. The feeling principle never offers itself for reflection except simply as feeling considered in its relationship of feeling activity that constitutes it. What feels, therefore, cannot be posited without what is felt, nor what is felt without that which feels. Both must be created simultaneously by God, and united. Feeling, I mean, must be created, and in feeling the distinct natures denoting that which feels and that which is felt, the 'sentient' and the 'feelable'.[125]

[125] We could ask if 'the feeling principle can have its roots in some other entity anterior to feeling'. Such a question, however, would take us beyond the bounds of human experience. It is sufficient for us to know that this principle would no longer remain if what is felt were removed. This truth is made known to us by our meditation on the nature of feeling.

264. This explains the common saying that life consists in the union of soul and body, and death in the separation of these two substances. In agreement with this common persuasion, we have considered life as the unceasing production of material and corporeal feeling.

This definition of life can be extended more generally by omitting the adjectives 'corporeal' and 'material', which we add to 'feeling' to characterise animal life. Life in general is then defined as *an unceasing production of feeling*, or even as *an unceasing actuation of feeling*.

265. In this definition, variety in the term of feeling, that is, variety in what is felt, will be the variable element constituting the different kinds of life.

If something *extended* is felt, *corporeal life* is present.

If something *extended* and *material* is felt, that is, subject to alterations produced by matter, *material life* is present.

If a spiritual object is felt, *spirit life* is present.

266. Both *animal* (corporeal-material) and *spirit* life vary in degree and nature according to variations in what is felt. The feeling principle which, as it were, draws its existence from what is felt, remains constant and simple.

267. This helps to clarify the other three definitions of life.

The feeling soul lives only through feeling, without which it would cease to be.

The body is said to be alive only in so far as it possesses the act with which it produces feeling in the soul.

The definition of life which we have given merits further consideration in so far as life is attributed to what is commonly called body. We said that in this case life is 'the unceasing production of all those extrasubjective phenomena which precede, accompany and follow in parallel the corporeal and material feeling'.

We have already seen how the subjective and extrasubjective phenomena are revealed in the same space. Thus we are in the habit of judging that when we see and touch the extended being in which we feel also, we see and touch our own body and nothing else, although the extrasubjective phenomena of touch and sight have no similarity whatsoever with the subjective phenomena.

Nevertheless, these two series of phenomena, which proceed

from the single principle we call our body, run parallel to, and in harmony with one another, as we have seen. In fact, our body exercises two actions, one on our spirit where it produces the fundamental feeling, the other on our organs producing the sensations of touch, sight and the other senses. As a result, a change in feelings (subjective phenomena) alters the power of our body in its operation on our senses. For example, terror is shown when others see us change colour. On the other hand, when our extrasubjective body changes, our feelings change. For example, sight of a wound is contemporaneous with a feeling of pain in the person wounded.

268. Granted a given complex of extrasubjective phenomena, therefore, we have a subjective feeling. In this case, extrasubjective phenomena are sure signs of life. Medicine, which is ignorant of the origin and formation of feeling, makes use of this very definite law operating between the extrasubjective phenomena and the vital feeling in order to produce and regulate the phenomena which inevitably accompany the feeling of life, and a healthy state of feeling.

13

THE GOVERNING PRINCIPLE OF MEDICINE

269. Medical practice restores, or attempts to restore, the extrasubjective phenomena which accompany a better state of health. This is achieved either by leaving nature to work unaided (doctors call this the *wait-and-see method*) or by applying certain agents to the body (the *active method*).

In the second method, the power of the active force, whatever it may be, is associated with the forces of nature to produce an effect common to the united causes.

270. This effect is known only through experience which reveals two things: first, the *extrasubjective* phenomena which appear in the body to which the agent was applied; second, the *subjective* phenomena belonging to feeling and life.

271. We have to remember here that the *subjective* phenomena are bound together in such a way that they constitute a single

satisfactory state in the animal. This depends upon the unity in the animal itself. As we have seen, the feeling principle constituting the animal, although unique, is not simply sentient; it is also *active* in such a way that, in virtue of its action, the extrasubjective body changes and takes on a state of life. Because the agent is unique, the extrasubjective phenomena themselves, which are the effects of this action, form a unity revealed by their association and harmony.

Hippocrates commented on this when he spoke about *a single consensus, a single harmony, a complete agreement*. Modern authors express the same truth in this way: 'Each part of the living body has its explanation in the body taken as a whole.'[126]

272. There is no doubt that even the mechanical organisation of the human body[127] is interconnected to support an extraordinary suitability for the communication of movement. Nevertheless, the mechanical design of the body, in which only material forces operate, would not of itself produce the unity of movement we do in fact see. Such a design would lack even the principle of movement. We could also take into consideration chemical relationships, and add these to the mechanical forces and organisation possessed by the body. A new lesson, the most wonderful provided by the Author of nature, would show us the chemical forces of fluids and solids united to the mechanical organisation and forces and producing the circular action which instead of consuming itself provides an unceasing vortex of particles where, according to Cuvier, life is to be found. Nothing superior to this unity could be imagined.

What we have described is however only the preparatory stage of the total organisation. Besides the chemical forces, we could add special, unknown forces apparently without feeling, and include opportune internal and external stimuli such as the

[126] Kant. The *Bibliothèque Universelle* (Geneva, July 1833) maintains that Cuvier was the first to state the principle: 'Every living being forms a complete system whose parts mutually correspond, working together towards the same definitive action by means of reciprocal action.' It is certain, however, that this principle was known long before Cuvier. Brown's attempt to simplify medicine by reducing it all to the principle of *incitability* presupposed Cuvier's more general principle.

[127] This mechanical organisation corresponds to a class of extrasubjective phenomena.

air, electricity, light and every kind of nourishment. And we would still have only a dead body, a statue as it were prepared for the life God would breathe into it but at the moment only a corpse. For this reason all truly great scientists realised that extrasubjective experience could offer no explanation of the principle of vital action, and appealed finally to a principle altogether outside the sphere of extrasubjective experience. They turned to an essentially internal principle that did not fall under external observation, and as a result we have Paracelso and Vanhelmont's 'prime element', Stahl's 'soul', Bordeu and Barthez' 'life principle', and the 'life force' of almost all modern physiologists.

273. Further observation showed that, given the principle of extrasubjective phenomena, these phenomena were posited in a suitably prepared body together with feeling. From this, it was deduced that only the feeling principle could be the source-principle of the extrasubjective phenomena, although this principle takes on the condition of recipient[128] relative to what is *feelable*, that is, to the interior body which serves as the term of the fundamental feeling. As a result, given the corporeal feeling and the space occupied by this feeling as a scene of the external, extrasubjective phenomena, the phenomena of life had to appear on this screen as action exercised by the feeling principle and manifested extrasubjectively.

274. We are now in a position to express in philosophical language the responsibility of medicine and its supreme principle.

1st. A person's state of health or fullness of life is known only by that person's conscious witness to the satisfactory state of his feeling of life. The aim of medicine, therefore, is to attain a satisfactory state of subjective phenomena, that is, the *normal state* of the animal whose essence is entirely subjective.

2nd. It is, however, impossible to act directly on this subjective state (at least, it is not the proper expression of medical practice). Medicine, therefore, directs its attention to a parallel series of determined phenomena, that is, the extrasubjective phenomena,

[128] Although the feeling principle is passive in corporeal sensation, it assists in the sensation, as we have said (cf. 248), and indeed *places* itself in a receptive state. Having done this, it often attains a new activity. As we shall see, movement originates in great part from feeling.

which constantly correspond with the *normal state of the subjective phenomena*. The series of extrasubjective phenomena accompanying the normal state of the subjective phenomena can rightly be called the *normal state of the extrasubjective phenomena*. The aim of medical science is to produce this normal state of extrasubjective phenomena in a living, human body in order to obtain the normal state of subjective phenomena which make up essentially the fullness of life, that is, a good state of health. The law we have enunciated makes it clear that this second normal state is always accompanied by the first.

3rd. If the extrasubjective phenomena were not bound together systematically, medical practice would be impossible. Taken individually, these phenomena are so numerous and of such variety that it would be totally impossible for human effort to assess or calculate all their possible variations, and take account of each one. Experience shows, however, that the variations and systems of extrasubjective phenomena are limited and determined, and even indicates that 'every partial extrasubjective phenomenon corresponds to a whole series, more or less extended, of different extrasubjective phenomena'. This law of *sympathy and synergy*, which binds the phenomena together, makes medicine possible and reveals its supreme principle.

275. In fact, the supreme regulating principle of experience in medicine can depend only on this general problem: 'Given a more or less extended phenomenon, or several phenomena bound together, how can we determine the complex or series of other phenomena which will follow?' All experience in medical practice seeks to solve this problem. If it could be solved, medicine would have reached its perfection.

276. What is illness? Simply a series of phenomena ordered according to certain consensual, synergical laws. That is, in every illness the presence of an initial phenomenon of varying extension (which may be simple or complex) immediately produces other phenomena which in their turn produce other phenomena and so on until health returns or the phenomena of death intervene. It is clear, therefore, that *pathology* would be perfect if experience could show 'which phenomena necessarily follow each

more or less extended phenomenon,'[129] granted, of course, that the state of the body were known in the first place.

277. The same can be said about any *special treatment*. Medication applied to the body immediately produces certain phenomena. These immediate phenomena are not, however, those which the doctor is aiming at. As a result of the law of synergy mentioned above, the first phenomenon or phenomena produce more numerous, *extended* phenomena which, bound together, produce still more phenomena. Each *order* or series of phenomena constitutes a better or worse state until signs of health appear, or the final order of fatal phenomena is reached. Only knowledge of the initial action of the medication, and of the chain of orders of phenomena which unceasingly follow one another, can bring *curative medicine* to perfection.

278. We can also see that in individual cases medical opinion embraces or at least indicates the universal principle of medicine. Doctors speak about *symptomatic* illnesses or of a state they call *irritative*. *Symptomatic* illness is an effect or sign of more serious, deeper illness; an *irritative* state is a disease of the body dependent for the most part on some localised cause. But if we take, for example, the inflammation produced by a dental abscess, we see that it is a second-order phenomenon following upon an initial phenomenon (to which it is bound by hidden laws of animality), and giving rise to third-order phenomena. On the other hand, a symptomatic illness is simply second-order phenomena dependent upon scarcely known first-order phenomena, and again giving rise to third-order phenomena.

In every illness, however, as we said, the phenomena follow one another in stages. This is not a characteristic of symptomatic or irritative illness alone, although it is easier to note the distinction

[129] This is valid for theory. In practice it is impossible to note all the phenomena because the internal phenomena of the body do not fall under external experience; they have to be conjectured through symptoms which are sometimes misleading. Doctors, therefore, study the effects of their medication (another source of conjecture about internal phenomena) according to their own principle: 'If it helps, use it; if it harms, discontinue it.' Medical practice can never be more than conjecture which, however, will approximate to the truth in so far as careful, daily experience indicates the way in which phenomena are bound together.

between the first and second steps in these illnesses. In irritative illnesses, the localised cause, when uncovered, soon draws attention to its effect, which normally provides more serious phenomena than those in the cause itself. In symptomatic illnesses, the phenomena connected with the effect are normally less serious than those constituting the cause. But if the distinction between first- and second-order phenomena is not obvious, an illness is not called symptomatic or irritative, although subject to the same law of linkage as all other illnesses. Discovering these links and what we may call the hierarchy of phenomena in this kind of illness must also be the aim of wise medical science.

279. These considerations seem to provide a governing principle for experience in medicine, which should no longer be ruled by chance. They show that the aim of experience is to indicate 'first-order phenomena, and the orders of all other phenomena'.

280. It is clear that this has not always be the guiding principle of medical science, and it is also clear that medicine is still a long way from achieving this aim, which is certainly difficult and perhaps never entirely possible. Nevertheless, it is the sole obligatory, essential aim for those who devote themselves to medicine, and every step taken towards it is a gain.

It follows that only this principle is suitable as a solid base for the philosophical classification of disease, and as a path for reducing *nosology* to scientific form. The different stages of phenomena associated with illness must constitute different orders and periods of disease itself.

281. One other important observation is necessary before I conclude this chapter, which is already too long.

Although there is a reciprocal action between the different parts or rather systems of the human body, it is certain that there is an order of phenomena even in a healthy state, and that concomitant actions result from this order. For example, it would be difficult to place a change of the different fluids separated out in the human body amongst phenomena that precede some defect in the organs of secretion. Rather, deleterious change would be found in an order following the normal change that takes place in the functioning of the organs of secretion. Nevertheless fluids inadequately or wrongly treated by the action of the organs separating them out would themselves become stimuli affecting and harming the action of these organs. In this case, the harm done to the functioning of the organs appertains to third-order phenomena, not to first-order.

If we now ask how stimuli produce this modification when applied to the organs of secretion, we certainly have to indicate at least the fibre contractility, swelling and other acts received by the body from the life principle, and maintained for some time by the body after the life principle has ceased to act. We have to point principally, however, to the relationship between the internal organs, especially their muscular bulk, and the nerve substance where the phenomena of life are more immediately evident. In all probability, we shall have to indicate modification in the nervous system as the principle of all other modifications.

In this case, the phenomena directly concern the principle of life whatever the place, part or system at which the disease begins. The principle of life reveals its activity principally in the nerves, the action of which is used to propagate the phenomena to other systems. It will be necessary, therefore, to investigate the action of the nervous system finally for the explanation of the universal consent of the various parts of the human body, a consent which gives rise to alteration in the whole mechanism when a single system, or a single part alone, is affected. Disease in the lungs, for example, provokes a whole series of ill effects which we call symptoms of tuberculosis. Here it is very obvious that a single agent irritated by a localised lesion then works throughout the body, producing its deleterious effects, and it is certain that the total, multiple change, accompanied by various complications throughout the mechanism, cannot be produced by the immediate, mechanical or chemical effect of the localised wound. We have to say that the wound stimulates the principle presiding over the whole complex, debilitates it, and prompts it to react by propagating the disturbance throughout the entire complex, communicating it to the different systems which in turn act successively and reciprocally according to the laws underlying the immediate influence of the life principle, or the laws' reciprocal influence.

The reaction of the life principle, immediately visible in the whole mechanism, to a single lesion in an important part of the

[281]

extrasubjective body is certainly a very mysterious matter. It is, however, a fact without which such a harmonious response of the phenomena in all the parts, organs, systems and complex of the body to a single lesion-phenomenon could not be explained. The unity and harmony of the response is such that it must follow from a single, first cause whose action is then modified and changed by the various states of the different organs in which it takes place.

282. It may be objected that the action which produces so many extrasubjective phenomena cannot be the same as that with which the soul feels. We must therefore presuppose in the soul some power, other than the feeling principle, to modify the external body.

Careful attention, however, will show that all the activities of the soul can be rooted in the single activity of *feeling*. As we have already noticed, the feeling principle does not lie inactive in feeling. Although it has a degree of passivity, it concurs actively in the production of feeling (this perhaps explains why certain insensitive parts of the body become sensitive, while sensitive parts sometimes lose their sensitivity — the soul contributes its action in different degrees). This action of the soul, which is necessary for the generation of feeling, is without doubt the same as that which gives the body its aptitude for manifesting extrasubjective phenomena. The vital state of the external body, therefore, is an effect of that act with which the soul concurs in producing feeling. Feeling and the state of external vitality or animation of the body as commonly understood is brought about by this same first activity of the soul. If such a connection between the extrasubjective phenomena of vitality and those of feeling exists without their being cause and effect of one another (although they both depend upon the activity of the soul for their first cause) we should not be surprised if, on the occasion of a forced change in the extrasubjective body, the activity of the soul reacts according to its own hidden laws and places itself in a different attitude towards the whole body manifested extrasubjectively.

14

OTHER IMPORTANT QUESTIONS ARISING FROM THE RELATIONSHIP BETWEEN THE FEELING SOUL AND THE BODY

Article 1.
The more important questions

283. We have said that the body acts, and that its action has a double effect. One effect is on the *feeling principle* (when the body is united to the soul), producing the corporeal feeling; the other on the *feelable* element of feeling, changing feeling itself by changing its term.

We also know that the *feeling principle* itself acts, in a double way, producing two effects. First, its action co-operates in producing its own *feeling*. Second, it modifies the action of the body, because the body, in its *material* action, receives from life the capacity to present a series of extrasubjective phenomena different from those of a merely material body.

Thus, the soul acts *directly* in the production of feeling, but *indirectly* in the production of extrasubjective phenomena by modifying the force exerted by matter.

The body also acts *directly* in the production of feeling, but in its role as matter it acts *indirectly* in the change of feeling by changing the feelable element, the extended term of feeling.

284. These complex, mutual actions of the soul and body, which are usually perceived solely by their effects and in an imperfect way, deserve the careful attention of serious thinkers. One of the difficulties, of course, is language; we still lack a vocabulary for the precise expression of ideas formed at a high level of reflection. If we try to invent a language, it becomes pretentious. I am forced therefore to mix precise with popular expressions. The latter may be true for the level of reflection to which they belong, but they falsify concepts at a higher level without drawing attention to the problems in hand. The only way I can supply for this defect, which arises from our imperfect

state of knowledge, is to explain frequently the popular language which I mix with philosophical language, so that the transition from one to the other can be made more easy.

In discussing the relationship of the mutual actions of soul and body, therefore, I shall nearly always use the language of physiologists to present some of the most important questions. However, I must point out that in speaking about corporeal molecules and their organisation, popular language uses these words to mean only *material* beings, while I use them to mean beings that have the double action described above, that is, beings which by acting on the soul become the extended term of feeling (the sensiferous, feelable *body*), and by acting on this extended term assume the notion of *matter*.

Granted, therefore, that the extension in which the primal, corporeal fundamental feeling finishes is identical with the extension of the corresponding matter, let us consider the following questions.

285. First of all, physiologists, in dealing with the intimate production of feeling, ask: 'Is subjective sensibility attached to the elementary molecules of bodies or to a certain organisation of the molecules?' Expressed in philosophical language, the question would be this: 'Does the proximate term of feeling correspond to the extension in which either the elementary molecules or an organised complex of them is perceived as extrasubjective matter?'

A second question asks: 'Does that which is feelable, by its mode of being, have movement as well as extension?' or, in the precise language of philosophy: 'Is the extended term of feeling necessarily in continuous motion, and do moving molecules correspond to this term as extrasubjective matter?'

If we suppose that the term of feeling is an organised body with a certain characteristic movement, we must also examine both the primary and secondary structures of this body, that is, the nature of the first living, organised molecules, and the nature of the molecules organised from these first molecules. This gives rise to the question: 'Is feeling attached to solids and fluids?' or, expressed philosophically: 'Is the term of feeling ultimately something extended which corresponds to what is perceived extrasubjectively and called "solid" or "fluid"?'

Finally, we must ask: 'Does the extended term of animal feeling always constitute a unity, and if so, what kind of unity: a unity arising from the continuity of the term, or from the harmony found in the balance of its elements, or from some centre that must always be affected by feeling itself?'

286. It is very important to understand how all these questions are possible in my theory of feeling. If the term of feeling is that which is extended, nothing prevents this term from corresponding, in its external, extrasubjective perception, to elementary particles of space, or to elementary particles bound indivisibly together, or to particles at rest or in motion, or therefore to particles corresponding to solids or fluids, just as nothing prevents the term of feeling from having a unity, or at least, sharing in a unity through the feeling principle — in fact this seems most fitting. The questions, which can be solved only by means of observation and faithful induction from experience, require an answer so that we can come to know fully 'the law of harmony between the order of subjective and the order of extrasubjective phenomena'. Knowledge of this law alone can guide us to the formation or understanding of a complete, explicit definition of animal nature.

287. Summarising the questions about the term of feeling, we have asked:

1st. Which is the term of feeling: the basic elements of bodies or specific *molecules* composed of the basic *elements* of bodies, according to a certain order and composition called *organisation*?

2nd. Or must these specific molecules themselves be organised into molecules of a second order so that they can be the term of feeling or at least of certain feelings? And if there is a first organisation (specific molecules) and a second organisation (second order molecules) for certain feelings, must there be a third or fourth organisation in order to have other species and genera of feelings (more perfect animal bodies)?

3rd. Is the organised, felt body a solid or a fluid, or can either be the term of feeling?

4th. Does the term of feeling always require a centre to give it unity, or at least a harmonious accord which unifies it in some way, perhaps by means of the feeling principle?

5th. Must the term of feeling be in continuous, harmonious movement for feeling to exist? And granted bodily organs, do certain kinds of determinate movements become terms of certain sensations, so that other kinds of movements could only be terms not of the same but of other sensations or none?

These are some of the principal questions of fact that have to be solved in a discussion on the production of the corporeal feeling. However, even if the questions were solved, they would not help us to penetrate the mystery of life entirely, although they would enable us to know the law and connection of facts by which feeling begins and continues, and upon which it depends for the conditions of its existence.

Without claiming to solve the questions, which in any case is not necessary for my purpose, I would like to make a few observations on them.[130]

Article 2.
The first question: is the term of feeling the first elements or organised bodies?

288. The first elements of bodies considered in themselves, even though extended,[131] escape the external perception of our senses. Consequently, we cannot know, by means of direct advertence, whether these minute elements taken individually are the term of feeling. We are totally unable to advert to such small sensations, and we have no reason for positing sensations which as such are absolutely beyond advertence.

On the other hand, where these elements have been united in the form we call animal organisation, I cannot doubt that feeling reaches down to the first elements of bodies,[132] so that life is truly present in them.

289. Nevertheless, if life invests and, as it were, enfolds the atoms, we cannot conclude that the extrasubjective phenomena corresponding to feeling can be reduced solely to the atoms taken individually, or that there is less need for the production of the animal feeling, or for a first, second or even more complex organisation of the indivisible elements. Such a composition of atoms forming the living molecules of living bodies is clearly

[130] These questions are discussed more fully in my *Psicologia*.

[131] *OT*, 846 ss.

[132] *Ibid.*

supposed by Gallini's system, although he seems to think that life is a primitive property adhering to atoms themselves.[133] Gallini explains all the phenomena of life by means of the changing *attraction* and *mobility* between the particles composing the structure of living bodies. The action of these forces presupposes a multiplicity of elements, choice, distances, right positions, and, in a word, organisation [*App*., no. 5]. We can therefore say that even the first elements of a living body have life, but we cannot say that they have it as individual animals do. Life can indeed reveal itself in a more or less multiple, variously organised body, but it must also diffuse itself and terminate in all the primary elements of the same body.

Article 3.
The second question: are the molecules of a first, second or higher organisation the term of feeling?

290. Even if a certain amalgam of molecules is necessary for us to notice the *production of feeling*, how could the nature of this more or less complex aggregation or organisation be determined? The only safe guide is experience and logical induction.

And if we want to see where experience will lead us, we need to investigate the simplest structure or organism to manifest definite signs of sensitivity. For example, there certainly seems to be no contradiction *a priori* in affirming that monads and other microscopic beings, which are apparently homogeneous in substance and of very simple, indeterminate shape, are endowed with sensitivity.

291. Experience definitely shows that the matter[134] of feeling can be reduced without the complete annihilation of sensitivity.

[133] This kind of proposition in physiology always contains a double error: 1. the elements physiologists speak about are simply and solely external, extrasubjective elements — feeling does not terminate in any way in an external, extrasubjective element, because this element has nothing real except the property of acting as matter; 2. if atoms have life, they must receive it from a feeling principle of which they are the term — life cannot be one of their properties as matter is.

[134] 'Matter of feeling' means the extended term of feeling, and should not be confused with corporeal matter whose concept has been given earlier (cf. 247–257).

In the more perfect animals a great deal of the matter of sensitivity can be removed without the total destruction of the animal. Sensitivity can be divided and split, as it were, into its different species, so that sometimes one organ exists independently of other organs, while one sense is independent of other senses in what it communicates to the feeling principle. The experiments of Magendie on various kinds of mammals are well known. He claims that if the hemispheres of the cerebrum and cerebellum are removed from a mammal, it becomes blind but remains sensitive to odours, tastes, sounds and tactile impressions. If the posterior nerves of the spinal cord are cut, sensitivity in the trunk disappears; if the fifth cranial nerves are cut before they leave the skull or on the sides of the fourth ventricle, all sensitivity in the face is lost. From these experiments we see that certain kinds of sensations cannot take place unless some organs are more complex than others. For example, visual sensations need the whole of the hemispheres of the optic thalami, the opthalmic branch of the fifth cranial nerves, and perhaps the anterior, quadrigeminal tubercles. On the other hand, other senses need only all the fifth cranial nerves common to all senses along with the nerve special to each; for hearing, this nerve is the soft portion of the seventh cranial nerves; for smell, the first cranial nerves; and for taste, the ninth cranial nerves.

292. This possibility of reduction in feeling is verified by many other observations. The following quotation describes the stages by which sensitivity in old people diminishes and finally ceases.

> They die bit by bit. Their external functions cease one after the other; all their senses gradually function less, so that the ordinary causes of sensation no longer arouse them.
>
> Sight grows dim and confused, and finally stops transmitting images with the onset of senile blindness. Sounds are first received in a confused fashion and then become meaningless. The skin — shrivelled, hardened and without vessels (which have disappeared) — becomes the seat of a vague, indistinct touch, to which habit itself has contributed by blunting the feeling. All the organs dependent on the skin weaken and die: the hair and beard become white, hairs fall out profusely, and odours produce only a weak impression on the nostrils.
>
> Taste continues for some time. Because it is tied with both organic and animal life, it is necessary for the internal functions.

> Thus, while old people lose all pleasant sensations, and the absence of these sensations has to some extent already severed their union with exterior bodies, the sense of taste remains the last thread on which existence hangs.
> Old people, isolated in this way in the midst of nature and partly deprived of the functions of their sense organs, soon experience the loss of their brain functions. Perception is virtually extinguished because its exercise is no longer determined by the senses. At the same time imagination weakens and soon ceases.
> The movements of the old are slow and few. It is difficult for them to change their posture. They will remain sitting next to the fire keeping themselves warm, all the time turned in on themselves, oblivious of their surroundings, bereft of desires, feelings and sensations. They do not speak, because nothing stimulates them to break their silence. And when all other feelings are practically extinguished, they are satisfied with whatever feeling remains.[135]

293. We can make another observation about the variety in the animal kingdom. We grant that the existence of animal feeling has not been verified in sponges, monads, polyps, medusae and zoophytes, but there is certainly a very wide range of beings, from vertebrates to radiaria, from mammals to infusoria, endowed with feeling and with a more or less complex organisation. Only experience, accompanied by strict induction, can establish which of the simplest organisations endowed with feeling constitutes an animal.

294. Our third observation concerns the less complex animals; they seem to indicate more readily that the matter of their feeling can be removed without their being destroyed. The fact that tortoises live for a long time after the removal of their brain, frogs live without both brain and heart, worms and polyps multiply when cut in pieces, shows that feeling does not need many organs for its subsistence, and, as we have said, only a careful observation will be able to determine which is the simplest animal organisation in nature.

295. In carrying out this investigation we must be careful to note that determining the minimum matter necessary for animal

[135] Bichat, *Ricerche fisiologiche intorno alla vita e la morte*, pt. 1.

feeling is quite different from determining what is required for the conservation of this matter. If an animal dies when it loses a given part, we must not infer that the part was necessary for feeling in general; we can infer only that the rest of the animal could not be maintained without it; it did in fact perish. The body of a mutilated or wounded animal seems to me to resemble a stocking in which a tear 'runs'. We see this particularly when a part becomes gangrenous and spreads its infection to adjacent parts. This does not prove that feeling needs these organs, but that they are needed by the kind of feeling proper to the animal, that is, the organisation and composition of the matter of that feeling, in order to keep itself together and endure.[136]

296. Finally, Professor Rolando's efforts to discover the ultimate vital organisation under discussion should be mentioned. He examined the first stages of organisation in moulds and funguses, and found only a union of globules or granules which sometimes vaguely resembled a particular arrangement but more often looked like filaments forming a net. These filaments spread through the fluid and seemed to have much more delicate roots formed by a succession of globules, measuring between 0.07 and 0.08 mm. These results convinced him that beings of a simple form exist

> in which all we can observe are variously composed masses of globules united together. These globules form the simple, basic elements from which the viscera, organs, systems and mechanisms develop in molluscs, reptiles, birds and mammals.[137]

297. Nevertheless, we still need:

1st. To verify whether the contractility and distension that accompanies feeling proper to animals is sometimes present in nature without this feeling.

2nd. And, granted that the organisation presented by the

[136] What has been said in this article removes the objection against the simplicity of the feeling principle. The limitation of the feeling indicated in this chapter concerns only the extended term of sensation. We do not deny, however, that the activity of the feeling principle can vary in intensity. In fact, the *specific* difference of animals must be principally sought in the degree of intensity, and in the nature and laws of this activity.

[137] Cf. Luigi Rolando's dissertation: *Del passaggio dei fluidi allo stato di solidi organici, ossia formazione dei tessuti vegetabili ed animali, dei vasi e del cuore.*

phenomena of contractility and distension is sometimes found in nature without animal feeling, to determine the signs indicating that the organisation is accompanied only by contractility and distension without animal feeling, and the certain or probable indication of the presence of that feeling.

298. We must therefore pay a good deal of attention to the being to which the rudiments of imperfect, initial organisation belong. If these rudiments later develop of themselves into an animal, we have to accept that feeling has never been lacking. It would be a far greater mystery to accept that the feeling principle began at a certain level of a body's development than that it was present right from the beginning. We would also be unable to explain the body's development.

Article 4. Comments on the third question: is the term of feeling a fluid or solid?

299. Experience is of little help in answering the question: 'Is the term of animal feeling, in its extrasubjective manifestation, a solid, or a fluid, or a body formed by a mixture of both?'

Soemmering has proved to his own satisfaction that no solid part of the human body can be the seat of the common sensory,[138] and that only fluid is capable of receiving promptly and

[138] The term 'common sensory' is incorrectly applied to parts of the body. Any corporeal part can be a seat of its own feeling but never of the feeling of other parts of the body. It was shown in my *Rinnovamento* (bk. 2, c. 36) that the common sensory must be simple, and that to imagine it as a corporeal organ is absurd. Physiologists use 'common sensory' inappropriately to name the organ considered necessary for all the sensations proper to an animal. These sensations are *aroused sensations*, not a *feeling of continuity*. — If, instead of the organ necessary for arousing these sensations, we seek 'the term of feeling and whether this term corresponds to a solid or fluid', we find that the term cannot be limited to one part of the body (for example, to the fluid in the brain ventricles); it must be present wherever feeling is present in the body. — Before Soemmering, the Italian Fr. Toffoli had demonstrated that the nerves of different senses do not unite at one centre in the brain. He hardened a brain by soaking it for a time in alcohol, and was thus able to observe the line of the nerves more deeply within the brain than had been done previously. Cf. *Opuscoli scelti sulle scienze e sulle arti*, t. 13, p. 390 ss., and t. 15, p. 98 ss.

with the necessary variety the modifications of impressions. Thus, he regards the fluid in the brain ventricles as the common sensory, and says that most of the nerves terminate on the walls of the ventricles, or very close to them. The fluid is always present in living bodies and can be drawn off only at the cost of death, as Haller and others found.

300. Lamarck also claims that the awakening of feeling does not depend on the vibration or ruffling of the nerves, but on a certain modification of the nerve fluid analogous to the weightless electro-magnetic fluid. Cuvier says that this fluid 'constitutes real animal essence, while all the rest seems destined to serve only the nervous system'.[139]

301. Other observations and experiments seem to indicate that the term of stimulated feeling is in the movement of a substance in the blood. For example:

1st. If red blood ceases to reach and permeate the brain, the brain is bereft of its sensitivity, and although the encephalic mass has suffered no lesion, it dies at once.

2nd. All the nerves are richly supplied by a large number of capillaries. As soon as the blood no longer permeates parts of the body, they become insensitive. This lack of feeling is followed by paralysis and gangrene.[140] Thus, a limb dies simply by the suspension of its blood supply.

[139] Cuvier and other well-known naturalists who attribute sensitivity to zoophytes find only an homogeneous pulp in these beings, but no organs or nerves used for sensation. They say that 'irritable and sensitive substances are mixed indistinctly' in the pulp. Judged *a priori*, this does not seem absurd to me, although other naturalists claim that sensitivity cannot be conceived without formed nerves. Cuvier's understanding of feeling would be confirmed by the fact (if proved) that molluscs smell with the whole surface of their body. All these investigations, however, depend solely on the verification of the fact: 'Are there definite vestiges of sensations in beings commonly considered more imperfect and simple than animals?'

[140] Stenone, Albino, Vieussens and others showed that when the main blood vessels serving the nerves were tied, the nerves lost all their activity, and that the limbs they served became paralysed. — Bichat asked 'which system, in the case of various asphyxiations, principally controlled the influence of the harmful substances mixed with the blood'. He concluded that 'everything indicates that their action is generally effected on the nervous system, and in particular on the system regulating the functions of animal life, because the organic functions were disturbed only later' (cf. *Ricerche*

3rd. All the organs which receive only white fluids but no blood, like the hair, nails, cartilages, etc., have no animal feeling.

4th. When inflammation increases the quantity of blood in a part of the body, sensitivity also increases in the same place.

5th. When inflammation makes the blood flow accidentally into the organs containing white fluids, the organs become sensitive. Is this perhaps the explanation of a phenomenon which causes so much difficulty for physiologists — a phenomenon in which sensation sometimes appears in places of the body entirely devoid of nerves?

6th. Another important observation concerns the passions of animal life. The movements called 'passions' are accompanied by feeling, yet, according to Bichat, they affect only the organs that are per se devoid of feeling, not the brain and nerves. He says:

> For example, anger accelerates the circulation, and often increases the power of the heart disproportionately. In other words, anger exerts all its influence on the force and speed of the blood's movement. In the same way, joy, although it does not alter the circulation to the same extent, can markedly change it. Joy develops the phenomena with greater activity, accelerating and directing the circulation towards the cutaneous organ. Fear acts in the opposite way, and is marked by weakness in the whole vascular system. It prevents the blood reaching the capillaries, resulting in a general pallor visible over all the body, especially the face. These effects are practically the same in people affected by sadness and sorrow.The influence of intense passions on the circulatory organs is such that it is capable of suspending activity. This gives rise to syncope, whose basic location is always in the heart and not the brain. The brain ceases to function solely because it does not receive the necessary stimulus of blood. During the Revolution, Desault saw heart troubles and aneurisms of the aorta multiply. This was due to, and in proportion to the misfortunes of the Revolution.[141]

fisiologiche intorno *alla vita ed alla morte*, pt. 2, art. 9, §1).

[141] *Ricerche fisiologiche intorno alla vita e alla morte*, pt. 2, art. 6, §2. — Among ancient writers, Empedocles and Critias located the common sensory in the blood (cf. *Empedocles* by Sturz, Leipzig, 1805, §15). Porfirio claims that Empedocles took this opinion from Homer (*In Stobaei eclog. phys.*

7th. Finally, Le Gallois, of Paris, observed in his experiments that when he had cut off the heads of many animals and tied the blood vessels, the trunks continued to live for some time. He also experimented on a human foetus and claims that after decapitation at the moment of birth, he stopped the haemorrhage by tying the vessels of the neck. Death did not follow at once in the trunk but only in the head, with the phenomena of impeded respiration. However, it seems improbable that the life of the trunk was truly animal life, endowed with an individual, comprehensive feeling, because the stimulated feeling lacked a dominant centre — unless the spinal cord could imperfectly supply for it.

All these observations, which would favour the opinion that 'fluids are the term of feeling', seem to be confirmed by the work of Rolando, who posits fluids as the origin of all the solids in the animal body.[142]

302. These inductions and experiments deal with the quality of the fluid, or generally, of the elements that circulate with, and are part of the blood. This fluid is possibly the same nerve fluid suggested by other naturalists, some of whom — including particularly among the Italians, Fontana, Della Torre and, before them, Malpighi — claim to have seen the fluid through

c. 52). Tertullian (De anima, c. 15) goes further back, claiming that the opinion came from Egyptian thinkers. Το ηγεμονικον, he says, is 'not in between the brows, as Strato the Physician states, nor in the whole chest cage, as Epicurus says, but' (here we must understand "in the blood") 'as the Egyptians, who seemed to be exponents of divine things, proclaimed it, and according to the line of Orpheus or Empedocles:

For the blood surrounding the human heart is feeling'.

The opinion that the soul and feeling are in the blood is a universal opinion of the earliest times. The oldest document containing the opinion is Leviticus, at the place where it says that 'the life of the flesh is in the blood' (c. 17: [11]). Empedocles himself, it must be noted, did not accept that life and feeling were in every principal component of the blood but only in the element *fire*. Thus, according to Plutarch (*De Pl. Phil.* V, 24) and Galeno *(Hist. Ph.)*, Empedocles defined sleep as 'a diminution of heat', and death as 'a privation of heat'.

142 Everything Roland says about the tiny globules which form different patterns and organic systems should be related to what Fr. Della Torre states in his *Nuove osservazioni microscopiche*. He says he examined some nerve segments under very powerful microscopes and discovered that their filaments were composed of minute globules joined together, and that a great number of similar globules moved between the fibres (p.63). — It is well known that Monro located the origin of all the nerves in the arteries.

microscopes.[143] If the inductions and experiments are to be continued, the following facts must be the special focus of attention:

1st. In animals with red blood, especially the warm-blooded kind, feeling is not maintained by dark blood. Only red blood brings feeling and life wherever it circulates. Bichat, who clearly proves this fact by many experiments, doubts, however, 'whether the insufficient, mortal action that dark blood exercises on the nerves and fibres is due to elements abundantly present in it (carbon and hydrogen) or to those it lacks (oxygen) but which are present in the red blood bringing life and feeling to the nerves and fibres'.[144]

2nd. The instinctive breathing of an animal which, while causing the reddening and warmth of the blood (to some extent at least), separates the hydrogen and absorbs the oxygen by means of contact of the air in the lungs.

3th. The acceleration of the respiration whenever an animal fears for its life. In sick people, close to death, respiration is accelerated and increases in volume, 'boccheggiare', as it is called in Italy. Hales showed by many experiments that whenever a large quantity of blood is drawn from an animal, its rate of breathing increases in an attempt to hold on to the life it feels ebbing away. It is also a constant fact that great pain increases the rapidity of respiration. Weariness, which is the effect of a sluggish circulation, causes us to yawn and spur on the blood by deeper breaths. When the animal breathes, therefore, it is obtaining life, as it were, from oxygen which it incorporates in its blood, while the blood itself simultaneously separates other elements out from itself.

These facts are simply clues or indications that we need to follow in our investigation of unknown truths [*App*., no. 6].

143 Bogros has recently revived the opinion concerning the cunicular formation of the nerves and the fluid moving in them. But Breschet and Raspail disagree with him. They repeated Bogros' experiments and concluded that the nerve channels were not apparent. According to them, we still lacked the observations necessary for affirming that feeling is exercised through some particular nerve-fluid (cf. *Nuovo Giornale de' Letterati*, Pisa, no. 39, May and June 1828). In any case, the question of the cunicular formation of the nerves differs from, and must not be confused with the question of the existence of a fluid proper to the nerves as minister and term of sensations.

144 *Ricerche fisiologiche intorno alla vita e alla morte*, pt. 2, art. 6.

[302]

Article 5.
The fourth question: does the term of feeling require unity?

303. It is very important to observe 'whether the concept of the animal fundamental feeling (the feeling that constitutes it) requires a single, extended, continuous term'. I believe such a term is required by the fundamental feeling; otherwise I see no way of explaining how a feeling which by its nature has many separate, extended elements could be a single, simple feeling rather than substantially separate feelings constituting individual animals.

304. I am not saying that we cannot conceive a feeling principle which, while one and the same, perceives different things and even entirely separate spaces. But I think it is impossible to conceive this in a *corporeal feeling* which must be essentially indivisible from its matter whose limits it cannot exceed.

305. Nor can we begin with what is found in human consciousness in order to make a judgment about merely animal feeling. As human beings we are more than animal; we have more than animal unity. Our unity and individuality is founded in intelligence, which is something much more sublime. Intelligence enables us to turn back upon ourselves and perceive our person impersonally. We can perceive ourselves in the way we perceive any other being, that is, as *objects* and, as it were, individuals of the great 'arch-category' of beings. We are able to distinguish ourselves from all other things, to compare ourselves with them and counter-distinguish our unity from their multiplicity.

306. The merely animal can do nothing like this. It does not perceive itself, nor reflect upon itself, nor distinguish itself from the things it feels, from what is *feelable*. What is felt and what feels can never be separated in the merely animal; they form a single feeling and cannot be thought as existing separately. We cannot say that the feeling element feels itself, because its feeling-act does not terminate in itself but in the *felt element*, where alone we could perhaps say that it feels itself (we cannot conceive totally passive feeling; although feeling is one, it must exhibit activity and passivity and hence some kind of duality, but without ceasing to be one). The purely animal could never say the word 'I', which expresses so effectively not only the unity and individuality of the human being but also their causal unity and

their consciousness of this unity. Consequently, it would be impossible to demonstrate the *identity* of what is purely animal if its feeling terminated in separate, extended elements. And I do not mean animal identity perceived extrasubjectively, which is demonstrated in the same way as the identity of material elements or brute bodies. I mean real animal identity, the identity of the fundamental feeling.

307. This identity can be founded in only one of two things: 1. the feeling principle, or 2. the matter which is the extended term of feeling.

The identity of the feeling principle is certainly necessary but insufficient for constituting animal identity, which is not something in itself. Neither the existence of the feeling principle nor a fortiori its identity can be conceived separately from matter. The identity of a thing clearly depends on that on which its existence depends. Thus, the identity of the feeling principle is a condition necessary for animal identity, but can arise only from the connection between the feeling principle and the matter of feeling, a connection from which the principle draws its life and origin. We must therefore examine the matter of feeling and note the kind of identity with which it can maintain the identity of the feeling principle.

I have already shown that the identity of the matter of feeling, a necessary condition for the identity of a feeling principle, is not the identity of absolute space.[145] Nor is it the identity of the material principles composing the term of feeling. The identity of the term of feeling must be found solely in all the conditions necessary for the continuity of animal feeling, without interruption in *time* and *space*. Continuity of time, which is clearly necessary, needs no further comment.[146] *Continuity* of space is also

145 *OT*, 806, where I showed that our absolute movement is *unfeelable* and that *absolute space* cannot be the term of our individual feeling.

146 The duration of the feeling principle, that is, *its identity at different times,* constitutes a kind of simplicity or unity. This unity, arising from the *identity* of the feeling principle during different, uninterrupted lengths of time, cannot be attributed absolutely to a purely material body but only to the body's relationship with the feeling principle itself. In fact the only way of conceiving the identity of a body at different times is to consider it in relationship to the subject perceiving it, that is, to attribute to it only a relative *identity* or unity of existence at different times. An extraordinary truth results from this: '*Continuous duration* has its seat in the feeling principle which

obviously necessary for the identity of animal feeling; a characteristic of this feeling is its self-diffusion in the *extended element*, which cannot exist without *continuity*.

Feeling, therefore, relative to the continuity of the space in which it terminates, can be identical in two ways: 1. through the stability and immutability of a portion of what is felt, even if the rest of what is felt changes; the identity in this case would be relative only to the unchanged part, not to the changed parts; 2. through the stability of the whole of the felt term, when change takes place only in the *quality* of the feeling. In this case the identity would be total. Thus, animal identity has its seat, relative to extension and its characteristic, dominant excitation, in the permanent term of the fundamental feeling. Variation consists in the qualitative modifications of this feeling.

In all these cases, any animal identity whatsoever would be found in the *term*, never the *principle*, of feeling. This identity, therefore, must be sited not in the 'sameness' of the *feeling element* but in the 'sameness' of the *extended felt term* and the characteristic excitation it produces.[147] The feeling element would follow whatever happened in the extended felt term and thus have its identity or mutability dependent on the term.

308. Even if we wished to place animal identity directly in the identity of the feeling principle rather than in the extended term, we would reach the same conclusion, provided we kept our mind firmly fixed on essentials without drawing on our imagination or arbitrary principles. The feeling principle either feels or does not feel itself as feeling. If it does not feel itself, it cannot in any way constitute the identity of animal feeling because it would be outside such feeling. If it does feel itself, the feeling principle cannot constitute animal identity unless everything it feels is simply modifications of itself. Felt things or, as we have called them, the *felt*, have an extension in animal

communicates this duration to its term. *Continuous extension* has its seat in the felt term, which communicates the extension to its principle.' Kant glimpsed something of this when he said that space is the form of external sense, and time the form of internal sense. But this does not alter what I have said elsewhere, namely, that both *time* and *space* can be conceived only on the condition that spirits exist.

[147] This theory of excitation caused by internal movements will be discussed in my *Psicologia*.

feeling. If the extended felt element were a modification of the felt feeling principle, we would have to say that this principle itself is extended, because an extension can be only a modification of something extended. In the first place, this is absurd, since we have shown that the feeling principle can only be unextended. In the second place, the hypothesis would make the feeling principle a modifiable extended felt element, and thus simply the term of the fundamental feeling. The only reasonable explanation, therefore, for the foundation of animal identity is the identity of the extended term of the fundamental feeling.

Hence, the unity of feeling depends on the continuity and permanence of its term, in the same way that the identity of what is felt cannot be determined unless we suppose its continuity and the stability of its organism and rhythmic movements. For this reason I said that the term of the fundamental feeling in every animal must be continuous.

309. We must note, however, that continuity is not necessary for the various stimulations of the fundamental feeling. Nothing that we have said contradicts the fact that a pain in my hand has no continuity with a pain in my foot, or that I have surface sensations not extended in a solid space.

310. Moreover, although the term of animal fundamental feeling, in order to be one, must be an extended, continuous element, the continuity can result from the contact of many extended, continuous elements touching one another.

However, experience demonstrates that if the feeling parts of an animal are separated from each other, no matter how small the space between them, one of two effects result: either the parts lose their feeling and the animal dies, or, if they do not lose their feeling, two animals take the place of one, as happens with dissected worms and polyps; two totally separate and independent feelings exist, precisely because there is no continuity. But if we suppose the continuity of the parts in the term of animal feeling, a certain unity is imparted to what is animate, because what is continuous is by this fact one. We cannot assign parts in a continuum; we can divide it, but if we do, we produce several continua in the place of one.[148]

[148] *OT*, 807, 808.

311. Granted, however, that the thing felt must be continuous in order to be one, and thus constitute a single fundamental feeling, a single animate being, we must ask: 'Does it need to be of such a composition or homogeneous organisation that the feeling is also evenly and homogeneously diffused throughout the continuum?'

If the question means: 'Are the external, extrasubjective characteristics of the compound which is term of the feeling sufficiently constant to allow us to believe that what is feelable is a single substance?', we must reply that generally this would not seem necessary, although experience shows it to be so in the higher animals relative to excitable sensitivity, because feeling is found, at least in the case of mammals, only where there is blood and nerves. Thus, the feelable substance which supposes the appropriate stimulation could be certain molecules found in and composing the blood; these penetrate, feed and, possibly, themselves produce the nerves and brain.

312. On the other hand, we may ask: 'Is this excitable substance disposed equally everywhere and endowed with organs?' Experience clearly shows that this substance is not everywhere. Hence, feeling in the higher animals, particularly human beings, is not stable and homogeneous but various and multiple. To remove all doubt about whether the matter of sensation can in this sense be various and not homogeneous, it would be more appropriate to ask if it were possible for the matter to be fully homogeneous. If the homogeneity of a felt continuum is in fact found in nature, it must be found only in very simple organic beings. But because it is very difficult to carry out experiments on such beings, we cannot make definite statements about their excitable sensitivity, and consequently must remain doubtful about their being truly animals.

313. Granted, therefore, inequality in the composition and form of the matter of feeling, the most we can hope to investigate is its fundamental law, the explanation of which must lie deep in the intimate and entirely unknown nature of the act of feeling. This fundamental law must ultimately be as follows: 'All these differences exist in feeling without destroying its unity.' Experience certainly tells us that a fundamental feeling, if granted, supposes only certain variations and modifications in its matter (in accordance with hidden laws), and excludes others.

Just as the unity in the homogeneous matter consists in the perfect *continuity* of the parts, so in the varied matter, the unity must consist in a certain kind of *harmony* between the density, mobility and movements which gives rise to a single feeling. All the different parts are involved in producing this feeling, or at least all the feelings of the different parts are referred to it and, as it were, cling to it.

314. This perhaps explains why, in more perfect animals, there is a part essential for the production of every particular stimulated feeling. Although there are organs for producing particular sensations, their ability to exhibit the phenomena of these sensations depends on a principal organ with which they have a hidden relationship. This organ is more correctly called a *common organ of feeling* than the usual 'common sensory'. For example, if Magendie's experiments were confirmed, the posterior cords of the spinal column would form part of this organ in mammals because all feeling would seem to cease when the cords had been cut. In the same way the fifth pair would be the common organ of facial feeling, if this feeling ceased when the nerves had been severed.

315. All these experiments generally support the presumption that in perfect animals an organ common to every kind and variety of feeling exists together with organs common to only some kinds of feelings. Hence there is a gradation of organs necessary for producing different kinds of sensations, entire classes of sensations, and classes that are variously limited; and finally, an organ necessary for producing all feelings. If, instead of this organ common to all the classes of feelings, there were simply organs for particular sensations, we could well imagine the possibility that an animal, when dissected, could multiply into many animals, or at least as many animals as there are independent organs of feeling.

316. And this seems to be the correct way to understand not simply the multiplication of polyps and worms but every kind of animal multiplication and generation. Ultimately all animal generation would consist in the production and development in living animal matter of a new common organ, independent of the previous organ, without any third organ superior to and encompassing the two of them. Clearly, a new fundamental feeling can detach itself from the animal element and constitute an

animal of its own. The production, or at least the development, that gives activity to this new centre of organisation, is the formula of all generation in those animals whose continuum of felt matter is not homogeneous.

If, however, the continuum as term of feeling is homogeneous, having the same structure, as it were, throughout, and the continuum itself is the only centre and unity, then animal multiplication becomes much easier. Dissection is obviously indicated as the means of multiplication, provided we know that the even, homogeneous organisation necessary for the matter of that particular kind of feeling will not be altered or destroyed by mechanical or chemical forces as a result of the dissection. I shall, however, make further observations about this in a later article.

317. We have therefore the following results of our theory:

1st. It does not necessarily and absolutely follow that because we do not feel certain parts of our body, they lack feeling, but only that they do not form a part and term of our individual feeling, although they could possess feeling of their own.[149]

2nd. Some animals, born without some principal part, for example, the head, give signs of life; or signs of life can be seen in a trunk severed from its head, as we mentioned in the experiments of Le Gallois (cf. 301). But we cannot deduce from this that the head is not a necessary part of animal fundamental feeling. Even if the existence of only one feeling had been proved, we could not affirm that this feeling was identical with the feeling present in bodies with parts missing. If I turned a viola into a violin, I would no longer have the viola; I would have a new instrument, giving a different sound and played with a different technique.[150]

[149] This perhaps is the case with entozoas.

[150] Cases of human beings born headless or with an ossified brain are not at all rare. Haller notes, however, that such cases are found only in foetuses (*Comm. in Boerh*. II, 625). A recent case of anencephalia has been described in the *Nuovo Giornale de' Letterati of Pisa*, March and April 1829, Nr. 44. The author, Tommaso Biancini, apparently sees a contradiction between the fact of living anencephalics and the experiments of Charles Bell, Philippis, Magendie, Serres and others, which indicate that feeling depends on certain parts of the cerebral-spinal system. We must bear in mind, however, that the question 'Are the parts of the cerebral-spinal system necessary for the feeling

3rd. It is not absurd that some living molecules possessing feeling and composing our body change from not being felt to being felt and become part of our feeling by placing themselves in continuity with the same extension to which our feeling is propagated.

4th. Nor is it absurd that an animate being be formed of a single molecule, whatever the organisation of the molecule, or that atoms themselves have life, as we have already said (cf. 288, 289).

5th. Finally, although animal *unity* is founded in the non-extension of the feeling principle, its *unicity* rests on three foundations: i) the continuum of the felt space; ii) the harmonious unity in the action exercised by the felt body on the feeling principle so that it always produces a single feeling in which the body's modifications are virtually contained; iii) the identity relative to the duration of time, which is proper to the feeling principle and communicated by the principle to the term of its feeling.

Article 6.
The fifth question: is continual movement the term of feeling?

318. While the concept of *feeling in general* requires no more than a feeling principle and a continuous, extended term, the concept of animal feeling undoubtedly requires an organised extended term, which is apparently more homogeneous in lower animals and more varied in higher animals. Hence the higher animals have a greater number of organs according to

of the being that has them?' differs from the question 'Are they necessary to the feeling of another, perhaps entirely different, living being that lacks them?' Interestingly, the *Roman Ritual* prescribes that the baptism of such horrifically deformed beings can be administered only under the condition 'If you are human'. The Church therefore does not reject but rather presupposes the opinion that human generation can be so disordered that instead of a human being a non-intelligent being is generated. Le-Cat reports the constant observation that headless foetuses are very lively in their mother's womb and make violent movements during delivery, but when delivered seem to suffocate and soon cease all movement. He also cites the observations made by Denis and Vaissière (*Dissertation sur la sensibilité des meninges etc.*, art. 3).

their kinds and classes of sensations, and in addition a single organ common to every kind of sensation.

But we have not determined whether the matter of stimulated sensation is a solid body, or a fluid, or a mixture of both. We have simply offered some observations which make us think that this matter could, at least originally, be a fluid, provided the living particles form a perfect continuum by contact. This is a necessary consequence of the principle that 'the extension of feeling does not exceed the extension of the body which is its term'.

We must now deal very briefly with the last question: 'Is a continual, vortiginous movement, or other kind of movement, required in the felt molecules in addition to their perfect proximity? Is the movement intrinsic, producing a kind of friction between the elements of each living particle or between the particles themselves?' The question does not concern feeling in general but animal feeling, a feeling that gives extrasubjective evidence of its existence. The following are some facts which have a general bearing on the question.

319. It is certain that in all living bodies, particularly in perfect animals, there are countless, continual movements. Are these incessant movements necessary terms of feeling, or is their purpose solely to prepare and produce continually the matter of feeling, maintain it in the act necessary for it to be term, replace unceasingly the particles it is continually losing, and increase it? Such functions are probably fulfilled by all or many of the movements of the animal body, but evidently we have to suppose movements in the term itself of feeling which, together with the movements that stimulate and animate the body, also become a necessary term of the feeling.

320. It is clear, however, that all particular, adventitious sensations need the application of stimuli to the sensory parts; and that the stimuli cause certain impressions or movements, in response to which feeling takes place. It also seems that, although particular, adventitious sensations are adapted to a particular organ and its movements, they are adapted only to determined movements, not all the movements.

Thus the sympathetic nerve and the pneumo-gastric nerves show signs of feeling in response to strong, unusual impressions. Various cervical and thoracic nerve ganglia can be removed without pain, but are found to be sensitive when irritated for a few days and then cut and torn. Perhaps these nerves, although unresponsive to external impressions, are the instruments of an internal, subjective feeling, or possibly they are rendered more sensitive by a greater influx of blood to the inflamed nerves, as we said earlier. These two suggestions, however, seem insufficient to explain fully the laws of sensitivity of the different organs and of the determined kinds of movements necessary to produce a feeling responding to their impression and capable of being adverted to.

The two suggested solutions would also seem insufficient to explain the phenomenon exhibited by the retina of the eye, as well as by all the nerves of the four external senses. These nerves, although insensitive to a sharp point, are highly sensitive when acted on by light, a movement of air, etc. The only satisfactory answer seems to be that the particular, proper stimuli of these organs cause a particular movement.

321. Experience therefore clearly shows that no special sensation exists which is not preceded by some movement in the animal organ. But it also seems probable that the fundamental feeling itself, by which the animal feels the mode of its own existence, is associated with innumerable movements taking place unceasingly in the bodily machine. Thus the nerves are everywhere accompanied by countless stimuli continually acting on and exciting the nerves. Principal among these incessant movements are those produced throughout the brain-mass by the stimulus of the blood carried by the large arteries at the base of the brain. The brain ceaselessly moves up and down, and if the movement stops, it dies. The same can be said about the other principal parts of the animal body supplied by blood.

'In both animal and organic life,' Bichat says, 'the parts, in order to act, need an habitual movement which can support their action.' He notes that besides the principal action of the blood, which strikes and stimulates all the nerves, there is close to every organ 'a large number of agents to supply for any heart-impulse they lack. Thus, in the chest we find that the ribs and diaphragm alternately rise and fall (this is in addition to the successive dilation and restriction coming from the heart and lungs). Respiration keeps the abdominal wall in continual movement while the stomach, intestines and bladder alternately expand and contract. The different positions we assume also continually displace the free organs. Finally, the limbs bend and stretch, move in and out, and up and down. These movements take place at every moment, both all together and separately.'[151]

It is also clear that all the molecules composing an animal body act internally with ceaseless movements to produce all the secretions and other animal functions to which the mechanical, chemical and animal forces also contribute their own continual action. Nor must we forget the extremely rapid movements of electric currents which certainly seem to be present in the different parts of a living body — relative to our question, they call for serious consideration.

322. These briefs remarks suffice to show that greater attention must be given to the solution of the two questions: 'Is the term of animal feeling always an extended element in continual movement?' and 'Are the alteration and movement found in the sensitive parts of a living body so governed by their own laws that they cannot be confused with either chemical affinity or simple mechanical movements, and must therefore correctly be called animal alteration or movement?'

15

THOUGHTS ON THE COMMUNICATION OF LIFE

Article 1.
Animate beings are part of nature; they do not result from the amalgamation of their elements

323. We must sum up some of the things we have said.

We located the essence of the animate being in corporeal feeling.

We then analysed this feeling, and found that it resulted from

[151] *Ricerche fisiologiche intorno alla vita ed alla morte*, pt. 2, art. 2 and 4.

two elements: 1. a feeling principle (the form of feeling); 2. a felt extended element (the matter of feeling).[152]

Finally, we examined the connection between these two elements (this connection gives rise to feeling and, as it were, creates animate being). Our analysis showed a supremely intimate connection culminating in true individuation: if one of the elements were removed, the other would cease to be.

This wonderful union requires unending reflection. As we said, the nature of the feeling principle observed in animate beings is such that the principle is no longer conceivable when all its matter is eliminated. If we remove all matter from the act of feeling, feeling itself ceases. And if feeling ceases, the feeling principle also ceases. Any surviving principle that feels nothing is no longer a feeling principle.

Only our imagination allows us to posit something in the place of absent feeling. We imagine something that either still feels, or does not feel. In the first case, some feeling persists, against our supposition; in the second case, what remains has no connection whatsoever with the preceding feeling.

On the other hand, the matter of feeling is no longer such when it ceases to be the term of feeling. It can be perceived only in true or imaginary, actual connection with the feeling principle itself.

324. It may be objected that this matter could be felt, even if it were not actually felt, and thus enable the matter to be called 'matter of feeling'. The same objection can be made about the feeling principle if it is defined as a principle capable of feeling rather than a principle which actually feels.

Objections of this kind, however, indicate serious neglect of philosophical method and fundamental misunderstanding of what we have tried to explain. Overcoming them requires care on the part of those who raise them.

One of the neglected laws of sound, philosophical method states: 'Take care not to deny to your opponent what you yourself need in order to prove your supposition.' The objectors state: 'The matter

152 The *sensiferous principle* remains outside feeling, according to the distinction we made between *sensiferous* and *feelable*. Nevertheless, the *sensiferous* principle acts in the soul with which it co-operates to produce *what is feelable*.

of sensation can exist without actually being felt.' But what is this matter? Inanimate bodies not actually present to our senses? In this case, we have to ask what is understood by 'inanimate bodies'? If such bodies are understood as shaped, resistant, coloured, and so on, we see immediately that this definition of body can be the result only of sensations. Inadvertently, the body has been defined as the matter of feelings by its being imagined in actual union with feelings, not separate from them. And it could not have been defined in any other way as long as it is considered as the matter of feeling.

The matter of feeling, therefore, has an essential relationship with the feeling principle. If this relationship is removed, the matter of feeling, the felt element and the feelable element are also removed. It is true, of course, that actually feeling this matter is not in question, but in speaking about it I nevertheless either imagine or think the matter as actually felt. In other words, it is in an actual relationship with a possible feeling. If it were not, I could not form any thought about it for myself.

325. This shows that in the *order of real things*, the two elements composing animate beings cannot be posited separately and then united to form animate beings. United, they have to be posited as part of nature's datum. Feeling (animate being) must be given together with its two elements, which can be distinguished by us only mentally. This, however, is not the sole case of such *synthesism* in nature. *Synthesism* is the law and key sustaining the nature of all things in the universe, as ontology shows.[153]

Article 2.
The law of conservation governing animate being

326. The elements of animate being do not pre-exist animate being itself, nor is one element in existence prior to the other. The elements subsist in unity to form animate being.

Animate being exists: this is the primary fact.[154] And because

[153] Cf. *PE*, 21–42. And P. Gioachino Ventura, *De Methodo Philosophandi*, where the author speaks of *substantial composition* in beings.

[154] In the book of Genesis, animals spring already formed from the earth in

it exists, its elements are present within it: this is the second fact which we find by observing animate being present in nature.

327. But *animate being* falling under our observation presents more than the two elements of feeling and felt which are sufficient to make up the concept of animate being. It also reveals other laws and conditions of its existence. These laws complete the concept of animate being which is then expressed through the word *animal*.

328. *Animal* existence is principally conditioned by two of these laws which indicate respectively the animal's *subjective* and *extrasubjective* subsistence. The first law states: 'In its external and *extrasubjective* appearance, a body must order its particles in a certain, determinate matter (organisation), and undertake certain determinate movements, etc., for it to be matter of the stimulated feeling.'

329. The second law states: 'A certain series of extrasubjective phenomena must correspond in a body to the series of subjective phenomena for a body to be known as animate and matter of feeling.'

330. Note that not all these *extrasubjective phenomena*, nor everything present in each of them, appertain to the animalisation of a living, organic body. The body of the individual, animate being contains, besides the *life force*, other mechanical, physical, chemical, organic forces, etc.[155] which can be considered as different operative principles, essentially independent of the vitality of the whole individual. These foreign forces can alter the matter of the animal feeling by drawing it away from the normal state in which it is capable of being a term of feeling. The

which God had placed their fecundated seed; in this sacred book the *spirit* of animals is never separated from their *matter*. This is not the case with the human being. God first formed the body of this king of nature, and then breathed the soul into it: 'and breathed into his nostrils the breath of life.' Here we have a principle, the intelligent soul, that can stand by itself, independently of matter.

155 I use *mechanical* force to indicate collisions amongst the various parts, *physical* force to indicate general attraction, *chemical* force for affinities, and *organic* force for distension, contractility and so on. I call all these forces in general *material forces*. *Sensitivity*, however is a subjective faculty, not an extrasubjective force, and cannot be confused in any way with the forces we have enumerated.

normal state is itself constituted and determined in general by the two laws given above.

331. The subsistence and conservation of animals, therefore, requires 'an amalgam of all the necessary mechanical, physical, chemical, organic forces and so on which, together with the life forces, are suitable for continually preserving the matter of feeling in a state capable of allowing the matter to act as the unique term of animal feeling'. If the harmony and balance between these forces breaks down as a result of a defect in even one of the forces, extinction of the individual feeling results inevitably.

Observation and experience, therefore, bring us to conclude that a certain state, determined by the two laws we have mentioned, is necessary in the body if the animal is to be sustained. The different kinds of forces and the continual movements they produce have to act ceaselessly and, as it were, with continual, supportive, interior, circular effect in order to realise the unending conservation and refurbishing of the external, material, extrasubjective condition of the body that signifies the complex life of the organic whole. Where such forces are balanced and harmonised in this way, animal life can exist and be preserved.

Article 3. Nutrition

332. It is clear that the simultaneous action of so many different forces and changes in the animate body will bring about within the body a constant tendency to abandon the normal state needed for the conservation of life. The activities of individual forces, together with the movements of individual particles, are ceaseless attempts to change place and state, and hence to draw the animal body to some other mode of being. This takes place without regard to the normal state of the body required for the maintenance of life. Only the life force, unique in its capacity for reaching out to the whole being, tends to subject matter to life. Other forces — mechanical, physical, chemical and organic — are governed in their nature only by the need to carry out blindly their own urges without regard for the complex life of the body to which they adhere.

333. We have within the body, therefore, an amalgam of brute forces which tend continually to its destruction. These alien forces have to be restrained and directed by equivalent forces tending continuously to conserve the body, or producing effects that balance those of the destructive forces. This state of *animal antagonism*, as I call it, furnishes the animal with what it needs for its conservation, balance and progress towards perfection.

334. One of the effects of the brute forces continually acting within the animal body is the living body's constant loss of particles which, when ceasing to share in the life of the whole, no longer form part of the same organism. This deleterious effect, which needs to be overcome and corrected by forces of conservation, could if uncontrolled lead to continual diminution and final destruction of the united animate matter. Nature has, however, established a way of entry into the animal body for other particles which compensate for the losses. These particles, continually introduced and inserted into the body, are 'animalised', that is, they become new matter for the feeling of the animal. 'Nutrition' is the means by which the particles come to receive the life common to the whole body. In the more perfect animals the whole digestive system is ordered towards nutrition.

335. The three following operations certainly form part of nutrition.

1st. The food must be broken down and decomposed to the final elements suitable for contributing of themselves to the organisation of the animal molecules.

2nd. These elements must be carried to the orifices of passages and tiny ducts scattered throughout the animal body where they can be received and introduced into the blood or into any place suitable for turning them into molecules that can be assimilated along with the other animal molecules.

3rd. Finally, these elements arrange themselves and unite with the body as a whole in such a way that they become part of the single organic whole and thus communicate their own life to the life of the whole. At the same time, they receive from the whole being an equal communication of life, stimuli and vital activities, and participate in the single life proper to the whole animal body.

336. Little imagination is needed to visualise tiny elements entering the pores and ducts of the body and organising

themselves, when viewed externally, so that they change into parts of organs. The truly extraordinary difficulty lies in the communication of life, through which particles foreign to the animal become its felt and feeling parts. And this gives rise to the profoundly mysterious question: 'How do particles, lifeless in the animal's regard, come to share the animal's life?' or 'How does brute matter change and become matter for the animal's feeling?'

337. Speaking in general, I think the following can be said without positing any hypothesis.

We have already shown that it is intrinsically necessary for the felt body to form a true continuum. As we said, we obtain our idea of extension from felt continuity, without which the idea of extension would be inexplicable. Consequently, the animal's appropriation of foreign molecules can take place only on condition that they first put themselves into perfect contact with the particles already animated by the animal's own life.

The molecules that are to become the term of the animal feeling must take a form allowing them continuity with the matter that is already term of the feeling, whatever this matter may be (perhaps something in the nerves). The particles that have to become feelable relative to the fundamental feeling must penetrate the matter already felt by the fundamental feeling, perhaps by inserting themselves between pre-existing animated particles in such a way as to mingle with and become assimilated to the former matter. This cannot happen, however, without the following law: 'Where one or more similar particles insert themselves between particles composing the matter of feeling, and separate the particles very slightly without breaking continuity, the single, dominant feeling principle does not abandon the particles to which it has given life, but continues to vivify them by passing with its action through the new particle lying between them.' This particle becomes a kind of conductor of feeling, when the feeling principle, through the same law of continuity of sensation, comes to feel the new particle or particles which it now makes its term along with the already animated particles.

As far as I can see, this explanation does not go beyond a description of fact. Whatever causes may intervene in such a event, the fact does not seem possible in any other way.

Article 4.
Animal growth

338. Having found through observation of fact that the activity of the single feeling principle is extended to matter which it had not previously reached, we have also found the way in which the animal grows and develops. To explain growth and development we simply need to add: 'The animal assimilates, organises and invests with life-activity a number of inanimate particles greater than the number it is continually losing.' In this way, if we grant the presence in nature of some first animal matter, however small, we find that this matter contains a capacity for forming other matter indefinitely. When the fundamental feeling is provided with matter and suitable conditions, the feeling principle must be unrelentingly active.

Article 5.
Generation

339. What we have said, taken with what was shown previously, clearly demonstrates 'the feeling principle's dependence on the matter of feeling'. We may express this dependence in the following way: 'The feeling principle is modified in accordance with the modification of its matter and its organism, which determine its mode of being.'

340. On the basis of this wonderful law furnished by experience, the multiplication of animals is no longer difficult to explain, generally speaking — or rather, it is not difficult to find a general formula to express adequately this multiplication. If the feeling principle takes its mode of being from the matter of feeling, and is modified in accordance with the modification of the disposition and quantity of the matter, the following cases can be verified.

1st. If the matter is entirely destroyed, the feeling principle of which it is the term, will also cease to exist because it cannot exist without matter.

2nd. If some given matter decreases quantitatively without being destroyed, the feeling principle of the remaining matter expands its feeling activity in a lesser extension.

3th. If, on the other hand, the continuous matter increases, the feeling principle necessarily expands its sensitivity in a more extended space.

4th. If, finally, the matter of feeling is divided without its being destroyed, and two independent continuities provided with the necessary conditions for preserving their continuity and organic disposition take the place of a single continuum, the feeling principle is also multiplied and becomes two principles. In other words, the animal is multiplied as animate matter multiplies.

341. The final case explains *generation*, and provides a general formula covering the different kinds of generation to be found in the animal kingdom. It is a new proof of the feeling principle's indefinite capacity (cf. 338) for extending, multiplying and stimulating itself, granted certain conditions, all of which depend upon the presence of some matter suitable as the term of the feeling principle.

342. As we have seen, different forms of perfection in animals depend upon the variety, unity and intensity of their fundamental feelings. In turn, greater *variety* of feeling presupposes more complicated organs; greater *unity*, a lesser number of centres amongst the sense organs; and greater intensity, a larger quantity of excitatory motion. Perfect animals, therefore, have a single feeling centre, and their multiplication can depend only upon the formation of a new centre independent of the first.

Article 6.
A difficulty arising from the simplicity of the feeling principle

343. The teaching we have outlined may easily present a difficulty arising from the simple, unextended nature of the feeling principle. Is it possible to divide something simple if only that which has parts can be divided?

The objection would be insuperable if the two or more elements were parts of the so-called simple being; that which is made up of parts cannot be simple. The objection is not valid, however, if simple and unextended beings are not *divided* into parts, but *multiplied* so that the resultant entities are each entire, perfect and simple. And this is what we are dealing with.

344. The whole difficulty experienced in understanding this fact arises, as we have said repeatedly, from the false concept we form of that which is simple and unextended. People cannot conceive a being without extension unless they consider it in relationship to a mathematical point, which has no parts. If the unextended being of which we are speaking were only a mathematical point, it would indeed be difficult to think of it as capable of multiplication — although some kind of multiplicity can be associated with it as the term not of one but of many lines, such as the centre of a circle in which many radii terminate.

But the simplicity of the feeling principle is altogether different. It excludes both extension and every relationship with extension, even the relationship found in a point as the end of a line. This non-extension consists in a *power* capable of producing certain effects, and is called simple and unextended because it pertains to a group of things entirely different from those in space.

345. The kind of simplicity proper to the feeling principle does not prevent the principle's terminating its operation in some extended continuum, as observation shows. We have already noted there could be no continuum whatsoever without its being perceived by a simple principle (cf. 94–97). As we said, the concept of the continuum requires that all its parts appear mutually contemporaneous and uninterrupted. This is impossible unless we suppose that they are presented to some simple principle whose comprehensive power is such that it can diffuse itself simultaneously to all the points of the continuum while remaining identical.

The feeling principle is then said to adhere to all the parts of the continuum which form the term of a feeling. Its adherence is such that the same identical power is found simultaneously in all points of the felt, extended thing. And I have to repeat: it is only under these conditions that an extended, continuous thing can be felt.

The co-existence of the feeling principle in all the assignable parts of what is felt and extended can indeed seem mysterious and truly singular, but this should not deter us from accepting the fact for what it is. And it cannot be otherwise, granted that we have a continuous sensation and an idea of the continuum.

346. If, therefore, we accept this fact as we find it in nature, can there be any difficulty in imagining that if a felt continuum divides in two, its feeling principle can be assigned to both continua? The principle was present in all the points of the continuum before the division. After the division, the feeling principle must be found in all the assignable points of the two smaller continua. But the feeling principle found inherent in all the points of one continuum cannot have any communication with the feeling principle adhering to all the points of the other continuum because the two continua, already divided, no longer form one but two things.

If we supposed that a single, identical principle terminated its action in the two separate continua, this could depend only upon the imagination's adding to the feeling principle something not contained in the concept of a feeling principle. If the same feeling principle were to feel the two separate continua, we would have to suppose that this feeling principle felt itself, and in the feeling of itself felt also the two continua. This does indeed happen, as we shall see, when the feeling principle not only feels, but possesses a higher and more general activity such as intellection. If, however, the feeling principle only feels, we have to be careful not to suppose that it can feel anything except an extended body. If it could feel something other than what is extended, it would no longer be merely a feeling principle, such as an animal, but something superior to animal, which is against our hypothesis.

We must remember that we are dealing only with animal feeling and take great care to acknowledge that in such feeling the thing felt is always and *solely* extension.[156] The nature of animal or corporeal feeling is found here. If, therefore, the animal feeling principle feels only and solely what is extended,[157] and does

156 We do not deny that the feeling principle feels, in extension, its own activity. It feels it, however, as in-existing in extension.

157 It is imagination, as usual, which prevents our feeling the entire force of this argument. On the basis of an analogy with bodies, we imagine a kind of *sub-stans*, or root, underlying the feeling principle. While not denying in any way that the feeling principle may be rooted in something other than itself, we must be careful not to confuse this 'something', anterior to the feeling principle and lacking individuality, with the feeling principle itself. In fact,

not feel itself or anything else separate from the continuum, it has to be granted that two separate continua, forming two things felt separately, form two separate feelings and, therefore, two separate feeling elements. This kind of multiplication is no more contrary to the simplicity of these entities than the feeling principle's capacity for being present simultaneously to all the assignable parts in a continuum.

347. Rather 1. the capacity of the animal feeling principle for being present simultaneously to all the assignable parts of a continuum and 2. the principle which makes the identity of feeling dependent upon the continuity of its extended term, result in the capacity of the feeling principle to multiply in the same way as the continuum. Simultaneous presence to all the parts assignable in a continuum does not detract from, but reinforces the argument for the simplicity of the feeling principle — nothing extended could be present in several places because that which is extended has by essence one part outside another. In the same way, possible multiplicity without self-destruction, as we have explained it, is a consequence and evident proof of the total simplicity and non-extension of the feeling principle

Article 7.
How new discoveries can perfect the given definition of animal

348. Our observations in this chapter on *conservation*, *growth*, *nutrition* and *generation* show clearly that the definition of

although the act by which God creates is a kind of root of all things, this act should not be confused with the things themselves. This would be illogical and pantheistic. We must posit in the nature of things only that which experience and rigorous induction reveals. This means finding the feeling principle where it is, in the feeling, not in something prior to the feeling. The feeling principle will then have to be defined as 'the feeling itself considered in its relationship of activity, not of passivity'. This definition removes all difficulty impeding our thought. It does not imply that we hold God's creative act to be the immediate root of feeling, although it is its final root and final cause. We leave room for possible intermediate, unknown causes which, however, have to be understood as links in a single chain finally dependent upon God, the Author of all things in the universe.

animal can be perfected and made more explicit through the progress of natural sciences. Animal properties, however, which can be indicated in a definition must be distinguished into two classes.

Some properties form the essence of animal; others, although not absolutely essential to the definition of animal, could be shown by experience to be common to all existing animals. The essential properties are contained in the definition we have already given of animal; the other properties, which might be found common to all animals without constituting their essence, could form part of the definition which would then be continually perfected through new discoveries.

These common animal properties, which are not strictly speaking essential, could be, for example, nutrition and generation, or a flexible, bulky, cellulose structure. Research could also show that characteristics thought common to all animals are not really so.[158] The definition of animal could then be expressed in different ways in accordance with variations in natural science. Nevertheless, the modifications brought about by progress in experimental sciences could never change the fundamental definition which is always that of an individual, organic, activated feeling. As we have said, only the accessory, non-essential parts of the definition could be changed.

Natural scientists who deny the possibility of a definition of animal, or expect it as a result of some perfect, future research, have overlooked the easy, undoubted experience proved by the

[158] There are immense variations in animal nutrition and generation, as we know. Many animals 'have no signs of a mouth, and would seem to take nutriment through their pores by absorption' (Cuvier, *Le règne animal*, t. 2). Sponges, for example, and certain gelatinous forms, which contract when touched, show no trace of any digestive apparatus but have pores scattered over their body which seem to act like little mouths absorbing any tiny animal that makes contact with them. So-called *infusoria* have been classified as animals principally because of their cellulose texture and their signs of movement. Nevertheless, they seem to lack eyes, muscles, nerves, organs for respiration and generation, mouth, and digestive apparatus. They are small, gelatinous, transparent, contractile and homogeneous, yet irritable at all points. Initial indications of a stomach only begin in vorticellae and rotifera. There is no intrinsic reason why these beings should not feel, but the presence of feeling needs to be proved without doubt before they can be classified with certainty amongst animals.

[348]

constant existence of stimulated corporeal feeling. This is sufficient for forming a stable concept of animal, and for an unchangeable definition. Our inability to perfect accessories to the definition, or our lack of knowledge of the order of extrasubjective phenomena flowing from the activated, material feeling (in which the definition of animal is founded), does not prevent the definition from being true or essentially complete.

349. Finally, I note that the additions to the definition of animal which depend upon persevering observation and experiment can only determine better the law of relationship 'between the order of subjective phenomena and the order of extrasubjective phenomena'. It is certain that in common usage the word 'animal' indicates the subjective order, accompanied however and revealed by the phenomena of the extrasubjective order (if I may speak in this way). From improvements to the definition, we can rightly expect this connection between the two orders to be clearly described and delineated.

16

DESCRIPTION OF THE FACULTY OF PHANTASY

350. So far we have considered the fundamental feeling and those modifications of the fundamental feeling which constitute the *external sensitivity* of animals. However, the feeling is also subject to the modifications of the phantasy which we must now try to describe. The marvellous power of our imagination enables us to reproduce or re-excite previous sensations so vividly that it is sometimes impossible to distinguish them from the sensations themselves. This is especially the case in dreams, mental illness and imaginary visions.

351. First, we must try to clarify the concept of this renewal of sensation which the soul, through its own power, can arouse internally. Let us, therefore, consider the nerve filaments as though they had two extremities. The exterior extremity extends all over the surface of the body, and terminates in its sensitive endings under the epidermis, in the skin. The interior

extremity will probably end in the brain or spinal cord, or anywhere we care to place it. The law which governs the awakening of sensation in the animal states: 'An oscillation, or trembling, or movement of some sort must take place in the nerve filament or sensory substance before the sensation can occur.' This movement or disturbance of the substance may be caused by two kinds of stimuli, one beginning at the outer extremity of the nerve, the other at the inner extremity. In the first case, exterior bodies stimulate the nerve from outside and produce feelable impressions; in the second case, the stimulus is the soul's own activity which has the power to move the sensory organs and to communicate movement to the outer extremity. If this action of the soul produces in the nerve a vibration or alteration similar to that produced by the exterior stimulus, a feeling will arise similar to that of the sensation already experienced. The root of this phenomenon is to be found in the law of parallelism (which we have already described) between the extrasubjective movements of certain parts of the body and sensations.

352. This way of conceiving the faculty of phantasy is the result of factual experience combined with induction. First, it is indeed a fact that the soul has the power to move parts of its own body. The parts it moves are not only the legs, arms, head and the trunk, but even tiny members — although it is not easy to see, without very careful attention, how movement proceeds from the soul in cases like these. Let us imagine that someone receives a letter bringing unexpected good news. It is the person's soul, his *understanding*, not his body, which perceives the joy of the occasion. But the rational soul does not keep the joy to itself: the heart beats faster, and the face glows. If the sudden news is bad, the face loses its colour, a sure sign that the soul has diminished the force it exercises on the heart and the arteries. This would explain why the soul produces extremely varied and complicated movements either directly in the nerves, or indirectly in organs which seem impervious to sensation. Sometimes this takes place where it would be least expected.[159] I have seen

[159] A sudden fright is sufficient to turn the hair white, as one can see in Schenck and others who have described such cases. Fright also makes the hair stand on end. The soul, therefore, has the power even to affect the hair, which

Giuseppe Bartolomeo Stoffella, a fellow townsman of mine, move his ears (as they say that Albino and that Mens, a Parisian surgeon[160] did) as a result of long practice. The aperture of the iris opens and closes instinctively to shelter the retina from exposure to excessive light and to take as much advantage as possible of dull light. But even this was learned and freely practised by Felice Fontana[161] and others.

353. I firmly believe, therefore, that 'all the movements carried out *instinctively* in our bodies (that is, all those upon which we depend for life and action) could be carried out as the result of an *act of our will*'. This 'exercise' of the soul, which produces some determinate movements rather than others, is an art learned as a result of practice. The soul must not only have the power to move the parts concerned, but must also acquire the habit of using it in such a way that the power can obey habitual instinct or even the command of free will.[162]

This is not the place to investigate how the soul learns the art of moving different parts of its body, or to examine the laws governing these voluntary movements. Here it is sufficient to know of the existence of the soul's power over different parts of the body in order to conclude inductively that the soul has the capacity for moving the nerves and the brain with the same movements as those accompanying sensations. In this way it reproduces the sensations, giving rise to what we call phantasies or images.

experiences life at a lower grade than other parts of the body.

160 Cf. Le-Cat, *Trattato de' sensi* (2 vols. Paris, 1767), where the author proves that the ears can be moved, and maintains that only lack of practice impedes voluntary ear-wagging.

161 Cf. Felice Fontana, *De' moti dell'iride*, a fine book. — I realise that the majority of modern anatomists deny the presence of muscles in the pupil. In this case, the will could not play any part in increasing or decreasing the pupil. According to these anatomists the enlargement of the pupil exposed to light is the result of an increase in the blood flow, due to the irritation produced by the light. But there is no doubt some individuals have been able to make the pupil diminish or expand at will. I am not saying that they used muscles to do this. I am simply stating a fact, which could also be explained by the power of the will over the supply of blood to the pupil.

162 Roberti, in his delightful letter about a sixteen month-old child, describes how children learn the art of moving their eyes which, before the soul has taken control over them, are immobile and supine.

354. Another fact on which we may base our conjecture about the explanation of the soul's power of phantasy is the vividness and clarity of images produced by the phantasy, which we have already mentioned. These are often powerful enough to induce a firm conviction of the presence of the imagined object (cf. 350). Dr. Pinel, after describing a female visionary whom he had kept under observation for a long period, commented on the nature and effect of her imaginary visions and on her complete conviction that the things she saw were as real as those in everyday life. He concluded: 'This is definitely not a mere memory. It is an instinctive knowledge, an interior fascination akin to that which would be stimulated by a vivid impression on the organ of sight.'[163] The same fact occurs in dreams where normally we have no doubt whatsoever about the reality of what we see, do and think. Superstitions, especially idolatry, have their principal source in the phantasy power of our soul, and we can affirm truthfully that this faculty is the principal occasional cause of our errors.[164]

[163] *Tratt. della alienazione mentale*, sect. 2, 7. — Dr. Lorenzo Martini suggests that use of the imagination could explain the heat sometimes felt by a sick person despite the coldness of the skin. 'It is not difficult to explain this phenomenon. It is subject to the laws of the imagination. In order to have a sensation in the first place, some power must either make itself felt or withdraw its pressure. Later, the same movements can be renewed in the common sensory, and the same perceptions awakened. A warmer body than our own acts upon the skin. The resulting impression sent to the common sensory enables the soul to experience a heat sensation. A cooler body now acts upon us in the same way, and our body loses some of its heat either in a part of its surface or all over. The soul is now conscious of a change in its state and feels the cold. The same movements can now be aroused later in the common sensory, the first group making us feel warm, the second cold. We need to note that the renewal of the cerebral, sensory movements, upon which the feeling of warmth or cold depends, are not noticeably willed, but result from some disorder' (*Lezioni di fisiologia*, lesson 77).

[164] Cf. *Certainty*, 1285–1298, on the seven occasional causes of error.

17

THE POWER OF PHANTASY IN DREAMS

355. One of the extraordinary phenomena associated with phantasy is its extremely active presence in sleep when the whole body is weak, and the exterior senses are, as it were, shut down. I do not want to attempt an explanation of this fact, however, but offer my own simple way of conceiving it, which may perhaps be of assistance to philosophers wanting to develop a better understanding of it, and more in conformity with all the facts that further observation may bring to light.

I imagine the whole nervous system as possessing two extremities, one which terminates principally in the cutaneous organ, and the other in the brain and in the spinal cord (cf. 351). These nerves, organs of feeling, are then moved by two kinds of stimuli: *external* stimuli, foreign to our body or rather consisting entirely of matter foreign to the organs of sensation; and *internal* stimuli, that is, the motor force of the soul.

Let us now suppose that the nerve filaments have two periodic movements. In the first movement, the nerve filament extends very slowly from the inside to the outside, and moves the tiny nerve endings forward — rather like the outward movement of the snail's antennae. This slow, but continual outward movement of the nerve endings must however have an extreme term in which it comes to rest. When it has reached this term and attained the maximum activity possible to external feeling, the tiny nerve ending cannot remain long under extreme tension without relaxing. When this relaxation of the outwardly poised nerve has reached a certain point it causes contrary movement in the nerve itself. The nerve retreats inwardly, and draws in its wake all the tiny endings it had expanded and pushed outward. This reverse movement continues until the nerve has withdrawn as far as possible to the opposite extreme, and the interior extremities or endings have expanded and pushed outward as the exterior ends did. The nerve remains at rest only a short time before it resumes its natural movement outwards. These two very slow, periodic movements alternate unceasingly in human life .

356. It must be clear to everyone that such a supposition about two unfeelable movements of the nervous system would explain periods of sleep and wakefulness. We would be awake when the nervous system, active and alert, is drawn by its own natural inclination towards sensation, is prepared to encounter external stimuli, and is open to outward expansion, which would permit it to receive impressions easily. After prolonged enjoyment of this state the nervous system, tired by its vital action and consequent straining forward, would insensibly retreat and turn back on itself. Action would cease, and the nervous system would concentrate itself in rest while the extremities of the nervous protuberances closed in on themselves and no longer accepted exterior impressions — as happens in sleep. To help this periodic movement, the Creator decreed in his infinite wisdom that day should be followed by night, when the stimuli of light and heat cease and even the impact of the air on life lessens because there is no light to draw oxygen from plants (oxygen is perhaps the principal stimulant of life).

357. What we have said also furnishes a very easy way of conceiving the powerful increase of phantasy during the night and in sleep. In the first place, by removing many stimuli from our exterior sensitivity, darkness must render our phantasy more active, in accordance with the law stating: 'The soul's power is more forceful when it is concentrated in a lesser number of faculties.' When people lose a sense — blind persons, for example — their remaining faculties become more acute.

However, although this would help in some way to explain the greater power of the imagination during the hours of darkness, it does not explain the extreme power present in dreams. But the supposition from which we start does lead, I think, to a very clear explanation. As the nerves are withdrawn from exterior stimuli with the onset of sleep, they gradually retreat inwardly and come to expand and extend their internal extremities in the brain or the spinal cord. Here they are more apt to receive the action and movements of internal stimuli, which may be either the bodily fluids or solids, or the power of the soul itself which, seconding the first movements of these fluids and solids, orders the nerves to move, and effectively moves them with sufficient force to produce images. And I think it likely that the movement caused by the soul must begin in the internal extremities which are at the heart of our supposition.[165]

358. My way of conceiving the imagination and its phenomena depends, of course, upon supposition and conjecture. Nevertheless, it cannot be denied that it has some basis in certain facts that give it a degree of probability. One fact is that the soul undoubtedly contributes its own activity when it receives feelings. Moreover, it contributes especially by assisting the nerves to provide the tendency and opening needed to receive the impression in a better way. The soul applies and adapts the nerves to the object and joins it, as it were, in undertaking the operation more effectively. For example, we stare when we want to see something clearly; or we look more intently when light is dim;

165 An excellent field for observation and research would be provided by the electrical condition of the two supposed nerve extremities. Matteucci's experiments on torpedo fish have provided a fine basis for such work. According to him, he has proved: 1. that the electricity producing the charge in the torpedo fish comes from the fourth lobe of the brain which is the source of the nerves that go to the electric organs; 2. that if these nerves are cut or tied, all electrical effect ceases; 3. that ligaturing the leg of a frog results in suspension of the current proper to the animal; 4. that on the contrary ligaturing the nerves does not suspend the passage of simple electro-chemical current either in the torpedo fish or in the frog. This shows that *animal electricity* has its own laws which do not coincide with those of ordinary electricity.
— Professor Stefano Mariannini maintains that his experiments on frogs lead to the following important conclusions: 'Electric fluid, when permeating a nerve in the direction of the nerve's movement, produces a muscular contraction, but when it ceases to flow, a sensation. When the fluid permeates the nerve in the opposite direction of the nerve's movement, it produces a sensation, but when it ceases to flow, a contraction' (in a Memorandum presented to the Academy of Rovereto as early as 1827 and printed the following year by Alvisopoli at Venice under the title: *Memoria sopra la scossa che provano gli animali nel momento che cessano di fare arco di communicazione fra i poli di un elettromotore, e sopra qualche altro fenomeno fisiologico dell'elettricità*). This shows that sensation corresponds with determined movements of the nervous system, not with every movement. As a result, it also shows that 1. it is possible for certain parts of the body to seem void of sense capacity when stimulated, simply because we do not succeed in causing those particular alterations which alone accompany sensation; 2. the soul can indeed use sensory nerves for movement, without necessarily exciting vivid sensations when moving these nerves.

or screw up our eyes when we want to see something tiny, and become

'Like the old tailor threading his needle'.[166]

Something similar occurs when we strain to hear faint sounds or voices, or the words of an eloquent speaker; or when we want to taste or smell something.[167] The same thing occurs even in our touch. I have no doubt that when we want to feel subtle differences in things we touch, we not only accommodate the hand to all the surfaces of the object, but also extend and expand the nerve protuberances in which the impression is brought together. Blind people soon become expert in this.

These facts seem to support our belief that the soul, avid for sensation, moves to meet the objects providing sensation as soon they are even slightly perceived. It pushes the tiny nerves towards the objects, prompting the nerves to receive the objects like flowers opening to receive light, air and dew. The same desire and inclination for feeling, and for renewed, vivid feeling, turns the child's eyes towards every variation of light, and in general explains all infantile movements whose sole object seems the perpetual attainment of vivacious, varied sensations.

359. Let us make another conjecture. I think it highly likely that the alternating movement of the nerves, which I have posited in the animal, begins at birth when the animal comes in contact with light and air. As long as the subject is a foetus, it would seem to lack this movement. Its nerve state prior to birth may be that of sleep or constant stupor from which it is aroused by the new external stimuli of air and light that provoke nerve movement and breathing. The baby's need for a great deal of sleep could be another proof of the gradually awakening to

[166] 'Looking' means acting upon the nerve of the eye so as to present it suitably to the object we want to see. Physiologists, therefore, classify sensation as *active* and *passive*. But it would be more accurate to say that every sensation is passive, although the soul contributes with a given degree of activity to the production of this passivity. Languages indicate this activity of the soul with special words. For instance, when the activity is considerable we do not say that we *see*, but that we *look*; not that we *hear*, but that we *listen*. Such differences are found in all languages. Latin, for example, as videre and *aspicere*, *audire* and *auscultare*, and so on.

[167] Haller maintains that when we taste something, the nerve protuberances rise visibly.

which the animal has to accustom itself little by little as it activates its nerves in the way suggested.[168]

360. Many other facts fit in well with our conjecture about the existence of this alternating movement. For example, the soul's tendency to 'go out' to sensation would account for our waking at the sound of some unusual noise, or when powerful impressions affect us as we sleep.[169]

361. Another fact harmonising with our supposition is that an over-strong impression, especially if applied to the whole body, causes sleep rather than awakens. Excessive cold,[170] pain and tiredness all make us fall asleep. This phenomenon can easily be explained if we grant that being awake consists in nerve extension towards the attraction of sensations, which always delight the soul if they are not excessive. If they are excessive, the nerve retreats from them into itself for two reasons. First, the liveliness of the stimulus has accelerated the movement of the nerve so that it reaches its extreme development too soon, and begins to turn back. Second, the action of the nerve in moving instinctively away from its disturbed state appears to be similar to the action of the aperture of the iris when the eye is struck by excessive light.

362. Our supposition would also help to explain partial sleep, to which a part, not all of the body is subject. Generally speaking, the same would be true of all diseases associated with sleep. These must depend upon a change in the movement of the nerves, alternating like a weaver's bobbin.

363. Another exceptional fact which seems to support my

168 Buffon and other naturalists think that the foetus in the womb is asleep almost continually.

169 Verduc and others have observed a phenomenon that merits further consideration. A sound or other impression on the skin that serves to wake us forcefully is felt more strongly at that moment than when we are awake. Does this happen because of the speed with which the nerve-head hurries to accept the impression? Or is the vividness of the sensation to be attributed mainly to this *rapidity* rather than to the nerve fibre itself? Is the *rapidity* of the nerve movement the effect of a greater degree of activity contributed by the soul to the production of the sensation?

170 It would be frivolous to object that cold is not a stimulus. For *sense*, any cause of change is a stimulus. A clock or mill stopping rouses a person from sleep as effectively as a loud noise. When we speak of 'sense', it is the soul rather than the body which receives the stimulus.

supposition is that brain compression precedes sleep in an animal. Haller's experiments on brain compression in animals are well-known, but sleep followed upon brain compression has also been signalled in human beings. On opening the cranium of sleepy people, Bonnet, Vallins, Fantoni. Wepfer, Bautin and others noted tumours within the skull that were exerting pressure on the encephalic mass; Willis found that meninges were inflamed and covered with blood in several patients; others found the brain ventricles under pressure from serum. Planque testifies to sleep caused by wounds penetrating the brain. Atkins explains frequent lethargy in hot climates by higher than average expansion of blood in the brain, and its consequent capacity for exerting pressure. It is clear that our supposition about movement in the nerves would harmonise exactly with these observations. If the entire nerve system retreated towards the brain, it would inevitably swell and produce the kind of pressure we are considering.[171] On the other hand, while there is no evidence to show that this compression comes about through the flow of blood to the head, there is evidence that sleep is connected with causes diverting the blood from the head and increasing it elsewhere, as we can see in the case of poultices or when feet are immersed in hot water.

364. Another fact meriting careful consideration could also be weight absorption, which is greater during sleep than in periods of wakefulness. Other kinds of absorption also increase during sleep. This seems to harmonise particularly well with our supposition about the retractory movement of the nerves.[172]

365. A difficulty arises when we observe apparent extreme wakefulness combined with very active phantasy and drowsy external feeling in people suffering from mental alienation. The wakefulness is, of course, due to extraordinary arousal of the nervous system which allows no rest to the nerves and the brain.

[171] A. C. Lorry differs from Haller in attributing sleep to compression of the cerebellum, not the brain. D. Hartley has recourse to compression in explaining drowsiness in children, which he attributes to overloading of the head.

[172] Hippocrates' dictum: 'Movements in sleep have an internal direction' is quoted in a book I have before me but, lacking the works of Hippocrates at this moment, I cannot verify the meaning he gives to these words.

But in this case, retraction of the nerves will be equally violent and irregular. It will not be the characteristic, natural slowing down suitable for producing phenomena accompanying sleep. People suffering from insanity can in great part be compared with somnambulists.

18

THE WAY WE THINK OF THE IMAGINATION (continued)

366. Our way of explaining how we conceive of phantasy can also help us to understand how images sometimes differ either in vividness or in quality from sensations, which they may surpass or belie. Notable differences will cause no surprise when we realise that the movement or nerve alteration which precedes feeling depends upon a stimulus of images differing from that of sensations. The internal stimulus acts according to different laws from those which govern bodies acting upon our external senses.

But it helps us to understand not only the difference between images and sensations: it also explains how they are sometime so similar that we cannot distinguish them in any way, nor decide whether an object is present or not. There is nothing to prevent the nerve alteration produced by the internal cause from being so perfect that it is the same as the change produced by the external cause.

Many other questions could be raised about the faculty of imagination. For example: 'Why is the soul capable of arousing only sensations already experienced, but completely incapable of arousing new sensations?' This, however, would lead us too deeply into the study of the activity of the sensitive soul and the laws according to which it operates. We shall examine the matter in the second section of this book, therefore, which we begin immediately.

SECTION TWO

THE ACTIVE ANIMAL FACULTIES OR INSTINCT

1

THE TWO BASIC FORCES OF ANIMAL ACTIVITY

367. We have said that feeling could not arise unless a feeling principle contributed its own activity to feeling (cf. 358). In fact, sensations could not conceivably be aroused in a principle devoid of all activity. Such a principle would be dead and as unfeeling as a stone. Corporeal feeling, although it requires passivity in the feeling principle, does not postulate a passivity which is entirely inert and devoid of action. It depends on a *spontaneous* passivity, a receptivity that co-operates to allow the reception. Strictly speaking, we are dealing with co-operation, not *relationship*. Both the feeling and sensiferous principles co-operate to produce the felt element; and given this element, *feeling* is present.

Nor must we mistakenly suppose that the *feeling* and *sensiferous* principles precede the *felt* element in time, as they do in their concept. We have shown that we have no evidence at all for such prior existence. Unless *feeling* is given by nature, there can be no progress in ideas. This fact must be the object of our reflection which, by means of analysis and reasoning, discovers in feeling a double, continuous, immanent action incessantly producing feeling. Thus, by examining the product, that is, the *felt* element or *feeling* itself, we arrive at the real existence of two acting principles (feeling and sensiferous).

368. But the co-operation of the *feeling principle* in producing feeling is shown not only by reflection on the constitutive elements of feeling but also by many other easily observable facts.

For example, greater pain, by attracting the activity of the feeling principle from lesser pain, diminishes or removes the disturbance caused by lesser pain simply because the greater attracts the activity of the feeling principle from the smaller.

Again, when a foreign body is first in contact with a mucous membrane, we feel pain, but as the contact is repeated or prolonged, the painful sensation gradually diminishes until it disappears altogether. The soul, by withdrawing itself from the very painful sensation, seems to play a large part in producing this phenomenon. Our skin, for example, feels acutely any sudden change from hot to cold, but becomes insensitive to a constant temperature. Certainly, many causes are involved here, but in my opinion a principal and probable cause is, as I have said, the soul's withdrawal from its initial contribution with its own action to the movement of the nerve. The soul may even positively resist and obstruct the movement of the nerve which is necessary for feeling to take place.

Another demonstration of the feeling principle's action in producing feeling is the totally different state of an animated body from a body deprived of the soul. The difference clearly indicates that the soul or feeling principle informs the body, giving it tone and mobility. In other words the soul gives the body the qualities which the body presents to extrasubjective observation. There can be no doubt, therefore, that the first activity of the soul is its co-operation in producing feeling.

369. The soul, however, has another energy, by which it acts after feeling has been produced: it is moved to action by the very fact of feeling. For example, the only explanation for an animal's being moved to suckle immediately after birth and perform other movements and tasks is the urge to experience pleasure and avoid pain.

That which is animal, therefore, has two activities: *its contribution to the production of feeling*, and *its behaviour as a consequence of feeling*. These two basic, universal energies are the source of all particular, active, animal faculties and actions. When acting harmoniously, they explain all the facts of animal activity. Although each of them can correctly be called *instinct*, the first is better called *life instinct*, and the second *sensuous instinct*.

2

THE RELATIONSHIP BETWEEN THE TWO BASIC ANIMAL FORCES AND THE ALTERNATING MOVEMENT OF THE NERVOUS SYSTEM

370. In order to determine better the nature and characteristics of the two basic animal forces, we must first examine their manner of activity in a particular case.

We have supposed that the whole nervous system alternates its insensitive movements in the direction of both extremities or poles of the nerve, so that the movement is either to the external extremity or pole, or contrariwise to the internal extremity or pole (cf. 355). These two unceasing movements in fact correspond to the two basic animal energies we have indicated (cf. 369). The extension of the nerves towards the external extremity is clearly a movement that presupposes a fundamental feeling in act, and can only be the effect of the *sensuous instinct*. This instinct, aroused by stimuli, uses spontaneous movement to obtain new sensations to which it is inclined. Hence the withdrawal of the nerves to a state of rest is produced solely by the *life instinct* because this instinct governs both the *production* and *conservation* of feeling, and therefore relaxes the nerves, returning them to their original and, as it were, natural state.[173]

[173] According to Boerhaave, sleep is so natural to human beings that they would go on sleeping if no stimulus disturbed their body. This great man's opinion would seem to agree with what we have said, namely, that stimuli arouse the nerves, whose movement therefore begins with respiration at the moment the foetus makes contact with air and light. Brown's opinion would also seem true. According to him, life is a kind of forced or excited state, produced by certain stimuli. Whatever the truth of these opinions, we must say that the exercise of external life cannot be incessantly continued, because it requires a certain effort whose continuation brings about changes in the organs and corporeal structures. Prof. Medici suggests that these changes, to which he thinks the structures are subject, are *mechanical* and *chemical*. He thinks the alteration of the mechanical state of the structures 'consists in a change of disposition, forms or adhesion in the integral particles of the structures themselves as a result of long, repeated movements of the organic filaments'. The alteration of the chemical state of the structures 'if indeed it takes

3

THE LIFE INSTINCT

371. A general description of the *life instinct*, as I have called it, has already been given. This instinct has its origin in the act by which the feeling principle or soul co-operates in the production of the fundamental feeling and feels the body considered subjectively.

372. A body felt in this way is the same as a living body. The act therefore by which the feeling element intervenes actively in the production of its feeling is also the act of animation of the body.

373. Animation of the body exhibits extrasubjective phenomena, by which our external senses distinguish whether a body is animate or not. The act therefore by which the feeling element acts in feeling is the first cause of all the extrasubjective animal phenomena of the animate body.

374. Such considerations might have settled the well-known controversy between Stahl's followers and their opponents. The objectors maintained that animal movements such as circulation, irritability, etc., took place without any feeling experience in the soul, and without any co-operation on the part of the will; consequently, the soul played no part whatsoever.[174]

place, arises from a greater loss of matter, the effect of the same vital movements of the structures. Because of this loss the organic compound would not be sufficiently preserved' (cf. *Manuale di Fisiologia*, Bologna, 1835).

[174] These are the kind of objections made against Robert Whytt and others by Haller in his dissertation on the sensitivity and irritability of parts of the body. Stahl's followers certainly did not defend their cause adequately by saying that irritability was explained by particles of the soul entering the irritable fibre (this makes the soul material and divisible), nor by positing an unfeelable feeling (a contradiction in terms) (cf. Whytt, *Opusc.*, Berlin, 1790). Le-Cat's opinion, in his *Dissertazione sulla sensibilità delle meningi e delle membrane ecc.* (Berlin, 1765), is also inaccurate. According to him *irritability* is an effect of animal *sensitivity*, so that every part is both irritable and sensitive; the soul produces irritability and feeling, even in limbs separated from the body, although we are not conscious of this because communication of the nerves with the brain (the organ of thought, according to him, art. 6) has been severed. I shall not stop to show, as I could, that such a way of speaking is seriously deficient. On the one hand it exaggerates by its apparent

However, the soul's lack of feeling and will in these actions does not exclude the possibility of its co-operation with the vital functions. I do not mean that the soul contributes with its will, because will presupposes knowledge of a purpose; therefore the soul must have some knowledge for the will to be activated. Moreover, the soul can withhold the co-operation of its feeling, which is generated, but not preceded by the action of the two principles we call feeling and sensiferous. But this does not remove the soul's capacity for contributing to the extrasubjective life phenomena of the body with the act by which it intervenes in the production of feeling — an act which cannot be felt by the soul itself. If, moreover, the soul intervenes in this way as co-cause of the extrasubjective life phenomena, it does so without *willing* or *feeling* the co-operation, of which it is totally unconscious.

4

THE LIFE INSTINCT ACTS IN EXTENSION

375. A principal property of the *life instinct's* mode of operation is its action in the continuous, extended element. This property is shown by the fact that animal feeling naturally diffuses itself in a continuum, as we have seen. The feeling principle therefore acts in all points of the felt continuum (cf. 94–103). We note that the action of the life instinct must be simultaneous and without the least interval of parts in its term, because the continuum cannot exist unless its assignable parts are contemporaneous and without any interval between them.[175]

We see therefore that the nature of *animal feeling* requires the action of the *life instinct* to be simultaneously, not successively,

spiritualism; on the other it is tainted with materialism. If, instead of speaking about consciousness, Le-Cat had said that a feeling not belonging to the animal itself can be present in the parts composing the soul, he would not have proposed something so patently untrue.

175 The action under discussion can indeed restrict itself to a more or less extended continuum.

diffused in a given extension, because the *life instinct* is precisely that which is generated by feeling throughout the whole extension occupied by feeling.

376. This fact is important, and explains many phenomena of animal activity. For example, if we grant for certain that the tonicity of the capillary vessels carrying the blood to the skin is an effect of the life instinct of the soul, such an effect will be contemporaneous, not successive. Pallor, for instance, as an effect of fright, does not appear first at one point on the face and then gradually spread; it appears simultaneously over the whole face or in an extended part of it, because the frightened soul removes simultaneously, not successively, the capillaries' force to carry the blood to the extremities.

In the same way we understand how different limbs of a living body can all undergo variation and change in the same place simply by the soul's change of action, which is unimpeded by the mutual distance of the limbs.[176]

5

THE DOUBLE EFFECT OF THE LIFE INSTINCT

377. If we observe the effects produced by the soul's act, which diffused in extension animates the body, we see that some are subjective, like feeling, and others, as I have said, extrasubjective (cf.

[176] Serious consideration of this would have prevented the introduction of strange hypotheses to explain the action exercised by the soul in different parts of the body. According to these theories the soul *acts at a distance*, which is a contradiction in terms. Moreover, there is here, under the form of excessive spiritualism, a material concept, because action at a distance presupposes real proximity and distance of place between soul and body. But relationships of this kind can exist only between bodies or extended elements. Johann Jakob Hentsch published a dissertation, *Meditationes de harmonia mentis humanae cum corpore sibi juncto, cujus causae exquiruntur*, whose principal thesis is the following: 'The human mind is endowed with a force or energy to move the fluid matter in the nerves of the body by means of ACTION AT A DISTANCE without any energy passing into the body' (cf. the Leipzig *Acta*, 1759).

374). We see that certain parts of the body are modified both subjectively and extrasubjectively, and are therefore the seat of both subjective and extrasubjective phenomena. However, other parts are seen to be modified only by particular, extrasubjective phenomena, and give no sign of subjective phenomena. The parts modified both subjectively and extrasubjectively are sensory parts, that is, organs of sensation; the others are the parts of the animal body which indicate only a share in life, but not feeling, at least not animal feeling.

It seems that the act by which the soul contributes to the production of feeling makes sensory only certain parts of the body, although it exerts its action on all parts, and tries, so to speak, to give them all feeling, but without success. This is probably due to lack of the necessary dispositions in the body itself rather than the direct weakness in the activity of the life-giving act, which is naturally inexhaustible.

378. Some physiologists posit a hidden sensitivity in all parts of the body. If this opinion had any foundation (and I believe it has, provided 'hidden sensitivity' is understood solely as 'not belonging to the individual feeling which constitutes what is animal'), we would no longer have any difficulty in explaining the fact under discussion. We could correctly suppose that the activity of the individual instinct, as it tried to join to itself and dominate every partial feeling of the animal body, would contribute to the production of the extrasubjective phenomena which all parts of a living body with their varying capacity for stimulation offer to our observation.

Such a supposition receives firm support from all those facts which show that even naturally insensitive parts manifest feeling under certain circumstances and when acted on by certain agents. Thus, we can say that extrasubjective phenomena even when lacking feeling can be considered as signs of certain dispositions of the parts which by the dispositions are prepared for becoming sensory.[177]

This opinion would be further strengthened if we could verify whether the passions were situated not in the cerebral nerves but

[177] It will be helpful to recall here Tommasini's opinion about the relationship between muscles and nerves. He considers muscles as a kind of expansion of the nerves, which accept other elements, especially fibre.

in parts entirely devoid of feeling. It is claimed that the brain is never affected by passions. But 1. passions certainly show their effects in the organs of circulation, respiration, digestion, secretion, exhalation and absorption; 2. it is equally certain that passions are not accompanied by feelings of *surfaces*, such as those caused by external impressions, but of *solids*, such as internal feelings and the fundamental feeling itself; 3. it is also certain that we acknowledge these feelings to be located in the region of the organs just mentioned. 'Gesture, as a mute expression of our feeling and mind, is a convincing proof of this,' says Bichat appropriately. 'Thus, in order to indicate an intellective phenomenon related to memory, imagination, judgment, etc., our hand moves involuntarily to our head, whereas to express love, joy, sadness, hate, it goes to the region of the heart, stomach and bowels. It would be a mistake for an actor speaking about sorrow to gesture to his head, and when speaking about some bright idea to gesture to his heart. He would bring down on himself the ridicule we sense but cannot explain.'[178] Feeling connected with passions is therefore located in organs considered as non-sensory. This fact would greatly help us in showing that the act by which the soul vivifies what are considered unfeeling parts of the body is the very act that produces feeling, which here is either less observable or follows other laws.[179]

Other facts confirm the teaching I have put forward, facts which are supported by the authority of well-known writers, and should be further verified.

The first fact, attested by Dr. Bertrand in his *Trattato sopra il Sonnambolismo*, is that in somnambulists 'organic sensibility' (we would say "organic vitality") 'is heightened and changed into animal sensibility'.

The second fact, which resembles the first and is corroborated by several writers, especially German writers, is that through

[178] *Ricerche fisiologiche intorno alla vita ed alla morte*, pt. 1, art. 6, §2.

[179] Cuvier attributes *irritability* itself to the nerves and unhesitatingly affirms that 'the internal network of the nervous system exercises other functions, of which the animal is unaware and which are independent of its will. These functions impart the necessary irritability to the fibres covering the internal organs and vessels so that the fibres can act in accord with their purpose and play a part to some extent in all secretions and other vital functions' (cf. his article, *Animali*, in the *Dizionario delle scienze naturali ecc.*).

[378]

the action of animal magnetism human beings fall into a kind of sleep in which organic vitality is changed into sensoriness. Moreover, the same people feel and know all the internal parts of their body and the relevant remedies for the diseases affecting the parts.

379. We conclude: the *life instinct* co-operates with *organic life* and is the source of *sensory life*. Organic life is equally proper to all parts of the animal body; sensory life, as far as can be ascertained, is proper only to certain determined parts.

6

ORIGIN OF THE LIFE INSTINCT

380. Animate being is found in nature. If we want to divide it into its two elements, we destroy both it and its elements. But this does not prevent us from examining the reciprocal action of the co-elements which produce feeling and animate being. In fact, if we succeed in distinguishing one element from the other in feeling, we should also be able to observe their mutual aptitude and reciprocal action.

381. We have seen that the first element, the feeling principle, is *passive* relative to the second element, the sensiferous principle. Vice versa, the sensiferous principle is *active* relative to the feeling principle. We have also seen that the feeling principle, although passive, is not inactive (*inactivity* and *passivity* are different and should not be confused). Indeed the feeling principle could not be passive and receive feeling if it did not co-operate and contribute in large measure to the act. These conclusions result from an analysis of animal feeling.

382. However, if we put feeling aside and consider only the extrasubjective phenomena of an animal body, another question arises because the extrasubjective phenomena of an animal body differ from those of material body. We must therefore conclude that animation influences the extrasubjective state of a body, although it is simply the act by which a body acts on the feeling principle by becoming its term. We have to establish the origin

of this act, an act which is prior in nature but not in time to the animal feeling principle.

We have attributed this act of the body to the action of the feeling principle itself, an action prior in nature to feeling but not in time. We did this because the difference between the extrasubjective phenomena exhibited by what we see of an animate body and the phenomena presented by what we see of an inanimate body shows how the body is modified. To this extent, therefore, the body is passive; and if passive, the animating principle must be acting as an active principle. Thus we see that in animation both body and soul are active and passive in turn.

When we speak about an animal body in which life is visible, the first action is that of the soul. The purpose of this action is to direct the well-prepared body to that actuation in which the body, thus constituted, acts on the soul itself, inducing animal feeling. The second action therefore is that of the body (now an animal body) on the soul. The soul therefore is first active and then passive; the body is first passive and then active. The co-operation of the soul in the production of animal feeling consists in an act prior to the act of the body. This act has the double effect of making the body active and the soul itself passive.

Our understanding of this reciprocal action of the two constituent principles of what is animal is helped by an illustration taken from Dobereiner's lantern. When we open the tap of a container in which hydrogen has been produced by the immersion of a small, solid cylinder of zinc in acid, an inflammable liquid is released. Although the liquid is cold to the touch, it has the property of immediately making red-hot a piece of platinum held to the tap. When red-hot, the metal ignites the hydrogen issuing from the tap. The flame of the burning hydrogen then ignites the wick of a lamp placed close by for the purpose. This lamp, or rather the lamplighter, is a similitude of the reciprocal animal action of the soul and body. The platinum is cold, and cannot therefore ignite the hydrogen. But the hydrogen, as it forcefully strikes the platinum, has the property of making the metal red-hot and thus conditioning it to ignite the very hydrogen which had made it red-hot. In a similar way the body cannot stimulate the feeling of the soul unless the soul, by first acting on a body endowed with organs, makes the body suitable for acting on the soul itself and thus give rise to the proper

[382]

induced animal *feeling of excitation*. In this way action produces passive experience, and passive experience produces action. This goes on continually, and can be noted not simply in our case but throughout nature, as *Ontology* shows.

383. It may be asked how the first act of the soul by which the sensiferous principle is brought into act can itself be posited. We must note that, prior to the induced feeling (which requires some stimulus from the sensitive body — a stimulus in which the soul then co-operates), I presuppose the *feeling of the continuum*. When stimulated, the principle of this feeling is effective in animating with induced life a suitably prepared body, endowed with organs.

384. But what is the origin of the act of the principle which feels the continuum? — The act is the essence itself of the soul; and nothing exists prior to the essence of a thing except the act by which the Creator posits the essence. The soul therefore is passive in its first act (if by passivity we mean indeed the reception of existence) but only relative to the first agent who makes it be what it is.

Granted its first act, therefore, the soul, by giving the body life and feeling it, works throughout the whole body endowed with organs. This is the origin of that activity of the soul which we have called *life instinct*.

7

ORIGIN OF THE SENSUOUS INSTINCT

385. The act by which the soul gives life to a body endowed with organs produces the animal fundamental feeling, the term of which is an extended element stimulated by internal movements, subjectively feelable, and simultaneously ministering to feeling, that is, sensory. This feeling is a continuous act, whose term is the whole living body, especially the whole body felt with its excitatory movements. The fundamental feeling is therefore immanent.

But the term of the fundamental feeling is modified not only by the soul but also by material forces, which gives rise to the modifications of the fundamental feeling, that is, to various, acquired sensations. Experience shows that, given feeling and particular sensations, a new activity, which we have called *sensuous instinct*, reveals itself in the soul.

386. This instinct teaches the baby to search for light with its eyes and, with its mouth, food from its mother's breast. It governs all the baby's movements and the few actions of its young life, charming it with pleasant sensations and withdrawing it from unpleasant sensations. There can be no doubt that feeling causes an instinct, and that many movements arise from the desire to feel intensely and pleasantly.

387. It is easy to see how this second activity of the soul, the *sensuous instinct*, is in some way a continuation of the first, the *life instinct*. The life instinct posits the primary, fundamental feeling, while the sensuous instinct seeks other feelings; it is always feeling to which the soul's activity tends. With its first activity the soul breaks into, so to speak, the movable, feelable, extended element. This movement always tends to new feelings, and spreads wherever it can.

Thus, the primordial power of the soul is reduced to a single power. All the soul's acts are virtually contained in the act with which it first feels. Like a drawn bow, the soul's power is contained in this act, ready to shoot forward when released, and show itself in movement.

388. Hence, 'animal' could appropriately be defined as 'an individual being, which acts by feeling'.

8

THE ACTION OF THE LIFE INSTINCT

389. We need to consider more carefully the action of the two instincts, and in particular their extrasubjective phenomena. We shall begin with the *life instinct*, bearing in mind the following:

1st. The term of its act is the animate body; the action of the soul is received contemporaneously in all parts of the term.

2nd. The effect of the soul's action is to produce in the body certain extrasubjective phenomena which are observable only in animal bodies and indicate that the body is in the state and act necessary for it to be felt immediately by the soul with a feeling of excitation.

3rd. The organic body is subject both to the soul's action and (granted the material properties of a body) to mechanical, physical, chemical, organic and other forces. These forces can alter the body and destroy the condition and state of the individual life furnished by the soul's action.

4th. The soul, in imparting to the body unique, individual life must find the body endowed with organs and structured according to certain hidden laws, so that it may give the body such an act of life. If the body lacks the required organisation and composition, the soul cannot exercise its wonderful function of fully vivifying it.

390. In the preparatory state necessary for the body to receive the soul's vivifying action, we can identify two extremes, and between the extremes, certain conditions or intermediary states. We must now consider these.

One extreme is the perfect, material state of the body. Granted this, the soul vivifies the body totally with a unique, individual life without any resistance or obstacle on the part of the body; perfect health is the result.[180] The other extreme is the state of the body in which the material condition necessary for receiving this life is completely lacking. In this case the body cannot be animated in its organic entirety.

Between the two extremes, there is, as I said, a gradation of intermediate states. The necessary condition and organisation of the body for receiving the act of unique animation is not entirely absent in these states, but is defective in some part. The result is ill health and disease.

All this can easily be verified by experience.

391. Let us suppose an animal to be in perfect health. All its parts and the whole of its body are perfectly disposed to receive the life-giving action of the soul. Nevertheless, death must result if a material principle so upsets the body that it is taken to the opposite extreme. Death must be the result because the soul no longer has an organic composition suitable for receiving its unique, vital action.

If, on the other hand, the disturbance does not render the body completely incapable of receiving the soul's action, a state

[180] The perfect state of a body enjoying fullness of life and health is apparently not related to size, nor is it entirely unique. A living body can present a perfect disposition at any age, from infancy to mature adulthood.

of disorder (disease) will result. Although the soul vivifies the body, it finds obstacles to its action, which tend to fragment it and destroy its unity. Although it tries to overcome these obstacles with its own action, it does not always succeed because its action is limited. The body is now affected simultaneously by two contrary forces: the *unifying* and *multiplying* principles. The phenomena of different diseases must find their explanation in the opposition between these two forces.

9

THE ACTION OF THE SENSUOUS INSTINCT

392. We must now deal with the activity that we have called *sensuous instinct* and discover how this new activity and its various functions arise after the unique feeling has been produced and the animal constituted.

We must first note that our enquiry does not concern the origin of particular sensations. They arise in the life instinct which, as the animal activity producing the fundamental feeling, must feel the modifications of the fundamental feeling caused by an alteration of its matter. We are simply asking for the explanation of spontaneous animal movements which are made in response to the experience of animal feelings, and which in great part tend to produce a better, animal state.

393. We must also bear in mind that spontaneous animal movements are the effect sometimes of a single feeling and sometimes of many feelings which, as modifications of the single fundamental feeling, are unified through the unity of the feeling.

394. Later we shall discuss the association of feelings with the spontaneous movements that follow them. Here we simply want to suggest how a simple feeling can stimulate a spontaneous movement in the animal without its having recourse to knowledge and intelligence. The animal is not endowed with these faculties; it is totally limited to feeling alone.

In reply we say that every partial animal feeling is by nature connected with a feeling of the nerves. Moreover, it is a fact that a movement stimulated in the organs used for feeling is communicated to the organs used for spontaneous movement. Drowsiness and sleep is a good example of this union and connection between the nerves used for feelings and those used for external motion. The nerves controlling *exterior sensitivity* withdraw for respite, and at the same time the muscles cease their activity. For example, when a person falls asleep, the muscles holding the head erect slacken, the head droops and the lower jaw sags leaving the mouth open. The knees become limp, and the lower limbs no longer support the person, who begins to slip, and would fall if not held. Hence the natural position for sleep is lying down and straight, because this position does not require any use of muscular energy. Many other similar observations show how muscular energy and movements increase or decrease in parallel with the activity of external sensitivity.[181] Indeed, physiologists have firmly and incontrovertibly established the fact we are discussing, namely, that nerve movement exists where there is partial feeling, and that this movement can extend to and affect the muscles.

395. This fact allows me to argue that when the living members of the body receive an external impulse to movement, the principle or soul vivifying the members also receives the movement. Consider the kind of feeling we experience if someone else's hand or some other external force moves our leg, for example, to a different but natural position. We cannot remain entirely indifferent to the movement caused in us. If we co-operate with the movement of the leg and with the force affecting and displacing it, we are clearly active. If we resist the movement with our leg muscles, we are active in the opposite direction. Even if we neither resist nor co-operate positively with the intended movement of our leg, we are still not indifferent (this must be carefully noted); we are passive, feeling that we experience some disturbance. We feel, not without some displeasure, that our dominion over our leg is being violated, as it were. If, however, we keep the leg firmly in position, not as something dead but as something living, it remains where it is because our living energy

181 Animals whose feeling is very acute respond more quickly in their movements. This explains the extraordinary agility of the bat to change direction and avoid the smallest obstacles, such as the minute threads which Spallanzani hung in a room.

determines it to that place and not elsewhere.[182] To displace it, the force would have to overcome the vital energy holding it there by applying some form of constraint. When, therefore, a muscle or part of our body receives initial motion from a foreign force, the animal has three choices: to resist the movement, to permit it to spread throughout the muscle without any co-operation (as if the muscle were inanimate), or to assist the impulse of the motion imparted to the muscle. Constraint is present in the first two choices, spontaneity in the third. To assist the movement in its initial stages is to alienate the constraint, the level of which depends on whether we resist or not. Normally the animal chooses to set itself spontaneously in motion, because spontaneous movement is less tiring and troublesome than the first two kinds of resistance. Moving becomes its natural state, just as previously when there was no impulse to movement from any direction, rest was its natural state.

396. Sleep is a good example for explaining more clearly the action of the sensuous instinct. By this action the animal determines itself to move when it assists and continues the *minute movements* of the nerves accompanying feelings. In human beings the nerves of the ear have a special bond and harmony with the muscles of the lower limbs: the movements of the acoustic nerves spread to the legs and give them the impetus for movement. Thus, when we hear music, we have to make an effort to keep our legs still, and can do this only by positively resisting the internal disturbance and agitation communicated to them, or by allowing the movement to act on our legs as if they were dead. This second kind of resistance requires even greater effort for a living human being, and opposes nature. Very young children (who do not resist nature) can be observed to start dancing as soon as they hear rhythmic sounds; animals, like the monkey and the bear, will do the same. This is the origin of dancing, which has been practised throughout history and by all peoples, particularly those closest to a state of nature.

182 We should carefully note the observation made by physiologists that muscular action is as much present in the positions assumed by human beings as in movement. If we remain in a given position, the antagonistic muscles are equally and simultaneously active. When we move, the antagonistic muscles alternate in their action, and movement results.

397. We can conclude that the animal principle is subject to a law of inertia similar in some way to the law explaining the phenomena of movement in bodies. If a body is at rest, it remains so until a force impels it; if it is moving, it will continue in motion until another force returns it to rest. In the same way, if a living principle is set in motion by sensation and the tiniest movements of the accompanying nerves, it will continue in this state of activity which, in its turn, produces muscular movement that increases with the mobility proper to the muscles. Hence the human spontaneous movements that we have described.

398. Consequently, we do not need to suppose intelligence or will in the animal in order to explain this kind of movement. Instead, we must suppose a special law of inertia by which the animal spontaneously assists and continues the movements produced in it by external stimuli and its own internal *vital activity* (which is the real starting point of every animal function).

399. The problem of small, unfeelable nerve movements on the one hand and large muscle movements on the other (apparently a mystery to physiologists) can also be explained. The smallest movement, which becomes large by spreading to the muscle, could undoubtedly find a favourable disposition in the irritability of the muscular fibre, but irritability would certainly not suffice to explain the phenomenon because the extremely small nerve movement would never be a sufficient stimulus to arouse such great contractions in a muscle. Furthermore, it would not explain how human movements, which contain nothing violent, oscillatory or vibrative, are smooth, spontaneous and obedient to the animal element producing them. Clearly, the animal must continually co-operate with its own activity.

In my opinion the very slight movement produced in the nerve in company with feeling, together with the mechanical communication of the movement, is not the only direct cause of muscle movement, although it is the cause that *stimulates spontaneous animal activity*. This activity is set in motion as soon as it feels movement in one of the parts under its control. The movement, as we said, disturbs the activity and attracts it by means of its own state, so that if the activity itself did not co-operate by moving the part in response to the impetus, it would suffer further discomfort. Consequently, it costs the activity less to move the part; its action is less than that required to keep the part rigid, if we suppose the part is moved independently of itself. Once in motion, the activity, because of the law of inertia, must continue till it reaches a certain point. In addition to its own inertia there is also the inertia proper to a body. When a body is set in motion by larger movements, it does not come to rest quickly; it tends to maintain itself in motion according to its own laws. A baby, when it sees its mother smiling and caressing it, experiences a feeling of joy. The feeling, accompanied by unfeelable nerve movements, initiates muscular movements of its mouth and lips. The soul gives in to these impulses, and, assisting them spontaneously, produces the baby's smile.

400. We cannot therefore agree with Bichat, who denies animal life in the foetus and explains its movement as a simple expression of organic life.[183] We readily accept that the foetus' movements in the womb can start in the brain and nerves, and be stimulated by the sympathy between certain organs and the brain. But we maintain that these tiny movements and stimulations in the brain could never explain the large movements of the foetus and the very strong pressures it sometimes applies to the walls of the womb unless the soul itself, following the law of the sensuous instinct, were drawn into action to assist and increase the first small movements. When the soul performs such movements, it carries out a smaller action and needs less effort than when it omits the movements, granted that, if the soul remained inactive, it would experience something contrary to its nature. As we have seen, the soul is naturally so active throughout the whole body that the instinctive movement we are discussing is virtually included in the first activity itself, and depends on the law of activity which makes the soul naturally master of the body, and unwilling to suffer any loss of control.[184]

[183] *Ricerche fisiologiche intorno alla vita e alla morte*, pt. 1, art. 8.

[184] Sensists have made feeling a part of intelligence, and instinct a part of will. Seeing that the movements of the foetus and other animal movements could not be attributed to the will, they attributed them to the organic complex, without considering whether there might be something between organic life and the will. But if we observe nature carefully, we notice that the *pleasure-instinct* comes between *organic life* and the *will*. This instinct is not a part of the will but an essentially different faculty belonging to *animal life*.

10

NATURE'S *HEALING FORCES* ARISE FROM THE LIFE INSTINCT; DISRUPTIVE FORCES FROM THE SENSUOUS INSTINCT

401. We must postpone an explanation of the sensuous instinct's more complex actions, and deal with an important consequence of what has been said, namely, that the two primary, active animal faculties which we have called *life instinct* and *sensuous instinct* are the source of two kinds of forces which are occasionally opposed to each other: the *healing forces* of nature and the *disruptive* forces.

402. If this consequence had been carefully noted, the quarrel between Brown and the doctors who preceded him could have been solved. His opponents maintained as a certain principle that nature should be followed in the cure of diseases, because nature is endowed with a hidden power to restore what it has lost and to repair its disorders, and therefore never errs in its instincts. Brown claimed that sometimes nature erred, and consequently that its guidance should not be trusted. As proof he indicated the case of animals that have been starved for a long time: they refuse the food they need but will take water, which will only weaken them further.[185]

I believe that the constant tradition of medicine is true. There is a healing force in animal nature, and this force gives rise to a kind of infallible instinct which works to overcome illness and produce health. I also think that along with this healing power there is sometimes another force or instinct which disrupts the action of the first instinct, changing its healing effect into a harmful one.

403. I said that I deduce the *healing force* from the life instinct, and the *disruptive force* from the sensuous instinct. I do so as follows.

[185] I do not know if the example is sufficient proof. It is certain that water is not entirely lacking in nutrients, and that nature cannot be restored in one big jump; we have to build up gradually from a small beginning. People who have been frozen are treated in this way; if they were warmed all at once, they would die. Nature indicates this procedure by the natural desire for water; that is, we must begin with very light food and proceed gradually to solids.

The sole purpose of the *life instinct* in all its actions is to produce one, stimulated feeling. By doing so, it gives life to the body; it is essentially a vivifier. Perfect health is nothing more than perfect life. We said that the material forces of a body which has to receive life must be so harmoniously composed that they can receive without resistance the one, single action of the vivifying principle. Hence, if this harmonious composition is lacking, a struggle must ensue between the unbalanced, disorganised material forces, which are opposed to receiving the unity of life, and the soul trying to give them life. Thomas Campanella's opinion, which was later espoused by Stahl's followers, seems therefore to be reasonable. He said that fever must be considered as a war of the spirit against illness.[186] We, however, go further and say that war is present in all illness, because the soul tries to subjugate the body to its rule and give it the form of life. Not only fever but all symptoms and phenomena of illness come from this source.[187]

If we consider the matter carefully, there is no doubt that the soul cannot exercise its action unless the body is first disposed

186 François Boissier, of Sauvages, in his Theoria Febris (Montpellier, 1738), followed Stahl's teaching. According to him, fever is caused by the soul's efforts to remove the obstacles which deny it freedom of bodily movement. But it would be better to say that the soul tends to give the body that fullness of life which constitutes the purpose of the act by which the soul first informs the body. Campanella's opinion, written long before Stahl, can be seen in his *Medicina*, bks. 3 & 7.

187 The origin of pain is found here. Pain arises from the resistance encountered by the soul in its effort to animate the body and produce the unified, stimulated feeling. This opinion resembles that of Canaveri (cf. *Dell'Economia della Vitalità* in addition to his *Sul dolore*), who observed that our capacity to feel pain is increased by what weakens the body but decreased by what increases the vital energy. Pain robs us of sleep, appetite and the vigour of our limbs. He concluded, after many thorough investigations, that the efficient cause of pain is the diminution of vitality in some part. These observations confirm our opinion. According to us, whatever happens in any feeling also happens in the production of pain: two causes, the soul and the body, must operate. For the body to contribute to the production of pain, the conditions necessary for its animation must be present; otherwise, pain would be entirely foreign to it. The body must also lack one of the conditions which make it suitable for receiving the soul's action in all its fullness, an action which would give the body perfect health and impede any pain. Such an origin of pain explains the varying action of stimuli, the different kinds of pain, and the different levels and phenomena accompanying it.

[403]

to receive the action. The body's disposition consists in a fixed choice of principles and in suitable composition and organisation. Granted this, the soul simply gives the body a final, complementary act which constitutes the life it is capable of. The term to which the soul properly tends is that of giving this final act to the body, an act which certainly brings with it a complex of harmonious movements, a relevant mobility, tension, etc. But this final act requires preceding acts or (to use Tommasini's expression) *preparatory processes* as its condition. When the soul finds the body in imperfect possession of the preceding acts, it uses the same force with which it posits the body in the final act to impel the body to posit itself more perfectly in the preceding acts, of which the final act is a continuation and complement. The soul is helped in this by the wonderful compagination of parts prepared by the wise Author of the animal body.

We have said that the soul or feeling principle acts in the continuum (a necessary condition, as we have seen, for the existence of extended feeling). If we consider this carefully, we have no difficulty in attributing principally to this vital animal action the digestive, circulatory, secretory, absorbing and nutritive phenomena, in fact, all the phenomena of animal life.[188] Similarly, we have no difficulty understanding that a lesion in some part of the animal can immediately bring about a disruption in the circulation and all other bodily functions. In the same way we explain the extraordinary activity not only of remedies but also of poisons. We can also understand why a grain of tartar emetic or ipecacuanha, minute in proportion to the effect of its mechanical action, notably disrupts the whole body when taken orally. It is always the vital action of the soul that is affected and that reacts according to its laws. Because

[188] We have only to consider secretory phenomena for a moment to be convinced of what I am saying. All the excretory ducts, the stenonian, warthonian, choledoch, pancreatic, etc. have their orifices open on mucous surfaces in contact with many kinds of fluids which pass over or lie on the surfaces. However, the only fluids that penetrate the ducts are those suited to each duct. This wonderful, selective affinity between the ducts and the nature of the fluids cannot be explained by any mechanism or chemical affinity. Once the animal is dead, the activity of these ducts and fluids ceases. The effect is principally an effect of the vital act which the animal imparts to the organic body.

the soul has *extension* as the term of its action, it can make its energy simultaneously felt in many parts and organs.[189] But this energy is never harmful; it continually strives to bring the body to the act of greatest life.

404. If this energy is allowed to act unhindered, it never fails in its purpose, although its operation can be disrupted by the *sensuous instinct* which, as we have said, is the source of harmful animal forces.[190] The *sensuous instinct* is of course designed by nature to act in harmony with the *life instinct* and to help it in every way. We cannot doubt that it will act in this way, unless sense is defective or unduly stimulated. For example, smell and taste are clearly ordered by nature to inform animals of both suitable and unsuitable foods. Cattle at pasture distinguish principally by smell the poisonous grasses and avoid them. They rarely eat the tussock-grass that grows in great quantities in the Alps or the white hellebore that abounds in the fields of Piedmont. Even in the case of harmful grasses, cattle choose what best suits their species. Moreover, smell is used by the instinct of animals to guide them to medicinal plants. Dogs can be seen searching the countryside; they find and eat a plant which they normally never eat, and then they vomit and have diarrhea. But despite these harmful effects they are in better health. We cannot doubt that the sensuous instinct, in its normal state, helps and

[189] Stahl's followers went too far by making *will* intervene in everything (the faculty is completely absent in animals, which have only *instinct*), but others, like Joubert, also went too far by attributing everything to material forces. Joubert's opinions are reported by Sprengel in the sixth volume of his history of medicine. Furthermore, the following fact is clear proof that the soul intervenes in producing extraordinary effects of remedies: when the soul's action on the body is suspended, or better, greatly restricted (as happens with *cataleptics*), emetics and drastic remedies have no effect.

[190] We have seen that pain arises in the soul from its struggle to animate the body totally, while the body, because of some lesion or other absent condition, is not fully disposed to receive complete animation (cf. 403). But if the pain reaches a certain level, it can produce some disruption in the life instinct where it originates, and can thus damage health even more, particularly through the apprehension or general affection it causes in the animal. However, if the pain sometimes causes harm to the healthy state, we must note that everything the animal does as a result of this pain belongs to the *sensuous instinct*. It is therefore the *sensuous instinct* itself that causes disruption in the vital animal forces.

acts harmoniously with the life instinct in which it originates. What I am saying, however, is that this instinct is sometimes subject to generally momentary alterations which disrupt the action of the life instinct itself.

405. We should not be surprised at this. Although the sensuous instinct draws its energy from the life instinct, it has another purpose. The life instinct tends towards the fundamental feeling and produces it; the sensuous instinct tends to the enjoyment of the modifications of the fundamental feeling because they give it a more varied, intense pleasure. Properly speaking, the *end of animality*, that is, the enjoyment of the greatest delight possible, is to be found in this more intense and ever new pleasure extracted, so to speak, by modifying the fundamental feeling. Obviously the reckless, over-excited tendency to possess the extreme pleasure found in the modifications of the fundamental feeling can upset both the fundamental feeling itself and the action of the life instinct controlling the fundamental feeling, especially if the organic composite is already defective in some way. Similarly, the sensuous instinct, for the opposite reason, can be too violently stimulated and flee the consequent pain, which is also a modification of the fundamental feeling and animal nature's greatest evil. And because the effort to avoid the pain is so great, the vital activity can be upset. Hunger, for example, sometimes makes an animal eat something harmful. The stimulus drives it so hard that time is denied for the use of the senses which would allow it to avoid the danger. Hunger has been given as the reason why Swedish, but not Italian goats, devour tussock-grass.

406. We must investigate the action of the *sensuous instinct* and see how it can directly alter and harm the action of the *life instinct*.

It is true that this happens less frequently in animals than in humans whose intelligent principle gives an extraordinary impetus to the passions. It thus upsets the balance which, according to the wisdom of nature, ought to be continually maintained between the *sensuous* and *life instincts*. Although intelligence gives this unbridled thrust to the passions, which are acts of the sensuous instinct, the passions themselves are the proximate cause of the change that follows in the life instinct. In other words, feeling-instinct, not intelligence, is the sole remote cause.

Let us see how the sensuous instinct, by means of the different passions to which it is subject, disrupts and even entirely suspends or removes the action of the soul's life instinct.

407. Animal passions have mainly three sources: the external senses, the imagination and the association of the external senses with the imagination. By giving examples of three kinds of passion corresponding to these three sources, we can see how the sensuous instinct harms the functions of the life instinct.

Taste is one example of the *external senses* and is the source of the passion of greed; sadness is an example relative to the *imagination* and arises from a misfortune we imagine has happened but in fact has not; fear, or sudden terror caused in another, is an example of the *association of feeling with the imagination*. These three passions, *greed*, *sadness* and *fear* all belong to the sensuous instinct. Let us now examine the influence they have on the life instinct, whose beneficial action they can change or impede.

408. With regard to greed, we should note that an animal, when taking food, does not experience a feeling simply on its tongue or where the taste buds are located in its mouth. We tend to think solely of this feeling, but there is another feeling, unobserved and less local than the first, which seems to reach the entire nervous system or at least a large section of it.

In order to become aware of two simultaneous feelings, one local and the other general, which are aroused when food is taken, let us consider the effect of something sweet. If several people taste such a substance they will all say that it has a sweet taste. Their judgment is uniform, and therefore the substance is, relative to the local sensation of taste, the same for them all. But there will be some who like it, some who do not, and some in between. Simultaneously with the sweet sensation, therefore, which they all equally experienced, there is a different experience. The same can be said about a bitter substance: all will affirm the bitterness, but some will like it, others will not, in varying degree. The same will be true of any taste whatsoever.

Now, if only the simple, local sensation of taste is in question, it would seem that the sweet taste should please all, and the bitter no one. All evidently agree that the sweet taste considered purely in itself is pleasant, and the bitter unpleasant. This is so true that we usually accept 'sweet' as synonymous with 'pleasant'. We can conclude therefore that when people dislike a sweet taste but not a bitter taste, they do so not because they do not sense the sweet taste as pleasant, and the bitter as unpleasant, but because simultaneously with the final sensation of sweetness or bitterness in their mouths, there is another, contrary sensation which is propagated throughout all, or nearly all, the nervous system. This feeling is more universal, and because it pervades, as it were, the whole animal, it dominates the first, more restricted feeling. The animal, influenced by this stronger feeling, rejects the sweet taste not in itself but because of the almost hidden disturbance accompanying it, and chooses instead the bitter taste not in itself nor because it is bitter, but because the unpleasantness of the bitter taste in its mouth is compensated more than adequately by the pleasant taste diffused throughout the whole animal.

409. We must note that the feeling controlling the animal's good health is not the limited, local feeling of taste (this feeling merely indicates the effect produced by the substance in the taste buds of the mouth), but the other more widespread, less observable feeling, which follows the first. This more diffused feeling often reshapes and changes our judgments about the first feeling so authoritatively and decisively that our judgment about the local taste remains suppressed and unnoticed. Hence we say absolutely: 'I like the bitter taste', or: 'I do not like the sweet taste'. We do not say: 'I do not like the bitter taste in my mouth but I like it in its total effect all over me', or: 'I like the sweet taste on my tongue but not in my being as a whole'.

410. Therefore, when the feeling of universal pleasure or displeasure which follows the local sensation of touch prevails in the animal, the sensuous instinct of taste is in total harmony with and subservient to the life instinct. Vice versa, the sensuous instinct disrupts and harms the life instinct in its functions when the former follows the false indication of taste rather than the taste which, after the taking of food, is an indication of the total feeling, and a firm guide of what helps or harms the animal.

When an animal is perfect, as nature generally makes it, it is never deceived in its taste. Its sensuous instinct constantly takes the total feeling as its guide. This latter feeling can be called the *alimentary sense*,[191] and guides the sick animal to foods with an

191 Here we can also see the advantage of simple, natural foods and the disadvantage of mixed foods. The *alimentary sense* is obviously present in

insipid or unpleasant taste which it does not usually eat. The first effects in such a case are vomiting and diarrhea which upset the animal at first but finally restore it to health.[192]

411. The *taste* sensation, however, can and often does prevail over the *alimentary sensation*. This happens principally or solely in human beings due to the passion of greed. The sensuous instinct is deceived and, as the source of all the evils of intemperance, does great harm to the life instinct.

412. We pass now to passions arising from the imagination. The activity of the imagination is a branch of the activity of the sensuous instinct, and nobody can be ignorant of the effects of the imagination on our bodily health.

There can be few diseases in which the imagination is not involved, to both the harm and advantage of sick people. I shall take one case only, rabies. It is generally known that rabies sometimes develops through the action of the phantasy stimulated by belief in having been bitten by a mad dog. Such an illness can then be cured by the contrary persuasion.

Dr. Barbantini, of Lucca, described a case that took place in 1817. A 23-year-old hunter called Carmassi had a dog which was attacked by another dog. When Carmassi seized his dog by the tail and tried to pull it from the fight, the dog turned and bit him slightly in the leg. At first, the young man paid no heed to the wound, but later, noticing blood, he washed it and covered it with a medicinal herb. Three days later the wound was dry, and Carmassi decided to go hunting the next day. However, because the dog had disappeared he began to think it had rabies. The next day he was depressed and avoided his friends. Symptoms of rabies, particularly the abhorrence of water, started to appear. In the evening he heard that different people had been

simple foods and allows us to know which substances are healthy or harmful. But in the case of mixed foods the indication of the alimentary sense is confused, because the different foods of the mixture conflict with each other.

[192] A similar phenomenon can be observed in animals in the case of other senses also. Animals sometimes submit to actions that are painful to some part of their body because a universal sense informs them that such actions are helpful. The well-known lion which had a thorn removed from its paw must have felt an acute pain at the time of the extraction, but nevertheless allowed the action and later showed its gratitude to the slave who had done the good deed.

bitten by a mad dog in a neighbouring village. He became more upset, told everyone to leave, and refused all human contact. On the fifth day some people who had gone to the house because of the great noise he was making found him deranged and grasping his rifle. The local doctor arrived. Although Carmassi knew him well, he was frightened and asked who the doctor was. Eventually, after alternating bouts of dark gloom and violence, Carmassi was bound. His fits continued for two days, and he neither ate nor drank; he made an effort to drink but as soon as the liquid touched his mouth he violently threw it away. On the ninth day his dog was found, in perfect health. The sick man would not believe it and asked to see the animal before he died. With great joy the dog jumped on to the bed of his master and showed his affection in the usual way. Carmassi calmed down, and slowly regained his health. After four days he was ready to go hunting again.[193] In this case, we clearly see how the *sensuous instinct* disrupted the functions of the *life instinct*.

413. The next case of fear is an example of the passions that arise through the association of the external senses and the phantasy. It is another factual proof of the power of the sensuous instinct not only to disturb but, when stimulated in an extraordinary way, to suspend in great part the action of the life instinct. It is a case of catalepsy recently suffered by a certain Karl Haag, who was cured in the Viennese military hospital of the Emperor Joseph Academy. The case was widely reported in the newspapers of 1823 and 1824.

On the 6th June 1823, this 33-year-old had a fit. As I have said, such an experience or passion concerns the sensuous instinct. In this case it caused the patient to lose completely the faculty of moving his muscles, a faculty belonging to the life instinct. His limbs remained fixed in the position in which others placed them. For three months he kept his eyes rigidly open, then, for sixteen months, firmly closed, unable to make the least movement. Tears

[193] Cf. the *Giornale di Fisica, Chimica, Storia naturale, Medicina, ecc.* of professors Brugnatelli, Brunacci and Configliacchi, Pavia, 1817, vol. 10. Dr. Barbantini notes in his story that in the majority of known cases of delayed rabies the imagination is stimulated by the memory of some earlier, forgotten bite. He says this applied to the case discussed by Chirac and mentioned by the translator of Weikard's *Elementi di medicina pratica*, vol. 6.

sometimes filled his eyes and his pale cheeks flushed when his illness was discussed in his presence. He could take no liquid food.[194] The life instinct had suspended the action of his body in the case of the faculty of voluntary movements, and even generally, in the case of external sensations, but it continued to perform the essential functions of life, such as circulation, respiration, maintenance of natural heat, perspiration, etc. After nearly a year and a half of this almost total suspension of the action of the sensuous instinct, the invalid began to show signs of returning sensation. He slowly emerged from his deep coma and began to move, but speech returned only later and with great difficulty. The life instinct, therefore, regained control of certain muscles before others, and then finally its full activity which had been suspended for so long. In the end he returned to full health.[195]

All this indicates that the sensuous instinct can be excessively stimulated, and that this excessive action can disrupt, suspend and completely block out the action of the life instinct.[196] The sensuous instinct, therefore, is the origin of the forces we have

194 What happened in many other cases of catalepsy also happened in this case: the strongest stimulants such as cantharides, opium, valerian, volatile massages as well as emetics and other drastic internal remedies were ineffective. This shows that the medicinal activity of the remedies is due to the *co-operation of the soul's life instinct*, as I said earlier (cf. 403). When this co-operation ceases, the only activity left to the medicines is their mechanical or chemical forces. I generally call these forces *material activity*, an activity which is very limited in its effects when compared with the effect resulting from the association of these material forces with the life principle.

195 The two following incidents concerning birds illustrate the effect of terror in animals. After a cat had frightened a blackbird in its cage, the person who went to its aid found it lying on its back, bathed in sweat. Later its feathers fell out, to be replaced by perfectly white feathers. In the other case, a linnet bit the finger of a drunken man, who took it out of its cage and pulled out all its feathers. The poor bird survived, but grew white feathers (Bibliot. Ital., Dec. 1831).

196 Note that the action is not only partly suspended but entirely *removed*. Pliny the Younger relates (bk. 7, lett. 30; bk. 9, lett. 12) that a certain Publicius died as a result of his imagination: the man seemed to see Pliny attacking him with a dagger. Theodoric is said to have died from terror at the sight of a fish head served to him. He thought it was the head of Symmmachus whom he had had put to death. We all know that passions can reach a point where they cause death, and passions, as I have said, are always acts of the *sensuous instinct*.

called 'disruptive' of animal life, and they should be seriously investigated by professors of medicine.

414. It is not within the scope of this work to examine the many ways in which the sensuous instinct can disrupt the action of the life instinct, although research of this kind would be most worthwhile. Instead, we shall conclude this chapter with the following comment. The relationship between the soul's *sensuous activity* and *life activity* is new proof that both these activities proceed from a single, unique principle and derive from the primitive act itself by which the soul exists, except that one proceeds from the other as a second act proceeds from a first.

415. To repeat: it is not extraordinary that the sensuous activity, although principally derived from the life activity, should have great influence over the latter. By acting on the organisation which is a condition of the life instinct, the sensuous instinct exerts a indirect influence on the life instinct.

11

A FURTHER EXPLANATION OF THE ACTIVITY OF THE SENSUOUS INSTINCT

Article 1. The conditions required for a satisfactory explanation of the activity of the sensuous instinct

416. We have to return now to the promised explanation of the more complicated activities of the sensuous instinct (cf. 401). This is undoubtedly a formidable task, and we are well aware of the difficulties we shall encounter.

The most serious difficulty becomes obvious when we consider that the explanation of the more complicated activities of the sensuous instinct has to be given without reference to intelligence and will. This is the first condition for any satisfactory explanation, although as far as I am aware it is not adhered to by those investigating the cause of animal activities. Normally, authors arbitrarily attribute some role to intelligence and will even in animals and, in doing so, eliminate the major difficulties encountered in positing the true cause of animal phenomena. In my opinion this is a very serious mistake. The concept of brute animal (which is the contrary of rational animal) totally excludes the light of reason together with all cognition and, consequently, every aspect of will (which, as a power operating according to what is already known, presupposes cognition).

417. The difficulty experienced in explaining the activities of animal sensuous instinct begins, therefore, with the first step in the investigation, that is, the formation of a correct concept of animal itself. As human beings, we use our intelligence to carry out many of the activities done by animals without intelligence. Hence, we can scarcely conceive mentally of a being entirely enclosed within the limitations of corporeal feeling and the instinctive activity which is the spontaneous effect of feeling.

418. In undertaking this difficult task, let us, therefore, first carefully examine the conditions required to explain satisfactorily the marvels of animal activity.

We see immediately that animal activities are not casual, disordered movements. Although taking place at various levels of complexity, these movements harmonise in an extraordinary manner and tend towards some purpose. A suitable and satisfactory explanation of these activities must therefore take into account: 1. the way in which such movements can originate from feelings; 2. the way in which the animal, without any trace of intelligence, can produce such suitably ordered movements for a given aim. The explanation of animal activity involves, therefore, two questions: How does motion arise? How does this motion attain a purpose? Both questions must be answered without reference to intelligence and will. If these conditions are not respected, the phenomena of sensuous instinct cannot be explained.

Article 2.
The general cause of spontaneous animal movement

419. The first of our two questions has partly been dealt with (cf. 394–400). As we said, the stimulus producing the sensation

by irritating the nerves is also the cause of incipient movements in the nerves themselves. These initial movements draw the sensuous principle into action and this in turn, by prolonging its action spontaneously, propagates and develops these extremely delicate movements throughout larger parts of the body. In my opinion, the initial movement of the nerves occasioned by a sensation is the general principle underlying every movement produced by the sensuous instinct .

The first feeling is the fundamental feeling. The movements permanently connected with the fundamental feeling are vital movements such as circulation. This is not sufficient, however, to explain spontaneous, partial movement in animals which, according to the principle laid down, requires a modification of the fundamental feeling, that is a new, acquired feeling, as we have called it.

The animal would remain perpetually immobile relative to these new, spontaneous movements if there were no new modification affecting the nervous system. This modification, which does not have its cause in the animal sense itself, must be a principle foreign to the animal and of such a kind that it produces new nerve movements parallel to the new feelings. Consequently the first cause of the instinctive movements we are considering cannot come from the animal itself; it must come from elsewhere. There is no necessity for supposing that the animal moves itself, which would certainly require the use of some kind of will. A sufficient explanation will be found in an excitatory stimulus foreign to the animal.

When animal activity has been brought into action through this foreign impulse or stimulus, it continues to act through the law of inertia, of which we have spoken. Far more is needed to explain cessation of action already present in the animal than would be required to explain how it continues in action.

420. We must now consider the law governing the propagation of spontaneous movement. In propagating itself, this movement increases through a harmonious alternation of feeling and movement. Let us imagine a local sensation. This produces nervous tremors, or some kind of extremely delicate movements in the affected nerve. In turn, these movements arouse and excite the soul to sensation which the soul spontaneously seconds and develops. This spontaneous action of the soul immediately gives rise to further propagation of the

tiny movements. The laws of movement then insure that the parts moved by the soul come into forceful contact with adjacent or contiguous parts and through mechanical laws cause them to move. This produces new stimulation for the soul which is now drawn to apply its spontaneity to these movements. In this way, the material impulse given to the parts near those already moved by the soul comes back to the soul as more and more parts are aroused and in turn make themselves felt. The minimal, hidden, imperceptible movements gradually develop, spread out and multiply.

Let us take a war-horse as an example. As soon as it hears the sound of the trumpet, the horse begins to tremble all over, even if it has never been in battle. If it is an experienced war-horse, its movements are accentuated. Obviously we can distinguish the local sensation of sound from the general movement coursing through the animal. The first movement aroused by the sound in the acoustic organ is definitely minimal. The spontaneity of the soul, stimulated by the rapid, frequent movements of the nerves governing hearing, immediately renders the movement spontaneous and amplifies them in a marvellous way. The reinforced movements then act forcefully upon the adjacent parts surrounding them, while these, having received movement mechanically, act upon the soul either by drawing or forcing it into further action. The soul, which cannot withstand the new pressure put upon it, frees itself from strain by seconding the movements it receives. These then become spontaneous, and lose all oppressive tendencies. This in turn maintains movement, which would otherwise soon cease, and indeed extends it throughout the parts. By degrees, but with extreme rapidity, both movement and agitation is generated throughout the horse which responds with all the alertness required for battle.

421. It seems likely that every local feeling gives rise in some way to this kind of propagation of sense and movement. In all probability it is also at the origin of that obscure, but extremely efficacious feeling (which we called *alimentary*, cf. 408–411) constantly accompanying the local sensation of taste.

Tracing the propagation of local feeling throughout the whole animal would provide a very rewarding field for highly skilled investigation. Each of the more obvious feelings would have to be studied individually. For example, a given scent pleases some and displeases others. The local sense and the scent are the same, but the feeling diffused by the scent — and usually inadverted to — is very different. This causes it to be pleasing to some, but not to others. The qualities of the diffused feeling are widely different, and too refined to be easily noticeable, but in a hidden way are very effective. They dispose the animal for different experiences and incline it in different ways. A pain, for example, will render one person reflective, others sad or joyful, or affected in similar ways even independently of the association of ideas.

422. An equally delicate field for research, connected with that already suggested, would be to follow the propagation of the minimal nerve movements dependent upon the stimulation and movement of the various local interior or exterior senses. The aim would be to determine the progress of movement from different starting points in the nervous system, and explain how the final movement was propagated in perfect harmony with the nature of the minimal movements received in the stimulated nerve.

For example, the researcher could try to explain why multiple, varied movements, rather than a single movement, are produced by sound, as we see in the case of the war horse. Because sound depends upon a certain number of air waves, the movements received by the acoustic organ (movements which cannot be reduced to a single movement) vary in an orderly way according to the different impulses of air. A tremor, and perhaps a contraction, is produced in the horse. The nerves, vibrated by frequent movements, must cause the varied, agitated and frequent movements in the animal. Movements dependent upon rhythmic sound will give rise to dancing, by retaining and reproducing on a larger scale the wonderful order already invisibly present in the first nerve movements.

423. Let me make an observation on the feeling and effects of ticklishness, a phenomenon which perhaps has not yet been properly explained. Tickling begins with the stimulation of many tiny, multidirectional movements in the cutaneous organ. We should keep in mind what was said about the spontaneity of the soul which, on feeling some movement in a part of the body, co-operates in the movement spontaneously in order to free itself of pressure that it would otherwise be unable to sustain. Given the innumerable, tiny, conflicting movements, the soul must be in a state of great agitation as it strives to follow them and make

themallspontaneous. New movements, taking place before the soul has time to respond to the previous stimuli, would give rise to contrasting activities and motions, and to convulsive movements (which are truly contrasting movements) first expressed in laughter, and then widely propagated. It is not improbable that these mutually opposed movements found in tickling, and generally in convulsions, could be sufficient to kill a person. Nor is there any doubt that the special constitution of the cutaneous organ, in which the most delicate nerve endings are to be found, plays a great part in this strange, complicated phenomenon.

424. The same kind of research into the propagation of movements arising from nerve disturbance simultaneous with feeling should be applied to the problem of 'shared feeling' (or 'sympathy'). Doctors use this phenomenon to indicate the extension of pain or disease in widely spaced parts of the human body, but it is not known if the phenomenon is founded in the anatomical connection of the nerves and muscles, or whether the life and sensuous instincts of the soul have some part in it, as would in fact seem certain. As we know, the unity and continuity of the soul permit it to act of its own power simultaneously in places distant from one another.

425. But undertaking such research would take us too far from the scope of this book. For our purposes it is sufficient to have indicated and demonstrated the general principle according to which the soul exploits feeling in order to impart movement to the muscles. We should note, however, that what has been said is valid for all feelings, internal and external. Consequently, we should apply the principle of spontaneous movement to phantasy images, which also give rise to movements in the way we have described. This would explain why a war-horse already accustomed to battle would be more daring under the direction of its rider than a horse which had not experienced the din of war.

Article 3.
Explanation of the continuation of the movement produced by the sensuous instinct

426. What has been said explains the origin of movement from

feeling, and the development and propagation of movement from minimum to maximum. But the propagation of movement must finally reach a limit beyond which harmony and spontaneous action ceases in the soul. Our explanation would seem insufficient, therefore, to explain cases in which the duration of movement appears to transcend this limit as, for example, when an animal in its eagerness to prolong some pleasure continues to act.

It seems to me that this persistence in continuing pleasurable activity has to be sought in the animal's *synthetic* or *unitive* power which in its simplicity joins the animal's *act* with the *pleasure* it receives from this act. Just as the animal naturally remains in a pleasurable state, so it perseveres with its act which, associated with pleasure, becomes a single thing for the soul perceiving this unity.

427. The soul's unitive power must also be the origin of the animal's effort to reinforce its act as it strives to reproduce and strengthen the degree of pleasure it receives. Experience reveals to the animal, which is directed by its apprehension of the whole scale of degrees of intensity, that its pleasure increases according to the intensity of effort that it devotes to its act. This apprehension in the animal generates sensuous expectation of something similar in the future — and it does indeed seem that the animal connects the past with the future in this way. In other words, the animal's successive experience is re-presented in its sense-faculty as 'something unified', from which arises the *sensuous expectation* already mentioned as the cause of continued movement and of the reiterated action the soul puts into movement. The sense-faculty itself achieves this synthesis of feelings, by joining within its own unity 1. both the action which produces and the pleasure which accompanies movement; and 2. the successive degrees of intensity of movement which it feels actively, and the growing intensity of pleasure, which it feels passively. And even this multiple apprehension is an incitement to further movements. It is an animal affection, the basis and principle of constantly growing movement through which the animal maintains itself in spontaneous movement towards pleasure.

428. This affection, the total effect of all the animal's feelings, cannot be one of the particular feelings which serve to make up the affection and act as its source. It is a unique affection

springing up from all these feelings; it entirely dominates the animal as the animal moves and contributes to the continuation and increase of its own pleasurable movement. A good example of this can be seen in the baby's way of feeding at the mother's breast.

First, the baby feels the act by which its lips strain on the nipple. This act, although composed of simultaneous movements of fauces, lungs and other parts of the body, is a single, very simple act for the baby whose partial efforts and movements are unified by means of the animal *unitive power*. The result in the baby is a single, simple, internal action. Along with the feeling of its activity, the baby has pleasant feelings arising from the flow of milk into its body and from the nourishment it receives. This, too, is made into a single feeling by the unity of the animal although it can be analysed into as many partial feelings as there are parts renewed by the feed, and nerves stimulated by pleasure.

The animal's unitive power, which has made a single, internal, original action of the many external actions, and a single, internal, final feeling of the many external feelings, now apprehends in a single, very simple act both the active feeling of its internal, universal action and the passive feeling of its internal, universal pleasure. As a result, the animal finally possesses in the depths of its being a single feeling (active and passive) of these two complex feelings. This final apprehension and feeling, the deepest of all feelings, informs the animal essence, and provides the principle of instinctive movement which, although simple in itself, extends its effects to several powers. Various parts are then moved simultaneously by a single thrust or pressure or slight internal movement. Each part or power, according to its own nature, receives and shares in the movement to the extent of the impulse given by the animal element to its internal parts, which are the first to participate in the stimulus arising from the unification and final completion of so many simultaneous feelings in the single feeling just described. In the same way, the movements of the act of sucking, of which the animal element has an active feeling, and the pleasurable sensations of the milk in the body, are prolonged and repeated as they succeed one another with varying degrees of intensity. This gradual succession of actively felt movements and of passive feelings is also unified internally by the animal unitive force which makes of the succession a single (active-passive) feeling and apprehension. The animal element, either by continuing or reinforcing the movement, perseveres with this single apprehension as long as pleasure lasts. In other words, it continues what it has begun, and according to its experience gradually adds to it. In this way, *time* (as something *feelable*, not as a *concept*), although successive externally, is simplified in internal animal apprehension. A single internal feeling extends to embrace an entire succession; from that single feeling, movement expands in a simple act to produce a whole succession and progression of multiple acts [*App.*, no. 7].

429. This whole artifact of feelable nature is necessary if the baby is simply to carry out the apparently easy task of feeding at the breast. One defect in the activities of the *unitive force*, however, would be sufficient to impede proper feeding. We would have to say that the difficulty in breast-feeding experienced by the cases of mentally defective children in Switzerland depends upon some defect in the unitive force. This would also account for their general difficulty and imperfection relative to first needs. When ten years old, these children are still incapable of putting food in their mouths and chewing it, so that they have to be subject to forced feeding.

Article 4.
Explanation of the order found in movements of the sensuous instinct which are commonly believed to depend for their formation on some degree of reason

430. The two preceding articles have clarified the *origin* of animal movements, which require neither a rational nor a volitive principle. We saw that animal *spontaneity* is aroused by two causes: 1. the need felt by the animal to avoid any painful state such as that of resistance or inaction in one of its living members when this is moved; 2. the tendency the animal feels to prolong and enhance any state of pleasure experienced in some determined activity.

Whichever of the two causes is operative, the principle of movement depends upon animal passivity which arouses itself to movement only through the intervention of some outside cause or impulse. This *passivity* then stimulates *spontaneous activity* in the animal. But once aroused, spontaneous activity continues and itself becomes a cause of new movement. In turn this movement becomes a stimulus to spontaneity, and a circular operation, combined with increasing interchange of *movement* and stimulus, takes effect. This explains the growth and endurance of animal movements.

The first of the two causes (by which the soul seconds the nerve movements) explains directly how the underlying spontaneous movement begins; the second (by which the soul perseveres in pleasurable action) provides a particular explanation for the expansion and *continuation* of movement.

But all this is not sufficient to explain the phenomena of the sensuous instinct. As we have said, it is not enough to indicate how movements can manifest themselves in the animal. We have to go further and show *why* these animal movements arise with such order, harmony and cohesion that they obtain some useful purpose for the animal itself. These movements are so far-seeing and wise that we are almost persuaded of their direction by some extraordinary intelligence. Perhaps this is the greatest difficulty in explaining adequately the functions of the sensuous instinct. Certainly, it is a field of philosophy still quite unexplored by mankind.

This does not discourage us, however, but provides greater impetus as we find ourselves in such fruitful, uncultivated territory. And we can hope for greater understanding and indulgence from the learned in this area where even to attempt such a beautiful, but arduous task, calls for sympathy.

§1. Three causes explaining order in the functions of the sensuous instinct

431. First, I need to describe my approach to the problem. I do not believe that the order noted in the various movements of the sensuous instinct depends upon any light of reason in the animal, nor that it can be explained by positing a single cause. This order springs from three distinct principles

which,taken together, can only show how the wonderful *order*, present in each and every complex animal operation, is generated.

The first principle by which animal movements attain such order must be found, I think, in the *natural order of* external *stimuli* and their consequent actions which incite the animal and produce in it the first movements.

The second principle positing order in animal movements must be sought in the *construction and cohesion of the animal body* which is characterised in all its parts with exquisite harmony and pre-established concord amongst its movements as they work to the advantage of the animal itself.

Finally, the third principle necessary for the order in animal operations is the nature of the spontaneous activity of the animal itself.

432. Therefore:

1st. There is something *foreign* to the animal which originates its movements. This consists in the natural or artificial stimuli which cause sensations and movements in the animal.

2nd. There is something *in the animal body* which orders the animal's movements. This is the harmony of forces and parts making up the body.

3rd. There is also something in the *soul itself* of the animal which orders and governs animal functions.

All three causes of order in animal operations have the wisdom of the Creator as their primary source. He imposes order upon all things — an order in inanimate matter, an order in the living body and a more wonderful order again in the feeling, animating principle, that is, the soul.

We have to speak about all three principles or causes of order. But we must preface our remarks with a comment.

433. As we have seen, the *movements* under discussion are always a consequence and effect of preceding *feelings*. If order is present in the movements, it has to be found previously in the feelings. As a result, we have to say that if the three causes of order put order in our movements, as we have indicated, they also posit it first in the feelings. We shall see this as we discuss each cause in turn.

§2. The first cause of order in animal movements: the order found in external stimuli arousing the animal to feeling and movement

434. We hinted at this cause when we showed that the order arising in dancing depends upon the order of sounds aroused in the acoustic organ. In turn, the order of the sounds depends upon the order of air waves which strike and stimulate that organ (cf. 396–400, 422–424). The same could be said about almost all animal movements. They always have an *order of succession* relative to the time in which they are distributed.

All natural stimuli at work in the animal follow certain immutable laws: day succeeds night; the seasons follow one another continually; each day brings an almost regular series of degrees of temperature, of atmospheric qualities, or wind direction, of electrical conditions in surrounding bodies, of cycles to which the animal body is itself subject. The supremely wise Author of nature has harmonised everything so that each has its role in bestowing a certain order on animal movements.

Even the animal body, accustomed to producing movements at appropriate times, offers well-ordered stimuli to itself and other animals living with it. The animal, finding this order satisfying, perseveres in it because the order is advantageous and pleasurable; disorder is odious, and avoided by instinct.

§3. The second cause of order: the harmony existing between the different parts and forces of the body

435. The wonderful harmony found between the different parts and forces constituting and activating the animal body also has a role in establishing order. The parts and forces of a body combine so well that a given feeling must be accompanied by a definite movement (simple or complex) extremely useful to the animal itself. Let us consider a few facts illustrating this harmony.

If we obstruct an animal's breathing by tying something around its neck, the animal is immediately stimulated by instinct to use its paws in an effort to remove the restriction; if we secure an animal by the leg, and impede its freedom of movement, the animal tries to bite through the rope. A blindfolded dog has no peace until it succeeds in shaking off the blindfold. Animals instinctively lick a wound or a sore; irritation induces scratching. At teething a baby compresses and rubs its gums with its fingers and other bodies to ease the arrival of the new teeth, and so on.

There is no doubt that these and many other facts depend upon a single principle determining the animal to such well-ordered and useful actions. And we shall see later the significant part played in this by spontaneity and especially by the animal's *unitive power*. In the meantime, it is easy to see that animal spontaneity is considerably aided in its operation by the harmony according to which each organ works to the advantage of the others.

436. It is the physiologists' task to determine the amount of influence exerted in this way. I think, however, that their investigations and experiments will finally produce the following result: 'Where an organ is injured or impeded in its function, the other organs join in a series of movements directed towards the distressed organ. These movements are stimulated by the local pain, suitably affecting the nerve-endings and eventually the entire nervous system.' Such united movements are founded, I maintain, in the distribution of the material forces used by the life principle to help the animal's well-being. This movement, at once material and vital, is then perfected by the sensuous instinct for which the first material and life movements have to serve as a common stimulus. These operations, therefore, have a specific place: first, the dispositions of the material forces posit an element of order in the functions; another element is then added by the life instinct; finally, a third element, which subsumes and perfects the first two, is derived from the sensuous instinct.

437. This final cause, drawing the various animal movements to act advantageously for the animal, could also be illustrated by reference to lesions affecting different parts of the animal, and by observing the laws according to which the lesions remove or disturb the harmony already established by the wisdom of the Creator of animate being.

438. The order existing between the parts of the body (mechanical harmony), and between its forces (dynamic harmony), protect the animal against lesions and disturbance by simultaneously

stimulating and directing the movements of the two instincts. But it also assists the animal's well-being in numerous other ways.

If the nose were not situated near the mouth, or did not possess a strict relationship and continuity with the palate and oesophagus, animals could scarcely be directed in their choice of healthy foods by smell. The association of the two senses of taste and smell explain many facts which at first sight could make us believe that animals, in their choice of food, were furnished with extraordinary intelligence. The association of these two senses is considerably assisted by their nearness to one another. This proximity depends only upon the wisdom of the Creator in connecting the parts of the animal which have to help one another mutually.

When one bird sings, all sing. And in general animals reply to sounds that they hear. We imagine, perhaps, that they are speaking to one another. It is clear that these phenomena would never take place if the vocal organs were not situated near the acoustic organs, or at least if they did not have some connection with one another. The connection and proximity of nerves causes the air which strikes and disturbs the acoustic nerves to initiate simultaneously movements of the nerves and muscles affecting the voice. Indeed, the movements of the acoustic nerve stimulate and start corresponding movements in the vocal organs — movements completed by the spontaneity to which they give rise and from which the voice proceeds.

The preludes to generative action are due to the physical, dynamic connection between the generative apparatus and the nerves of the eye and touch, their various movements and corresponding image-phantasies.

In a word, every single animal function, however wonderful and complicated, depends in great part on the order present in the arrangement of the body. This order necessarily results in variously ordered and extremely wise animal actions without our needing to presuppose intelligence of any sort in the animal.

§4. The third cause of order: the nature of the animal's own spontaneous activity

439. Finally, the nature of the animal's very own spontaneous activity is the third, chief principle giving rise to the order of

operations of the sensuous instinct which appear to depend upon reason.

Animal spontaneity has its own determined properties, and is subject to fixed laws. As a result, its operations naturally bear the mark, as it were, of these properties and laws, and of the regularity and marvellous order dependent upon them.

The properties and laws of spontaneous animal activity are profound, and would require lengthy study even for a tentative development. I shall confine myself, therefore, simply to mentioning them sufficiently for an adequate understanding of our present work.

440. The laws of spontaneous animal activity are principally derived from three sources:

1st. From the condition of the organic body to which spontaneous activity is tied in its operations. — The laws deriving from this source are highly mysterious; and effective work on them will have been achieved (even though they remain unexplained) when they are accurately described, and their existence is well established by factual observation.

2nd. From the *inertia* to which the spontaneity of the sense-instinct is subject.

3rd. Finally, from the *synthetic* or unitive *force* of the animal.

I
Laws of spontaneous activity in the soul arising from the union between soul and body

441. The soul, because of its adhesion to the organic body, is subject to many extraordinary laws. In particular, its spontaneous operations proceed with the same degree of regularity as that manifested in the state of its body.

We have already noted that the more perfect animals are twofold, that is, composed of duplicated parts, more or less equal, at least relative to the principal organs of feeling. Moreover, the greater the conformity between both parts, the more distinct and perfect the animal's feelings. In the same way, perfect imagination depends to a large extent on equality between the two hemispheres of the brain. An injury to one, or even inequality between them, causes confusion and disturbance of the judgment which of course depends upon material provided by judgments associated with cerebral movements. But if inequality in the brain hemispheres, say, causes defective images, it is clear that equality between the hemispheres leads on the other hand to regularity in the operations of the soul.[197] The same can be said about any lesion in the brain or in the nerves. The nature itself of the complex being formed by body and soul, and the nature itself of the union, conceal a law according to which the operations of the soul are determined in one way rather than another. A reason explaining order lies in this law.

442. But the laws to which the soul's activity is subject as a result of the action it receives from corporeal nature differ in their depth and wonder. Some are of the utmost delicacy. For example, let me remind the reader of the phenomenon of residuary colours. If I fix my eye for some time on a red object, and then suddenly look at something black, I see a bluish-green tint in it. If instead I first look at something orange, my eye then sees purple where the black is. If the pupil is affected by something greenish-yellow, the impression becomes violet when we place ourselves in darkness. On the other hand, if the eye has looked for some time at bluish-green and is then placed in the dark, it sees red. Likewise, purple looked at intensely is changed into orange in the eye, and violet into greenish-yellow.

Moreover, if the eye has been fixed for a long time on something white, and is then plunged into total darkness, the white sensation changes after a short period into different colours until it vanishes. First, the white sensation changes to yellow, then to red, purple, blue and finally green, when it disappears. Such a phenomenon shows clearly that the optic nerve is engaged in an action which changes in determined ways. To each of these changes corresponds a different sensation in the soul.

Now it is obvious that there must be a natural order amongst the colours themselves, that is, an order founded in the physical nature of the sensations if there is: 1. a stable law according to

[197] Dr. Miraglia, in a paper read to the medical section of the 7th Italian Congress (Naples, 1845) maintained: 'If the action of an entire hemisphere, or part of it, is altered, the exercise of all the functions is necessarily disturbed; but if the action, either of the entire hemisphere or part of it, is annihilated, activity is concentrated in the other hemisphere' (Cf. Polto, *Relazione dei lavori, ecc.*, t. 53, 54).

which movement (the condition of the retina affected by light) changes; and 2. another law according to which the soul modifies the action it posits in receiving the sensation of colours.

But colours are feelings and, as we said, where there is order in feelings, there must be order in movements deriving from them. The action of the feeling soul, relative both to the life instinct and to the sensuous instinct, receives a determined order from the profound, hidden laws resulting from the union of soul and body.

It may indeed be impossible for us to offer a principle, or first reason, to explain the source of these laws, but it is sufficient to have verified them carefully through experience and observation of the facts. Who can say why the nature of things is what it is? Does not this nature depend in the end on the eternal, *intrinsic order of being*?

II

Laws of spontaneous activity in the soul arising from inertia

443. The activity of the feeling soul is also regulated and ordered in its operations by laws arising from *inertia*. It is scarcely necessary for me to say that by inertia I understand the soul's disposition for remaining in a given state, or for persevering with a given action until an exterior cause makes it change state or action.

444. Both *inertia* and *spontaneity* are present in the soul. The latter tempers the former. Inertia maintains the soul in the same action until a foreign cause produces change; spontaneity provides the soul with an aptitude for changing its state or action, without resistance on the part of the soul, as soon as a foreign cause moves the soul.

445. Matter is *inert* and lacking in spontaneity. Hence it resists any force wishing to change its state of rest to one of motion, or its state of motion to one of rest, or to change a state of lesser motion into one of greater motion, and vice versa.

The feeling soul, which is simultaneously endowed with *inertia* and *spontaneity* needs on the one hand some exterior cause to induce it to change state. On the other hand, if this cause is present, it gently follows its invitation without resistance.

As we said, this arises because the first act of the soul's life instinct[198] operates continually upon the body (cf. 371–384). In this initial act,

[198] Our *life instinct* corresponds exactly to Hippocrates' ενορμον.

the soul possesses an impulse towards all future movements. The impulse, however, remains undetermined to any particular movement. Consequently, it does not move; it lacks a sufficient reason determining it to one rather than another movement. The universal impulse to all movements and all directions involves an equilibrium impeding movement in any specific direction.

Hence the causes drawing the soul to move the members of the body do not, properly speaking, provide the soul with motion, as happens in matter, but only with some determination towards motion. As a result, the soul is said to cause movement *spontaneously*, although we also attribute to it inertia in so far as it needs an external cause to determine it.

446. With these clarifications in mind, we see that inertia provides certain laws regulating and ordering the instinctive movements of the soul.

The two principal laws are:

1st. The soul determines itself to those movements which give it most natural pleasure.

2nd. The soul determines itself to and prefers, other things being equal, those movements which it can perform more easily.

The first law appertains to the soul's *feeling*, the second to its *activity*. Both correspond to the two causes we have already assigned to spontaneous movement, that is, the need to avoid disturbance, and to pursue pleasure (cf. 426–429).

447. Careful analysis shows that these laws are mutually inclusive: it must naturally be more *pleasurable* for the soul to do what is easier, and easier to do what is more pleasurable. But I have made two propositions of this one law because pleasure is sometimes found towards the end of an act, and effort at the beginning. Moreover, *ease* and *pleasure* can be considered from different points of view, and thus become the sources of more particular laws about the soul's activity. But we have no time to enumerate these laws here.

448. We note only that *pleasure* and *ease* are qualities sought by the soul of its very nature. They are rooted in the soul's *inertia* and spontaneity. *Spontaneity* tends towards what is pleasurable; inertia towards what is easy.

449. It is clear that these two laws must posit some order in the animal's instinctive movements. One result of the laws is that the soul is moved to choose whatever is easiest and most pleasurable; it does not operate by chance, nor is it indifferent to a

choice of movements. We might almost say that its choice is made intelligently, although this is not the case. It is guided only by the laws of inertia and spontaneity.

We cannot wonder, therefore, if every animal carries out the movements most suitable to its nature. For example, most animals walk on four feet; human beings walk upright because this is easier and more pleasant for them. Every animal has its own habits and its own ways of lying down, stretching, taking food to its mouth, eating and drinking and carrying out other natural activities. In each action, animals prefer what is most natural, and therefore easier and more pleasurable for them.

450. We have to consider that an animal which feels any need whatsoever — hunger or thirst are the obvious examples — also experiences some kind of disquiet. The need produces tiny, unrelieved, multi-directional movements. Amongst these movements, the animal finds some which are suitable for satisfying its need and bettering its state. It follows these indications and gradually finds itself feeling better as it removes the cause of its distress. Put something on a dog's back, for example, and you will see the animal take up whatever position it finds suitable for removing the burden. If it discovers that lowering its back provides the freedom it desires, it will finally sit down and remove the weight altogether.

More often than not, animal instinct is very quick in choosing the movements and actions required for attaining the most comfortable and pleasurable position, for removing discomfort, and for bettering its state. Sometimes, however, a certain amount of effort and experiment is needed. The child, for example, spends much time finding its balance and directing its muscles in such a way that they help it walk and keep it walking. This is a case where the most comfortable and pleasurable position is tiring at the beginning, and requires effort for success.

451. Animals, therefore, can be trained, and would seem capable of grasping the *art* of movement and action, although this in fact depends entirely on the modification of instinct and on the *sensuous retentive faculty* accompanying instinct.[199]

[199] Darwin and others decided to deny the presence of instinct, pointing out that animals *learn* certain activities. But what they call *learning* is not true, human, intellectual learning. Instinct is not just a faculty initially determined

Everything can be explained easily enough by reflecting that the sensuous instinct moves the animal to direct itself towards the easiest and most pleasurable movements and positions, and that every need experienced by the animal arouses in it, as we said, a multitude of tiny movements. These give rise to discomfort, and the animal, according to the laws we have detailed, pursues and develops whatever movements it finds easiest for attaining most satisfaction from the feeling it experiences.

The reader will see immediately how profound a source of stupendous order this is for instinctive animal movements.

452. Other extremely beautiful laws can be discovered by observing all that renders certain movements easy and pleasurable to a determined species of animal. It is also possible to explain why certain things, disposed in a given way, seem ordered harmoniously, while others do not. Such an investigation will succeed in establishing the principle of a natural passage in animal movements and feelings, that is to say, of the existence of certain steps determined by nature, making the passage from one determined feeling or movement easier and more pleasurable than the passage to any other feeling or movement. Only natural steps enable a passage to be made smoothly; effort is required to make the passage where nature has placed neither stepping stones nor signposts. In other words, there is a law, based in animal nature and sensitivity, which renders the passage from one state to another, or from one feeling

in its acts so that it has to do everything in the same way from the first moments of the animal's existence. Instinct, like other capacities, depends for its operation on many circumstances. In the first place, it needs *stimuli* and *external occasions* in order to act. As these vary, the instinctive activity also varies. Moreover, instinct also needs *phantasms* and the sensuous retentive faculty. The phantasy is the animal's means of carrying out actions when objects are lacking. The dog searching for its master is one example; imitating what it sees is another. Finally, *habit* provides another law of animal activity which has immense influence on instinct. What we normally call animal *learning*, therefore, is only the acquisition by the instinct of certain modifications and new attitudes dependent upon three main causes: 1. the stimulation of the exterior senses; 2. phantasms, together with their mutual associations and relationships with sensations; 3. the force of habit. Nevertheless, these three causes presuppose the existence in the animal of the instinctive principle which is then modified and, as it were, educated by them.

to another, either smooth and delightful or difficult and distasteful. Granted this, it is certain that everything leading the animal to experience a series of feelings and movements ordered according to the steps decreed by nature will be extremely pleasurable and harmonious. Ignoring nature's way of passing from one state to another means losing this pleasure and harmony.

453. Rameau's splendid observations on sound, and Giambattista Venturi's on colours can be used to illustrate this point.

Rameau noted that as a sound dies in the ears it gives a sensation of a twelfth, that is, of a fifth above the octave. This shows that the natural passage for the sensations of the acoustic organ is from first to fifth. Playing a fifth after hearing the first interval, therefore, finds the ear already naturally inclined and disposed for what it hears. This is the obvious reason for the delight found naturally in a jump of a fifth, and the same is true for every other chord, as Rameau shows. We can see, therefore, that harmony of sounds is founded in the hidden laws of the union between soul and body, and in the principle of the sensuous instinct which, by reason of inertia, always seeks to enjoy what is easiest and most natural.

Our own G. B. Venturi noticed that the same occurred relative to residuary colours. Red harmonises well with green because the pupil, before losing its red sensation, passes naturally to green. Orange and purple, violet and yellow also form harmonious associations, as Mengs observed, and in general imaginary colours harmonise with the true colours that precede them. The sensation of one colour disposes the soul to pass so naturally to the sensation of another colour that the second sensation, once determined, not only costs the soul no effort, but helps it to carry out what it would have done of itself, although less vividly.

454. Something similar may take place in other sensations, but it is more difficult to observe.

However, the facts we have indicated are sufficient to show that there is a principle of order and harmony in the very nature of the sensitivity resulting from the union of soul and body. This principle must have an incredible influence on the movements proceeding from sense.

III

Laws of spontaneous animal activity which depend upon the unitive force with which the animal is endowed

455. I have already demonstrated the simplicity of the feeling principle (cf. 92–134) and shown that its *unity of action* springs from this simplicity. Every animal activity emanates from the first act of the life instinct; the sensuous instinct is only a second act, as it were, of the life instinct itself. I have also made use of the animal's *unitive force* to explain how an animal perseveres at length in a pleasurable action, or even gradually increases the degrees of intensity of this action in order to derive more pleasure from it (cf. 370–400).

We now have to consider this *unitive force* as the principle of *order* in animal activity. This is an immense subject which I cannot hope to exhaust, but I shall have done sufficient if I succeed in opening a door on the matter and allow others a glimpse of a marvellous world in which so much delicate work remains for careful, discerning researchers.

456. The unitive force under discussion is present, I think, in all animals, although it does not seem to exist at an equal level in all species. The quantity and quality of the unitive force, therefore, could perhaps serve as a foundation for the philosophical classification of the animal kingdom. It would be a surer foundation than those already discovered, and could serve as their meeting point and perfecting principle.

This animal unitive force should be subject to careful analysis in the hope of 1. indicating all its functions; 2. showing which of these functions is found in each animal species; 3. describing all cases of possible lesion that could render the force unsuitable for its functions; and 4. thus classifying imperfections or defects in the animal in so far as the animal is a feeling and instinctive being.

457. This last work would moreover offer a solid foundation for the classification of lesions in the human intellective and volitive faculties in so far as they require for their matter what is prepared and submitted to them by feeling and instinct.

Here I shall indicate only the principal functions of the unitive force which, however, will serve to show clearly that every operation of animal instinct, whatever apparent signs of intelligence it offers, can be explained on the basis of the animal's own intrinsic properties, and especially of the properties of the unitive force with which the animal is endowed.

The first function *of the animal unitive force: to join together the sensations of different senses, especially those of sight and touch*

458. In *The Origin of Thought*[200] we have described at length how sight, by administering *signs* of corporeal tactile properties to animals, assists touch and movement. An animal without sufficient unitive force to bring together and unify, as it were, touch sensations (associated with movement) and sight sensations could never perceive the solidity of exterior bodies with sight alone. On the other hand, when touch sensations (united with movement) are associated with sight sensations, the latter are coupled indivisibly in the animal with a phantasy-retention of the corresponding touch sensation (it is touch which, through movement, possesses the property of perceiving any determined, corporeal solidity). As a result, sight sensation then represents and suggests to the animal's internal sense the solidity of bodies whose size is given by movement and touch. In other words, the sight sensation now offers more than is actually seen. The person born blind described by Cheselden perceived only a bodily surface adhering to his eye when he recovered his sight; he did not perceive corporeal solidity. Use of touch then taught his eye to discern solids intuitively. This could not have occurred, however, if the person were not endowed with the *unitive force* enabling him to associate several sensations, that is, visual sensations with touch sensations and images of touch sensations. Acting according to a specific law of association, he formed a single, internal affection aroused in him as the eye received colour. This affection enabled him to perceive solids through colours alone when he realised that colours are distributed in solid space, the term of the fundamental feeling, where movement traces limited corporeal solidity.[201]

[200] Cf. 907–921.

[201] Cheselden's experiments have been fully corroborated recently by T. H. Brett, who restored sight to many Indians born blind. Reports of his work

459. Lack of harmony between sight and touch sensations is often observed in congenital or contracted mental illness. Dr. Pinel, in describing some of the mentally ill amongst his own patients, says:

> Sometimes I have observed a kind of disharmony between sight and touch which do not act together on some new object that seems, however, to have attracted attention. One mentally ill person whom I know looks immediately at any painted image or solid body presented to him, but he then tries to touch it in an awkward way, as though the axis of vision were totally undirected to the object. His gaze is either not fixed upon it, or is turned vaguely to the brightest part of the room. The sensation experienced by such a person must be either very obscure or nil.[202]

The same can be said about sight perception of distances which depend upon perceptions of touch and movement. This kind of sight perception, unaccompanied by touch and movement, requires some *unitive force* in the animal in order that the perceptions produced by touch and movement may be associated and stably tied to the sight perception. As a result, sensations produced by touch and movement are aroused in the phantasy when the eye receives its own proper, corresponding sensation. The internal sensation of the phantasy, a reproduction of the external sensation, is an indication and measure of the corresponding distance. This association must come about according to a certain proportion and an instinctive law so that an internal image of the exact distance is aroused in response to the corresponding eye sensation.

Cabanis speaks of a boy completely unable to judge distance, although his eyes were perfect. The defect must have been in the *unitive force* which was incapable of carrying out the function we are describing. However, an observation is necessary before we can induce anything definite from this fact. What criterion was used in deciding that the child could not distinguish distance with sight? Probably the conclusion depended upon

can be found in the *Giornale Asiatico* (January 1837) and in the *Biblioteca Universale di Ginevra* (September 1837). Brett's experiments are important as a corrective to other oculists who questioned Cheselden's experiments (*OT*, 622).

202 *Trattato medico-filosofico sull'alienazione mentale*, sect. 2, 11.

his being unable to direct his movements on the basis of sight alone without the help of touch, which would have been needed to allow his movements to correspond to the distance he wanted to cover. But this would only prove, absolutely speaking, that the child did not know distance with sight alone, and that he was defective in *unitive force* capable of connecting sight and touch sensations. In order to move according to the distances perceived, the child's *unitive force* would have to perform yet another function about which we shall speak later, the function uniting *passive* with *active feelings*.

460. In answer to questions about the law according to which sight sensations are harmonised with those of touch and take their place, we say that the first condition for such a law is the unlimited solid space given by nature as the term of the fundamental feeling. Granted this, the law then depends upon the equal *proportions* according to which colours seen by the eye are distributed in the visual orbit, and according to which objects felt by touch are distributed in space, as we have already shown at length in our theory of knowledge.

461. Consequently, any sudden change in the proportions of the colours in the visual orbit would lead to mistakes. For instance, we would reach out to touch bodies which, although seen, would not be where we placed our hand. Illusions of this kind cause us to place our feet wrongly, and stumble.

In passing, I could mention something that happened to a servant of Monsignor Sardegna, retired bishop of Cremona. After losing an eye, this servant no longer cut all the tonsures of the bishop's resident priests in the middle of the head but on the side. When he wanted to light the altar candles with a taper, he mistook the distance of the wick and held the taper about six inches away from the candle.

The reason for this will be clear if we remember that the total visual orbit had been diminished and rendered defective on the side where the eye had been lost. The servant, who, presumably, was used to putting his hands on objects in the centre of what had been presented by the visual orbit of two eyes, now put them in the centre of the orbit presented by his one remaining eye. As a result, he put his hands towards the side on which the good eye was, and went further than necessary.

462. Nevertheless, I must add another observation connected with the unitive activity enabling the animal to connect sight sensations with touch sensation and movement. Although it directs its movements solely according to the tenor of its sight sensations, and therefore in harmony with the requirements of touch and movement, another synthesis is needed if the animal is to complete this operation. The animal, in carrying out this action, does not simply unite and harmonise actual sight sensations and mobile touch sensations (this is the first synthesis we described, in which the animal appears to use its sight without constantly comparing the size and shape of the spaces it sees with its touch experience); it also unites *actual sight sensations* with *past touch sensations* now re-activated in the phantasy. This is precisely the reason why it can succeed in knowing what effort to put into jumping a ditch, and how to measure its own movements according to the spaces in which it does them. But the following reflections on this second synthesis will help us understand it better.

The second function *of the unitive force: associating sensations and images (the bond enabling images to co-exist)*

463. This function presupposes as a law of operation that external sensations already felt by an animal are easily re-aroused in the internal sensory faculty, that is, in the imagination. This law is revealed by experience.

464. But explaining the law is not easy. My own opinion is that the explanation is not to be found solely in the nerve fibre, nor in the feeling principle, but in both together. The feeling principle, or soul, having been moved at one time to experience a given sensation retains its inclination or tension towards that sensation through the law of spontaneity; at the same time, the living fibre retains greater mobility relative to the movement already suffered than to other movements. This, however, is mere conjecture on my part.

465. On the other hand, there can be no doubt about the ease with which previously experienced sensations are renewed in the phantasy as a result of very slight stimuli. Similarly, it would

seem that the phantasy is incapable of furnishing the soul with images other than those already experienced in sensation. The imagination remains sealed, as it were, until sensation releases it.[203]

Granted this, let us see how this function is carried out, and examine the importance to the animal of the help provided by the function when the animal recalls and connects *present sensations* with 're-aroused *past sensations*', as I call the images.

The union of several sensations in the animal (the first function of the unitive force) comes about because these sensations are simultaneous. If all these sensations are taken together, and all the animal feels is taken as constituting a single sensation, their union gives rise to a single feeling, a single *feelable state* in the animal. This state is as simple as the feeling animal is simple, although many simultaneous sensations contribute to form it.

The whole of this single, complex feeling is preserved in the animal by the *sensuous retentive faculty*, as we have called it. This faculty retains traces, as it were, of the single feeling, of the 'feeling in potency', of its 'susceptibilities', its 'habit' — expressions which are more or less equivalent.

It follows that a single part of this multiple feeling (a single sensation of the many that went to form the feeling), when aroused in the animal by some external cause, is sufficient to revive in the animal phantasy all the other sensations originally

[203] It is normally accepted as certain that the phantasy cannot possess images other than those already provided by external sense. I would be inclined to qualify this affirmation and say that the phantasy can furnish only clear, definite images of that which has been experienced in the external sense. But I do not think it can be maintained absolutely that the phantasy can furnish no image whatsoever prior to the arousal of the corresponding sensation in the external sense. Take, for example, a person born blind with perfect eyes except for cataracts which cover them. He has never seen light. Nevertheless, I am not at all sure that he could not have, through some internal stimulus, the sense, say, of sparks of fire. In fact, such a sense is aroused not only by light, but by other stimuli such as pressure on the globe of the eye. We all experience this when, for example, we are struck in the eye, or feel pressure exerted even on other parts of the nervous system. 'That hurt,' we say. 'I can see stars.' Some physiologists have reported the presence in dreams of images which have had no corresponding sensation. I think such a phenomenon is possible provided that the sensory organs, although they may never have been used, are healthy and without defect.

[465]

felt along with the single sensation and forming with it the general feeling or *feelable state*. Nothing more is needed to revive the whole feeling and recall it to act.

Consequently, when an animal receives a sensation experienced on other occasions it does not move simply according to the requirements of that sensation alone, but according to the requirements of the general feeling which the sensation helps to reproduce and renew.

466. For example, a hunting dog, when it sees its master take a gun, becomes very excited, as though it understood that a day's shooting was to take place. But the dog does not in fact understand anything. Intelligence is not required to explain the dog's agitation; the association of pleasurable sensations already experienced by the dog when hunting is sufficient. The animal's unitive force associates many other pleasant sensations in the dog's phantasy with sensations of the shotgun and of the master picking up the gun. These sensations taken together compose and form a single feeling and state which is recalled and renewed by the animal as soon as a part of the feeling is reproduced in the external sense. It is this multiple feeling which causes the dog's excitement and consequent agitation.

Innumerable other animal activities can be explained in the same way. The dog, for example, tracks a wild beast by means of scent or finds its master, although he is a long way off; it discovers objects deliberately hidden; it learns tricks that seem to require great intelligence. But all this is carried out through the association of sensations and images. They are bound together in such a way that the experience of one sensation gives rise to other images connected with it which complete a feeling previous@'r the animal as a result of the co-existence in it of many things felt simultaneously. The animal, when it feels a part of the total feeling which has brought it such pleasure, spontaneously seeks the rest of the feeling. It experiences some discomfort as long as the feeling is incomplete, and is stimulated to search for what it still lacks.

467. This is the foundation of all animal training, which is mainly based on the following principle: 'Associate pleasurable sensations with actions required of the animal, and unpleasant sensations with actions to be avoided.' Such association is impossible without the animal's synthetic or unitive force,

which is one as the animal is one. Through this force the animal forms, from several simultaneous sensations, a single, pleasurable or disagreeable act or state. It then seeks or avoids the total sensation.

If the activity from which one wishes to dissuade the beast is very pleasant, disagreeable sensations have to be connected with it until they completely overcome the pleasure experienced in the activity. The animal now receives a single bitter-sweet feeling in which the unpleasant element is greater than the pleasant. The unity of the feeling and the prevalence of the unpleasant element makes the feeling as a whole unpleasant and to be avoided. In this way dogs are trained not to eat food thrown to them, and to undergo other privations. The training depends upon the image of the punishment meted out to them if they do what is forbidden.

468. All these matters seem at first to call for some use of reason in animals. We believe easily enough that like us they act on a calculation of pros and cons, or by understanding sufficiently to work from a sign to what is signified as though they knew rationally, for example, that the master's handkerchief was an indication of his presence. But there is no question of arguing from a sign to what is signified, or of weighing pros and cons. The animal passes from a state of imperfect, partial feeling to a state in which the feeling is entire and complete, and does this spontaneously through instinctive law.

The third function *of the unitive force: fusing several sensations and images into a single, well-ordered affection (the effecting bond)*

469. So far we have explained two apparent traces of reason in animal activities.

Animals seem able to *measure and relate proportionately forms and shapes seen by the eye with those presented by touch.* This phenomenon was explained by means of the first function of the unitive force. No intelligence is at work; sensations, which themselves possess proportionate sizes and shapes, encounter one another in the unity of the animal, as we have explained, and are their own mutual measure and proportion.

It would also seem that animals *recognise signs, and move from signs to that which is signified*. This second apparent act of reason was explained by means of the second function of the unitive force, without our needing to presuppose reason.

But there is a third apparent indication of reason at work in animal activity. Each operation is composed of various movements bound together for the purpose of producing a single effect. Moreover, many animal activities are ordered in relationship to one another. This harmony between animal movements and activities cannot be explained through sensations and images which are either separate from one another or at most connected by the bond of co-existence of which we have spoken. Such activities would seem therefore to require the use of some understanding and reason. We have to show that even here there is no need to have recourse to reason for an explanation of the phenomena.

470. Let us recall something we have already seen: movement in the animal does not originate directly from sensations and images, which only initiate the nerve movements that affect the soul's spontaneous activity (cf. 385–400, 419–429). In turn, this activity arises to prolong and perfect the movements.[204] These nerve movements first produce a diffused feeling, which I call an *affection* or even a *universal affection*. As we saw, the soul's activity is present throughout the body. Consequently, this affection expands more or less everywhere. But the very diffusion of feeling and activity is a third function of the animal unitive force in which several sensations and images are fused and harmonised into a single prevalent affection which, ruling the sensations and images, makes them subservient to itself. This is the unique, proximate cause of animal movements and activity.

471. We can now see why these animal movements and

[204] Niccolò Contarini in his splendid work *De Perfectione Rerum* (Somaschi, Venice, 1576) observed acutely that the imagination is a cause of motion, but only in so far as it arouses animal spontaneity: 'neither the latter (the phantasy) nor the former (the mind) is the cause of movement, but simply arouses the power of movement' (bk. 6, c. 2).

activity are sometimes well-ordered and well formed, and sometimes show signs of disturbance and disarray.

If the animal operates in virtue of an *affection* produced by several partial sensations and images, each of which possesses its own degree of natural force, the operation also reveals unity and order. In it one dominant, governing feeling presides over all the other partial feelings. If, however, one or several images take on unnatural, excessive strength, and thus control the sensuous activity, they necessarily weaken the action of the other images and sensations. These immoderate images take up the dominant position and themselves alone produce an exclusive affection generating partial, disharmonised and disordered movements. The unitive force is weakened in this state; it no longer has the energy to unite all the images and sensations harmoniously, each with its own correct proportion of strength so that it may contribute with the others to forming the single affection and its corresponding movements. At this point, the animal exhibits signs of disturbance, *rage* and in the human being even *delirium*.

472. But overwhelming constraint is not the only impediment blocking the *unitive force* as it attempts to carry out the function we have described, that is, to produce the *affection* by harmonising images and sensations. Very often the weakness of the images, or the extreme ease with which they can be eliminated from the sensuous retentive faculty, serves as an impediment to the unitive force. Very languid images are associated with *idiocy*. Excessive, but brief and momentary images which leave no trace, give rise to a kind of *dementia*, mixed with some form of *mental disability* and incipient rage.

473. Let us consider examples of all four cases.

1st. *Lack of unitive force due to weakness of images*, the cause of true idiocy.

There are many cases of people in this state who reveal such obtuse senses and languid images that *universal affection* is totally lacking in them. They remain in an almost absolute state of stupor and immobility, without giving any sign of spontaneous movement even for primary needs such as food. Everything has to be done for them. Even nourishment has to be forced down their throats (cf. 459).

474. 2nd. *Lack of unitive force due to the brief duration of*

images, despite the liveliness and strength with which they are impressed on the phantasy.

Dr. Pinel has given a description of one of his alienated patients in whom images must have been extremely forceful, but of short duration:

> I have never seen such chaos as that person showed in his movements, ideas, speech and his sudden, confused outbursts of moral affection. At one moment, he draws near me, looks at me and overwhelms me with a torrent of disconnected words. A second later, he moves away and approaches someone else with his never-ending, incoherent chatter. This time his eyes flash, and he appears to threaten. But he is incapable of anger, and incapable of any connected series of ideas: his movements are limited to rapid bursts of childish effervescence which calm down and vanish instantly. When he enters a room, he immediately overturns all the furniture; chairs and tables are lifted up, thrown down, moved around without any design or definite intention. He looks outside, and immediately moves elsewhere, swinging along, stuttering a few words, kicking stones, pulling up grass which he throws away to dig up more. He comes, he goes, he comes back again — endlessly. He remembers nothing, and does not recognise friends or relatives. At night, he sleeps a few moments at a time; when he sees food, he stops for an instant and devours it. He seems in the power of an endless series of ideas and unconnected moral affections which hardly appear before they vanish without trace.'

We cannot say that this unfortunate person was lacking in sensations or images, or that these were weak and incapable of producing the universal affection which is the proximate cause of instinctive movement. The images were extremely vivid, but of such brief duration that the unitive force was unable to connect them and produce a well-ordered, harmonious affection from them all. As a result, they formed only isolated affections, and isolated, disconnected movements.[205]

205 In cases of this kind, alienated people are brought back to sanity if sufficient effort can be made to block the diffusion of the images, and keep the attention fixed for as long as needed. This is done by external signs which can, I think, be usefully employed in the treatment of the severely deranged. For example, it sometimes happens that although these unfortunate people are

[474]

475. 3. *Lack of unitive force due to the extreme violence of one or a few images.*

If the violence of one or a few images is excessive, and produces an *affection* which governs instinctive movements, the outcome will be rage. We should note here that every passion present in the irascible part, such as anger, pride, ambition and excessive jealousy, degenerates into *rage*. Instances of this are not rare, and we do not have go to hospitals for the deranged to find them.

476. 4. The same lack of unitive force due to the extreme violence of one or a few images can induce *delirium* in the rational animal if the deficiency influences the will and through the will, the understanding. Unfortunately examples of this are very common.

477. *Rage* and *delirium*, therefore, normally have a common root, that is, the immense power of a few images. If the force of this power prevails only in the animal part, it causes *rage*; if it prevails in the understanding, it brings *delirium*.

478. We must note one other case in which the unitive force of the animal loses much of its activity without harm to the animal itself. This occurs in sleep. Barthez asserts that in sleep each organ exists on its own account without retaining its correspondence with any other. This is perhaps exaggerated, but it is clear that the unitive power decreases in sleep, and especially in cases of somnambulism when some senses are fully exercised, and others quite inoperative.

The fourth function *of the unitive force: to unite* passive *and* active feelings (*the bond of innermost sense*)

479. We saw that as a result of the animal's unity the third

completely incoherent in speech, they manage to reason logically when writing. The explanation must be that writing produces stabler signs to which the ideas of such persons can be connected. 'Some deranged people,' says Pinel, 'are capable of concentrating in the midst of their passing moods, and of writing outstanding letters, full of good sense and reasoning, to their relatives and to the authorities. One day I persuaded one of my patients, a very cultured person, to write a letter that I needed for the following day. It was full of logical, good sense although it had been written instantly in the midst of some irrational monologue' (*Trattato medico-filosofico dell'alienazione mentale*, sect. 2, 3).

function of the unitive force produced in the animal a single *affection* from several external and internal feelings. This affection is the proximate cause of spontaneous motion.

Nevertheless, such an *affection* would not itself be sufficient to enable us to explain fully how animal movements receive order and regularity. A fourth function of the unitive force is needed by means of which the animal itself proportions and balances its movements according to the intensity and quality of its affection. This takes place in the *innermost sense*.

480. In order to clarify this concept we must remember once more that I call feelings *passive* in so far as they are received by us and aroused by an external agent; *active feelings* are those to which our own activity, our own movement, has been joined (cf. 428).

481. A second observation. Positing feelings connected with our own activity is not opposed to what I have said about the feeling soul's not feeling itself as a feeling principle, nor to the fact that feelable extension is the soul's felt term. We can affirm that the soul does not feel itself as an isolated principle of its feeling without denying that it feels the activity it develops in feeling.

As we know, felt extension is the product of two causes, the body and the soul. Consequently we must recognise that along with what is felt, the soul must have a sense of its own activity provided that this activity is understood as felt in its term and effect, not in its principle. In this way, the soul feels itself as mingled, we might say, with what is felt. It does not feel itself as something separate and abstracted from what is felt, nor can it be conceived as feeling itself in this way.

Moreover, what is felt can suffer modifications by means of movement of its parts. This movement is felt necessarily because it is a change in what is felt. But when this change — movement in the parts of what is felt — takes place, the soul either experiences some kind of passivity if the cause of the movement is external, or itself acts if the very cause of the movement is the spontaneous activity of the soul.

These two states cannot be indifferent relative to the soul, which must feel not only the movement that takes place in the term of its feeling, but also some new passivity in itself. Force is exerted upon it in so far as movement arises without positive co-operation on the soul's part, although the soul must then feel what happens in so far as it contributes to what is taking place. The result is four feelings: 1. that which has for its term the extended felt element, *felt as extended*; 2. that which has for its term the *movement* taking place in what is felt as extended; 3. that which has for its term the *disturbance* brought to bear on the soul when its movement arises without its own intervention; 4. that which has for term the soul's own *activity*, if the movement is generated through its spontaneous activity. The first three feelings are passive; the fourth is what I call active feeling.

482. It is my opinion, therefore, that when the animal is about to move itself, it has the feeling of its own activity (active feeling), and with it instinctively measures the quantity of movement it begins to excite in the organs of movement. This quantity of movement is of course the direct effect of that feeling. Let us imagine that a brute animal has the passive feeling of some distance which has to be covered. Disharmony and lack of proportion will prevail between the animal's movement and the distance it has to travel, unless this feeling can influence and inform its powers of movement, and hence impress upon them the right quantity of movement necessary to travel the distance. If not, the movement will be greater or less than the distance, and the unitive force will have failed to fulfil its function of harmonising and balancing the *passive feeling* which prescribes movement with the *active feeling* which actually determines it. The active feeling has its origin in the depths of the passive feeling, and must be commensurate with it if the action is to be done well. The *feeling of the distance* could be present together with disproportionate *movement* towards it. This would depend not on lack of the unitive force necessary to produce the feeling of distance by sight alone (the first function), but through lack of the unitive force enabling the animal to apportion and balance its actual movement with the feeling of the distance it wishes to travel (fourth function).

For example, a person could have an ear for receiving the sounds and experiencing the emotions associated with music; he could also have a pleasant voice. Nevertheless, he may not have sufficient unitive force (of the kind we are discussing) to be able to accord and harmonise his active feelings (his vocal activity) with his passive feelings (the sounds heard). He may never succeed in using his voice to reproduce the sounds and cadences he hears; he may be incapable of discovering the cords in his throat or of impressing on them the movement or pressure of air necessary for singing the desired sounds and melody. And it is certain that he will appear to have a faulty ear and discordant voice until he learns to carry out sufficiently well this operation of unitive force.

483. This explains why music has to be learnt, although its elementary faculties may be innate. It is an habitual balance achieved by the unitive force between passive and active feelings, between sounds heard and sounds to be reproduced. Such balance is not easily attained by the unitive force.

§5. Summary: a description of the origin of instinctive movement

484. We must now summarise the principal elements in our study of the various functions of the unitive force contributing to the production of instinctive movement.

Instinctive movement is for the most part the effect of multiple, hidden activities. Although it seems to arise without much preparation, like an underground river suddenly surfacing, it is the gradual product of much delicate work on the part of nature. And the animal's *unitive force* plays an extremely busy part in this step-by-step preparation.

485. The following are the steps taken by nature to produce the instinctive movement on which it relies for reactivating a pleasurable act or state already experienced.

1st step: a state of motion or rest in which the animal experiences pleasure or satisfaction.[206]

2nd step: the union or association, brought about by the *unitive force* of the soul, between the *feeling of the animal's state* of rest or motion, and the *pleasant feeling* accompanying this state. This union or association consists (if the state is not pleasant in itself) in joining, in the animal, the feeling of movements and circumstances with phantasms of already experienced pleasant sensations, and vice versa. Consequently, the feeling of

206 Note that animals possess only *feeling* of these movements or circumstances; human beings soon become *conscious* of them.

movements and circumstances are represented in the animal imagination and accompanied by the arousal of enjoyment from pleasant sensations already experienced. Movements, circumstances and preceding pleasant sensations become, as it were, a single entity.

3rd step: the representation in the imagination of some of these circumstances and movements as a result of external or internal events. At the same time, the pleasure which accompanied the circumstances is also recalled in the phantasy.

4th step: the general effect or *affection* produced throughout the whole animal by the representations and phantasms together. This affection is like a feeling pervading the entire animal and initiating in it the movements which are direct or indirect causes of its pleasure.[207] In considering the beginning of movement, we need to reflect on what we have repeatedly stated: that is, the *sensation*, *imagination* and *affection* arising from several sensations and images contain in themselves and of their own nature whatever local change — tremor, slight impulse, contraction or extension — is needed in the nerve filaments or fluids governing analogous movements. The intimate connection between *feeling* and *instinct* is characterised by the prior presence, in the feelable passive experience, of the beginning of instinctive activity. *Instinct* is generated in the depth of *sense*.

5th step: the beginning of movement initiates a disturbed, pressurised, and hence restless sensation. A need is felt, therefore, to perfect these tenuous, initial movements by means of *spontaneity* and according to the laws of *inertia*, as we have explained. Consequently, a new *synthesis* is forged, as we mentioned above, of the progressively increasing degrees of *movement* and *pleasure* which through synthesis are grasped by a single apprehension, itself the source of progressive movement.

[207] I say *direct* or *indirect* because the movements which commence in the animal may not tend directly to pleasure, but to finding places, objects, positions and attitudes in which pleasures are enjoyed by animals. If this is the case, another *synthesis* or operation of the unitive force intervenes between circum*stances, movements and pleasures* (three separate things) or between *first movements* intended to search for the circumstances, the *circumstances* themselves, *second movements* required to produce pleasure, and the *pleasures* themselves. These four things are gathered together in a single apprehension by the unitive force so that once the perception of one of them is aroused in the animal, the other three unite to complete the single, complex apprehension.

[485]

We note that in the animal (where spontaneity is united with inertia, unlike the case of inert matter where no spontaneity is present) a normally progressive action can be retained in its forward movement by the animal's own inertia. The movement, once begun, would prolong itself according to both mechanical and animal laws. Nevertheless, it finds obstacles first in the inertia of the corporeal parts still at rest (to which it attempts to communicate itself), and secondly in the instinctive activity of the animal. Although the movement would tend to communicate itself by mechanical law to contiguous parts equally and without distinction, the instinctive activity producing the movement does so only for the sake of the pleasure it expects to derive from the movement. Hence, this activity is bent on propagating the movement only in the way, in the parts, and in the mode suitable for causing pleasure. At the beginning, the animal does not succeed in finding these parts easily, nor has it any expertise in directing the movement, stimulating the nerves or vibrating the fluids needed to obtain the pleasure it desires. Consequently the animal, as long as it continues to make efforts of this kind, and until it finds the right path to controlled movement, manifests signs of troubled, disturbed, stressful feeling. This passes when, having taken the necessary trouble to activate its movement, the animal finds full satisfaction.

The *6th step* is the instinctive movement itself, the final effect of the dispositions and attitudes taken up by the animal in the preceding steps.

486. The instinctive movement, therefore, cannot arise if one of the five preceding actions is lacking. For example, let us imagine that no *affection* is produced, so that this effect of the fusion of several feelings, or of the propagation of a single feeling (4th step), is lacking. In this case, spontaneous movement, which has its source in affection, cannot be generated. And this defect may be the cause of the case described by Pinel: 'I saw a seven-year old girl whose acoustic organ was extraordinarily sensitive to even the slightest sound. Nevertheless, she seemed unable to distinguish articulate sounds or the difference in sounds expressing joy, menace or love.'[208]

208 *Trattato medico-filosofico dell'alienazione mentale* (sect. 2, 2). This child received physical impressions in her ears, and possessed local sensations

§6. Explanation of the imitative instinct

487. Finally, I want to deduce the explanation of the phenomena of the imitative instinct from what has been said.

Imitation is one of the most wonderful guides given by Providence to animal activity. Through imitation, animals seem to possess reason itself; it is extremely strong in some species — monkeys, for example — and can produce extraordinary results in the human species; it is effective at any age, and in entire social bodies; and infancy is guided almost exclusively by the two needs of *feeling* and *imitation*.

488. We must turn once more to the animal unitive force for an explanation of the phenomena of imitation, and especially to the fourth of the functions we have described.

Imitation, in fact, is reduced finally to *active* reproduction through movement of what has been perceived *passively* through feelings. Imitative activity therefore consists in that function of the synthetic force by which the animal unites, balances and measures its active with its passive feelings.

The *passive feelings*, united and balanced with the active feelings in the functions of imitative instinct (that is, with feelings springing from the subject's own power and action), are of two kinds: 1. *pleasure* and *pain*, according to which the *quantity of movement* is proportioned and balanced (motion and its accompanying pleasure, as we have seen, become a single thing in the animal and a state in which it perseveres) (cf. 485); and 2. *phantasms*, according to which the *quality of movement* is proportioned and balanced. *Quality* refers to the direction and form of movement, and is the principal source of the imitative instinct.

489. This will be seen more clearly if we recall that phantasms initiate the nerve movement which stimulate the soul's spontaneity. This explains *sympathy*, the phenomenon which makes us share in another's sorrow or contentment as soon as we see or imagine their suffering or happiness.

There is no doubt that reason plays a great part in such events;

which, however, produced no further effect. No *universal affection* extended throughout the entire animal system to arouse spontaneity, and consequently no corresponding movements were possible.

it is through reason that human beings come to know and appreciate others' joy or misery. But reason is neither the sole nor proximate cause of what takes place. Rather, reason simply reinforces the imagination and makes it more active than it would be otherwise. In itself, the phenomenon is part of animal life because sympathy always concerns physical good and evil which we not only conceive abstractly, but really feel in ourselves as we imagine it in others. Such a phenomenon, therefore, is an entirely animal effect whose origin is the first nerve movements stimulated by the imaginative apprehension of another's pain, and by the spontaneity of the soul which immediately arises to support and propagate these first movements. This leads to the production of a painful or sad affection more or less similar to what has been seen or imagined by us to exist in the unfortunate person. The intensity of such a sympathetic effect depends on the delicacy of the organs and the way in which they are habitually activated. And perhaps this would account for the story told about Mindyrides of Sybaris who ordered a labourer to stop digging a ditch in his presence because the heavy work oppressed him![209]

490. Something similar takes place in every *imitation*. Actions imitated by an animal are first perceived by the animal with its senses, especially the sight. Such things are first seen, that is, become sensations and are then made images; they are passive feelings from which corresponding active feelings have to be produced along with activity reproducing the action which has been seen. The passive feelings, however, begin the movements at the nerve apices. These movements are followed by greater movements, complementing what has already been initiated in the imagination by means of minimum nerve movements. These minimum movements, as we said, are seconded by animal spontaneity leading them to reproduce and imitate the perceived action in precisely the same way that a sound is reproduced by an animal that has heard it (cf. 438).

209 'They say that Mindyrides came from Sybaris. When he saw a man digging and raising his mattock, he felt the strain of the effort put into the work, and forbade the labourer to work in his presence' (Seneca, *De Ira*, bk. 2, c. 25).

§7. How *passive* and *active* elements are intimately united in the essence of the animal

491. Another observation has to be made about the correspondence between *active* and *passive* elements in the animal, that is, between what the animal receives in feeling and what it produces in space.

I have already noted that one cannot say with propriety: 'The body is outside the soul', but only that the body is essentially distinct from the soul. That which feels and that which is felt, the constitutive animal elements, are not situated or united in any place, but concur in reciprocal action. I also said that active feelings must be classed amongst felt things which include the following: that which is extended, the continuum, size and shape, and even movement, which changes size and shape.

If all these things are united with the soul in such a way that the soul acts upon them all, that is, acts in what is extended by changing the size and form of what is extended, it can obviously unite in itself and balance its active with its passive feelings. It can also make certain movements follow upon determined feelings and reproduce in space what it beholds in the imagination. We do indeed marvel at such occurrences, but they are all contained in the first notion of animal and confirmed by experience.

492. Let us consider carefully two obvious facts presented by experience.

1st. A person throws a stone at a given target, and succeeds in hitting it.

In throwing the stone, he must first have measured internally the space between himself and the object, and then, relative to the distance, have employed the forces necessary for throwing the stone in the right direction and hitting the target. He will have calculated his throw and made it correspond to the space he has measured. But when he throws the stone, he has only the sensation of the space provided by his sight, that is, a *passive feeling* (cf. 168–170). However, this felt space is enough for him to determine (by means of an *active feeling*) the quantity and direction of muscular movements needed to throw the stone.

This shows that in balancing the active with the passive feelings and proportioning the feeling of effort to the feeling of visual space (something the animal must do in order to obtain the pleasurable effect), the passive feelings do not always provide the soul immediately with the real measure of the movements it has to make. Sometimes, as in our present case, they provide only a proportionate measure. The movements, therefore, are not reproduced mechanically by the initial nerve movements accompanying passive feelings, as though such movements were a physically necessary, immediate consequence. They depend upon the kind of influence exerted by the soul's spontaneity which in turn requires for its activity some measure proportionate to the desired movement. The soul, possessing solely this proportionate measure, easily reproduces the measure on a larger scale by means of its own unitive force. In other words, the soul associates a great effort towards movement with a small nerve movement. This explains how animals can walk, run and jump in space accurately enough to avoid mistakes even in difficult and dangerous places.

This association of the quantity of motion with spatial sight sensation is of course brought about by exercising the appropriate faculties and by experience. Experience itself is possible in the animal through its *sensuous retentive faculty* which shows the animal the measure of motion corresponding to every visual space and thus balances the *visual sensation* and *movement* directly, without the mediation of *touch*. In fact, even animals like the horse, with almost no touch in its hooves, are very safe jumpers.

2nd. A blind person walks without stumbling.

Persons born blind, or blind for a long period, do not find walking difficult. And the even more wonderful feats of somnambulists could be mentioned here.

493. While sight sensation is totally lacking in these persons, we nevertheless have to say that there is a measure of external space in the *imagination* or in the animal *retentive faculty*. This internal or image mode of space is produced either by sight, by touch or by the other senses from the experience of movements undergone on previous occasions and provides the soul with a definite standard for determining the quantity and direction of movements that it has to command and activate in the real world.[210]

210 St. Thomas (*S.T.*, 3, q. 13, art. 3, ad 3) takes up Aristotle's teaching (*De Anima*, bk. 3, text 48 ss.) about the *imagination* as the principle of local motion. Niccolò Contarini, an Italian philosopher of the 16th century,

494. These facts and the preceding reflections easily explain many of the most difficult and complicated animal movements. The internal world of imagination is necessarily as complicated as the external, real world. In both cases, it is indeed the same world, but with two different relationships. The internal world can therefore give rise to any kind of complicated movement. When understood in this way, certain instinctive movements, which are otherwise inexplicable (for example, sexual intercourse), lose some of their mystery.

12

FICHTE'S ASSERTION THAT *ACTION* ALONE FURNISHES US WITH BELIEF IN THE EXTERNAL WORLD

495. What we have said so far about the nature of the animal offers a solution to the great question posed by idealism. Fichte, persuaded that the subject had no possibility of going outside himself, followed Kant and others in maintaining that *theoretical reason* offers no way of demonstrating the existence of the external world.

Frightened by this strange conclusion, Fichte (who considered the conclusion as the inevitable result of theoretical knowledge) turned to the *practical reason*, that is, to the human need to act. He maintained that human beings were made for *action*, not *knowledge*, that action should prevail over knowledge, and that action was impossible without prior *belief* in the external world. *This need to believe* in the exterior world in order to make possible the action to which human beings are ineluctably called by the intimate voice of conscience, constitutes the *practical reason*

examines the question of the cause of local motion in his admirable *De Perfectione Rerum*, which we have already quoted. Although he acknowledges that the intellective will can also be the cause of movement in human beings, he affirms that it is never more than a remote cause. For him, the proximate cause of movement is always the imagination. 'Hence, we maintain that the remote cause of motion is the mind and the will; the proximate cause, about which Aristotle also spoke, is the imagination itself' (bk. 6, c. 2).

of transcendental philosophy. The practical reason is thus a *belief* induced in us by our need to act.

496. But what Fichte called the *conclusion of theoretical knowledge* was only the conclusion of *his* theoretical knowledge, not of knowledge considered in itself. Offering to replace universal knowledge with one's own knowledge was a very bold move, but German philosophy, with Kant at its head, has never been lacking in boldness.

497. As we said (*Teodicea*, 146–147), transcendental idealism is guilty of a material error. We have only to consider the phrase *exterior world*, which this form of idealism uses and interprets rigorously, not metaphorically. Strictly speaking, there is no *external* world relative to the soul (cf. 491). The relationship between soul and matter cannot be expressed by the words *inside* and *outside*, or *interior* and *exterior*, but only by words indicating different entities. If we abandon the expression, *external world*, the arguments of the transcendentalists have no further meaning, and the captivating scene presented by this otherwise eternally memorable philosophy vanishes.

498. There is no doubt that the soul could not act unless there were something different from the soul itself. Space, extension, the continuum, etc., is an absolutely necessary condition for animal activity. But this is neither the first, nor the only argument to reveal a world endowed with breadth, height and depth, to reveal, that is, the existence of matter and bodies. *Sensation* precedes *action*, and we have shown that in sensation itself we are given immediately *that which is extended*, along with body and matter, and all feelable qualities. These things, which are essentially distinct from the feeling principle, are the term of sensation and thus intimately necessary to sensation.

This is sufficient to prove with the utmost clarity that the *conclusion of theoretical knowledge* coincides fully with what Fichte and others of his school attributed to some mysterious, inexplicable *belief*. The divorce between *knowledge* and *faith* can be upheld no longer; knowledge and faith are forever reconciled.

Book 3

SPIRITUALITY

DEFINITIONS

I

499. The intellect, as an element of human nature, is the human subject in so far as it intuits indeterminate-being.

II

The intellect as a power[211] is the faculty which intuits determinate-ideal beings.

III

500. *Reason* is the faculty which applies indeterminate-being to feelings, and to real and ideal beings. This application gives rise to reasoning.

IV

501. *Will* is the faculty which inclines towards a known object. The act of will is called *volition.*

V

Freedom is the faculty which determines the will to a volition or to its contrary.

502. All our previous considerations about animality are simply a commentary on the first part of the definition of human being (cf. 22, 23), that is, of the human being as an *animal subject.* We now have to continue our work by commenting on and clarifying the subsequent words of the definition according to which the human being is also an *intellective* and *volitive* subject. For the sake of brevity, these two qualities of human nature are grouped under the single word *spirituality.* On the other hand, everything pertaining to the intellect is immune from all admixture and contact with body, and as such constitutes in its own right a spiritual substance.

[211] Occasionally the word *intellect* is taken as synonymous with *understanding* to indicate the whole complex of intellective faculties.

503. The words *intellective* and *volitive* fall into place in the definitions in so far as the natural division of this third book needs to harmonise with that of its predecessor. Having considered first the passive and then the active animal faculties in speaking of the animal part of the human being, we now have to do the same when dealing with the spiritual part.

We shall divide this book into two sections, therefore, and deal first with the human being as *intellective* and then as *volitive*. All the *passive faculties* of the higher part of human nature are included under the heading 'intellective', the active faculties under the heading 'volitive'.

SECTION ONE

THE PASSIVE FACULTIES OF HUMAN UNDERSTANDING

504. We have already dealt with the passive faculties of human understanding in various writings on the theory of knowledge[212] which we need not repeat. I shall restrict myself, therefore, to recalling some of the principal matters already demonstrated, and in particular the nature of the different faculties of human understanding. Any new observations will be brief and in accordance with the requirements of this book.

1

THE INTELLECT AS AN ELEMENT OF HUMAN NATURE AND AS THE SOURCE OF ALL THE INTELLECTIVE POWERS

Article 1.
The intellect is an element of human nature

505. As we have seen, human beings in so far as they intuit being are said to be endowed with intellect (cf. 39). The intellect, therefore, is not merely a power, but a constitutive element of human essence. This is why we have included intellect in the definition of human being.

We do not want to investigate here how this intuition of being is produced. It is a primordial fact, and truly transcendental. What we can say is that the intellect, if deprived of the intuition of being, no longer exists. It has been annihilated. If, on the other hand, we consider the intellect as endowed with this intuition, we find that it is *receptive*, and that understanding consists

[212] Principally in *OT* [666 ss.], *Certainty* [1205 ss.] and *Rinnovamento della Filosofia in Italia*, etc.

simply in receiving intellectual light, that is, the idea. But we can also see that, given this intuition, the subject itself, in receiving that light, has to contribute some activity. Of its very nature every reception presupposes some degree of activity in the recipient. A being without any activity whatsoever could neither receive nor experience anything — although the activity itself does not have to precede the receptivity. Both can be brought into existence at the same instant.

Article 2.
The difference between the essentially *felt* element in animal feeling and the essentially *understood* element of understanding

506. Understanding presupposes the intelligent principle just as feeling presupposes a sentient principle.

The first act by which the intelligent principle intuits being, that is, cognoscitive light, is that by which its nature as intelligent is constituted. The understanding, therefore, contains the *duality* already discerned in feeling where our analysis presented us with two elements, that which feels and that which is felt. In a manner perfectly analogous with feeling, understanding presents us with two elements, that which understands and that which is understood. But the difference is immense when we begin to compare the *felt* with the *understood* element.

507. The felt element in animal feeling, of which we are speaking, is real and contingent; the understood element is of its nature ideal, necessary and infinite. The difference, therefore, between what is simply felt and what is simply understood is nothing less than infinite.

What is felt is the *matter* of feeling, and as such inferior to that which feels; what is understood is the *form* of understanding, and superior to the one who understands. What is felt takes its desirability from that which feels; what is understood, on the contrary, makes the one who understands desirable. What is felt is a mere *term* of the activity of that which feels; but what is understood is a universal, unchangeable *object* to which the intelligent principle adheres.

Article 3.
Analogy between the *feeling principle* in animal feeling and the *intelligent principle* in understanding

508. If, therefore, we compare what is *felt* with what is *understood*, we find an immeasurable distance between them. This accounts for all the differences distinguishing and dividing animal feeling from human understanding. On the other hand, if we compare the other two elements, that is, the *feeling principle* and the *understanding principle*, we see a wonderful analogy between them.

We have already noted that all animal powers and activity proceed from a first act by which the feeling principle concurs in the production of the fundamental feeling. We may now apply a similar reflection to the intelligent principle. We shall find that all intellective powers — the whole of the human being in so far as this subject is a being endowed with intelligence — have their source in that first act by which the human spirit intuits being and so, together with being and aroused by being, concurs in positing its own intelligence.

509. In fact, an accurate analysis of our thoughts shows that in the order of mental operations any thought or mental operation whatsoever resulting in a new cognition is always reduced to a determination and limitation of some presupposed cognition. In other words, we learn explicitly what we already knew implicitly. An implicit cognition, from which all cognitions develop as from a seed, necessarily precedes these other cognitions which are only a limitation, continuation and further actuation of the first cognition. The spirit, with the activity by which it intuits universal being, also intuits every particular entity because everything is already contained in universal being. All that is needed is for universal being to reveal more of itself to the onlooker who like a spectator at a play sees everything that appears on the stage by the very act with which he sees the stage. And this stage, on which everything is manifest to our spirit, is *universal being* at which by nature we gaze steadfastly. The eye of our mind, which can never close or blink, is focused ineluctably on the scene before it.

In this way every intellective activity of the mind is explained by the single act with which the spirit intuits being in general. And this explanation coincides in great part with the way in which the activity of the feeling principle is presented. The variety of all partial sensations is received by this principle through that first act with which it produces the fundamental feeling.[213]

The activity of the human will also depends on the first, original act with which human beings understand. But we shall speak about this later.

2

THE INTELLECT AS A POWER

510. The human spirit intuits indeterminate-ideal being by nature. Such intuition constitutes not a human power or capacity but an act essential to the spirit. It is the intellect in so far as the intellect constitutes an element of human nature.

But if ideal being, present naturally to the human spirit, then acquires some relationship with the real world by means of sensations, the intellect in turn intuits ideal being furnished with some determinations. This new intellective act is that to which intellect is said to be in potency. In this sense we can speak of the *power* of intellect.[214] The *intellect* considered as a power will be understood better if we compare it with the other power of *reason*.

[213] It would be impossible to explain how the spirit could begin to think, that is, jump the abyss from not thinking to thinking, unless nature itself had provided the human spirit with a first act of intelligence. As St. Thomas says: 'Nothing can be brought from potency to act except through some being in act' (*S.T.*, I, q. 2, art. 3, corp.).

[214] The distinction we have indicated between the intellect as constituting human *nature* and the intellect considered as *power* seems to be noted by St. Thomas who says: 'The intellect can be considered in two ways: as apprehending being and universal truth, and as some particular thing and power with its own particular act' (*S.T.*, I, q. 82, art. 4, ad 1).

3

REASON

511. We have defined the essential intellect as 'that principle which intuits indeterminate-ideal being'.

We have defined reason as 'the faculty of applying indeterminate-ideal being to feelings, and to real and ideal beings' (cf. 499).

According to these definitions, the essential intellect furnishes us with 'indeterminate-ideal-being'.

Reason applies this indeterminate and ideal being to illustrate and render knowable things which of themselves are unknown to human beings.

512. Reason first applies the light of being to feelings. The first function of reason, *intellective-perception*, arises from this application.[215] By means of intellective perception we apprehend *real beings*. When felt, their action brings knowledge of an acting agent through the *principle of substance*.

513. When perceptions of *real beings* have been acquired, reason can apply ideal being in new ways. One of these applications enables it to pass from the contingency and limitation of real beings to acknowledgment of the existence of a necessary, unlimited, first Being. This second function of reason, *integration*, is carried out by means of what we may call the *principle of absoluteness*.[216] Through such a noble use of reason, we come into possession of new intellective riches formed by knowledge of the existence of God, which in some way completes our knowledge of real beings.

514. But we have to make further reflections on the real beings we perceive and know. We can exercise our power of abstraction on them by producing mental and ideal beings, new kinds of

[215] All these different functions of reason are described more fully in works already published by me on the theory of knowledge.

[216] It would be impossible for us to know with certainty that a being is contingent and limited if we did not first have some *knowledge* of what is necessary and unlimited. Nevertheless, although we require such knowledge, that is, the *idea* of necessary and unlimited being, we do not require to know that unlimited being subsists. This subsistence is what we deduce in the principle of integration.

objects, for ourselves. *Abstraction*, a third function of reason, creates the world of beings of pure reason, and concepts.

Reason thus becomes master of new material, that is, ideal and rational beings, to which it can unceasingly apply being in general. By applying it to ideal beings, reason creates what we call pure, abstract sciences.

515. Again, by applying the *pure sciences* of ideal beings to the real beings it has discovered, reason can derive all the *applied sciences* which regard real beings and can be pursued through abstract, scientific method.

516. The principle functions of reason, that is, of the faculty which applies ideal being, are therefore five: 1. perception; 2. integration; 3. abstraction; 4. deduction of the pure sciences; 5. deduction of complete sciences. *Reflection* is present in the last three functions, *reasoning* is clearly manifest only in the last two.

517. The aim and benefit of these different functions of reason is to provide us continually with new cognitions which must, however, be distinguished from the *operation* by which they are formed. We have to posit in the human soul a principle which intuits such truths after they have been formed, and a principle which forms them. This last principle, which draws one cognition from another, is precisely our power of *reason*; the principle which intuits the cognitions after their formation is our power of *intellect*, already defined by us as 'the faculty of intuiting more or less determined ideal beings'.[217] And St. Thomas seems to offer the same distinction between the powers of intellect and those of reason. He says: '*Intellect* and *reason* differ relative to the way in which they know. The intellect knows by means of simple intuition, reason by discourse and by passing from one thing to another. Nevertheless, reason comes to know through such discourse what the intellect knows without discourse.'[218]

[217] The intellect is always related to ideal beings. Our only communication with real *beings* is by means of *sense* and of *judgment*.

[218] *S.T.*, I, q. 79, art. 8, corp. These words would draw us to believe that St. Thomas intends here to speak rather of *reflection*, one of the more general functions of *reason*. Strictly speaking, reflection takes place when we consider what we already know [Rosmini provides a summary, rather than a translation of St. Thomas' words at this point].

518. Certainly, the principle which intuits truth is not properly and essentially different from that which discovers it, because the truth is discovered when it is intuited for the first time.[219] Nevertheless, the distinction we have made between these powers, although not radical, is well founded in their various ways of functioning, and should be preserved.

519. Critical philosophy, with the German school in its wake, made *reason* a power superior to *intellect*. Kant, led by what he saw of the Platonists' use of the word, considered *reason* as the power of the absolute and placed it above the intellect (the power of concepts). But the Platonists understood the word λογω as the *objective reason* of things, not as a mere power of the soul (although they were not entirely consistent in giving it this meaning). And there is no doubt that reason, as understood by Plato, who took it as objective reason and a synonym of 'idea', is infinitely superior to the intellect.

520. If, on the other hand, the discussion is about powers, and consequently about subjective reason, Plato and Aristotle seem to agree on the position assigned to reason. Marsiglio Ficino, who in his preamble to Plato's *Meno* intended to distinguish the powers of the soul according to the mind of his mentor and author, gave pride of place to *mind*, which corresponds to intellect, and second place to *reason*.[220]

The two powers were consistently placed in this order by the whole of antiquity. Plutarch, who did not adhere exclusively to any school, is an impartial witness: 'There are two altogether special assets possessed by human nature: intellect and reason. The intellect commands, and reason follows it.'[221]

Even the etymology of the word *intellect* indicates something already grasped by the mind (*intellectum* [literally 'read through', 'understood']); reason (*ratio*) from an etymological point of view simply points to an act of investigation. In the same way, the Greek word λογος, which corresponds to the

219 This is why St. Thomas maintains that *intellect* and *reason* are not two essentially distinct powers. Cf. *S.T.*, I, q. 79, art. 8.

220 'The first power of the soul is *mind* whose act is perpetual contemplation of truth. The second, *reason*, whose act is the investigation of truth' (*Argum. in Menon*).

221 *On the Education of Children*.

Latin *ratio*, has its origin in λεγω, 'I gather'. In other words, it represents an unfinished act, a search for the elements with which to form some cognition. In Latin, *mens* is the word best fitted to the meaning we give to *intellect*; in Greek, it is μενω, from which *mens* is certainly derived. Μενος expresses impetus, or ardour of spirit, and is understood as a force with immediate direction, just as the intellect naturally flies straight to the truth standing before it.[222]

4

THE TWO SERIES OF POWERS, OBJECTIVE AND SUBJECTIVE, THAT ORIGINATE FROM THE INTELLECT

521. We now have to take into account the more particular powers in order to see how they are attached to the intellect and how they originate from it in due order. We shall examine the nature of the intellect, therefore, to discover how all other intellective faculties are conceived within it. Such an examination shows that these faculties can be divided into two groups: *objective* and *subjective* faculties. In order to complete the listing of these faculties, we shall consider the passive faculties, as the title of this section requires, and the active faculties as occasion demands. In the following section, we shall examine further the active faculties.

[222] Νους comes from νεο which properly speaking means *necto*, 'I join', *cogo*, 'I bring together' (from which *cogito* is derived). J. Lennep affirms: 'νους is derived from the perfect middle νενοα. It indicates that highest part of human nature which connects, as it were, ideas conceived by the spirit and in this way reasons.' The word νους, therefore, although it may be translated by 'mind', expresses in its initial meaning a power which *discourses* and reasons, not a power which *intuits*. Hence Giov. Aug. Ernesti acutely places it in contrast with μενος which, as he says, 'is permanent and stable in a sentence or proposition'.

Article 1.
Objective and *subjective* faculties

522. The intellect results from the union of two terms, the *intellective principle*, the subject, and *being* as understood, the object.

Being manifests itself to the subject; its own proper activity consists in this manifestation. It does not act, however, as real substances do, but simply manifests itself without undergoing any alteration or change whatsoever. We call such a way of acting, which has nothing in common with the action of real substances, the *intelligibility of being*.

The intelligent principle cannot withdraw itself from the presence of this self-manifesting being. Being shines in the subject which cannot raise any opposition to what it sees. But the subject is not merely passive in its union with being. It is in fact intensely active in this first act, its very act of existence.

523. On these two united elements, that is, on the two activities of subject and object, two series of powers depend. It is, of course, true that in the rational or moral order no power is posited without requiring for its production harmony and concurrence between the two activities. Nevertheless, two series of powers can be distinguished, each of which has one of the two elements as its principal or dominant agent. The first series of powers (*objective* powers) comes into play if the manifestation of being dominates in such a way that the subject concurs in the manifestation only with the activity required by natural necessity; the second series of powers (*subjective* powers) results where activity greater than that required by natural necessity is found in the subject.

524. Let us analyse the act of the intellect, and see how it contains the root of both objective and subjective powers.

As long as being, and being alone, is manifest to the human spirit, only the manifestation of being is found in the spirit which does not yet feel itself. The *object*, in manifesting itself, acts only as something *intelligible*. It does not change but rather creates the substance to which it manifests itself. At this point, the human spirit does nothing more than *understand*. The sole result is an *objective power*.

525. But now the spirit *reaches out* to being as seen. *Sense*, an intellective sense which modifies the subject itself, begins to operate in the spirit. This sense is a *subjective* power.

This is the source of the two kinds of human powers, *objective* and *subjective*.

Article 2.
The identity of the feeling and intellective principle, the condition for developing *objective* and *subjective* powers in human beings

526. These *objective* and *subjective* powers develop in human beings, therefore, according to the development of the two principles from which they originate, namely, the *object* which manifests itself and the *subject* which reaches out. The object has to manifest new forms and aspects of itself to the spirit; the subject must pass to new modes of being and undergo diverse attractions. We have to investigate how the *object* changes itself before the mind so that the spirit may move from the vast, uniform intuition of indeterminate being to the vision of being in its various determinations and limitations; we also have to see how the *subject* changes by adhering with different degrees of intensity to the intuited or perceived objects. As we said, all the operations of the objective and subjective human powers are reduced to change in the object and the subject.

527. The *object* develops before the eye of the understanding only on condition that new feelings, to which the object can be applied, arise in the *subject*. The object is determined by the relationships these feelings have with it. In the same way, the subject acquires new states and modes of being only by obtaining new feelings. The feelings of the human subjects are in turn provided by their animality.

528. The human subject can develop in the order of intelligence only on condition that it is identical with the animal subject.

529. Let us first see, therefore, how it is possible to conceive that the feeling or *animal principle* and the *intellective principle* are not two, but one and the same principle in the human being.

The possibility is understood easily enough if we consider the analysis already provided of the feeling principle and the intellective principle. As we saw, the nature of the feeling principle is determined by the nature of what is *felt*, while the nature of the intellective principle is determined by the nature of what is *understood*. Feeling in this case is called 'animal' feeling because the thing felt is endowed with extension, while the understanding is called 'human' only because the thing understood is indeterminate being (cf. 504–507).

We may now consider the relationship of the feeling principle and the intellective principle with the felt element and the understood element. Here the activity of the two principles is subject to a relationship of passivity. Because this is so, there can be no repugnance in conceiving that the same principle is the subject of two kinds of passivity instead of one. In other words, a single principle is passive relative to two different agents each of which exercises its own mode of operation upon the principle.

This most simple, undivided principle, which is subject on the one hand to the passivity produced by the action of the body, and on the other to the passivity, or better, receptivity of universal being is precisely what we call the *human spirit*.

Article 3.
Development of the *objective* and *subjective* powers

530. In the human spirit (the feeling-intellective principle), therefore, are virtually contained all the powers which later, at given opportunities, show themselves as distinct through their various operations. The very act by which the spirit exists is its universal thrust for action which takes place in as many different ways as its activity later develops and manifests itself.

We have already seen the order and mode in which the animal powers develop but we still have to examine the way in which the spiritual powers come to act. The process presents us with a wonderful alternation between *objective* and *subjective* powers, both of which receive continual impetus and movement from what occurs in the feeling and animal element of human beings. Our present task, therefore, which we will undertake immediately, is to see how, as animality develops, intelligence also is activated.

§1. The faculty of intellective perception

531. Universal being, intuited by the mind, receives its determinations from relationship with feeling. Through feeling, human beings communicate with real being; and every reality echoes and relates to some corresponding ideal entity. To feel, to pass to the idea corresponding to the felt reality and simultaneously to advert that the felt reality is a determinate *being*: this is what we mean by intellective *perception*.

532. The elements of perception, that is, universal being and the fundamental feeling, are first given to human beings by nature: once united, they would bring about perception of themselves. As a result, classical writers said that self-perception was given by nature; and St. Thomas rightly teaches that we know ourselves *habitually*.[223] This means that the elements of self-perception are always present to us, enabling us to unite them easily and promptly when occasion arises, and so arrive at self-perception. All this takes place naturally and spontaneously so that we do not seem to acquire any new knowledge, but rather to reflect on what we already possess as though it were something completely familiar and natural.

When a baby understands for the first time the meaning of the monosyllable 'you' addressed to itself, it has such an easy, spontaneous perception of itself that it experiences no sense of wonder in discovering the perception. It does not and cannot realise that at this moment its intellective state has taken a great step forward. It would have to reflect in order to advert to what it has done, but is as yet incapable of such reflection.

We need to distinguish, therefore, between the *immediate perception of ourselves* and *reflection upon ourselves* which takes place after we have perceived ourselves. The second function is very different from the first, and is carried out only much

[223] Cf. *OT, App.*, no. 1; *Certainty*, 1181–1190.

later. But some self-perception, whose elements are given by nature, is soon present through the use of language.

533. If we consider exterior perceptions, we see that the external senses furnish the matter of these perceptions by means of the feelings with which they provide us. These senses begin to function as soon as we exist; they are prior to and independent of what we learn from articulated language.

534. Self-perception and the perception of exterior things are two functions of the same faculty of perception. Our first faculty to develop, therefore, is the *objective* faculty of perception. Its purpose is to provide our spirit with determinations and actuations of being, with new objects, and with determinate, real beings.

§2. The faculty of intellective sense

535. Generally speaking, the intellective spirit is inclined and directed from the beginning to the act of understanding, just as the sense is avid for feeling. We may believe, therefore, that a degree of vital pleasure is naturally and essentially connected with all intellective perceptions just as a degree of pleasure accompanies all sensations, as sensation. What we have called *intellectual sense* begins to reveal itself along with the perceptions of real things; it is a *subjective* faculty corresponding to the *objective* faculty of perception.

§3. The faculty of rational spontaneity

536. Nevertheless, this intellectual sense is still only a passive faculty, a pleasing, diffused feeling that the percipient subject experiences as a result of communication with another being by means of the intellect. Each *passive faculty*, however, has its counterpart in an *active faculty*.[224] Consequently, some activity

[224] The correspondence between active and passive faculties did not escape St. Thomas' acute observation: 'Appetitive powers must be in proportion to apprehensive powers' (*S.T.*, I, q. 83, art. 4, corp; cf. also I, q. 64, art. 2, corp.

proper to the intellective principle, which we normally call *intellective* or *rational spontaneity*, must correspond to this *intellective sense*.

537. Rational spontaneity is first drawn into activity by *animal instinct* just as the intellective sense originates by means of the *animal sense*, which provides the matter for rational perceptions. When a baby is drawn by animal instinct to carry out certain operations proper to animals, the subject undertaking these actions is both a sensitive and intellective principle. If this principle encounters difficulties in the execution of its animal operations, it uses all its powers to overcome the obstacles. Amongst these powers are those of its intelligence which the subject then makes use of in order to satisfy its animal instinct. *Rational spontaneity* is first roused in this way.

§4. Will — Choice and command — The faculty of affective volition

538. But we need to consider carefully the components of this first function of rational spontaneity. The abstract ideas of *end* and *means* play no part in it. Its formation depends on a simple act of will and on a command given to the very actions to which the baby is drawn by instinct. The first function of rational spontaneity is indeed the cradle of the will, but only in so far as will has perception as its guide. The baby perceives intellectually the movements of instinct, which it simply wills and commands.

539. These first volitions do indeed contain an *act of choice* and an *act of command*, in addition to the intellective sense united with diffused feeling.[225] However, they contain no *evaluation*. The willed and commanded instinctive movements are simply an object which gratifies sense and is loved. No judgment is made about its worth. This would require an abstract rule not yet formed by the baby.

and q. 80, art. 2, corp.).

225 'Choice' is an act of volition which does not exceed the limits of the will; 'command' is that act with which the will directs the movement of powers different from itself. A third kind of act, which is propagated to human powers but without any positive command, could be called a 'stimulated act'.

We call this first function of intellective spontaneity *affective volition*.

540. The subjective faculties corresponding to the objective power of perception are, therefore: *intellectual sense* (a passive faculty) and *rational spontaneity* in its first function, namely, affective volition (an active faculty).

§5. The faculty of abstraction — Reflection

541. After this level of subjective development, another objective faculty, *abstraction*, begins to develop, stimulated by the use of language coupled with animal instinct, as we have shown.[226]

542. Abstraction, which simply fixes attention on perceptions and on ideas if they have already been formed, always presupposes an act of reflection concerned with the observation of certain common properties and qualities in the perceptions and ideas to the exclusion of all the others. By means of abstraction, *specific* ideas are first drawn from *perceptions*, then *generic* from specific ideas. Generic ideas can become ever more generic and abstract until the universal and most abstract of all ideas are attained. Abstraction, therefore, is a function of *reflection* and *attention*, and develops through innumerable degrees almost to infinity; it moulds and marvellously embellishes the *ideal world* of the human mind.

§6. The faculty of evaluative volition — Judgments on the value of things — The spiritual instinct — Decrees of the will

543. If we consider that abstraction alone provides human beings with all the *rules* by which they act, we can see the extent to which any new activity of rational spontaneity depends on this power of abstraction.

544. The ideas of material or spiritual good and evil are abstract ideas.

[226] *OT.*, *ibid.*

By *material good*, I understand what is good for the body; by *spiritual good*, I understand opiniative good, or even what constitutes enjoyment for the spirit. Note that a real *good* or evil is not to be confused with the abstract *idea* of good and evil.

Our perception of real good and evil is enough to enable us to want or to reject them (cf. 539, 540), although we may still not have any distinct idea of a species or a genus of good, nor of good in general (all these are abstract ideas). Real good can be *desired* by means of what I have called 'affective volition'; but it cannot be *valued* without some specific, generic or universal idea which serves as a rule for our evaluative judgment.

For example, how can I judge that a loaf seen by me is something good? Note that I am not asking how I can *desire* the loaf, but how I can *judge* it to be good. Abstract ideas are not needed to desire it; the animal appetite, whose act or desire can be perceived and willed immediately by the rational principle, suffices for this. But desiring the bread is not of itself sufficient for judging that what I see with my eyes is good. In addition I need at least the specific idea of nutrition as good, and I must also know beforehand that bread is something to eat, something nourishing. Then I can judge. And this judgment is always a syllogism, whose major is given by abstraction, and would run: 'That which nourishes is good.' Only when this major premiss has been formed by me mentally, and I know that the object perceived with my senses is nourishing, can I make my judgment and conclude that the object is good.

All the rules, therefore, rendering judgments possible are provided by abstraction which has its own possibility in indeterminate-ideal being, the most universal of all rules. This being, provided by nature, is the source of our perceptions, that is, of our primitive judgments.

The objective faculty of abstraction is therefore the principle and cause of 1. a most noble subjective faculty which follows in its wake, providing another function of rational spontaneity, and 2. another level of will which I call *evaluative volition*

545. Abstraction, therefore, in offering new objects to the mind, obviously provides the will with new stimulation.

All objects of abstraction are ideal, and hence universal. They are the universal good and evil of every species or genus; pure, essential good and evil in that species or genus, without admixture of any determinate object; unlimited and unrealised good and evil which, pure and abstract, is a kind of common form shared by the real objects of different species and genera.

The worth of these real objects depends, in turn, upon the extent to which they share in this common form. Objects which share more extensively in that form of good are judged better and valued more highly. Such judgments can be made by us only through comparison and confrontation of the objects with the abstract form which therefore is needed as a rule for the evaluation of objects. But an object, when it is esteemed by us as good, can be desired and willed not only with our animal instinct, but by means of a totally spiritual instinct arising as a consequence of this judgment, and completed and confirmed by an explicit decree of the will.

Such is the nature of *volition*. As we can see, it is composed of three acts: the *evaluative or value judgment*, the *spiritual instinct* that draws human beings towards good as soon as they have valued it, and the *decree* of the will that decides it wants to satisfy this instinct.

§7. The faculty of choice — The formation of opinions about the value of things

546. This evaluative volition takes new forms as abstraction increases. The first abstract ideas of evil and good are the specific ideas of physical good and evil. Consequently the first ends the baby puts before itself, and the first rule it follows in its activity, is to to obtain the physical good and avoid the physical evil of which it has formed a concept for itself. At this level of development, the baby's *evaluative volitions* completely agree with his *affective volitions*, just as these harmonise perfectly with his *animal instincts*, which they strengthen and assist. At this age, the baby's powers are in complete peace and concord.

547. Nevertheless, even at this stage, *choice*, a new form of evaluative volition, begins to appear. The baby, who cannot reach out to all physical good as he would wish, has to choose which he judges best for satisfying his instincts.

548. These repeated acts of choice already begin to produce in

the baby *opinions* or habitual judgments about the value of things. For example, fruit that the baby has greatly enjoyed will be noted mentally as very worthwhile. This opinion, formed very early on, will induce him to choose the same fruit without trying any other, even much later in life when its real taste has diminished for him. He seems to taste and savour the fruit, if not with his palate, at least with his memory and through the opinion he retains of it.

§8. The faculty of practical force

549. The factual existence of *opinions* requires the greatest attention because it shows the presence in a subject of an altogether singular force capable of increasing or diminishing the value of objects. If the fruit of which we are speaking is esteemed extremely pleasant by the child not because it is so now but because it used to be, it is clear that the habitual esteem retained in the child's spirit is founded on and caused by the energy of the subject, the child himself, not by the present reality of the object. It is the subject who has created for himself, as it were, a quality that is no longer real. It is precisely at this point that what I call the *subject's practical force* begins to make its appearance. Mental retention of *habitual*, lasting and active *opinions* about the value of things, even when the real things have diminished in value, or lost their value completely, is the first act of the practical force. The object retains its worth for the subject, not because the object merits the worth, but because the subject continues to provide this worth by adding to it something of his own — his *persuasion*, his *belief*, his own act of *creation*.

§9. Development of choice and of the practical force

550. New kinds of good soon manifest themselves to the child's mind as the objective faculties continue to develop and present him with new objects. Although he first esteemed only that which brought him *pleasure*, he soon begins to appreciate

also the things which he knows to be *means* for obtaining, preserving and renewing the pleasure.

551. Hence, the child reaches out to all the objects around him, to everything in fact that will serve some purpose: house, garden, rooms, clothes and toys — all help to develop in the child's spirit the idea of *property*, of *that which is his own*.

552. Feelings and needs of a totally different, spiritual kind begin to develop in him contemporaneously with the opinion he forms about the value of the good which surrounds him, considered as a means to his own physical pleasure. These needs can all be embraced under the heading *desire for one's own greatness*, which very soon takes three special forms: an *instinct for superiority*, an *instinct for power*, and an *instinct for glory* or esteem from others.

553. This inclination of human nature for self-aggrandisement springs from two causes. First, the more human beings feel, and feel their own activity and capacity, the more their enjoyment increases. This cause of greatness is instinctive and immediate, the offspring of the intellective sense. It is included in the subjective faculties amongst *affective volitions*.

But the human being is also endowed with ideal being and capable not only of perceiving many beings but also of comparing them in order to discover which has more and which has less entity. Having a greater degree of entity means having greater worth. Human beings desire to acquire the greatest possible quantity of *entity* because they want to be worth a great deal, and to tip the scales of intelligence heavily in their own favour. This second cause, the offspring of the intellect as objective power, has its place amongst *evaluative volitions*.

We want our own greatness, therefore, in equal measure with an *affective* as well as an *evaluative volition*. The affective volition of our own greatness is revealed as soon as we come to perceive ourselves. Evaluative volition, however, requires in addition reflection upon ourselves and comparisons between beings and with ourselves. When all these new kinds of good manifest themselves to us, our sphere of choice is immensely extended.

554. Our choice no longer lies amongst physical goods alone; it now falls between physical and spiritual good which, as

different kinds of good, soon come into collision with one another. Our act of choice now differs greatly from what it was.

As long as we had to choose between physical goods, our choice was directed by the animal instinct itself, which always selected what was more pleasurable. Now, however, the choice lies between physical and spiritual good, which are not of the same kind. A true conflict breaks out between the various active powers because different powers preside over the two kinds of good, the animal instinct over physical good, the spiritual, volitive instinct over spiritual good. One of these powers has to surrender, sacrificed to the victory of the other.

Victory can go to the spiritual good in two ways: either because the spiritual instinct (affective volition) conquers, or because the decretorial will conquers (evaluative volition). In the first case, the spiritual instinct takes on prevalent, but accidental vigour. In the second, the *practical, decretorial force*, by which the will subjects instinct, exerts increased strength.

555. But this practical, decretorial force draws much of its vigour from the reality of the objects themselves, and from natural spontaneity — or rather, this force is itself simply a power for using valiantly, and directing, the constitutive elements and inferior forces of human nature.

556. We must note, however, that whenever the practical force of human freedom turns towards evil by following a wrong opinion or formal error, it exercises special energy. In this case, the practical force itself creates the object, and acts according to its own creation.

557. In order to know the full range of command exercised by this spiritual power which we call *practical force*, we have to consider the stages by which it moves from its seat in the most elevated part of human nature, and specifically in the act of judgment, in order to reach, move and dominate the lower powers. Its influence falls upon them mediately, not immediately, as it communicates its impulse down the line from one power to another until it reaches the lowest.

558. The first, proper act of the practical force is that with which it forms its *opinion* of the good or evil in some thing. Note, however, that this opinion is not concerned only with good considered in itself. The practical judgment of which we are speaking affirms the quantity of good present in something

something obtainable. Our judgment is indeed practical, not theoretical if, after affirming that a given thing contains an immense good, that this immense good is good for us and that it can be obtained by us, we then go on to will it.

This first act of our practical force moves the power nearest to it, that is, our power of *spiritual affectivity*. It is impossible for us to judge that a given thing contains an immense good, and a good that is good for us and obtainable by us, without our spirit's being filled with joy, hope, courage, and so on. These spiritual affections communicate themselves with their own special effect to human *animality* which they render active, by giving rise first to internal and then to external animal activity with which human beings tend towards the attainment of that good.

559. If, however, these spiritual affections are sometimes barely feelable or perhaps even unobservable, the evaluative judgment induces the relative action in our members either immediately or by means of an express *decree*.

§10. The moral faculty

560. At this point a completely new extension of human activity is revealed. So far, the human being has known different kinds of good which have drawn his powers into motion. But he has thought only of himself. Now, as he finds himself in society with others, he realises that the things he has judged good for himself are also good for beings exactly like himself.

Here we find an order of things — the moral order — far more sublime than anything already encountered. The human being soon realises that he cannot be content and happy at the cost of making others miserable. On the contrary, he must seek the happiness of others as though it were his own. What inner light shines, enlightening him in this sublime way, leading him to limit his own enjoyment by ordering it in harmony with the enjoyment of others?

561. He discovers this law revealed in his heart along with the knowledge of the existence of other human beings by means of his faculty for esteeming and evaluating all things *objectively*,

that is, as they are, rather than as related to him. This faculty of objective evaluation, the essentially objective and absolute faculty, is a consequence of the first and most sublime of his powers, which intuits being and constitutes his intelligence.

There are now two ways in which the human being can judge things. He can evaluate them relative to himself, and relative to human nature in general; he can evaluate them subjectively, or evaluate them objectively by weighing the degree of entity they possess in themselves.

Prior to this, only the first kind of judgment had been available to the human being; actual morality was therefore impossible for him. Now, as he develops judgments of the second kind, he immediately feels moral necessity, knows the law and experiences the sanction of interior approval and remorse. His *activity* has two ways open before it which arise from the two rules revealed to him. He can act either according to his *subjective* or *objective esteem* of things.

562. The two rules, which sometimes agree, can also disagree and clash. The second is authoritative, and commands the first as a master commands his subject. The first only attracts, it never commands the subject. We must now ask, therefore, how human beings can obey the commands of the second and repudiate the attractions of the first, and how they can sacrifice their own good for the sake of the respect demanded of them by the absolute good.

These questions are not easy to answer. To do so, we have first to understand that there is a hierarchy amongst absolute entities and good, and therefore an absolute order or absolute disorder. Secondly, we must grasp that the human being as intellective feels and perceives only ideal being and absolute being, as we have said. He does not even perceive himself except absolutely. His existence as an intellective being, therefore, is not to be found in the subject, but in the world of absolute beings and in objectivity. Consequently, the objective order, in so far as the intellective subject procures it, is the proper order of the intellective being; objective disorder, in so far as he procures it, is his own order.

If the human being were simply a purely intellective, volitive being and possessed only the act by which he saw and adhered to beings, he would be naturally moral just as the animal is naturallysensitive.[227] Moral necessity exists in the objective, absolute world; the human being shares in moral necessity in so far as he shares in this objective, absolute world. Such necessity is of its nature invincible and insuperable precisely because the nature of beings which form the objective, absolute world is invincible and insuperable. Moral necessity demands, prescribes, commands, orders, chastises and rewards as part of its own necessity. If we ask, therefore, how the human being can act according to the objective esteem of things without regard to their subjective esteem, we have to reply that he draws the strength to do so from the objective and absolute world itself in which he exists and lives as an intellective being.

563. At this point we can view the extent of this moral power in the human being and see how it decreases and increases.

The strength of moral power with which we conquer the attractions of subjective good depends upon our share in the absolute world of beings. Because of this, Christianity points to our weakness in doing good as long as we exist in the natural order where we share only incipiently and tenuously in essential being, the principle of the absolute order of beings; it also indicates that we can do all things when helped by divine grace through which we share abundantly in essential, absolute being.

§11. The choice between subjective and objective good — Freedom

564. When our powers reach the stage at which we act morally, the act of *choice* takes on a new form, the third of those to which this function is susceptible. We no longer compare different aspects of physical good (the first form); nor do we compare physical with spiritual good (the second form); we now compare *subjective good* with something that has its own *objective* dignity, and choose between them.

565. Our *practical force* also extends itself in new, more wonderful ways. Putting the objective dignity of things on one side of the scales, and their subjective worth on the other,

[227] Cf. *Teodicea*, 390–415.

it inclines the balance in favour of the former as though all the weight were on the side of objective dignity alone. But the practical force can also draw us into error by creating an illusion of weight which leads us to give the advantage to subjective good.

566. We shall examine later the way in which 'freedom of indifference', as it is called, is manifested in this choice between subjective and objective good. Here it is sufficient to conclude by pointing out once more that the development of human powers, which we have described very briefly, takes place through an unceasing alternation of *objective* and *subjective* powers. Objective powers, however, always precede subjective powers in their development so that the human spirit always puts forth some new kind of activity after new kinds of objects have been revealed to it.

And here we must pause to examine each of our active faculties. These require more attention because they have a closer connection with moral discipline.

SECTION TWO

THE *ACTIVE* FACULTIES OF HUMAN UNDERSTANDING

567. Because we cannot consider *powers* without first considering *acts*, we must first determine the nature of *human acts*.

1

THE HUMAN ACT

568. Every act proper to a human being is called 'human', and is carried out with powers found only in human beings, not in brute animals.

569. Intellect and will are powers found in human beings, but not in brute animals. Hence, a purely intellective act must be called 'human', because it is done by a power proper to human beings but not possessed by brute animals.

Amongst theologians, Giuseppe Antonio Alasia recognised that intellective perception must be placed among human acts. He says that human acts 'include the act done solely by the intellect, that is, simple perception, the act with which the human assents to the truth known manifestly as true'. He adds: 'Although these acts do not spring from free will, they are called "human" because they result from powers which distinguish the human being from other animals. They proceed, that is, either from the intellect alone, or from the intellect and will simultaneously. In the latter case, the will tends towards a thing with a movement that is necessary but not free.'[228]

570. However, despite this clear teaching, even Alasia did not give an accurate definition of the human act which he defined as 'a movement in the human being proceeding from knowledge

[228] *Comment. Theol. Moral.*, Dissert. I, c. 1, n. 3.

of the end as end'.[229] The human being does not begin to act for an end known as end without first exercising the power of abstraction (cf. 541–550). But long before we form abstract ideas, we act with our intellect which has different functions prior to the function of abstraction. All the acts of these functions are human, according to Alasia's own principle.

2

THE WILLED ACT

571. To include will in the definition of human acts is not, therefore, entirely accurate. Properly speaking, *human acts* are the genus, *willed* acts the species. 'Will' was included in the definition of human acts for two reasons: first, because moral authors wished to define acts which were not only human but also moral; second, because 'will' was understood as a general faculty by which human beings can move all their powers. When 'will' is understood in such a wide sense, every intellective act must simultaneously be conceived as willed.

In my opinion, however, the will is not simply that which moves the understanding. We must define it more strictly as: 'The power by which the human being tends to known good,' or more generally: 'The power by which the human being tends to a known and pleasing object.' Consequently, I think that it is philosophically inaccurate to extend the meaning of the word 'will' excessively; such a use results in equivocations and useless discussions. Declaring the will to be the sole mover of all other powers means including instinct in the definition. A similar extension of meaning is given to the word 'knowledge', when it is made to include corporeal sensations.

People are generally inclined to broaden the sense of the words 'knowledge' and 'will' because they tend to attribute to external objects what they experience in themselves. For example, primitive nations attribute a soul to all the objects of nature because they cannot understand how natural beings are

229 *Ibid.*, no. 2.

moved without a spirit in them; and in this respect perhaps they reason better than philosophers. Thus, in order to explain the phenomena of brute animals, popular philosophy makes analogous use of what is seen to take place in human beings, attributing *knowledge* and *will* to animals solely because in human beings the same effects are seen to arise from knowledge and will. The reasoning is certainly false, but we must not be surprised at finding such loose terminology (in which sensation is taken for knowledge, and instinct for will) in the earliest philosophers. What is surprising is that it still exists.[230]

572. The Scholastics' general acceptance of the will as the principal mover of all the powers gave rise to an extraordinary and truly insoluble question: 'Does the intellect move the will, or vice versa?' On the one hand, they said, the will moves the intellect because the will is that which moves all the powers. On the other, the will tends only to what is known; the intellect therefore must move the will, presenting to it an object to which it tends. St. Thomas deals with the question in his *Summa Theologica*. He first grants that 'the will, acting like an agent, moves all the powers of the soul to their acts except the natural, vegetable forces which are not subject to our will'.[231] This was the common opinion. Here the word 'will' has the broad meaning which produces the confusion we want to dispel. But the difficulty arising from this principle could not escape the observation of a genius like Thomas. He himself states the difficulty: 'We cannot will anything which the intellect has not first known. Now, although the intellect cannot move without being moved by the will, the will that moves the intellect must have some prior cognition present to it. And so the process continues to infinity if every act of the will must be preceded by an act of the intellect and every act of the intellect preceded by an act of the will.' Thomas replies that the process to infinity is avoided by stopping at the first movement of the intellect. But who

[230] St. Thomas is quick to observe that knowledge and will can be attributed to brute animals only when these words are used in a metaphorical sense. Certain places in his works, where he seems to attribute knowledge and will to animals, must, according to the intention of the Saint, be interpreted with this observation in mind.

[231] *S.T.*, I, q. 82, art. 4, corp.

causes this first movement of the intellect? God himself, answers St. Thomas, not the will.[232] 'Intellectual apprehension necessarily precedes any movement whatsoever of the will, but a movement of the will does not precede every intellectual apprehension. Thus the principle that moves us to consider and understand is an intellective principle higher than our intellect: it is God himself'.[233] This means that the will is *not* the sole mover of the human intellect.

St. Thomas saw and maintained the strict, rigorous definition of the will. He says that it is 'a certain inclination consequent to the form of the intellect'.[234] Hence, the intellect first acts without the intervention of the will, and according to the natural impulse which it posits in its first act, as we have said. By this first act, the intellect is always drawn to intuit being (which is necessarily present to it) and the determinations and realisations of being, that is, of particular, real beings.

573. This natural inclination of the human spirit is exactly like the inclination which moves the animal's life instinct. Just as animal instinct posits feeling, which is the essence of animal, so the first act of the intellect posits understanding, which is the essence of the human being as an intelligent being. In the way that the life instinct, when it changes its matter, shows its activity with different effects, so the intellect, when sense presents it with some determined actions of being, displays its activity with the immediate perception of real objects. Thus the intellect is in continuous act even before the forces of the will move. This intellective activity, devoid of the will's control, embraces the intuition of universal being and the perception of feelable things. As Aquinas says, therefore, the cause of the first act of the intellect, as well as the cause of the act of the life instinct, is found only in God, the Author of nature.[235]

232 Sensists, who claim to have St. Thomas in their favour, should note this.

233 *S.T.*, I, q. 82, art. 4, ad 3.

234 *S.T.*, I, q. 87, art 4, corp.

235 In the *Summa* St. Thomas also teaches that the natural instinct of brute animals is moved by God (*S.T.*, II-II, q. 83, art. 10, ad 3).

3

THE MORAL ACT

574. The *human act* is the genus; the *intellective act* and the *volitive act* are the species. There is, however, a third species, *moral acts*, which contains the *eminently human* acts.

575. For an act to be moral, it is not sufficient for it to be intellective and volitive. The first intellections and volitions of children cannot be called moral because the law is not yet promulgated in these children who are ignorant of the objective order of beings, that is, of the order to which duty is directed (cf. 560–563).

We have seen that volitions or acts of the will are divided into two very different classes which we called 'affective' and 'evaluative volitions' (cf. 563). A *concept* formed by the intellect must precede both classes of *volition*, because, as we said, the will is simply the power by which human beings tend to a known good.

But not every volition need be preceded by many concepts, or by concepts of the same quality. Affective volitions require less intellectual development than evaluative volitions. This is indeed what precisely differentiates them from the latter and makes them the first to be activated in human development.

Affective volitions in the intellective part require only perceptions of animal good. *Evaluative volitions* require much more. In order to desire something as a result of its evaluation, we need more than perception. The thing must be evaluated by us, that is, judged. This judgment on the thing's value needs a rule which is always an abstract idea. Thus, *abstraction* must precede the evaluative volition (cf. 541–544).

576. Purely *affective volitions* cannot be called moral, because they contain no value judgment; the will co-operates in the act solely to gratify and assist animal instinct.

577. Nor are all *evaluative volitions* moral. To be moral, the evaluative judgment must be regulated not by any rule, but by a moral rule. As we saw, there are three kinds of *rules* according to which human beings in their first development judge the value of things — three *criteria* of good, which we form

successively. The first rule states: 'That which satisfies our animal senses is good.' In this case the rule is 'the abstract idea of animal good.' Next, we discover new good manifested to us by a human instinct, and the rule of our judgments becomes the principle: 'That which pleases us, whether it be animal or spiritual, is good'. These first two rules are used solely for measuring and evaluating subjective good; the moral rule, lying deep within our soul, has not yet assumed an external, explicit and really effective form. It is activated only when we become aware that there are other intelligent beings in the world besides ourselves whom we must treat with the same regard as we treat ourselves (cf. 546–554).

When we have discovered the existence of other beings like ourselves, we quickly arrive at the mental conception of the first intelligence by the faculty of integration[236] and at what is owed to supreme intelligence, God himself, the source of all intelligences. In this way, we attain full possession 'of the abstract idea of objective good'; the idea in our mind has become determinate and been applied. In a word, it is suitable for guiding our judgments, and by means of them our volitions, and finally our actions by means of our volitions. The moral act begins, therefore, when this idea speaks in us for the first time.

If we now go on to call 'law' this abstract, specific idea of objective good, this rule of the absolute value of things and actions, we shall have a clear definition of a moral act, namely, 'the act of the will in its relationship with the law'.

578. In *moral acts*, therefore, we can distinguish three elements: the first, appertaining to the intellect, is the *perception* and *conception of any thing* towards which duty is exercised; the second, *evaluative volition*, appertains to the will; the third element, the *law* or idea of objective good, which is superior to both the intellect and will.[237]

[236] *OT*, 623, 624.

[237] It is traditional teaching that moral good consists in preferring *objective* to *subjective good*, and moral evil in preferring *subjective* to *objective good*. It is an essentially Christian teaching. St. Augustine says: 'A will turned from unchangeable good' (objective good) 'to its own good' (subjective good) 'sins' (*De Lib. Arbitrio*). His follower, St. Prosper, repeats the same sentiment to explain sin: 'Changeable nature, which depends on unchangeable essence for its preservation, turned away from the supreme good to be wickedly enthralled

As long as none of these ideas of objective good is formed in us, our acts cannot be moral. But from the moment that only one of the ideas is formed in our spirit, human acts have acquired the characteristic of morality.

4

THE ELECTIVE ACT

579. We have distinguished the *moral act* from *human*, from *intellective* and from *volitive acts*. We must now distinguish it from *acts of choice*. The concept of acts of choice is not entirely the same as that of moral acts or of volitive acts. The will can wish without choice. This happens in all affective volitions. Hence, choice is not an essential characteristic of acts of the will.

580. The act of choice is not necessarily included even in evaluative volitions. If only one object were present to our minds, we could evaluate it indeterminately as good and desire it, but no comparison would be made with other objects nor would any kind of choice be involved in this action of our will. The act of choice or election takes place solely in those evaluative volitions in which we give a value to several objects present to our spirit. We choose one of them because we cannot have them all.

We have distinguished three levels of choice, because three kinds of conflict can arise between the good things from which we must choose. There can be conflict: 1. between things good for our animality which we cannot possess simultaneously; 2. between animal good and the subjective spiritual good proper to human nature; and finally, 3. between subjective good on the one hand and the objective order on the other. The first conflict reveals itself in us before the second, and the second before the third. This same sequence takes place at the three levels of choice.

It is clear that as long as we have not conceived the objective order of things, we feel no moral obligation. Hence, there are

by its own good,' which is subjective (*De vocat. gent.*, II, c. 34).

two levels of choice in the child before the child reaches the age of morality. The concept of the *elective act of choice*, therefore, is quite different from the concept of the *moral act*.

5

THE FREE ACT

581. We must now distinguish some very closely related and easily confused ideas.

The *act of choice* cannot be confused with *free act*.

In fact, the first level of choice is truly devoid of freedom because choice is determined by the prevalence of animal instincts, to which the will spontaneously accedes.

Relative to the second level of choice, freedom seems present because we choose between *real*, physical *good* and *opiniative good*. The latter is not always indicated by natural human instinct; it is created by us and is a product of our practical force. But can the practical force, which creates what we think is good, truly act as long as we are confined to the sphere of subjective good? And if it can, is it free within this sphere? I doubt this very much. If the practical force acts while we are confined to the sphere of subjective good, I think it would indeed create a chosen good for us, but not freely. Accidental causes would determine the practical force to boost one good rather than another. These causes, which could be very slight and could perhaps pass unobserved, would remove the exercise of free will because spontaneity would immediately accede to them.

582. However, the real and clear location of the power of human freedom is the third level of choice. At this level *freedom* is called to exercise control over all that is *subjective*, by conforming it to the *objective*, absolute order; it is called to make what is unseen and ideal — truth and justice — dominate over all that is visible and real, over the universe and, in the universe, over everything beautiful, great, seductive and captivating.

583. In my opinion, St. Thomas must be understood as speaking about this third level of choice when he posits human freedom in the act of *choice*, because it is clear that he is speaking

about choice relative to morality, that is, a moral choice. But, as I have shown, choice is moral only at its third level.[238]

584. Freedom, therefore, strictly speaking consists in not experiencing necessity. A free act is an act of the will, an act not determined by any necessary cause different from the willing principle.

585. This *freedom* is the source of the *merit* (in the strict sense) of human actions. There are, however, other kinds of *freedom* appropriate to the will, which explains why 'freedom', or 'free will', is given different meanings. And these meanings must be carefully distinguished if we are to avoid discussing insoluble problems, a trap into which many authors have fallen in their treatment of freedom.

And I think it worthwhile, for the sake of avoiding confusion, to separate *meritorious freedom* from every other kind of freedom appropriate to the human will.

6

THE DIFFERENT KINDS OF FREEDOM APPROPRIATE TO THE HUMAN WILL

586. 'Freedom', generally understood, means the opposite of 'servitude'. But just as there are different kinds of servitude, there are also different kinds of freedom. Perfect freedom

[238] According to St. Thomas, and as we ourselves say, freedom is a characteristic not of all, but of certain acts of the will. St. Thomas reduced the principal acts of the will to two: *volition* and *choice*. Simple volition is not free; freedom, according to St. Thomas, is rooted in choice: 'Choice is proper to free will. Thus we say it is characteristic of free will that we can accept one thing and refuse another. This is choice, and therefore the nature of free will must be considered from the point of view of choice' (*S.T.*, I, q. 83, art. 3, corp). The places in which St. Thomas teaches that freedom has its seat in the act of choice have been published together in Petavius, bk. 3, c. 4, *De opificio sex dierum*. An examination of all these places does not show that Aquinas intended to affirm that every choice was free, but only that choice is a characteristic of freedom, and that without choice there can be no freedom. Lastly, St. Thomas does not normally speak about choice in general, as we said, but about moral choice.

excludes all servitude — as Seneca says: 'Freedom consists in serving nothing.'[239] Let us distinguish carefully the various types of freedom.

Article 1.
Freedom from all violence

587. We said that the human will is always free. This must be correctly understood. If the expression means that the will cannot be *constrained*, it is true without qualification because it is simply a result of my defining 'will' as 'desire tending to known good'. A will, therefore, that acted as a result of violence used towards it would be a contradiction in terms. We would be saying: 'Willing what is not willed'. To will something is to regard that thing as good; to will something is to love it. But what is regarded as good, what is loved, is willed without constraint. On the other hand, to apply violence to the will means so to operate that the will, which by its essence is the tendency to good, tends to evil as evil.

Hence, no external force, no *violence* whatsoever, acts on the will. External force and will are opposites which never meet in any way. There is no middle term: either the object of the will is considered good and the will loves it without any constraint, or the will considers the object evil, in which case it is no longer the object of the faculty.

588. For this reason, St. Thomas says that even God (who cannot do contradictory things because they are not things) cannot constrain the will. 'Violence cannot be done to the will, relative to the will's proper act, because an act of the will is simply an inclination which proceeds from a knowing, internal principle. On the other hand, constraint or violence come from an external principle. Hence, clearly, constraining or violating the will is contrary to the notion of its act.' From this truth, St. Thomas immediately deduces that God can indeed move the will in some other way, but not by doing violence to it. If God moved the will

[239] 'You ask what is freedom? It is to serve nothing, to be necessitated by nothing' (*Ep.* 47).

through violence, the will would play no part: 'It would not be the will that was moved but something contrary to the will.'[240]

Article 2.
Freedom from all necessity

589. Nevertheless, the will, although it cannot be subject to violence, is not always free in the strict and proper sense. It could be moved from necessity without suffering violence.

Hence, theologians distinguish two kinds of liberty which they call: 'freedom from violence' (*libertas a coactione*), and 'freedom from necessity' (*libertas a necessitate*).

590. Although they apply the word 'freedom' to both kinds of liberty, they teach that absolutely speaking the word cannot, without qualification, be applied properly to a will which is free from violence but nevertheless under necessity to some extraneous principle.

591. In order to avoid all equivocation, therefore, it will help to distinguish *spontaneity* from *freedom* in the faculty of will which, although it can never act except spontaneously, does not always act with complete freedom.

Nor is the distinction between completely free action and spontaneous action of little importance. It has been solemnly approved in the Church by the decisions of Councils and Popes in condemning the teaching of Calvin, Jansen and Baius. This teaching was grounded in the confusion between *will* and *freedom* which is an accident of will. To eliminate the confusion and correct the error, 'freedom' (in the strict, absolute sense) was reserved specifically for the human ability to act without any determining necessity, that is, without any impulse outside the volitive principle (cf. 584). Baius' proposition 'Violence alone is opposed to the natural freedom of the human being'[241] was condemned; its opposite therefore must be true and approved, namely, 'Not only violence but every necessitating impulse is opposed to natural freedom.' Consequently, whenever the will

[240] *S.T.*, I-II, q. 6, art. 4, corp.

[241] Baius' 66th proposition, condemned by St. Pius V, Gregory XIII and Urban VIII.

acts under necessity, and precisely because it is under necessity, there can be no freedom. We are left only with a non-free will.

The same use of the word 'freedom', taken to mean exclusively a state or condition of the will in which no violence is experienced, is confirmed by Baius' other proposition (also condemned by the Church): 'Whatever is done by the will, even if under necessity, is done freely.'[242] If this is false, its opposite is true, namely, 'That which is done by the will, but done necessarily, is not done freely.' Here, use of the phrase 'to act freely' is clearly rejected as an indication of an action which merits in the strict sense, although it is carried out simply with *will* and *spontaneity*. The Church's decision also declares that the word 'freedom' and the expressions 'acting with freedom' and 'acting freely' are best used to indicate the function or act of will in which the power of will is not under necessity to anything, but determines and moves itself towards any one of the choices before it.

592. If, therefore, certain writers, including St. Augustine, sometimes use 'freedom' or 'free will' to mean the will's spontaneous but necessitated action, their meaning must be interpreted according to the context in which these phrases are used, and by comparison with parallel places. Attention must not be fixed on a single phrase, or on any phrase taken out of context, but on the total teaching, on the core of the whole system, and on the understanding to which the author's thought is seen to be finally directed. And because anything that can help the true, correct interpretation of such an outstanding, authoritative and penetrating author as St. Augustine must be of great importance, I beg the reader's patience if here and elsewhere, while dealing with *freedom* or *free will*, I try to explain the concepts and expressions of the great Father.

In the following passage St. Augustine uses the expression 'free will' in the sense of 'the will acting spontaneously', as the context clearly shows: 'The congenital, enduringly human free will we are looking for is that by which all wish to be blessed, including those who refuse the means leading to beatitude.'[243] Here we clearly have a definition of the will in general, that is,

[242] [Proposition 39].

[243] *Operis imp. contra Jul.*, bk. 6, c. 11.

of that power which, as I frequently assert, tends to good as such, and consequently to happiness. St. Augustine does not say simply 'free will' but 'congenital, enduring, human free will'; he has made additions which clearly show that there must be another free will. He defines the special characteristics of one free will, and indicates that it must not be confused with the other.

The same can be said when he uses the word 'freedom' instead of 'spontaneity' which is clearly intended by the contest. Augustine says: 'The immutable freedom of will with which the human being has been and is created is that with which we all wish to be blessed, and which we cannot not will.'[244] He adds immediately: 'But this freedom is insufficient for us to be blessed, or to live uprightly and so become blessed. The freedom by which we can do good is not immutably congenital in us in the same way as the will by which we wish to be blessed. We all want to be blessed, even those who do not want to do good.'[245] Clearly, then, there are two distinct freedoms, the first of which appears to be synonymous with 'will'; only the second, however, can properly be described as 'moral will' and 'meritorious freedom.'

593. In conclusion I note that the word 'free' is taken to mean both 'free to do something' and 'free from all subjection, not under any necessity, free not to do that thing.' In the first case, 'free' means being master of a situation, that is, 'having the power and capacity to do something'. This is the opposite of the second case. In fact, it is possible to have the power to do a given thing and at the same time be under necessity in doing it. St. Augustine took this view in the passages quoted above where he called human will 'freedom' or 'free will', and in doing so indicated our power to tend to happiness. We certainly 'have the power to tend to happiness' although, because we are under necessity to tend towards it, 'we are not free not to tend to it.' It is proper, therefore, for someone who is free, that is, not subject to the power of another, to do what he finds most pleasing; one who serves, however, is prevented from doing many things he would like and desire to do. Hence *freedom* is used to describe what is properly a consequence of freedom, that is, human

[244] *Ibid.*, c. 12; see also c. 26.

[245] *Ibid.*

dominion to tend towards and desire the things we like, irrespective of any necessity.

Article 3.
Freedom from all servitude

594. Authoritative writers gave other meanings to the word 'freedom', considered as a quality of willed action, and made whatever distinctions were needed to ensure their writings would be correctly understood. As we said, freedom was first applied metaphorically to mean a quality of willed action, and thus detached from its proper sense which simply indicates the opposite of servitude. But we could expect it to retain some of its original meanings. These will be rooted in the threefold understanding of servitude, which we must now examine: 1. servitude with a basis in right alone (servitude *de jure*); 2. actual or *de facto* servitude alone; 3. servitude with a basis in right combined with enforced actual servitude.

595. Three kinds of freedom correspond to these three kinds of servitude. We can be 1. free by right, but actually bonded; 2. actually free, but not by right; and finally 3. free neither actually nor by right. In this last case, when persons freely remain subject to a master, they can be called 'free' because they are subject to servitude without any pressure from force or coercion.

596. All three meanings were applied to the freedom of the human will. First, the will is said to originate as not free but subject to the law. Second, the will that does not wish to serve the law is said to be free from the law in so far as it has thrown off subjection to the law. Third, although the will obeys the law, it is said to remain free in the sense that it obeys of its own accord, without external force, and effectively.

597. The three species can also be considered as three degrees of servitude and of freedom. The first degree depends upon the presence or absence of rightful subjection; the second upon the presence or absence of actual subjection; the third upon the presence of rightful and actual subjection, which may be either enforced or willed.

598. Writers always considered such subjection and freedom in relationship with justice and injustice, and thus distinguished three states of will. In the first state, the will is the servant of justice and therefore free from sin. In the second state, the will is the servant of sin and consequently free from justice. In the third state, the will has the power to serve either justice or sin, but does not necessarily serve one or the other. The first two states could be called states of *unilateral* freedom, the third the state of *bilateral* freedom.

599. The three degrees of servitude or freedom we have indicated can each be distinguished in the first two states, that is, those which concern justice and sin. The service of justice can be understood from the point of view of right, or factually (because of an act by a non-necessitated will), or finally according to necessary servitude. Those who are admitted to the beatific vision serve justice by willed necessity, just as the damned in hell are necessarily the servants of sin.

600. St. Paul speaks about unilateral freedom and servitude when he says: '*Freed* from sin, you have been made *servants* of justice; — hence, on the other hand, when you were *servants* of sin you were free from justice.'[246] In these words the Apostle points to the kind of freedom and servitude that is rooted both in right and in act. Relative to freedom and servitude by right, he argues his case on the basis of the titles by which we have been freed from servitude to sin and become servants of the justice of Christ, that is: 1. the title of purchase, and 2. the title of willing dedication. The Apostle had already said about the title of purchase, by which Christ redeemed us from servitude of sin: 'Do you not know that all of us who have been baptized in Jesus Christ, were baptized in his death?'[247] About the title of spontaneous dedication he had said: 'Do you not know that to whomsoever you make yourselves servants by obeying him, you are servants of him whom you obey, whether of sin unto death or of obedience unto justice? But thanks be to God, you who were servants of sin have sincerely obeyed the form of the teaching into which you have been changed.'[248] The passage shows that

[246] Rom 6: [18, 20].
[247] Rom 6: [3].
[248] Rom 6: [16, 17].

he is not speaking about freedom and servitude dependent simply on right, but also about that which actually exists. He exhorts Christians to maintain themselves in this freedom from sin, obtained for them by Christ.

The third degree of servitude (necessary servitude to sin) is also indicated by the Apostle in the same place. Without the grace of Jesus Christ, there was a necessary servitude to sin and it is of this that he is speaking when he says: 'Because sin will not rule over you, since you are no longer under the law but under grace'[249] and again: 'We know that the law is spiritual; but I am carnal, sold to sin.'[250]

601. These different meanings of the word 'freedom' should be borne in mind if we want to understand certain passages of the Fathers, and especially of St. Augustine. It is easy to see that human beings can never be without one or other of the three kinds and degrees of freedom and servitude. There can be no difficulty, therefore, in the following passage: 'A free will is always present in us, but it is not always good. It is either free from justice when it serves sin, in which case it is evil; or it is free from sin when it serves justice, and in this case it is good.'[251]

St. Augustine, the 'doctor of grace' indicates this triple freedom in very many places. I shall quote two passages as a key to understanding many others. He asks: 'What will be freer than free will when it is unable to sin? For human beings, this state should have been the reward of merit, just as it was for the holy angels. But when the good which was to be merited had been lost through sin, that which was to have been the reward of merit became, in those who had been freed, a gift of grace'[252]

249 Rom 6: [14].

250 Rom 7: [14]. The reformers of the 16th century, particularly Beza, misapplied these passages of the Apostle which, according to them, demonstrated that human bilateral freedom had perished with original sin. But this is quite foolish. St. Paul exhorts his Christians not to give themselves to the servitude of sin, especially after baptism. This presupposes possible falls. It is true that without the grace of Christ we can perform no work meriting eternal life, and that, as St. Paul says, we are servants of sin. But this does not mean that we have been deprived of the assistance necessary for salvation; even before the time of Christ God's mercy provided in various ways.

251 *L. de gratia et libero arb.*, c. 15.

252 *L. de corrept. et gratia.*, c. 11.

(that is, it became the happiness of not being able to serve sin). He continues: 'For this reason, we must carefully and diligently note how much "being able not to sin" differs from "not being able to sin" . . . The first human being was able not to sin . . . The first freedom of the will, therefore, was "being able not to sin"' (it was a bilateral freedom from both good and evil); 'the last freedom will be much greater, "not being able to sin"' (this is servitude to justice). ' . . . The first was the possibility of perseverance; . . . the last will be the happiness of perseverance.'[253] He also says: 'A free will without sin was given to him (the first human being), and he turned it to the service of sin. On the other hand, these (Christians) had a will which served sin, but then was freed by him who said: "If the Son of man frees you, you will be free indeed." Through this grace their freedom is such that although they may have to struggle against the concupiscence of sin as long as they live they no longer serve the sin that brings death.'[254]

These passages clearly show that St. Augustine distinguishes:

1st. The kind of freedom which renders human beings free from the happy service of justice and makes them servants of sin. This is the wretched freedom of the damned, and is partly inherited by the children of Adam from their unfaithful father.

2nd. The freedom which renders human beings free from the miserable service of sin, making them servants of justice. This is the blessed freedom enjoyed by those enlightened in heaven, or confirmed in grace, or infallibly and irresistibly moved to some holy act by a dominant, effective grace.

3rd. Finally, the freedom in which we are free to serve one of two masters, justice or sin, according to which pleases us most. The first human being possessed this freedom in the state of innocence. It is also possessed by those redeemed by Christ. Grace has restored to them the power to conquer evil fully and to do good in the supernatural order also.

602. It is true that it is not easy to follow St. Augustine's mind on the matter of the bilateral freedom possessed by human beings after the sin of Adam. But if we concentrate sufficiently, I think we can confidently summarise his thought as follows.

[253] *Ibid.*, c. 12.

[254] *Ibid.*, c. 12.

Adam as innocent, constituted in the state of nature and of grace, was able to sin and not to sin, that is, he possessed bilateral freedom.[255] After turning his freedom to evil by sin, he put himself and his descendants in servitude to sin. From that moment, neither he nor his descendants had the kind of freedom which allowed them to save themselves by doing good fully and perfectly. In this sense the human family had lost free will. But God came to their aid, and through Christ freed them from sin, giving them grace to do perfect, saving good.[256]

In this state the ability to do perfect good comes from God, while the ability to do evil is proper to the human being. Thus, bilateral freedom was restored to us.

But in this new state the will cannot be *indifferent*; it cannot be neither good nor evil but must be good or evil.[257]

If the will is good, it comes from God; if evil, it comes from us. The *disposition* or power of the will must be distinguished

255 'If he wished, he could have persevered. That he did not wish to persevere depended on his free will, which then was so free that it could wish both good and evil' (*Ibid.*, c. 11).

256 'As long as the human being used his free will well, he had no need for grace to raise him since he could not rise. Now in his ruined state, he is free of justice and servant of sin. Nor can he be a servant of justice and free from the dominion of sin unless the Son has freed him' (*Op. imp. contra Jul.*, bk. 1, 82). Note carefully that St. Augustine is continually speaking about *perfect* moral good, not about moral good in general. He describes that good which renders the human will completely good, pleasing in the eyes of God, and able to save him. Some would like to deduce from this that 'the works of unbelievers are sins', but this is ridiculous. St. Augustine's teaching does not deny that we can practise natural virtue, even if deprived of grace. He denies that these virtues can be so perfect that they make the will of the doer justified and acceptable in the eyes of God.

257 'The will cannot seem to take up any kind of middle stance between good and evil. If we love justice, our will is good. If we love justice more, our will is better; if we love it less, the will is less good. If we do not love justice at all, our will is not good, and we have no hesitation in saying that a will which does not love justice in any way is not only evil, but greatly evil. If the will, therefore, is either good or evil, and no evil comes from God, we must have our good will from God. Otherwise I do not see in what other gift of his we are to rejoice, since we are justified by him. This, I think, is why it is written: "The will is prepared by God." And in the Psalms: "The steps of man are guided by the Lord, and he decides his way." As the Apostle says: "It is God who acts in you, and wills and acts in favour of a good will"' (*De peccator. merit. et remis.*, bk. 2, c. 18).

[602]

therefore from the *real fact* or act of the will. Now bilateral freedom relates to the disposition of the will which, however, in *fact* is always in some determined state either of goodness and salvation or of sin and loss of salvation.

The grace of the Redeemer is so powerful that it moves the will to act; the grace given to Adam provided him only with the ability to move his will of himself. However, although the grace of the Redeemer is sufficient to move effectively the will of anyone not opposed to it, it does not follow that the human being cannot resist it most of the time. It is not the same to say on the one hand that a cause is sufficient to produce an effect, and on the other that this cause cannot be obstructed by another cause while producing the effect for which of itself it is sufficient [*App.*, no. 8].

Article 4.
Freedom from all sin

603. There is yet another meaning given to 'freedom.' As we noted, serving justice is justice itself. But this kind of justice cannot aptly be called servitude in the normal sense of the word. Servitude normally indicates an unpleasant condition, or at least the privation of some good such as freedom. On the other hand, serving injustice means serving an unjust master, who has no right to subject us. Because it entails every kind of trouble and unrest, servitude to sin is servitude at its worst.

It is in this sense that St. Augustine maintains God's freedom even in respect of moral relationship, although God cannot be unjust.[258] This explains why the Saint says: 'What can be freer than free will, when it no longer serves sin?'[259] For the same reason St. Leo says that 'true freedom exists when the flesh is ruled by the judgment of the soul and the spirit is governed by God.'[260] It explains why the saints in heaven are said to be free,[261]

[258] *Op. imper. contra Jul.*, in many places, and amongst others, bk. 1, c. 81, and bk. 6, c. 10.

[259] *L. de corrept. et gratia*, c. 11.

[260] *Serm. 1 de quadrag.*

[261] *Op. imp. contra Jul.*, bk. 4, c. 10.

and gives meaning to the well-known dictum: 'To serve God is to reign.' Scripture speaks in the same way, as we can see simply by referring to the place where Christ says that the truth will set us free.[262]

604. This is a most noble and sublime form of freedom, and can fittingly be called 'freedom of intelligence' because the intellectual element of our humanity provides our relationship with the objective world of beings. In so far as we live in this world, we feel the moral necessity, founded in our intellectual nature, of conforming ourselves to the objective, absolute world. The human being, considered simply as intelligence, needs this moral order, and essentially desires it. Because our *intellectual will*, deeply rooted in and forming the noblest part of our nature, constitutes our nature, it follows that our essential, intellective human will, when contradicted, opposed or in the grip of passions which tend to subjective good, is locked, as it were, in a narrow prison and made a servant of subjective good (that is, of good enclosed in an infinitely narrow sphere compared with the vast sphere of objective being). But simultaneously the will wishes to expand in the universality of objective, moral good which alone constitutes its delight; it wishes to extend in the vast domain from which every narrow limit cuts it off; it wishes to be free in that sphere where it has all that it desires and where nothing is opposed to its sublime aspiration.

In the human being, therefore, we can distinguish two kinds of natural inclinations of will. First, *subjective* inclinations which incline the will to satisfying the tendencies of its own nature as subject. Second, *objective* inclinations or the moral *necessity* felt at a certain level of development of human intelligence. This is an infinitely precious need by which the noblest part of human nature desires to conform with the known truth, the order of beings. It is a need to acknowledge all beings for what they are, and give each its due.

The subjective inclination restricts us to a limited sphere, the objective extends us towards the infinite. The sphere of the subjective inclination is a real prison in which our lot is servitude; the sphere of the objective inclination is the mansion of heaven where we enjoy freedom.

[262] Jn 8: [32].

Universal intelligence contains the principal, sovereign part of the human being. Subjective pleasure is the essentially subordinate, less important part. We can say therefore that as human beings we are free when our better, naturally dominant part is free. We are servants when this part has to submit to the less important, naturally subordinate part.

The human will called by nature to prevail is that which follows intelligence. When its desires are implemented, we are free because we are not prevented from doing what we most desire. The triumph of our higher will is then joined with happiness which satisfies all human longings. When nothing more restricts our will and we possess and do all we desire, we have reached true, fullest freedom. It is the freedom proper to those who have attained heaven.

605. Such freedom, perfect in every part, cannot be obtained in this present life. The freedom possible here is always mixed with some kind of servitude. Nevertheless, the free human being is the virtuous human being, whose noblest part is free and is valued for its own sake; in the virtuous person only the lowest part is servant, that is, the part containing the passions or limited, subjective instincts destined for servitude. And for human beings dominion over these is a desirable and glorious good.[263]

If, therefore, submission to justice is a indeed a yoke, it is sweet and light, as Christ tells us.[264]

263 'Freedom is threefold', says St. Bernard. 'First of all, it is the opposite of natural necessity, and as such free will' (bilateral freedom). 'Third, it is the opposite of death and the ills of this life, and as such confers blessedness on human beings' (the freedom possessed by those who have gained heaven). 'Second, it is the opposite of sin, and as such makes human beings just and holy' (the freedom of the just on earth) (*L. de gratia et libero arb.*). St. Augustine is of the same mind: 'The freedom possessed by the just to do good perfectly (*ad perficiendum bonum*) in this life is not as great as that to be found in the life where we will no longer say: "I do what I like".' (*Op. imperf. contra Jul.*, bk. 1, c. 99).

264 Matt 11: [30]. St. Anselm indicates how obedience to justice can be called freedom in one sense and servitude in another: 'This freedom relative to justice is said to be and is freedom relative to the justice found in upright action which is done freely; at the same time, it is also servitude relative to obedience to a precept. Similarly, good servants serve their masters freely and willingly so that servants both good and bad maintain their free will while they serve.

7

THE NATURE OF BILATERAL FREEDOM

606. Having distinguished the various kinds of freedom, we must now examine more carefully what we have called 'bilateral freedom' in so far as it is the source of merit. We begin by clarifying its nature.

What we have said elsewhere is already sufficient to show that the nature of this kind of freedom does not consist in acting without a reason (which would make the action irrational). Rather, several reasons or motives for action are present in our spirit, and it is within our power to make one prevail over the others and thus become the motive determining our will to act (cf. 581, 582).[265] The different *reasons* for willing and acting present to our spirit do not contain in themselves a cause sufficiently capable of necessitating action. On the contrary, it is the spontaneity of the will which adds what is lacking to one or other of the different reasons in order to make the reason a determining cause of the will itself. Fr. Ercolano Oberrach's ingenious definition, 'the power to supply what is lacking to the motivating reason' refers, therefore, to *spontaneity* rather than *liberty*.

607. For greater clarity, we must first distinguish *reason* from *impulse*. The word 'reason' simply means an idea according to which we are able to conclude that to will or do a given thing is good or bad. 'Impulse' indicates a real cause, not a mere idea, which stimulates and attempts to put will and act in motion efficaciously.

608. It is clear that the will can never be inclined and moved necessarily when *reasons* rather than *impulses* are in question, unless the will puts itself in motion, as it were, through its own spontaneity. The same cannot be said when we are dealing with real, effective impulses.

609. We shall speak later about impulses and their degree of

Surely we retain our free will whether we serve justice or sin?' [*Dialogus de libero arbitrio*]. And so Jesus Christ in the gospel sometimes describes the observance of his law as a pleasing servitude or as a light and sweet yoke, and sometimes as freedom: 'The truth will set you free.'

[265] See *PE*, 171–176, 181.

efficacy in moving the will one way or another. For the moment, we intend to describe only the way in which the will determines itself when there is no impulse necessarily determining it.

Let us begin by considering the nature of *spontaneity*. This is a way of acting common both to the will and to animal instinct, as we have seen. We shall first consider it in instinct.

The *spontaneity* of instinct differs from the *mobility* present in brute matter in which the movement communicated corresponds exactly to the thrust impressed upon it. Here the cause or moving force and the effect or quantity of movement together form a perfect equation. The same equality is not present between these two things in the case of the spontaneity of the animal instinct. A very light movement imparted to certain parts of the living body propagates and enlarges itself: the external cause of the movement is small, but the quantity of movement is great. The little force or cause of movement applied to the living body does not, properly speaking, produce solely the material movement proper to it. Simultaneously, it arouses and draws to action another *cause of movement* which, once stimulated, itself adds a certain quantity of movement to that produced by the material cause. In this way, what was originally a little movement now becomes much bigger. The movement of the living animal is, therefore, the product of two causes: a preceding cause which is then accompanied by another cause. These causes are: 1. a material force, which simultaneously *causes* movement and *excites* spontaneity; 2. spontaneity, which in turn causes further movement that extends and continues the movement already present. Here there is no question of *will*, and even less of *freedom*.

610. In the human being two new causes, will and freedom, are to be added, as we have said. The human being, as soon as he acts as a result of knowing some good, performs an act of will. In this definition of willed act, there is no distinction between the case in which the will is determined as a result of some impulse, and that in which the hesitant will determines itself. These two cases, however, are very different. If the will is determined in its operation by some impulse, the force acting in it is wholly similar, as far as its mode of action is concerned, to the spontaneity of the animal instinct. What happens is that a suitable impulse, which we suppose to be applied to the will, acts in the will but not in the way that brute force acts upon anything material by

communicating movement equal to the impulse but nothing more; the impulse acts by awakening and arousing the energy of the will itself, and thus drawing a new cause into act, just as a new principle of movement is actuated in the animal instinct as a result of a material impulse. But if the impulse applied to the will is not sufficient to determine it — and this is the case when the will's spontaneity is not excited sufficiently to produce the full effect and overcome the obstacles before it — it is clear that the will either remains inactive, or determines itself to act. If it does determine itself, a fourth force comes into play from the subject's own resources. This force, added by the subject, tips the balance by determining the mode of activity. And this force is properly speaking *freedom*. Two forces therefore can be distinguished in the will: *spontaneity* and *freedom*.

611. *Spontaneity* cannot be the subject of violence, but it can be *necessitated*. It has its own laws, and is aroused in correspondence with the stimuli or impulses given to the will. *Freedom*, however, is a thrust or power of the subject which has no constant, determined relationship with the stimuli or impulses given to the will. On the contrary, it disturbs the stimuli which oppose it, sustains the weak against the strong, and determines the hesitant subject to a decision. Its opposites are both violence and necessity, to neither of which it can be subject.

8

THE WAY IN WHICH SPONTANEITY OF THE WILL ACTS

Article 1.
The first acts of the will, in which the intellect, without making any judgment, presents the object to the will

612. We have distinguished two kinds of motives in the activity of the will: *reasons* and *impulses* (cf. 607). Because reasons appertain to the order of ideas, they are of themselves isolated and naked, unaccompanied by images, feelings or passions.

They do not excite the will to action, therefore, but simply to contemplation. This is not the case with impulses, which appertain to the order of real things, are true, efficient causes and effective stimuli of the will. These impulses can all be reduced to instincts which are either aroused in us without our intervention, or have been excited in us by ourselves. In this last case, our freedom can play some part, but for the moment we have to consider instincts in themselves without reference to the cause which activates them; we consider them therefore as stimuli of the will.

613. There are two great classes of instincts, *animal* and *human*. Of their nature, the latter move the will to what we have called evaluative volitions, but the same cannot be said of the former.

614. We first ask about animal instincts 'whether the will, which allows itself to be moved by them, must not only perceive the object to which they tend, but perceive it as good.' At first sight, it would seem that this must be the case, but very careful consideration may show that in the human animal the instinct's enjoyment of its object is sufficient to move the will. The will may make no judgment on the goodness of the object which it perceives only as a being, and not yet distinctly as something *good*. We can grasp the possibility of these merely affective volitions (which, as the first made by babies, are totally non-evaluative) if we keep in mind the unity of our extremely simple subject which is simultaneously animal and volitive. When animal instinct moves the baby to an action such as sucking the breast, the entire subject wishes to receive satisfaction through this animal pleasure. Consequently all the baby's forces, of whatever kind, are brought to bear in the act. The will, one of the baby's forces, plays its part, therefore, although it has no need to direct the operation, which depends for its direction and determination on the instinct. The will simply abandons itself blindly, without need of any judgment, when it perceives what the instinct places before it. The entire action comes from the subject which simultaneously is the root of instinct and of will, and requires no more of the will than its co-operation in its instinctive act.

615. It will be helpful if we note the analogy that obtains between the first act of the intellect, that is, *perception*, and the

first act of the will, *affective volition*. In perception, the intellect does not first form the *subject* to which it may then add a *predicate*, but in one act adds the predicate and forms the subject. This occurs because the matter presented to the intellect is simply sensations devoid of every idea; the intellect's task is to carry out its act upon them by supplying the idea. In the same way, the sense-instinct does not present the will with some good judged to be such by the intellect, but only with pleasing sensations which do not form the proper object of the will. Nevertheless, the will carries out its act in their regard by blindly obeying the subject who rules it and moves it with physical movement. The subject *wants* that entity or those acts to which instinct tends because it feels them as pleasing, not because it *judges* them as good.

616. I admit, however, that this is a very subtle question. If the solution I have offered is true, the adage, *Voluntas non fertur in incognitum* [The will does not tend towards the unknown] is still valid, but has to be understood in the sense that while the will must know the *object* in order to desire it, it has absolutely no need to judge it as good. It is sufficient that the *subject* move the will physically to want the object. This the subject can do when the object is pleasing and because it is pleasing to the subject's animality. In this case, the will would act knowingly relative to the desired object, but blindly relative to the reason for desiring it. The reason for its act would be found totally in the movement of the subject to which the will belongs as one of its powers.

Article 2.
The second kind of acts of the will, in which the intellect presents the object to the will together with a very general judgment about the object's goodness

617. The baby soon begins to judge, however, that what pleases its feeling is good, and what displeases it is bad. Nevertheless, these first judgments can only be of a most general kind. Although the baby realises that what feeling finds acceptable is good, he conceives this simply as good without classifying it any

further. The *specific and generic ideas* of good still remain unformed in the baby, who needs more experience and comparisons. The idea of good in general, with its foundation in the idea of being in general, precedes the ideas of specific or generic good in the baby's mind because being and good are in the last analysis the same thing under two relationships. In other words, any being whatsoever is known as good as soon as it is considered as a pleasing object of desire.

618. It is true that the attractive sensation experienced by the baby is itself a *particular good*. Nevertheless, although this proves that the baby perceives a particular good, it does not necessarily follow that he has the corresponding *specific* idea of such good. The particular aspect of the feelable good experienced by the baby remains entirely enclosed in the feeling; the intellect simply adds a general judgment that this sensation is good. The idea apprehended in this first intellective perception, that is, the predicate of this first judgment, is simply the idea of good, and not the idea of some specific good. The baby will be determined to a given choice by its prevalent instinct only when he experiences good of different kinds and has to compare different kinds of good in order to make his choice. And this instinct acts with extreme rapidity, of course, in determining the subject to action. But the baby soon makes the choice with his understanding, and for the first time begins to classify good for himself, although the only rule he depends upon is the preponderance of the instincts themselves according to *generic or specific* ideas formed for this purpose from the various kinds of good he has known.[266]

619. As long as a human being judges that an object is simply good or bad without using any generic or specific idea, I call his volition *affective*, not *evaluative*, although it does include a very general evaluation - if indeed evaluation can be present where comparison is totally lacking.[267]

According to this kind of terminology, affective volitions would be of two kinds: 1. those made without any judgment on the goodness of some thing; 2. those made on the basis of a very

[266] See the theory of *species* and *genera* we have developed in *OT*, 646–659.

[267] In this case, one *appreciates*, but does not *evaluate*. There are, therefore, three levels of volition rather than two: *affective*, *appreciative* and *evaluative*.

general judgment which concludes that some thing is good, but without determining its degrees of goodness. But such a general judgment can scarcely be considered 'evaluation', which implies determining the worth of something.

Article 3.
The impulse necessary to stimulate the first kind of affective volitions

620. Having distinguished the two species of affective volitions, we are now faced with the problem of the degree of impulse or stimulus required in order that the will may produce these volitions.

I do not think that every act of sensuous instinct is sufficient to excite the will to the first kind of volitions. Such an act does not, in fact, move the will directly, but exercises its activity immediately on the subject, the common root of instinct and will. The subject then calls the will to its aid in order to obtain full satisfaction for its animal, sensuous instinct. However, if this satisfaction can be obtained very easily by the instinct itself, the subject does not need to call upon the will, which it cannot stimulate without contributing some activity of its own. This degree of activity emitted by the subject in order to stimulate and move the will would have no sufficient cause if the instinct were already self-induced to carry out everything easily, immediately and pleasantly.

621. If, on the other hand, the subject cannot satisfy its animal instincts without their encountering difficulties and delay in reaching the fulfilment of their inclinations, it is frustrated by the obstacles it encounters, and needs to call in aid some new activity to fight and overcome them. The subject cannot altogether avoid some discomfort in this state because it must either bear with the contradiction it finds in the obstacles opposed to its appetites or activate some new degree of energy in itself in order to motivate the will. But both courses of action cause discomfort: moving from inaction to action always causes unease because it calls for a level of effort that the subject will not undertake without a sufficient reason. Consequently, the principle

governing the subject's movements is that applicable universally to instinctive activity as well as to spontaneous activity of the will: the subject 'determines itself to whatever action is easiest and requires the least activity, amongst all those actions which lead it to a state to which it is already determined to tend'.

622. We may conclude that in the baby the first kind of affective volitions requires the following two conditions: 1. the animal instinct finds some obstacle in obtaining satisfaction; 2. that in attempting to overcome these obstacles, the subject finds it less objectionable to move the will than to tolerate the obstacles or increase the degree of action of the instinctive forces.

Article 4. The impulse needed to move the second kind of affective volitions

623. If we suppose that the intellect presents the object of animal instinct to the will from the point of view of what is good, although without any distinctive evaluation, the will requires no special activity from the subject to determine it to act by desiring this object — it is already determined as soon as it is presented with an object judged to be good. The will, which we have defined as 'a power by which the human being tends to the good it knows' is such that the human being cannot know any good without the will's tending towards it as its proper, essential object. A human being will always want a good known to him unless he prefers some other good which he considers greater. In this case, it is not a question of his not wanting the first good, but rather that he wants the second good more and, in order to possess it, resigns himself to the loss of the first good.

624. As a corollary, we may conclude that the will is of its nature very mobile, or indeed infinitely mobile so that any known good, however small, is sufficient to move and determine it.

625. But we have to rely on certain presuppositions in order to grasp this. First, the will must be presented with a single good, and from one point of view. If a given thing were seen simultaneously from two points of view, one of which showed it as good, the other as evil, the will would possess two objects,

which is against our hypothesis, and would be moved by two contrary forces. The thing as good would not draw the will to itself unless the good overcame the evil which would also be present to the will.

Secondly, we have to suppose that the will is in a completely pure and virginal state, as it were, without any previously determined affections, dispositions or tendencies which deprive it of its natural equilibrium and incline it in one direction or another. Granted these two conditions (that the will is in a perfectly pure state, colourless as it were, and that only one good, of which the human being has had experience, is presented to it by the intellect), it appears indubitable that this good, however small, must be altogether sufficient to draw the will to an act of volition. In such a case, the good is like a minimal weight that serves to tip a perfectly balanced scales.

626. We must also conclude that the more the human will is pure and devoid of hidden habits and affections, and consequently free of objects that have to be weighed, the greater its agility and flexibility. This is the principal explanation for the mobility shown in children's volitions. Experience shows that even the smallest thing can move them: they want, they don't want, they come and go, run, jump — here, there, up, down. All these are effects of surprisingly rapid volitions which are also seen in their constantly new games, their disconnected speech, their frequent, strange questions. All that they do shows a desire to know, to experience, to see, touch, move and test everything.

Although it is true that what attracts the instinct initiates these actions, they do not pertain to animal instinct alone; they are completed and effected by volitions which arise and vanish with great rapidity. And this gives us a perfect picture of the incredible mobility of our power of will. We can see clearly how the smallest things — even the slightest use of imagination — experienced by children are sufficient to activate their will and draw it to innumerable acts, one piled upon another, as it were, in a jumble of childish disorder. We do not find any strong, constant act of will resistant to accidental impressions, or any act strong enough to impose itself on other acts (this comes about at a more mature age); the will yields obediently to the slightest impression. All this takes place because the child's will is still completely simple, and unaware of the utility of resistance; as yet the child, is still ignorant of the good that may be gained by ordering its unconnected and dispersed activities. This is not the case with the adult in whom a dominant design, a purpose and a general interest are the object of the will, enabling it to stand firm against any number of passing impressions which, if the will were altogether simple and natural, would draw it into movement.

This also explains the great mobility of the masses, which gave rise to the expression *popular acclamation* as a sign of the multitude's capacity for bending its will to whatever takes its instant fancy. The masses are indeed like children in many respects, and have a much more simple will than that of sophisticated people. There are also certain so-called mob passions which take possession of the people with extreme violence and rapidity, and disappear with the same rapidity.

627. It must be dangerous, therefore, for any jury to pass judgment in religious and political matters which vehemently arouse the popular imagination and will. The multitude, which is upright and decent when calm, unexpectedly conceives prejudices and affections and then, with its will already moulded and incited, manufactures the strangest, most unjust judgments. For example, it pains one to see how many decent persons, whose immense probity and virtue cannot be doubted, were condemned to atrocious deaths in England for reasons of religion and state under Henry VIII, Edward, Elizabeth, and James. They underwent the formalities of a regular trial, and were condemned by the unanimous decisions of juries who had been fed with evidence composed only of conjectures and suppositions. Bartoli's *Inghilterra* would move one to tears.

Article 5.
Can the pure *idea* of good act efficaciously upon the will, and if so, how?

628. We should now consider the natural impulse required for the spontaneity of evaluative volitions. However, the presence of the *idea* of good within these volitions as the measure for judging the value of a given object first prompts the following question: 'What force has the *idea* of good for setting the will in

motion?' The same question can be asked about the second kind of affective volitions. Here, too, the *idea* of good, that is, of good in general, presides over the volitions.

We first have to distinguish between the simple, pure idea of good, and the idea associated with the experience of good itself. By the sole, pure idea of good I mean the idea of some good which has never been experienced and consequently is unassociated with any image, memory or physical effect left in us by the enjoyment of that good. Moreover, the idea of some good presented to the will may be entirely negative. For instance, a person blind from birth may be told about a beautiful colour. In such a case, the person to whom the idea has been suggested usually composes the image of this good by referring it to some good of another kind which he has already experienced. The idea, however, is no longer pure and unique in this person. The action that it exerts on the will is accompanied by a completely false icon of good altogether different from the good that should be denoted by the idea. This fiction of the imagination, which is immediately associated with a negative idea — to give the idea a positive connotation and some efficacy over the will — has to be removed if we are to consider any pure, negative idea of good. We are not dealing with the support and force that can be associated with this idea, but with the power to move the will possessed by this idea when wholly separated from anything else.

But it is not sufficient to strip the idea of good of elements differing from it in order to arrive at this idea in its unique purity. It is possible that the subject may not add to this idea any icon of positive good fabricated in the imagination with elements of good he has experienced. Nevertheless, the simple consideration of what is held in common by the idea and by the good he has experienced (the simple consideration of their being good) must add to the idea some kind of efficacy relative to the subject's experience of various kinds of good. We have to prescind, therefore, even from the impulse that could be given to the will by the influence of any image or by analogy between the good proposed by the idea and the good experienced by us; we are as it were in a state in which we have never experienced good of any kind, or at least known it as good. It is true that a specific or generic idea cannot remain in our mind without some relationship with a feeling, and from this point of view our question

[628]

seems unreal. But in supposing the idea to be devoid of all feeling, we intend to ask: 'Can the will be moved by the pure idea without reference to any movement which may come from the feeling we have mentioned?'

629. We have to distinguish. If we are dealing with an *idea of subjective good*, such an idea cannot impart any motion or impulse to the will. Of itself, the idea is totally cold because it pertains to an order of things completely different from the good to which the will tends, that is, it pertains to the order of ideas. Subjective good as object of the will always belongs to the order of real things. If, on the other hand, we are dealing with an *idea of objective good*, which depends on the absolute order of being, such an idea can indeed move and incline the human will in its higher part, that is, in so far as the human being is an intelligence and as such adheres to being (to the absolute order of being) — in other words, in so far as the absolute order of being is good for him. This explains why a natural inclination to morality is revealed as soon as the human person is enlightened by the absolute order of being (which takes place when he first becomes aware the existence of other intelligent beings different from himself, whose good contrasts with that of his own). Human beings could not be other than naturally virtuous if the impulse received by their will from absolute, objective good were not opposed by impulses imparted to their will by experiences of subjective good.

Article 6.
The idea, associated with experiences of good, can act efficaciously on the will

630. We shall deal later with the struggle between the idea of absolute, objective good and the seductive attractions of experienced subjective good (the struggle, properly speaking, is the domain of freedom). For the moment we want to restrict our argument to the idea of subjective good and ask how this idea, associated with the experience of such good, can move the will?

It is clear that relative to subjective good nothing pertaining to the *ideal* order directly and of itself moves the will. Nevertheless, it can move the will indirectly. The intelligent subject can easily fabricate for himself some *opinion* about unlimited good by drawing together the various kinds of good he has experienced, his images of this good, the physical effects persevering in him as reminders of this good, and his animal and human instincts, especially those which, concerned with his own aggrandisement and happiness, generate exaggerated hopes in his heart and arouse the total activity of his powers.

This fictitious and often exaggerated *opinion* about good (and the corresponding expectation of evil) is an idea appertaining to the order of intelligence, but at the same time the product of the instincts, images, memories and passions we have mentioned. It is not a mere idea; it is not a pure idea. It is an *opinion* or persuasion rather than an idea; the subject has acted upon it with his creative force and added to it the result of what we have called the power of *persuasion*.[268]

631. This combination of *idea* and *opinion* acts by moving the will in two ways. As *idea* it acts indirectly by drawing together and uniting many elements with the intention of increasing the *value* of this multifaceted, unified good. In other words, the subject's forces are given a single *direction* without the creation of new forces. As *opinion* or *persuasion*, it acts directly because the power of persuasion springs from the activity of the subject, of which it is a function. The subject, now *persuaded* of this great good, moves the will directly in order to obtain it, while the will calls in aid all the other powers, increasing the forces of instinct, imagination, hope and any other passions suitable for contributing to the end in view.

It is clear, therefore, that *ideas* help the human being to form *opinions* about subjective good by uniting its elements and presenting them to his judgment for evaluation and enhancement; *opinions* about good or evil act upon the will which asserts itself in so far as it finds help from the other powers according to their own state and condition.

[268] Cf. *Certainty*, 1335–1361.

Article 7.
How the natural collision between subjective good and evil determines the spontaneous movement of the will

§1. Every opiniative good is an object of the will

632. The will, therefore, is an extremely mobile power (cf. 624–626). As a rational tendency to good, it must be stimulated by any good whatsoever, provided it is suitably presented, that is, known and thought of as good. And because every being is good in so far as it is,[269] the will is born of its nature to love all things. Such universal love is, we may say, the basis of the will and of the human nature which possesses it.

§2. The natural collision between different kinds of subjective good, and the preponderance of some kinds over others

633. Nevertheless, the will, although naturally inclined to the love of all things, cannot be said to love them all. The *inclination* to love is one thing; *love*, the consummation and conclusion of that inclination (from which the outward act follows), is another.

634. In fact, the different kinds of good capable of moving the will sometimes come into collision in such a way that one good can be loved only if another is rejected. The primary explanation for this fact is the limitation of created, contingent beings in each of which some part of being and good is lacking. Hence, the natural inclinations of the will must also be limited and come into collision in the way that different kinds of good conflict.

Secondly, although beings are good in so far as they are, they often lack some part of the good which is naturally theirs. This renders them defective, and the cause of defects in other beings. If we consider these beings from the point of view of the defects they possess or cause, they fall under the concept of evil, and

[269] Cf. *PE*, 16–31.

provoke the will's natural hatred rather than its love. The deeper the defect or evil discovered in the being, the greater the hatred. This is especially true of evil deep in the internal constitution of the being (as in the case of moral evil) where the author of evil is the subject himself.

Thirdly, the lesser good which impedes the attainment of greater good is itself regarded as evil and as such is naturally hated by the will.

635. As long as the will obeys these natural laws, which determine the degrees of its love and hate according to the comparison made between what is good and evil, the order of nature rules and determines the will's spontaneity. In this state the will is passive in so far as it cedes without opposition to the natural invitation causing its movement.

We have already seen that the will, when presented with a single object thought to be good, moves to desire that object however insignificant it may be. In the same way, when there is a collision between what is thought to be good and what is thought to be evil, the will comes down in favour of the weightier side, even if this is only fractionally more attractive. Everything else that is good, but deficient by comparison, attracts a *mere wish* and inclination of the will, but not the perfect act of volition.

We must remember that this argument is valid only for the case in which the human will is still enclosed in the field of merely subjective good.

9

THE METAPHYSICAL QUESTION OF FREEDOM

636. Having spoken about the spontaneous operation of the human will, we must now return to consider its freedom. The first problem is posed by the great metaphysical question: 'How can freedom be reconciled with the principle of causality?' The exceptional difficulty of the question, which cannot be gainsaid, must not deter us in any way from affirming the fact of freedom. As we said, freedom is a fact attested by internal observation and

by our inmost sense which we cannot and must not deny whatever marvels and wonders it places before us. Indeed, the most extraordinary thing of all would be for it to deceive us. We have constantly proclaimed: 'The faith that we must give to facts depends upon their being adequately verified, and is altogether independent of our ability to explain them.' This affirmation is valid for thinkers and non-thinkers, and enables us to maintain rightly that no difficulty brought against the existence of human freedom has the power to diminish our persuasion of its reality. Nevertheless, without prejudice to this persuasion which has its foundation in the verification of the fact, we can lawfully investigate the explanation of the existence of freedom in relationship to the equally necessary and undeniable principle of causality which seems irreconcilable with the principle of freedom.

637. Philosophers have elaborated three principal systems to escape from the maze in which the noblest intellects have been lost.

1st. Some maintained that human freedom depended upon making a choice without a sufficient reason. This is summed up in the common phrase: *the will takes the place of reason*. This provides a strong defence of freedom, but little protection to causality.

2nd. Others, including Leibniz, maintained firmly that freedom always favoured the side of the prevailing reason. Here, the principle of causality, or at least of reason, is undoubtedly saved, but at the cost of defeat for true bilateral freedom.

3rd. German critical philosophy appeared while philosophy was divided between these two camps, to which it offered itself as arbitrator and conciliator. It said that both parties were right. However, the former had to accept that the principle of causality was necessary and undeniable; the latter, that freedom was only freedom on condition that it was conceived as acting independently of the principle of causality. This school justified its decision by maintaining that all things were divided into two great orders, *phenonema* and *noumena*. The first are things in so far as they appear externally to the senses; the second, things in so far as they subsist internally in accordance with what reason posits about their internal subsistence. In the *phenomenal order* the principle of cause governs and rules everything; this is not the case in the non-apparent *noumenal* order which is produced for us by reason, and is governed by other laws, one of which is freedom. In other words, German critical philosophy maintains that the defenders of the principle of causality are right because they consider things in the phenomenal order, and that the defenders of freedom are right because they consider things in the noumenal order. But what is the relationship between these two orders? The critical school replies to this anguished question of both sides by saying that the two orders both emanate from the forms, or intimate laws, of the human spirit. This spirit, as *feeling*, makes up the phenomenal order; as *reason*, it produces the noumenal order. The two orders depend on the subjective laws of the spirit which must give credence both to exterior nature, to which the spirit itself gives extension through its own activity, and to freedom, to which the spirit attributes activity without any cause.

638. The novelty and obscurity of this language took the contending parties by surprise. But after their first shocked and thoughtful silence, they asked themselves about the final conclusion of this new self-proclaimed authority in the field of philosophy against which it seemed sententious to argue. If both sides were said to be right, it was more likely that both were wrong. In other words, both were being mocked. German critical philosophy maintained that phenomena and noumena, that is, freedom and the principle of cause, were equally the product of the human spirit from which they emanated and from which they demanded credence. There is no longer any absolute, objective truth, but simply credence given to blind, fatal fact. And the new critical philosophy found itself in total darkness. One party to the original dispute had asserted that the principle of causality was something absolute and necessary, independently of the existence of any human spirit. It was true in itself and not relative to human beings who see it as true and necessary, but do not form it as such. All this was now denied, and the principle of causality whose existence had apparently been assured now revealed itself as a lying mockery.

The other party had understood freedom as something real, and human activity as truly independent of any necessitating cause. Freedom, however, now became a mere *belief* that the spirit could not relinquish because it must believe that what it does is moral. It was no longer necessary to know or to ask if the human spirit were truly free or not; indeed, being free was blatantly in contradiction with the principles of theoretic reason, one of which was causality. Again the reality of freedom has been granted in words, but denied in practice. A blind belief in freedom would be an absurdity in the presence of reason, and was certainly not the freedom under discussion.

Hence the kind of reconciliation offered by German critical philosophy is a travesty. Those who defend causality might go on to show that affirming the principle of cause as valid for one order of things but not another, would result in the destruction of the principle, which cannot be necessary unless it is universal. A single exception would annul all necessity. This is, in fact, the reason why upholders of the principle of causality deny that freedom can determine itself except on the basis of some preponderant reason. It is clear, therefore, that the solution to the problem of freedom offered by the critical school succeeds only in greater philosophical confusion. An apparently ingenious conclusion turns out to be the worst conclusion of all. It honours neither the principle of causality nor freedom, and in place of a public execution, garottes them privately. But what solution can be offered? Which side shall we take?

639. I think we should first examine carefully the nature of the act of freedom, and strip it of everything extraneous. It will be much easier to explain when it is viewed in its purity and simplicity without any adjuncts.

We are dealing, therefore, with that act of choice in which the human being, having a subjective good on one side and an absolute, objective good on the other, chooses one in preference to the other. Both kinds of good, however, when present to the spirit, are capable of arousing the spontaneity of the spirit itself, as we have said. If, therefore, only one of these two kinds of good were present, the spirit would undoubtedly act without contradicting the principle of cause simply because the known, opiniative good is a suitable cause for arousing spontaneity, and spontaneity is a suitable cause for action. This is true for both kinds of good. Whichever kind the will chooses, therefore, its *volition* always has a cause, or better, a reason. It depends upon the opiniative good present to the spirit, and upon the spontaneity aroused by this good. The act of volition does not lack a suitable reason; the problem lies in knowing how the spirit *determines* itself to one of the volitions rather than the other.

What happens is this. While the presence of only one of the

two kinds of good is suitable for arousing the spontaneity of the human spirit (the good itself and the spontaneity together form a complete cause of the act), the presence of two or more of these kinds of good gives rise to their contemporaneous action in the unity of the spirit where they arouse a new spontaneity different from that aroused by each of the two kinds of good on its own account. This third spontaneity is that of choice; it is the spontaneity that moves the human being to form a choice.

We have to distinguish that which moves a person to make a choice from the act of choice itself. Although the human being is moved spontaneously to choose, this spontaneity does not determine the way in which he must choose. As we said, the spontaneity moving a person towards a choice is different from the act itself of choice which in its most simple state is still made up of *choice* alone without *volition*. It is this act of choice which determines one of the possible volitions, and which therefore must precede them all. Just as each power has its own proper act, so the act of that faculty which can choose between possible volitions is uniquely and essentially the act of determining between these volitions. This act, therefore, does not lack a cause: its cause is a special activity of the spirit, aroused to operation by the presence of several different kinds of opiniative good.

640. It may be objected that such an act of choice, which can be made in one of two ways, requires a determining cause. But the objector would show a lack of understanding of our distinction between *volition*, and the *choice* that first precedes volition. When we say that this act can be done in one way or another, we are speaking about *volition* and not about the first *choice*; an act that can be done in one of two ways is different from the act that *determines* one way or another. The determining act is superior to both ways; it is that in which the pure choice itself essentially consists; it is a proper, essential act of the faculty of choice just as volition is the proper act of the faculty of volition, and vegetating is the proper act of the vegetating faculty.

Freedom essentially resides in this supremely pure act of choice by which the volition is determined, and as such does not in any way offend the principle of cause. It is in this act, therefore, that is, through the nature itself of this act and through the nature of the faculty to which it appertains, that we behold the spirit as essentially lord, ruler and cause.

641. And this provides for full conciliation between freedom and causality.

But this kind of conciliation, and this way of conceiving freedom, is not new. We take great comfort from finding ourselves in full agreement on this point with the ancient traditions of wisdom and we are glad to be able to confirm all that we have said by appealing to the most trustworthy authorities. First of all, we find ways of speaking in the Bible, in ecclesiastical writers, amongst philosophers and even in ordinary language which show that the distinction between the *faculty of determining volitions*, and *volitions* themselves, is a truth universally recognised and admitted.

Let us begin with the Bible, and consider the phrase used by St. Paul to describe a free human being. He calls him one 'having *power* over his own *will*',[270] that is, over his own volitions. He expressly distinguishes, therefore, between the *will*, that is, the principle of the volitions, and the *power* that the human being has over it. This *power* of the human *will* can only be the power that the person has to turn one way or another and therefore to determine one or another of all the possible volitions. Freedom, according to St. Paul, consists in the power that a human being has to bend his will one way or another. This power is anterior to, and the cause of, the act of will.

642. We find a definition of the *power of the will*, or of free will, in the very early book *Recognitiones*, attributed to Pope St. Clement where it is called 'a certain feeling of the soul which has the energy capable of directing it to those acts which it wishes'.[271] Here we see *volition*, the act with which the soul wills, clearly distinguished from the principle that determines it to one or other of these acts of will. In the same way, St. Justin calls the faculty of *choice* between volitions 'a force or power to turn oneself one way or another'.[272]

The same truth is shown by the inability of authors to be satisfied in speaking without qualification of the will, or judgment

[270] 1 Cor 7: [21 (Douai)]

[271] In bk. 3 of *Recog.* these words are attributed to St. Peter.

[272] 'No created thing would be worthy of praise unless it had been given the power of directing itself towards something other than itself' (*Oratio ad Gent.*).

directed by the will. They consistently add that the human being has dominion over this will or judgment directed by the will, or that the judgment directed by the will is free,[273] or something similar, which clearly shows that the faculty of volition is different from the faculty by which we determine ourselves to one or other of the volitions. *Freedom* truly consists, as we said, in this second faculty. Here we find mastery of self which enables a human being to rule and as it were to possess himself.

643. Some writers have also noted the fleeting nature of the instant in which human beings abandon their hesitation in order to make a decision. Cyril of Alexandria says: 'Humankind, which is both its own master, and free and in possession of its own will, moves *in an instant* to do what it wishes for good or for evil.'[274]

The distinction between determination of the will and *volition* itself, which is my starting point towards a solution of the metaphysical problem of freedom, is not new, therefore, but constant amongst those who have reflected on the matter, and is moreover supported by common sense.

10

THE ORDER OF SUBORDINATION AMONG THE DIFFERENT HUMAN POWERS

644. We have considered the act of choice, the summit as it were of the human spirit and the most sublime of the subjective

[273] 'The free power of the will' (Ter. *De Anima*, 21); 'In my opinion human beings have been made by God free in their will and in their power to act' (Ter. *Adversus Marcionem*, bk. 2, 5); 'All freedom over the will has been given him in both directions so that he may consistently remain master of himself by spontaneously doing good and avoiding evil' (Ter., *ibid.*, 2, 6); 'Freedom of will has been posited in the will of the one who wills' (Arnob. *Adv. Gentes*, bk. 2); 'Although he left us freedom of will to merit goodness' (Hil. in *Ps* 2); 'It is indeed in the power of our free will to take the form a person wishes' (St. Greg. of Nyssa *in Cant.*, Hom. 4); 'God constituted human beings masters of their free decision and of their will' (Theodor. Ancyr. *Hom. in Natal. Salvat.*)); 'Freedom of the will remains intact in mortal beings' (Boet. *De Cons. Philos.*, bk. 5, pr. 6).

[274] *Contra Julian.*, bk. 8.

faculties. Now we have to pause and from this vantage point look down on all the other active powers in order to examine the wonderful chain that binds them, and see how, by relying on one another, they all finally depend upon the highest power of all which acts as their brake and their director.

We have seen how three kinds of forces manifest themselves in animality: 1. material forces; 2. the forces proper to the life instinct; 3. and the forces of the sensuous instinct. These three kinds of forces are manifestly subordinate to one another. The material forces are modified in their activity and dominated by the life instinct; at the same time, the life instinct is in its turn modified and dominated by the sensuous instinct as we have seen (cf. 401–415).

When manifested in a human being, the instinct for a new kind of *human* good, which is principally summarised in the desire for one's own aggrandisement, is seen to be superior to the sensuous instinct because of its intellectual condition. It extends a certain kind of authority and domination over the sensuous instinct itself which is usually unable to compete with such an opponent or master.

However, we have up to now dealt simply with ever nobler instincts, each one destined to govern the one below it. Above this sphere lies the *spontaneity of the will* which by natural right rules the other two instincts and prevents their collision. This spontaneity does not exist independently, however, in the human being. It soon finds a power greater than itself, to which it is naturally subject. This *practical force* influences and modifies spontaneity because it enables human beings to cling with varying degrees of strength to some known good which at their own pleasure they either enhance by exaggerating its worth and augmenting its activity, or undervalue by lowering its worth and decreasing its activity. But the *practical force* itself is simply the executive force of a preceding *decree* arising from the human being's faculty for determining his own volitions by choosing between them. This elective capacity was destined to be the highest of all the subjective powers and their focus point; it was to be the throne of human freedom, the power superior to every other human activity, by which we were to make ourselves like our Creator here on earth as we ruled ourselves, the other powers constituting us, and the activity of these powers.

[644]

645. It is precisely here that our human *active unity* is generated, just as in the *consciousness* of this union and unity between faculty and force our *passive unity* is generated. It was necessary that there should be a centre for the many elements making up the human being; the many phenomena and activities taking place in human nature had to have a primary, unique source. Moreover, this centre and source of all human functions would be insufficient if the functions themselves were not subordinate to one another, or did not form by mutual adherence the chain whose final link is human freedom as it makes its dominion felt over all the other elements, and perfects them through its own act, provided that the act is upright.

646. It is true that each faculty could attach itself directly to the subject even in the absence of this chain; it is also true that the faculties, which do not always preserve the intended subordination, sometimes act (drawing their forces directly from the subject) without awaiting a command from the highest faculty. This, however, would be insufficient to constitute human dignity, which resides in the natural order of subordination between the various faculties up to the highest.

The human subject, therefore, possesses a simple, unitive force as the root and mother of its faculties. Moreover, there is an order between the faculties themselves, some of which are destined to obey and some to command. As a result, the subject acts in two ways: either as the principle of each faculty or as the principle of all the faculties taken collectively. In the first case, each faculty acts independently of any other, and depends solely upon the subject as its principle; in the second case, the subject's action is communicated in order from one faculty to another just as electricity is communicated and passes through a whole series of metallic links.

647. When the subject acts as principle of all the faculties taken together, its work is more intimate, profound and essential; as the common principle of all the faculties, it must be the principle of principles in each faculty. Although the principles of each faculty can be activated separately from one another, they require to be moved according to their mutual order when the supreme principle reaches out to them all. This most intimate principle, which presides over all the faculties as the principle of their

order, has its root precisely in *freedom*, that is, in the faculty for tipping the balance towards one of its various volitions.

648. It will be helpful if, at this point, we show once more, on the basis of certain facts, that there is nothing in the human being over which *freedom* is incapable of exercising some command. This marvellous power makes its bidding felt even in the material forces which compose the human body although, as we said, this communication of the power of freedom takes place through intermediate causes. Of their nature, the *material forces* constituting the first rudiments of the body are subject only to the *life instinct* as their direct master and ruler. Nevertheless, freedom modifies them through this instinct over which it makes its power felt by activating the *sensuous instinct* to which the life instinct is subject. In this way, *freedom* exercises its influence and acts by means of *volitions*.

Animal passions, which pertain to the sensuous instinct, are very often willed and, as we have seen, modify the life instinct. In its turn, the life instinct disposes and modifies the material forces in various ways so that the organic, living body composes and decomposes, assimilates or disassimilates material substances. St. Augustine testifies that he himself had experienced the human capacity for sweating at will; here the will commands the instinct.[275] He also adduces as proof of the soul's innate dominion over the body the case of Restitutus, a parish priest of the diocese of Calama, in Africa, who could will to make himself comatose (he looked like a dead man) provided that someone sang to him sadly. The only feeling that he retained was for high-pitched voices which he heard as though they were some distance away. He also gave no sign of respiration.[276] Cardano, and

[275] 'I know from my own experience that a person can sweat when he wants', *De Civ. Dei*, bk 14, ch. 24.

[276] 'But there is something even more incredible than that, and many of the brethren have had recent experience of it. Restitutus, a priest of the church of Calama, could at will abstract himself from sense-life and lie prostrate like a dead man (he was asked to do this by people who wanted to see it for themselves), provided someone was prepared to imitate a person in pain. In this state, he was unable to feel people pinching or prodding him, and felt no pain even when slightly burnt by a flame (although he experienced pain from the wound afterwards). He felt nothing when he was pushed or moved, and like a dead man did not breathe. However, he said afterwards that he could hear

later Leibniz, were persuaded that the art of sense-alienation could be brought to the point where torture was no longer felt. Cardano affirmed that he had done this for himself,[277] although I am not sure how much credence we should give to this rather odd character. All this shows once more that free will is destined to dominate the life instinct which produces the feeling.

649. The fact remains that there seems no doubt whatsoever about the general proposition we have before us: 'Freedom is born to dominate all the other powers by communicating its action from one power to another right down to the lowest.' Ability to achieve this, however, is an art that has to be learned. We begin to learn and make progress when stimulated by some natural need (although we still have to contend with the internal and external obstacles that impede all practical learning).

11

THE LIMITS OF HUMAN FREEDOM

650. We have seen that the subjective faculties have an order amongst themselves, and that the highest of them, freedom, enables us to determine our volitions. At the same time, we saw that in human operations it is not always the supreme faculty that moves the others, all of which can move independently (cf. 646). This twofold operation of the different subjective faculties inferior to freedom provides the explanation for the limits of freedom itself. It is clear that every time a faculty inferior to freedom moves of its own accord, its action is not free, but withdrawn from the ambit of freedom.

651. We must therefore examine the laws according to which human operations are withdrawn from the influence of freedom. It is these laws that first put bounds to freedom itself.

We have seen that when considered in isolation every active power of the subject has two proper causes of movement. The

human voices from a distance if they spoke clearly enough.' *De Civit. Dei*, bk 14, ch. 24.

[277] *De Rerum Varietate*, bk. 8, c. 43 [11, 17].

life instinct, for instance, is moved by corporeal and material forces according to determined laws; the sensuous instinct receives its impulse from feelings; affective volitions are roused to act both by the spontaneity of the volitive, animal subject and by the intellective perception of what is good; evaluative volitions are aroused by a good known and approved. All these powers, therefore, when taken separately from one another, are capable of operating independently of the action that human freedom can exert upon them. Even if freedom were non-existent, each of them could act spontaneously in the human being.

652. The causes proper to each of these powers move the special power whose stimulus they are, provided the effect they cause naturally is not impeded by some other force, and in particular by the influence of some superior power, or of the supreme power itself. But how can the operation of freedom itself be impeded? This is the problem that now confronts us. Only by solving it will we be able to establish the laws which restrict human freedom within certain limits.

653. First, we recall that *freedom*, as we have described it, is composed of two acts, that is, it has two functions: 1. that of *choosing between volitions*, a function which consists in the first determining act proper to the will, according to which one volition is willed in preference to another; 2. that of the *practical force*, or executive force of choice, which consists in increasing the value and worth of the good determined by the will. These two functions have a very close connection which we shall examine later.

In the meantime it is clear from what we have said that human freedom can find obstacles impeding its operation in both these proper functions. The will can be impeded either 1. because the necessary conditions for *choice* between different volitions are lacking; or 2. because the *practical force*, which should augment the value of the good determined by the will, is incapable of enabling this good to prevail over other goods which simultaneously exercise their effect over the will. In a word, freedom is deficient in act either through lack of *choice* or lack of *practical force*. We must, therefore, consider the limits imposed on freedom from both these points of view.

Article 1.
Limits to freedom through lack of choice

§1. First limit: which depends upon lack of a reason sufficient to arouse the faculty of free choice

654. As we have seen, even the power of choice needs to be aroused if it is to be drawn to act. This does not mean, however, that a sufficient reason has to determine the choice in one direction or another. To do so would be to destroy freedom. We merely say that some reason is needed to draw the soul towards choice in such a way that the choice itself modifies the development of the spontaneous operations of the will.

655. As I have noted, the human being would have no cause prompting action on the part of his faculty of free choice if present, physical good alone were offered him. In this case, the animal instinct, and the spontaneity of the will which shadows such an instinct, would be a sufficient, and indeed, excellent guide enabling him to reach out for the finest good when many of the same kind are presented to him.

But the inclination of the sensuous instinct is not sufficient for making a choice when animal good is connected with a totally different kind of good. Another need, incapable of being satisfied by animal instinct — which has no perception of it — arises within the human being. Take, for example, the case of probable future good, even physical good. We grasp this probability with our mind, not with our feeling. Only the mind enables us to calculate whether physical good is better served by some immediate sacrifice of present good for the sake of longer, more abundant enjoyment. In making this judgment, we blunt the immediate, limited impulses of feeling, and submit them to the true or false *opinion* we have formed about some good through the use of our intelligence, assisted by our imagination and all our other inferior powers. Nevertheless, although it is clear that instinct has been subjected to human will at this point, we still cannot say that we have exercised freedom of choice which lies, still unobserved, in the depths of human nature. The principle of action that has emerged, although a power superior to physical instinct, is not freedom.

It is true that we have made use of a special activity in the action we have described, but this is connected with an *opinion* about some good, an opinion in which we balance present and future good with the intention of gaining the best available subjective good. We avoid sacrificing a greater to a lesser good, which is in accord with the laws of human spontaneity. Human instinct taken in the broadest sense of the term — not animal instinct — has acted as our judge and guide. However we have not yet acted of our own accord, independently of our tendencies, but as their obedient servants: the *spontaneity of the subject as a whole* has simply been substituted for *animal spontaneity*.

I realise that we could have determined ourselves in some way when we carried out the different actions needed to form an intellectual judgment about future good. But we did not necessarily do so, and even if we wish to suppose that we did, we still have to offer some sufficient reason for this kind of determination. As we said, we cannot move ourselves to some entirely free choice unless we have some sufficient reason for doing so. And that is precisely what we are seeking now.

Our next step is to affirm that what we have said about calculating future, physical good relative to present good can be maintained equally about every other kind of subjective good, whether it is the means for attaining physical good, or for satisfying the passions and instincts proper to human nature through various types of good — such as good that we hope for, or good springing from vanity, and any similar good. All these, although specifically different, constitute only one basic kind of good, that is, what is good for the human subject. As long as subjective good alone is presented to us, we have no sufficient reason for any truly *free choice* in our actions, even though we are offered various species of good.

Why should we make some free choice when this opposes our natural tendencies? If we are surrounded by a great quantity of subjective good, we must surely prefer greater to lesser good. If, then, we cannot reach out for all the good present to us, and will undoubtedly take what is greater rather than what is less, we need only esteem the greater through reason and experience before taking hold of whatever accords with our evaluation. In all

[655]

this we only obey the *spontaneity of the will* without an act of truly *free choice*.

656. In such an act, only the possible struggle between present good and greater future good may be likened to free action (provided that present, actual enjoyment attracts the will more intensely despite the reason's decision in favour of a future good less immediately attractive to feeling). Such a struggle would provide a stimulus for the human being, reasonable as he is, to use his autonomous power for the sake of reinforcing reason which, of itself, is cold and weak. It is undeniable that in such a case the *practical force* could be employed to some extent to fortify the desire of the human being, but there would be no obvious use of the *free choice* of which we have spoken. Giving way to the immediate desires of the sensuous instinct or deciding to reinforce the view taken by reason would be determined by circumstances according to the laws of spontaneity. Spontaneity would either succumb to the vehemence of instinct where the vehemence exceeds certain limits or, by drawing upon the practical force present in the depth of the spirit, suspend the effect of instinct by the degree of force in reason. On the other hand, the *practical force* is only an element of freedom when it goes hand in hand with *choice* between volitions.

It is possible, therefore, that in the whole sphere of subjective good surrounding and affecting the human being no sufficient reason is to be found capable of arousing an act of pure, free choice. If we had to live in this sphere, all our actions would be regulated by the laws of spontaneous will. The truly free force, which is really determinative in our volitions, would never be aroused or stimulated in us.

657. But this is not the case when we leave the circle of *subjective* good to enter that of *objective* good. Immediately we find ourselves engaged with two worlds, and forced to choose between them. We can no longer trust ourselves to our instinct or spontaneity because instinct, whether it is proper to one special power alone or embraces *human instinct* (which as a universal instinct reaches out to every kind of good that exists for human nature), never exceeds the limit of subjective good. Only within this sphere of good can it validly determine choice. But we are dealing now with a far superior kind of determination. On one side lies human nature; on the other the absolute world of

beings. We have to choose between two objects: ourselves and the world intuited by our intelligence.

In this choice, *spontaneity* properly speaking is all on one side, that is, on our side; on the other side lie ideas in their eternity and divine light — or rather all real beings seen in these ideas. If we prefer ourselves, we necessarily and sacrilegiously violate, abuse and attempt to destroy what is infinite; if we prefer what is infinite, we immerse ourselves in a sea of self-forgetfulness where we experience a kind of annihilation.

The two sides of the deliberation are totally different, without analogy or proportion between them; they cannot be compared. *Spontaneity* is wholly on one side; *authority*, obligation, law, on the other. If they differed in degree, a *spontaneous choice* could be made between them. But lack of any degree of difference is reinforced by total absence of likeness or affinity. It is impossible for them to share any common tendency.

If the absolute order were considered from the point of view of the delight it causes in the subject contemplating its incomparable beauty, that order would no longer be itself. It would become pleasure, not duty, and the choice of which we are speaking would lie between pleasure and pleasure, not between absolute duty and subjective satisfaction.

When these two orders of things, the subjective order and the absolute, present themselves to us for the first time, therefore, a sufficient reason is found for arousing within us and drawing into act our most noble power of free choice. This explains why writers hardly ever speak of human freedom except in reference to human moral action.

658. A 7th century Greek author observes with great acumen that in the human being freedom is contemporaneous with the development of virtue and vice. 'Freedom of soul never shows itself except in the presence of an impulse to vice or to virtue. If contrary things did not invade the spirit, where would free choice be?'[278] In the end, only virtue and vice are contraries; everything else can be subsumed, as we said, under a single kind. And this explains why the age at which a person begins to act freely is normally called 'the age of discretion between good and

[278] Anastasius of Sinai, in his οδηγου, or *Guide*.

evil', a phrase which proves that this opinion is already common amongst Christians.[279]

§2. Second limit: the lack of two or more good objects from which to make a choice

659. What has been said about the necessity of a sufficient reason for arousing the act of freedom also shows the need for at least two objects about which the free choice may be made. Nevertheless, this new condition for the actuation of freedom is different from the first which explains how the subject decides upon the *act* of free choice, and how the stimulus arousing the spontaneity of the determining acts of will comes into being. The second condition is that which makes the choice itself *possible*.

The difference between the two conditions is factual as well as conceptual. It could happen, for example, that moral order, or duty, when revealed to a human being for the first time, coincides perfectly with subjective good. In this case, freedom would not be exercised through a choice between opposing alternatives; the human being would simultaneously adhere to what satisfied his tendencies and to what was upright. The two motives, subjective good and objective good, would amalgamate and conspire to arouse a single volition in the spirit. If the free act were to take place, therefore, 1. there must be two objects of choice; 2. and these two objects must contradict one another sufficiently to arouse a free choice.

600. It may be objected that two objects or volitions from which to choose can never be lacking; although opposite goods may not be present from which to make a choice (*libertas contrarietatis*), it is always possible either to posit or not to posit the act of will (*libertas contradictionis*). This objection, however, neglects to consider that alternatives, in order to be the object of choice, must also be thought of. It is true that one can either accept or reject a single known good, but it is not true that such a choice

279 'Having come to the age of discretion, the human being, by means of his free will, can make use of good and evil just as he pleases '. St. Catherine of Siena, *Tratt.*, 1, ch. 14.

is always conceived by the intellect. An act of reflection is needed on the part of the subject if he is to deliberate about not willing some good presented to his intellect. In this reflection, the subject has to apprehend as good the act of not willing the good, and as evil the act of willing it — because the will never chooses anything except *sub specie boni* and never rejects anything except *sub specie mali.* I agree that the subject could deliberate about such a choice if, on reflection, he judged that it was not good to want an otherwise good object, but this is not the case under consideration. We are considering a period anterior to such reflection and intellectual judgment when only one of the alternatives, either good or evil, is present to the mind. Here, only the spontaneous, not the free will can intervene.

§3. Third limit: the experience of an infinite good

661. In the two cases we have indicated, freedom lacks the opportunity and the object for the use or trial of its powers. But there is a third case in which its activity is blocked because of the disproportion between its powers and an object which cannot be refused. Such an object is the infinite good, when it is experienced fully. This explains why those who have come to apprehend the vision of God in heaven lose all exercise of freedom between good and evil. According to Catholic teaching, they are fixed immovably in good. But this infinite good does not merely overcome every possible *practical force* in the human being. It radically impedes choice itself by annihilating, with its own weight, any contrary force. In fact, a free choice requires the presence to the spirit of two kinds of opposing good (cf. 659, 660). But if one of the alternatives is infinite good, it cannot be true to say that two opposing types of good are present to the spirit. Infinite good gathers all good to itself, and the loss of infinite good is an amalgam of all evil. When infinite good is known intimately, as it will be when perceived and experienced by a human being, no element, aspect or even appearance of good stands outside it And when the intellect no longer offers two kinds of good to the will, but one alone, the will can no longer err about good, nor be deceived by false good.

For the same reason, this state or condition leaves no possibility of two volitions about which to deliberate. The number of possible volitions are only as many as the possible kinds or aspects of good proposed by the intellect. But in our case, only one direction can be taken because only one good attracts the will.

In addition, because this good is infinite, it must draw the will with a certain infinite attraction, which is often more than sufficient to determine the will irresistibly and instantaneously. Freedom of choice at such a moment receives no stimulus enabling it to suspend its volition, and has no time or space in which to deliberate anything to the contrary.

Article 2.
Limits to freedom when the *practical force* is lessened

662. We must now consider the limits placed on the exercise of freedom by the *practical force*. As we said, this *force* is *free choice*, the executive faculty, and is very closely connected with choice itself. The first step, we might say, in the use of this force influences the choice itself in such a way that positing a faculty devoid of any degree of practical force on the one hand, but enabling us to determine ourselves freely on the other, is a simple contradiction. In fact, if we were to suppose that the faculty by which we determine one volition rather than another possessed no practical force, we would no longer be thinking of a real *determining act* of our will, but only of some *inclination* without any definitive outcome. It is impossible to determine oneself to will what one cannot will at all.[280]

663. *Volition* follows immediately upon the *determining act*.

[280] The very strict connection between the *determining act* and *volition* caused these two acts to be taken as one in the sense that the second must follow on the first, although even here a verbal distinction was still made between them. For example: 'DETERMINING the will is not an entity distinct from the will and its ACT' (Gregory of Rimini, a noted 14th century theologian, in *II Sent.*, dist. 34, 35, q. 1, art. 3). In this quotation, *the determining act* is not an entity distinct from *will* and *volition*, but even speaking about them in this way shows that they were at least considered as mentally distinct.

The practical force, which produces and informs, as it were, the volition itself, begins here. Volition pure and simple is normally called *choice*, the *elicited act* of will. It is followed by the *stimulated act*, and by the *command*.

The *command* is the movement of some power under pressure from the will. If I decide internally to move a foot, and actually move it, this movement is an act commanded by my will. If my foot is in chains so that I cannot move it, I can nevertheless will to move it. In this case (provided we do not take into account any effort to move the foot), the *commanded act* of will is lacking; only the *determining act*, which does not pass from the will to some other power, is present and terminates in the will whose proper act it is, and which alone it needs in order to run its course.

664. Here we have to consider that my *freedom* is not diminished if the acts with which I command my organs, for example, are impeded by external pressure or defective organs. Freedom is wholly interior, and has no natural communion with brute force, which can neither increase nor diminish its power.

665. The same could not be said if the commanded act were blocked not by a force external to the human being, but by rebellion on the part of the interior power which receives the command. Internal war breaks out: freedom begins to measure its strength against powers which by natural right are its subjects. In such a case the *practical force* is truly bound, and a limit is set to freedom.

St. Paul refers to this limitation of freedom when he says: 'I can will what is right, but I cannot do it.'[281] A clear distinction can be seen in these words between the *determining act* and the *practical force*, or better between the first degree of practical force, that is, the choice or simple volition, and the second degree, that is, the command or volition influencing the inferior powers. The Apostle, speaking in the person of human beings inclined to evil, affirms that he does indeed will what is good, but feels at the same time that he lacks the power to do good. Consequently his will remains sterile: 'For I do not do the good I

[281] Rom 7: [18]. St Bernard explains this as follows: 'Without the support of its *faculty*', (that is, without its practical force) 'the will is prostrate' (Serm. 88, *In Cant.*).

want, but the evil I do not want is what I do.'[282] We must, therefore, consider this limitation of the *practical force* and show how the executive power of freedom is internally blocked in its exercise.

666. The limitation of the practical force depends upon two principal causes: 1. the *ineffectiveness* of the practical force itself; 2. the superabundant *effectiveness* of the powers which limit the practical force and block its natural activity and effectiveness. It is clear that the entire relationship of which we are speaking depends upon the relationship between the efficacy of the practical force and that of the powers limiting it. An increase in the efficacy of these powers and decrease in the efficacy of the practical force determine the limitation imposed on the *practical force* of human freedom.

667. But the degree of efficacy of the powers limiting the practical force, relative to the degree of efficacy of the practical force itself, does not depend solely upon the intrinsic condition of the practical force and the other powers. It also depends upon two principal external circumstances: 1. lack of skill in moving and ruling these powers on the part of the spirit (moving the lower powers is an art for the most part, and can be learnt only through experience); 2. the tardiness with which the practical force comes into action and its consequent late reaction to the unexpected speed of the powers in competition with it.

These two circumstances have to be considered very carefully in any factual calculation of the practical force of liberty present in a human being. In particular, maximum importance must be given to the second condition because the success of the practical force depends very frequently upon its *readiness* for action. Later, I shall speak more at length about this important point and develop it as it deserves.

668. Meanwhile, we have to list the powers that can come into conflict with the practical force and render its action ineffective. We shall view them in order, and consider how they place a limit to the activity of the *practical force* of human freedom. These powers are: 1. the animal instinct, together with its passions and habits; 2. the spiritual instinct, also accompanied by passions, memories, associations and habits; 3. the theoretical judgment; 4. the practical judgment; 5. the general, habitual volitions that

282 *Ibid.* [7: 19].

have their place in the depths of the soul. Given certain circumstances, all these powers can subtract themselves from the command of freedom, or conquer its practical force. We have to see how this comes about, and with what limitations.

§1. The first limit, dependent upon animal instinct

669. The first question arising from the relationship between *animal instinct* and *freedom* is concerned with the activity of animal instinct considered in itself. In order to discover the extent of this activity, we need to examine it in brute animals, where it is unaccompanied by any act of will. If we were to examine it in human beings, where it is associated with the will, we would often remain unsure whether certain effects appertained to instinct or to will. Matters pertaining to instinct in the human being are often predicated of the will. When we have ascertained the sphere of instinctive activity in brute animals, however, we will be able to conclude rightly that instinct can act similarly in human beings in so far as they possess an animal nature.

670. In brute animals, instinct produces all movements — walking, eating, etc. — and every act and function of animal life. A human being, therefore, in whom the will was entirely idle or listless, or simply a kind of onlooker, would not lack external activity. He would be able to walk, eat, and carry out all the acts and functions of animal life as a result of pure instinct, without any need of will.

671. On the other hand, if the will begins to act, instinct is neither destroyed, nor changed in its nature, nor diminished in intrinsic power. What kinds of relationship exist, therefore, between the instinct and the will, and between their different activities? These relationships can only be three in number: either 1. the will acts as a mere spectator and leaves the instinct to proceed on its own; or 2. it adds its own power and helps the instinct to act; or finally 3. it opposes the instinct by attempting to block or modify its action with its own commands.

672. In the first case, the will could remain inactive either because it approves what the instinct is doing, or because it is held captive and remains incapable of moving itself, granted the speed

and vehemence with which the instinct acts. If it approves the act of instinct, the will is not altogether inactive; it *consents* to the action, although it does not positively *influence* it. If the will cannot intervene, there is indeed disharmony between will and instinct, but of such a kind that the instinct both prevents the will from opposing its own act, and silences, as it were, any opposition that might be forthcoming. We could indeed classify this last case amongst the third kind of relationship in which instinct and will are at war.

673. We said that the will could be overcome in its battle with instinct, but it could also conquer. The degree of difficulty it would experience in conquering depends upon the level of vigour present in the practical force.

674. A list of the different ways in which animal instinct could overcome the will in the human being would show that this occurs:

1. in the absence of will, when knowledge of any alternative is lacking, as for instance in the first movements of a baby;

2. when the will is present, but unable to act, as in sleep and sleep-walking, when the human being sometimes knows what he is doing, but is unable to judge his own activity or act according to such judgments;

3. when the practical force of the will is completely overcome and conquered by the pressure and swiftness of instinct. Something like this could happen in the case of rape, such as that mentioned by St. Augustine in *The City of God*. He affirms not only that the women in this case were without blame, but that their merit was in proportion to their distress. The opposition of their will, which absolved them from sin, did not block the effect of animal instinct.

675. The way in which animal instinct entirely overcomes the practical force of the will can be examined more clearly in the case of persons suffering from rabies or delirium.

The unfortunate victims of rabies feel an irresistible instinct to bite those who approach them, even their nearest and dearest. Not only do they not want to do this, but they beg people to keep away. Nothing is more painful for them than awareness of this urge to bite people and rage against them.

The same can be seen in attacks of delirium which often take place without any mental disorder or irrationality. Dr. Pinel describes the case of one of his patients in the hospital at Bicêtre:

> Before his committal, the patient suffered an attack of delirium

> at home. He told his wife, whom he loved dearly; she scarcely had time to flee and avoid a violent death before the attack overcame him. At Bicêtre there were other attacks of the same kind against the Superintendent whose compassionate care and gentleness the patient praised unceasingly.[283]

Instinct cannot be overcome by the will when it takes these forms, and I believe that in this respect it can be as savagely diseased in as many ways as there are animal passions that lose all restraint and normal harmony. In all these cases, however (provided we take no account of the cause of the excess of instinct which could depend upon some preceding, freely willed defect), the will, which is not the originator of the excessive act of instinct, plays the part of a weak and desolate, or strong and unwillng spectator. In every case, the will is an embattled, oppressed victim.

The vehemence of instincts in sufferers from rabies, delirium and mental disorder has its source in some diseased principle.

676. The instinct is sometimes disordered and diseased from birth. Cases have been known of people manifesting irrepressible instincts proper to dogs, cats, sheep and other animals. There is no doubt that the material composition of their bodies bore a likeness or analogy with that found in these animals. This would have modified their life instinct, and given it the characteristics we have mentioned. A few examples will help to show how the animal instinct can, within certain limits, overcome the practical force of the will.

1st. The *canine instinct*. In his secret memoirs of the reigns of Louis XIV and Louis XV, Du Clois describes the affliction of Henri Jules de Bourbon, son of the great Condé, who sometimes experienced an irresistible urge to act like a dog. On these occasions he would start to bark with all his might. Once, he was taken by a fit of this kind while in audience with Louis XIV. The king's presence enabled him to control the force of this instinct to some extent, but not to suppress it altogether. He had to go to the window and lean out while making a great effort to prevent the barking noise, although he still went through all the

[283] Philippe Pinel, *Trattato medico-filosofico sopra l'alienazione mentale*, Sez. 3.

canine actions connected with barking. It is clear that he employed the whole force of his will in the matter without its being able to help him overcome such strange impulses of instinct.

2nd. The *feline instinct*. I remember reading a memorandum of Dr. Ruggeri, professor of the medical faculty of the University of Padua, in which he notes the case of a young woman who exhibited instincts very similar to those of cats (animals which she detested). When she married, it was found that a considerable part of her body was covered with cat-like skin which she had managed to keep secret. The marriage was annulled.

3rd. The *ovine instinct*. Doctor Pinel observed the presence of ovine instinct in a mentally handicapped girl. He described it as follows:

> She was a patient at the Salpêtrière hospital for two and a half months. During this period, she showed particular repugnance for meat, but, like a sheep, willingly consumed vegetable substances — potatoes, salads, bread, and especially a local bread baked in her village and brought by her mother. She drank only water, and in her own way showed great gratitude for the attention she received from the nurse, although she was able to express her thanks only by muttering the words "baby", "auntie". Her lack of other words depended, I think, on a simple absence of ideas (her tongue moved normally). She also had a habit of moving her head up and down, and resting it against the stomach of the nurse as a sign of gratitude. Something similar occurred in her little quarrels with children of her own age whom she tried to butt. When she was in the grip of blind instinct like an animal, she had no control over her outbursts of anger; her excesses took place for the slightest reasons, or for none at all, and even led to convulsions. We were never able to make her sit down, or rest, or prepare her meals, and she slept with her body curled up on the ground like a sheep. Her back, limbs and shoulders were covered with a kind of flexible, dark hair about an inch and a half or two inches long, and fine like wool. It was a very distressing sight.[284]

Animal instinct, therefore, receives from birth a special impress which carries with it an inclination towards some peculiar activity, and a particular kind of arousal.

[284] *Op. cit.*.

677. But instinct is equally moved and excited by stimulation from principles which, as we have said, may be disordered as a result of contracted passions and habits. For instance, I could name a person of noble birth who developed a habit of interjecting something like 'coro-de-coro-coro' after every three words of conversation. It was very unpleasant to hear, but he was never able to correct it despite the ridicule it caused him in society. Another person, still living, has a habit of chirruping loudly like a bird whenever he is with others. The movements of his lips and mouth are so frequent and marked that people who do not know him are immediately put off. But each of us will have had occasion to observe a great variety of similar strange, habitual defects.

678. We have already hinted at a common cause of all the instinctive movements that become too strong for the will, that is: 'the extreme mobility of the nerve endings whose tiny movements cause the spontaneity of the life and sensuous instincts to produce greater movements which terminate in the strange facts we have examined'. This extreme mobility needs only the slightest stimulus to be brought into play. Sometimes the stimulus comes from the life instinct, sometimes from the sensuous instinct (especially in cases of acquired habits). The imagination, for example, which forms part of the sensuous instinct, is always being aroused and continually receives present sensations intermingled with those of the past; ideas, too, often reflect the content of our imagination and phantasy.

679. We may sum up by saying that instinct can withdraw itself from the command of the will, or overcome its force: 1. as a result of some special inbred condition; 2. through some diseased condition acquired after birth; 3. through an inclination resulting from contracted habits; 4. through heightening of animal passions; 5. finally, as a result of various combinations of these causes.

680. However, two very different cases have to be distinguished with great accuracy when we are dealing with the victory of animal instinct over the *practical force* of the will.

The instinct can conquer despite the will's continual opposition. In this case, the will posits the *act of choice*, the simple volition, despite the instinct, which overcomes and defeats only the *command*. The will, lacking the power to prevail and succeed in its determination, is weakened, but not completely misled.

681. But the instinct can also incline the will itself if reason does not intervene quickly enough. Again, if the will is already inclined to evil, instinct can not only block its operation over the other powers, but even mislead it by persuading it to posit an *act of choice* in its favour. In this case, the will is entirely overcome: its volition is weakened and rendered impotent relative to the other powers; and the will itself conspires with instinct against its own freedom.

The instinct succeeds in extracting from the will a volition opposed to the moral law; the will, through its act, places itself in an immoral state. We shall have to speak more fully about this when we see how not only the instinct, but even the *judgment* can in certain cases withdraw itself from the force of the will. As we have seen, an *act of choice* on the part of the will, or volition, is always based upon some judgment, that is, some practical judgent.[285]

682. However, we must continue here with our examination of the first kind of power of instinct over the will, that is, when the instinct acts without perverting the practical judgment. We cannot be content with establishing the fact that animal instinct sometimes conquers the will directly, and that the will in its weakness and quasi-paralysis permits instinct to act in its place. We have to describe the struggle between the two powers, and take careful note of what occurs. But because the conflict between the *will* and *human instinct* follows a similar pattern to that between the *will* and *animal instinct* (the laws of combat, the efforts made by the two sides, and the outcome of the struggle bear a close resemblance in both cases), we shall be able to describe together the accidental features of the two conflicts after saying a few words about the way in which the human instinct rises against the practical force of the will.

§2. The second limit, posited by human instinct

683. Under the name *human instinct* we have included the tendency towards one's own aggrandisement, towards society,

[285] Cf. *PE*, 182–192, and *Storia comparativa de' Sistemi intorno al principio della Morale*, c. 1, and c. 8, art. 3, §3–5.

honour, knowledge, fellow-feeling, love and other effects of the same instinct. All of these naturally incline the will from the beginning, and are occasionally in collision with it when it wishes to maintain the absolute, objective order of the law which is unknown to human instinct — just as it is unknown to every other instinct — and as such remains outside its sphere.

684. *Human* instinct exists at a higher level than mere *animal* instinct. Nevertheless it draws its operative material in great part from animality itself. Love, for example, has its material element in the physical attraction of the sexes; fellow-feeling depends to a great extent on the material provided by the imagination; friendship is often allied with love which colours friendship, giving life and vivacity to mere remembrances and images; the companionship proper to society depends upon the common likeness in human nature and upon its complementary needs. All these things come to us through the senses. The same is true of honour, which is nourished by the sound of human voices (fame is often depicted blowing a trumpet), and of the other subjective, human inclinations which, taken together, form what we have called human instinct. Animality, however, provides nothing more than matter. The form of human instinct is posited by reason, which works in wonderful ways on the matter furnished by the senses, transforming, amplifying, spiritualising and divinising it. Human instinct, which is unlimited because intelligence is unlimited, is therefore essentially different from merely animal instinct.

685. Consequently, human instinct cannot work under the same guise as animal instinct whose operation is totally blind. Human instinct, essentially a rational appetite, never acts without some light from reason. While animal instinct can and sometimes does withdraw its acts through brute force from the influence of the *will* and even of the *reason*, the human instinct cannot operate independently of judgment springing from *reason*[286]

[286] The distinction between the two instincts is expressed very clearly in the Bible. St. John, for example, speaks of a will *of the flesh* and of a *human will.* These two wills can only signify the will in so far as it obeys what we have called *animal* instinct, and in so far as it obeys what we have called *human* instinct.

686. But what provides the occasion for the struggle in which *human* instinct, as we have called it, engages with and sometimes overcomes the human will?

We have already described the two ways in which *animal* instinct acts in opposition to the will, that is, either by operating independently of the practical judgment of the will, or by toppling it. These ways are not open, however, to the human instinct which acts only on the will and whose inclinations cannot be actuated without the consent of the will, nor rendered effective without some determining volition and consequently without the judgment upon which, as we said, every volition is founded. The human instinct, therefore, does not struggle properly speaking with the *will*, but with the *freedom* of the will. Human instinct seeks to corrupt the will and to incline its spontaneity against the law; freedom opposes this, and battle commences.

We intend to consider this struggle shortly when we speak about the flexibility of the faculty of judgment and ask if there can exist within us any irresistibly false judgment (cf. 681, 682). For the moment, however, we wish to examine *human instinct* simply as a power reinforcing *animal* instinct which is unbelievably assisted, modified and sharpened by the unceasing activity of human instinct.

We shall first see how this *animal instinct*, reinforced by *human instinct*, struggles with and often overcomes the will.

§3. Causes of the weakness of the will in its struggle with instinct

687. We are dealing here with a *comparative* weakness of the will relative to the forces of instinct. The weakness increases as the instinctive forces grow on the one hand, and the forces of the will decrease on the other. We must, therefore, consider weakness of will from the point of view of instinct and from that of will. What stimulates and invigorates instinct, and what weakens and lessens will?

It is clear that the instinct's power to overcome and conquer the will depends upon the vigour and speed with which it acts.

688. Relative to the practical force of the will, we need to

consider the two functions of this force which we have already described, that is, the function of *choice or determining acts* and the function of *acts of command*, which are intended to move the powers naturally subject to the will. As we know, the will exercises one kind of force in simple volition, and another in communicating movement to the other powers. As a result, we have to deal with a double weakness: that found in the simple volition, and that found in the command moving the other powers.

We have to examine all these causes briefly (those dependent upon the instinct and those dependent upon the will) which prevent the will from reacting sufficiently against the urges and harassments of instinct. But we do this taking into account human beings as they come into existence and develop. We shall see that human instinct is undoubtedly disturbed from the very beginning.

I
The natural, self-assertive pride of instinct, and its growth through development and exercise

689. Christianity is not alone in teaching unhesitatingly that human beings contract imperfection and moral disorder by nature. Unbiased observation of infants and their development shows a clear imbalance between the dignity of their moral calling, with its irresistible command, and the force of will available for responding to this calling.

The most ancient traditions, all the beliefs asserted by the peoples, the symbols and the myths, proclaim with a single voice the hidden, fatal, moral disability of human nature. Pagan philosophy, sacred teachings and popular beliefs have always agreed on this point. Cebete, in his famous description, shows humanity emerging to life and contemporaneously brought face to face with dazzling attractions and errors. The souls destined to enter bodies are first well dosed with this poison. Plato has no hesitation in declaring: 'Humanity conceals in the depths of its heart a deadly disease which, springing from mankind's ancient, unexpiated faults, torments and crushes human beings.'[287] Radically opposing schools of thought

[287] *Laws*, 9.

hadnodifficulty in accepting such an evident fact. Aniceride of Cyprus taught, with Plato, that 'mankind has to accustom itself to all that is good in order to overcome the vicious affection diffused and inserted within humanity'.[288] Similar assertions are very frequent in the pagan writers who flourished before Christ. It is not surprising, therefore, if this truth is even more clearly maintained by the philosophers who came after him, and in particular by Seneca[289] and Plutarch. One example from Plutarch will be sufficient to illustrate the point: 'From the moment of our birth, a fatal dose of evil is diffused through all that we are and all that we do. Human seed bears its own mortality within, and in great part causes this misery of ours by giving rise to evil inclinations, disease, anxiety and other fatal disasters that burden mankind.'[290]

But there is no need, in fact, to depend on the authority of others when our daily experience provides clear proof of our state, and forces us, despite our unwillingness, to see that an unfaithful instinct captivates our heart from the beginning, involving it in evil.

690. Pleasurable sensations and natural instincts are in no way balanced by the power of reason. Their vivacity and blind impetus deceive humanity from the start by promising more than they can possibly provide, and human beings, in their credulity, light- heartedly abandon themselves to the government of instinct in a vain hope for happiness. Desires spring up, urging us to enjoy more than we are able, while we ourselves demand from the senses which have deceived us more than they can ever give. But we still go on believing, and immerse ourselves more deeply in sensuality. Longings are provoked and

[288] Diog. Laerz, bk. 3.

[289] Cf. *De Clementia*, bk 1.

[290] *De Consol. ad Apoll.* It comes as no surprise that this truth, asserted six thousand years ago and repeated ever since, causes certain people weariness and irritation. The desire to appear original prompted one writer to begin a work with the words: 'Human beings are born good; society corrupts them.' But how, if we are good, can we form a corrupt society always and everywhere (in the last analysis, society is simply the union of many human beings)? Rousseau, in avoiding the problem of the origin of human corruption, had to face that of the origin of corruption in society. He neither loosened nor cut the knot; he simply transposed it.

irritated, and assert their influence (through our imagination rather than in reality) to such an effect that the whole human body can be destroyed. Savages, people undoubtedly in contact with nature, drink themselves to death, for example.

Such excess may not show itself early in life, although gluttony, especially for certain foods, can be seen in quite young children. Nevertheless, careful observation shows that sensations are extremely lively from first infancy, and totally subject the human being. An infinite need of ever new sensations is produced, together with a morbid, but always unresolved desire to satisfy oneself through them. The rule of the animal over the intelligent part of human beings is consistently strengthened and finally manifests its own imbalance, blindness, irresponsibility and inclination to self-destruction. It is only too clear that in this situation the will, subject to immense pressure, is bound to go astray through a false judgment about the value of sensations furnished with such excessive and deceitful *vivacity*.

691. We also need to consider the rapidity of the movements of feeling and instinct compared with the slowness of our rational reactions.

There are, of course, moments of tranquillity in human existence when our intelligence shines in our hearts like the sun on a calm day. Such moments, however are brief and infrequent. Their place is soon taken by confusion and interior disquiet. Only the person who has never experienced the agony of passion, the vehemence of contempt, the onset of grief, the cold touch of fear, the ecstasy of beauty, bursts of joy, the anger of love, practical expressions of compassion and the joy of hope can deny that the human will is often under the influence of immense pressure against which it has no defence and no place of refuge. But no one lives without taking counsel from these perfidious friends and finding, in brief moments of activity, that their momentary advice has shut the door against every other counsel and transformed itself into active deliberation.

There is no doubt that we shall have to render an account if we are the authors of such a state and place ourselves in this miserable condition. But here we are dealing only with a fact, and asserting that both the *vehemence* and *rapid response* of the affections, passions and sensations sometimes take the will by surprise and eliminate the time needed for it to deny its consent.

Dante saw, perhaps better than anyone else, how love, delicate and sublime, could be at odds with the intellect and torment the heart. He describes such a situation with immense tenderness and lays the blame on the sudden awakening of passion, which leaves no time for defence against error. He goes on to speak about virtue, which he had adopted and taken as his safeguard against such love:

'The first assault was fatal.
Strength and space for arms withheld,
Virtue tried in vain to flee from battle,
To lead me, slow and weary, out of harm
Towards the saving rock too high for me to scale.
Today's the same. Her will to help's
Of no avail, her power unable to prevail.'

692. *Pressure*, therefore, and *rapidity*[291] are two characteristics of instinctive activity in animals and in humans, and as such are inherent to the nature of instinctive action. This pressure and rapidity of movement increases through habit. But what causes the increase?

693. In examining the growth of pressure and impetus, it will help if we distinguish the *passive faculties*, which are those of our feelings, from the *active faculties*. There is no doubt that the latter increase in vigour through moderate exercise while the former seem to diminish. In the case of an epidemic or spread of contagious disease, for example, we often see a number of doctors working with equal zeal for the sick in their care. In the younger ones, feelings of compassion (which, as feeling, is passive) are perhaps more marked; in their senior companions, courage, activity and constancy are found at a higher level, although there seems to be a drop in compassion and feeling for the patients. The more experienced doctors have perhaps lost something of their feeling, although their active care of patients has grown. The feelings moving them to care for the sick have lessened in intensity, it would seem, but increased in practicality.[292]

291 I do not mean that the *will* of itself acts less quickly than instinct. Rather, it is held back by the deliberation which precedes volition whenever several motives for acting, each one capable of moving the will, are present. If no deliberation or choice, but only spontaneous movement is needed, the will is as swift to act as the instinct.

292 Nevertheless, it is not unreasonable to ask whether benevolent feelings

694. In the case of *passive faculties*, it is a fact that the corporeal fibres weaken under the continued action of stimuli, and become less capable of producing sensations, which require movement and hence some kind of passage, not a constant, balanced state. If, however, the stimulated action is not too prolonged, and the fibres are given the opportunity of returning to their natural, primitive state, we have to go on to distinguish between painful sensations, which instinct tends to avoid, and pleasurable sensations, which it tends to enjoy.

As instinct grows in strength, pleasurable sensations become stronger and more vivid; troublesome sensations, on the other hand, seem to diminish in their degree of pain when instinct weakens. This would explain why pleasure gains uncontrollable mastery in persons enslaved by their senses, while pain seems to diminish in people who suffer habitually and for prolonged periods.

695. The reason explaining the increase of vivacity in pleasurable sensations as a result of use of the faculties of feeling is to be found in the soul's collaboration in the production of sensations, not in the material organisation of the fibres. The same applies in the case of diminution of pain. If such change were to depend on the organisation of the fibres, pleasant and unpleasant sensations would follow a constant law of growth and diminution. But the activity of the soul, which we have called the *sensuous instinct*, consists totally in seconding pleasant and avoiding painful sensations. Because activity on the part of the soul is required for the production of feeling, the soul

in older doctors are indeed less strong than in their younger colleagues. We could be misled here by another law that we have observed, which dominates the whole theory of capacity for feeling: 'Partial and superficial feelings are more accentuated and more apt to draw the attention of persons experiencing them than the same feelings developed at a more universal level, because such growth in feelings makes them less amenable to reflection although more efficacious in moving instinctively into action.' For example, when we eat we are governed in our choice of food more by the hidden indications of our rather general and less obvious *alimentary* feeling, as we have called it, than by the restricted *sense of taste* which is usually the sole object of our observation and thought. I think that the feeling of humanity which governs concerned action for our neighbour becomes more general and more profound as such action grows and, as a result, becomes less lively but more efficacious.

itself learns from experience to posit a greater degree of activity in producing pleasurable feelings, and to withhold as much activity as possible in contributing to painful feelings (cf. 367–369).

The very definition of sensuous activity explains, therefore, the diminution of vivacity in painful feelings and the growth of intensity in pleasurable feelings. As we know, the sensuous instinct is simply 'the natural movement of the soul towards what is pleasant, and the withdrawal of the soul from what is troublesome'. Even the lessening of the degree of habitual pain indicates an increase, not a decrease, in the power of the sensuous instinct. Precisely because this power has increased, the soul is able to flee, at least partially, from pain. If, therefore, the instinct grows in power through exercise, we have here an explanation for the increase in the active powers. Instinct is precisely the soul's activity.

696. This is true relative to the degree of *vehemence* in the instinct. But how and why does the degree of *rapidity* in instinctive activity increase through exercise?

We need to note with great attention that the active faculties are normally found in different stages of potential. I mean that the active faculty initially given by nature possesses a very different potential from that found in the faculty when it undertakes some particular act which can be posited only as a result of the faculty's passing through a series of grades or states until it reaches the act ('second act', as we call it). But the faculty could come to a halt and be found in a state or mode of being at any of the levels of activity which may exist between mere potency and mere act. It is clear, therefore, that the more the potency is activated, that is, the nearer its state to that of act, the more readily and easily it can posit the act. The passage from such a state to the act itself is shorter because the faculty is already to some extent habitually activated towards the completed act. The use or exercise of the potency draws it more and more from its potentiality, furnishing it with ever greater activity as it approximates to perfect act.

This explanation needs to be added to what has been said about the soul's increased activity towards what it finds pleasurable in pleasing sensations, and away from the pain of displeasing sensations. This, too, stimulates and excites the impetus of instinct towards action.

II
Weakness of the will in its relationship with instinct

697. We now have to see how the will may or may not be capable of holding its own against the vivacity, urgency and speed of instinct. We have already said that of its nature the will is extremely flexible and yielding, and that in children it gives way for a long time to instinct, which it serves as a humble companion obeying an overbearing master. Unarmed as it is, it cannot do otherwise. Reason, which forges weapons for the will, is *cold* of its nature and *slow* to operate. Its qualities are very different from those of instinct.

698. We must also note that the weapons provided for the will by reason, although intended to assist the will's moral rule and government of instinct, cannot be prepared and fashioned as soon as reason begins to act. Reason must first prepare itself for action. It can operate only when it has set up its own workshop, as it were, and made the tools it needs.

As we saw, perceptions and the specific ideas of things are the first realities associated with reason. The moral principle with which the will must rule the instincts begins to shine in the soul only when reason, having perceived intelligent beings, starts to reflect that they should be honoured as they deserve whatever the cost to instinct. Instinct, blind as it is, pays no attention to the harm it causes anything or anyone provided it succeeds in satisfying itself. Reason, however, begins to notice the deviations of instinct as soon as the norm governing what is just and upright shines before the human mind — even though the norm is not yet present in its abstract form. At this moment a rule appears which prescribes that all should receive their due according to the absolute, eternal order of beings. Reason then reproves the will for its softness, recalling it from the mistaken path to which it had strayed. Reason also tells the will to understand its own dignity and rebel against the caprices of instinct, which it must learn to command and govern.

From this moment the will has a new power enabling it to become the source of human actions. Everything done within the reign of the will now depends upon the will's desire and consent, which must be directed solely towards justice and virtue.

The will, however, which has already taken several hurried

steps in the direction of its own pleasurable satisfactions, has to be made capable of preferring the path of justice and virtue. This can occur only when it realises that the pursuit of moral uprightness is a greater good than all the attractions of subjective good. And here we are face to face with a serious difficulty. On one hand, we experience real, lively action from the good that we feel; on the other, stands a simple rule, a cold law, a kind of compass showing us the way without helping us to follow it. Reason never ceases to affirm, however, that this supremely worthy norm can never be changed or overcome. The norm commands, and goes on commanding with equal force whether it is obeyed or not. For those who disobey, its command stands as a condemnation.

The sublime, noble nature of this law is the immobile point used by the will for its leverage. From this point the will draws strength to overcome and disregard all sensible good, despite the immediate, real action exerted by this good. In other words, the will is capable of enhancing the law's authority in its own regard and rendering this authority more powerful than the attraction of things opposed to the law. The will can ensure that following the law becomes a greater good for it than anything the will could attain by breaking the law. In this way, the will increases the power that good has over it. This capacity for perceiving one of the things present to the will as a good superior to all other good forms the principal force underpinning the efficacy of *freedom.*

699. Summing up, we may say that the operation with which the will consents to rest in one good rather than another is the result of two elements: 1. the natural action on the will by the known, supposed, experienced good (here the will is *passive*); 2. the consent of the will without which the activity of the will remains suspended (here the will is *active*).

Moreover, this consent is either spontaneous or free. It is *spontaneous* if it does not resist what naturally attracts the will, and if it yields to a single felt impression or to the strongest when several impressions are experienced. It is *free* if it stands up to disordered attraction and uses the mastery described in Scripture: 'Lust shall be under you, and you shall have dominion over it.'

700. Such dominion can only be employed if the will perceives and experiences sufficient light of truth to reach the practical persuasion that this light is worth more than all possible subjective good. In order to attain this persuasion, however, and

through it disembellish the lively stimulus and felt attraction of contrary objects, the will needs *time* (it is understood that we are now speaking of the will's natural forces); it cannot carry through its persuasion instantly. Normally, prolonged meditation and exercise are needed to appreciate — at least at a certain level of efficacy — the extraordinary beauty of virtue. In general, we can say that *attention* to, *meditation* on, and *contemplation* of the value of things is the normal means used by the natural will to reinforce the perception of their worth, and to render such worth more immediate and operative. The action received by human beings from the good they know is not in proportion to this good in itself, but to the good as apprehended, considered and experienced by us. In a word, its value depends on the way it exists in our feeling, in our spirit, in our understanding and in our persuasion.

But, as we said, carrying out these acts requires time; here below our will acts only in time. Consequently it first needs sufficient virtue to withhold its consent for a moment from the importunate, feelable object stimulating and pressurising it. Only then can the will arm itself with the weapons forged through intense concentration, wise and careful meditation and loving, peaceful contemplation. Before beginning any deliberation about choosing between a more stimulating or a more authoritative object, the will must ask itself: 'Should I consent immediately, or should wait and think about what I am doing?' But it is precisely this which sometimes escapes the will. The question implies a mind at peace in moments when it is often distraught and goaded to action.

701. Unfortunately it can and does happen that the stimulus acts with overwhelming force and urgency; it first disturbs and then attracts all the soul's attention. In such a case, the stimulus becomes infinitely powerful relative to the law, which begins to be heard less distinctly, and finally fades completely as attention is removed from it. Opposition on the part of the law is swept away as though non-existent, and the will, apparently incited and moved by a single stimulus, reacts spontaneously as other resistance ceases. Suspension of assent is eliminated at such moments; the will is a prey to determination.

The fact that I am describing can be seen easily enough in the first movements of what are commonly called 'irresistible passions'. During the brief moment in which they take place, their power over the will is sufficient to eliminate the time needed for reflection and suspension of judgment, while the unreflecting will, taken off guard by the sharpness of the stimulus, follows the passions with spontaneous movement as they attract the soul's energy and prevent further thought. On the one hand, all the soul's energy is built up in a single direction; on the other hand, if the soul's total energy is built up by degrees and devoted exhaustively in one direction, any contrary stimulus is soon annihilated and the will gives its irreparable assent.[293]

702. But we have to examine more carefully this defect of *weakness* in the will, as we have called it, and uncover its intimate nature. We said that in free actions *choice* precedes all that the will does, and we called this executive force of free choice the *practical force*. The heart and the *energy* proper to freedom are found in this practical force which ecclesiastical writers have always distinguished from simple choice. It may be helpful, therefore, if we use some of their statements as witness to the admirable harmony between the conclusions we have reached through meditation on human nature and the teaching found in the most respected traditions.

The 6th General Council, held at Constantinople, considers that

[293] We have to pay great attention to the development of this act of will, which sometimes passes through three different stages. There is first a necessary stage constituted by the natural *inclination* towards all the good or particular elements which the will can choose. At the second stage of *choice*, the will is moving towards free choice. Then in the third stage, the will is no longer *inclined* or in a state of *deliberation*, but actually *determined* in one way or another. From this point onwards, it is no longer free. The passage to the final stage always arises as 'all the stimuli or good things competing with the *conquering* stimulus gradually lessen their activity on the will' in such a way that the action of this prevailing stimulus becomes sufficiently strong and dominating to render other things of little or *no value* compared with it. If we now ask whether the *absolute prevalence* of the single stimulus and the corresponding diminution of other stimuli comes about *freely* or through *necessity*, we find that it sometimes take place in one way, sometimes in another. Very often freedom prevails, but it cannot be denied that there are cases (of dementia, for example) when an impulse of animal instinct proves so strong and unexpected that it necessarily pressurises the will, leaving its judgment and activity open to the most extraordinary errors and eccentricities.

the integrity of human freedom is to be found in this *energy*.[294] Isidore of Seville, in distinguishing between simple *choice* and the *energy* proper to freedom, says expressly that when the human race fell through original sin 'it lost the *energy* of its free will, but not its power of choice'.[295] Consequently, the *weakness* we must analyse pertains to the practical force, although there is a close connection between this practical force and choice itself.[296]

703. We also said that the practical force is first used in the simple volition, that is, in the act of choice, and then in the act of command, that is, in the power exercised by the volition over the inferior faculties. We need to consider *weakness* of the will, therefore, both in simple volition and in the command which the volition exercises over the other powers. This weakness plays a great part in the disobedience shown to the will by the other powers although we cannot deny that, independently of this defect, the dominion of the will is limited by the poor disposition of these powers in their recalcitrant subjection to the will, whose yoke they do not easily bear. Hence *difficulty* in doing good, which St. Augustine describes as a wound contracted by human nature through original sin, depends equally on the weakness of our volition and on the insubordination of the other powers as they go their own ways.

A. Weakness of the will relative to the act of choice

704. First, let us examine the source of the weakness of simple

[294] 'The integrity of human substance is constituted by the essential will through which the ENERGY of free will is impressed in us.' 3rd Council of Constantinople, 680 A.D., in the opening sermon before the Emperor Constantine.

[295] 'After our fall from the good present in nature through seduction by the serpent, we also lost the ENERGY OF FREE WILL, but not however CHOICE' (*De Doctr. et Fide*, 20). Rabanus Maurus, the celebrated archbishop of Magonza, quoted the words of Isidore two centuries later in his great work, 'On the Universe', where he says: 'After Adam fell through Eve by the seduction of the serpent, he lost what was good in nature together with his ENERGY OF FREE WILL, but not however CHOICE' (bk. 4, c. 10).

[296] Normally, we choose not to do an action when we feel that lack of *practical force* prevents us from carrying it out.

volition. We are speaking of our volition for good, and asking why it is so difficult for human beings to want good in real earnest. We shall prescind, however, from the principal cause of the difficulty, that is, the natural inclination of the will to evil, of which we have spoken, and from the fatal attraction of external things. We simply want to examine the causes internal to the will itself, and confine ourselves to the intrinsic difficulties which often impede the will from positing a strong, decisive act in favour of what is good.

This can be done only by analysing *volition* which always has some *judgment* as its foundation. A *judgment*, by which we declare that something is better and preferable to its contrary, certainly forms the first part of volition. This *judgment* is the knot joining *volition* and *choice*, and the immediate object of choice itself. We deliberate, and choose to make one judgment rather than another. Having *chosen* to judge in one way rather than another about the value of the alternatives before us, we then make the *judgment* with which *volition* is initiated. Judgment and volition are here related rather as a line proceeds from the point at which it begins.

705. This analysis is important. And it coincides, we are glad to see, with the thought and meditation of those who have gone before us, and whose authority we now wish to use once more to confirm what we have said. Grasping carefully how a *judgment* may be both the proximate *term* of choice and the *principle* of volition requires concentration. The knowledge, therefore, that this teaching was understood and firmly established prior to our own thought on the subject can only support what we have said, and reassure us that we are walking the path of truth.

First, calling freedom 'free decision' [*liberum arbitrium*] shows that common belief considers the act of freedom to be essentially a *judgment*. The Latin *arbitrium*, as we know, can rightly be translated by *judgment* in English. Hence, the explanation given six centuries ago of the phrase, *liberum arbitrium*: 'We use *liberum* to show that the will is free, and not necessitated; and *arbitrium* because the reason *judges* and discerns that which the will desires.'[297]

[297] Caesarius of Heisterbach, bk. 8, c. 44.

Seven centuries further back again, Cassiodorus described how the soul deliberates about its act of will: 'The soul takes its seat on high as though it were about *to give judgment*. It sees itself moderating its own appetites, *judges* between good and evil, decides about doubtful matters and rejects what it finds harmful.'[298]

This explains why 'free decision' is also called a *decision of the mind* or *freedom of the mind* by ancient authors.[299] As Gregory of Nyssa says: 'Free choice lies in the freedom of mind and thought'.[300] Theodore of Ancyra is right, therefore, when he says: 'Human beings are free simply because their *judgment* is free.'[301] Denis the Carthusian offers the same explanation of human freedom: 'Human beings act in virtue of their *judgment* because they know things conceptually; and they act freely because their judgment consists in weighing pros and cons, and so enables them to decide in favour of one thing rather than another'.[302] Thus, because the capacity by which we determine our judgment about things in one way rather than another renders our volition free, our free volition rests upon the foundation of a judgment. This was the constant teaching of the ancient sages, and the reason why an unknown ecclesiastical author was able to write at the end of the 2nd century: 'Our spirit is free to direct its judgment whichever way it wants, and to choose the road it judges best. It is clear, therefore, that human beings possess freedom of decision.'[303]

706. The entire force available to free will in its fight against the seduction of passion is found, therefore, in a *judgment* which serves as the foundation and principle of *volition*. Through this judgment the will affirms and decides that it is better to take the path of what is just and right than that of easy attraction. But it is not sufficient for the judgment to affirm this

[298] *De An.*, c. 15.

[299] Jerome, *Is.*, c. 55; Cl. Maures Victor, *In Praef. Genes.*

[300] *Orat. catech*, c. 30.

[301] 'You were made free, you do what you wish, you are not under any compelling necessity. The judgment made by your spirit is free. The sun is under necessity; human beings have been allotted freedom of judgment' (*Hom. in Natal. Salvatoris*).

[302] *Summa orthod. Fid.*, art. 115.

[303] *Recognit.*, bk. 3.

speculatively, as it were. Because the faculty of *persuasion* is that in which the noble, practical force of judgment principally resides, the human subject must persuade himself that this is so.

In the judgment itself, therefore, two elements have to be distinguished: the *ruling*, or conclusion of the judgment, and the more or less effective *persuasion* that brings about our conclusion. Our free decision is in great part the source from which both these things arise. The authorities we have examined confirm what we have said about the *ruling*; and St. Jerome teaches explicitly that *persuasion* depends upon us and upon our consent.[304] Other authorities could be adduced to prove the same thing.[305]

707. The definitive judgment by which we oblige ourselves to what is just and upright rather than to what is base and seductive acquires greater power over the will: 1. according to the perfection with which our *ruling* or sentence is pronounced; 2. according to the effort made by the soul to *persuade* itself more intimately, profoundly and effectively about the decision.

708. The *ruling* pronounced by the soul in favour of what is just and upright depends for its degree of perfection on the level at which it is pronounced, and on the way in which justice is given precedence over all transitory and subjective things. There can be no possibility of exaggerating here. Justice is infinitely noble and beautiful, and cannot be compared, even from a distance, with anything that may be found in the universe. Without justice other things are less than nothing. Hence the infinite dignity and authority of the law is, as we said, an inexhaustible spring whence the will can always draw further strength against instinctive allurements. The more the will considers justice, the more its love of justice grows.

709. At this point we could usefully and interestingly ask: 'Does the moral law manifest itself from the beginning with equal light to all souls?' My own opinion is that the degree of

[304] 'PERSUASION does not come from the one who has called us, but from ourselves whether we consent or not to the one who calls,' (*In Ep. ad Gal.*, c. 5). In the order of supernatural things such persuasion is always impossible without grace.

[305] The little book of precepts for the education of royalty, written by Emmanuel Paleologos, c. 28, has this to say: 'Human beings decide whether they are going TO BE PERSUADED.'

light with which the law is resplendent in souls varies from the beginning, even in the natural order — at least in the present state of humanity.

Note carefully, however, that while the light manifesting the law in its beauty and dignity varies from person to person, the authority of the law is revealed as equal for everyone and to everyone. This authority is equally absolute, unchangeable, impassible and eternal because these are all properties essential to the law of justice and uprightness. Without them, such a law would not exist. I conclude, therefore, that although all humans beings feel equally obliged by the law, they do not all possess the same facility and readiness in rendering the law a powerful stimulus to the will. Those, however, are more fully endowed whose gaze, formed more purely and sharply by nature, absorbs at first sight greater light from the divine ray of justice.

710. It is worth noting that human beings, although often incapable of overcoming base desires with their natural forces, always presume they can achieve more than their possibilities permit. Deep in the spirit of all individuals lies an unshakeable belief that they are equally free to do good or evil, even when the contrary is true. This belief is tempered only slightly, even in the lives of persons prepared to reflect, by continual experience of their own weakness.

Such excessive belief in one's own freedom is undoubtedly due to the authority of the law and the rational nature of human beings. The law, in fact, shows us the path we have to tread, and does so with inflexible, unchangeable moral necessity. But if we were to believe ourselves incapable of conforming to the law, our own self-image would suffer the greatest indignity; we would despair of obtaining any moral dignity. This we abhor naturally, more than any other evil, and rather than think so badly of ourselves we put our trust in our own freedom. We are after all faced with a simple choice between alternatives.

On the other hand, our rational nature also draws us to put faith in our own freedom. The debased pressures and allurements which assault our will in an endeavour to deprave it and lead it into evil do not properly speaking come from the rational order, but rise up from the lower part of ourselves. The law, however, is revealed, and the decisions of freedom are made in the region of the intelligence. As intelligent beings, we cannot but consider ourselves as free because we are free within the borders of this region where nothing impedes or contradicts the exercise of our freedom. Consequently authors make freedom depend on intelligence, and speak of it as an outcome of intelligence.[306] Consciousness of our own freedom, and of the powers of this freedom, is proper to human beings as intelligent, although such consciousness is still speculative. But when we decide to act, we do so with all that we are, not with some part of ourselves. We do not act simply as intelligent beings, but as we are, animal and intelligent. And in our real, effective activity we discover obstacles arising from our animality which did not exist as long as we confined ourselves to speculation, nor in the concept of ourselves as intellective beings.

711. We have to distinguish, therefore, between *freedom* and the *exercise of freedom*. Human beings are always free even when the exercise of their freedom is sometimes curtailed. This explains why the Catholic Church decided on the one hand that *free will* had not perished[307] in human beings with original sin and on the other that we could do nothing relative to *perfect good*, that is, to good as sufficient for eternal life,

[306] St. Gregory of Nyssa expresses this concept as follows: 'Only inanimate beings and those without reason are led by the will of others towards visible things. If a nature which shares in reason and intelligence were to abdicate its free will, it would by that very fact lose its intelligence. What point would there be in using our mind and thought if our power to choose what we have decided through some judgment were vested in others?' (*Orat. catech.*, c. 30). Nemesius shares this opinion: 'If we were not the authors of our own activity, our faculty of thought and deliberation would be of no use to us' (*De nat. hominis*, c. 39). Hence Boethius' general remark: 'No rational creature exists without free will' (*De Consol. Philo.*, bk. 1, prose 2.). More recently a Greek author has repeated an opinion frequently recorded in the Greek Fathers: 'The more rational part of the soul has been given to us by God so that we could come to some decision. In our decisions reason and free will shine forth' (Nicetas of Chone, a 13th century author, in *Tesoro della Fede ortod.*, bk. 4, heres. 42.

[307] 'If anyone says that human free will is lost and extinct after Adam's sin, or that free will itself is only a name, and indeed a word without any corresponding reality, [or says] that it is mere imagination and hence forced upon the Church by Satan: let him be anathema' (Council of Trent, sess. 6, *De Justificat.*, canon 5).

without grace.[308] Thus, two conclusions, at first sight apparently opposed to one another, are reconciled, and we possess a key to the interpretation of many passages in St. Augustine and other writers which appear to be in contrast, but in fact are not.

712. Freedom, therefore, considered in its essence and its source, that is, in the intelligence, is never lacking to the human being. Intelligence, however, is only a *remote* power for doing good; as a *proximate* power it moves towards its act, the exercise of freedom, when it is not bound and impeded by accidental obstacles. And, as we said, we activate our *remote power* for doing good (the freedom proper to rational beings) and make it a *proximate power* (the freedom of the animal-rational being) by drawing strength primarily from the law we contemplate, whose intrinsic, absolute goodness and dignity we perceive. As we said, however, the time needed to make this move is sometimes eliminated by the overwhelming haste of our passions.

713. Moreover, our natural forces do not give us much assistance in advancing this work because the law, as an abstraction, cannot stimulate the activity needed to move our actions in the

[308] '. . . neither can human beings without the grace of God move of themselves and of their own will towards justice before God' (Council of Trent, sess. 6, *De Justif.*, c. 5). Hence St. Augustine's explanation of how we must understand that human free will has not been lost along with the sin of Adam: 'We do not say that free will has been lost to human nature by Adam's sin, but that it avails for sin in those subject to the devil. The human will is of no avail for good, holy living unless it has been liberated by the grace of God, and assisted towards all good in deed, word and thought' (*Contra duas epis. Pelag.*, bk. 2, c. 5). This passage shows that free will was not eliminated through sin, although its exercise was in part blocked in such a way that the grace of our Saviour was necessary to draw such exercise in the direction of freedom. St. Augustine himself says that our decisions are held captive through original sin until it is freed through grace: 'If we truly wish to defend free will, let us not attack the source of its freedom. If we really oppose grace, by which our free will is liberated to avoid evil and do good, we want our free will to be held captive.' (*Ep. 107 ad Vital.*). A 10th century commentator on Scripture had no hesitation in writing: 'Nor do we destroy human freedom by saying this. We are free if we are assisted from on high. For there is no freedom if we are without grace' (Rudolf Flaviac., *in Levit.*, bk. 12, c. 1). In these and many other places, where it is constantly repeated that after sin the human will can do nothing good without grace, we have to understand this as referring to supernatural good, that is, complete good, which alone can ensure our eternal well-being.

world of reality. Even within the sphere of natural virtue, therefore, our moral force is limited and incapable of resisting every temptation.

But we do draw strength for our practical judgment in favour of the law and against the seduction of the senses from sources other than the law as pure idea. This occurs in the first place relative to the objects themselves indicated by the law. These objects are real, and perceived by us in a real way. For example, love of our fellow human beings, which is commanded by the law, is assisted by the perception of our fellows. Such a real perception inclines us towards them, and helps to form within us kindness, friendship, loving reverence for our relatives, compassion for suffering and every kind of fellow-feeling. These things do not destroy the law, but rather promulgate it within us, give it body and life, activate it and add to it the efficacy proper to real things.[309]

714. This explains why we find great difficulty in carrying out duties relative to objects we have not yet perceived. Sometimes we see human virtues flourishing in human societies deprived of a true religion, and simultaneously a total lack of virtue in matters relating to God. This occurs because, naturally speaking, we can have only a completely negative idea of God who, as the supreme reality, cannot be really perceived. This thought was expressed by St. John where he said: 'If anyone says, "I love God", and hates his brother, he is a liar; for he who does not love his brother whom he has seen, cannot love God whom he has not seen.'[310] These words show that the vision and perception of objects is of considerable assistance in helping us exercise our duties towards them. Hence, according to Catholic teaching, we need grace principally for the sake of fulfilling our duties towards God. These duties are the root of all the good activities which save human beings because in the supernatural order all virtues are finally reduced to the love of God.

715. Finally, the practical judgment enabling us to prefer the path of justice to that of iniquity is reinforced by many accessory ideas and by reflection on all the consequences of

[309] See *La Storia comparativa e critica de' Sistemi Morali*, c. 5, art. 5, where I have treated this question at length.

[310] 1 Jn 4: [20].

virtue and vice. Interior peace, remorse, reward and punishment, the temporal advantages that are normally the natural accompaniment of an ordered life, the disadvantages of a disordered life, praise and blame, good example, habits formed during the process of a good education and other similar features unite to constitute a profound judgment in favour of what is good. They also add vigour to our deep-rooted resolutions to prefer an upright life to any kind of deceitful illusion.

It is true, of course, that these final reinforcements of our judgment and determination towards good are not all as pure and sublime as those we mentioned previously. But they do serve as accessory motives and as tiny helps providing extraordinary support for us, who by nature tend to gravitate towards vice.

716. It is clear that human beings who choose what is good find these final helps in society. And provided the society in which they live is not totally corrupt, the quantity of help they find will result from the extension, good order, development and civilised state of the society. This explains why savage or still undeveloped peoples, although possessing greater *independence*, or rather precisely because they are more independent, have less feeling for their own liberty than civilised peoples amongst whom the consciousness of free will is immensely increased and continually develops. This growth of free will in civilised societies is the effect of greater human activity within them. Virtue and vice also find more means and weapons, as it were, with which to sustain themselves.[311]

[311] This persuasion of one's own power and freedom, which increases in human beings as societies grow more civilised, is an undoubted influence in greatly modifying the materialistic views of *feticism* and *polytheism* which can prevail in such societies. Again, when a purer religion is brought to a people professing such idolatry, consciousness of its own freedom and power must suddenly increase together with civilisation. But history, it must be noted, does not present any definite case of a people practising fetistic religion and of itself advancing culturally to a stage where it could exchange this religion for a better cult. Nor is there any example in history in which superstitious, fetistic religion has shown any internal progress towards purer ideas about the deity. Movement in peoples of this kind always proceeds from without, that is to say, either *civilisation* is imported into these peoples who, as a result, modify their religious ideas for the better or a *purer religion* has been imported which generates progress in civilisation. The following quotation

717. We must now recall the distinction we made, in speaking of the practical judgment favourable to the law, between the *ruling* and the profound *persuasion* rendering the ruling efficacious in us.

First, the ruling, which has a speculative and a practical side. Relative to the speculative side, we judge the law to be infinitely authoritative as soon as we perceive it because this infinite authority is of the essence of the moral law which, without its infinite authority, cannot even be thought. In this respect, judgment about the law is necessary and equal in all human beings as soon as they conceive the law. But this *theoretical* ruling, which can be obscure, languid and very inefficacious in our minds, is only the foundation of the *practical* ruling. The practical element now to be added comes from the will and begins properly speaking in the act of determination which can be more or less strong and decisive. But the decisiveness and strength of the act determining the volition is confined within certain factual limits beyond which the force of the will cannot be extended. The will itself is a very limited power, and bears from the first moment of its existence limitations which, without doubt, are greatly increased as a result of the wound inflicted upon human nature by the first sin.

718. We find, therefore, a degree of force, applicable both to *rulings* and *persuasion*, posited by the will in its act of self-determination. Then come the other motives which we have indicated. These consist in experience and in the association of ideas,

from a modern author will help to reaffirm the matter for my readers, despite the onesidedness and consequent imperfection of the author's viewpoint: 'Only when religion has been considerably purified and has rejected the fetistic and polytheistic heritage of residual anthropomorphisms about God are we able to view the disappearance of all difficulties about destiny, fate and free will. At this moment, the notions of necessity and change — two hypotheses constantly at loggerheads in imperfect religions — are succeeded by a notion which unites all their advantages, and rejects only what it finds gross in them. Then, in order to applaud self-conquest more vigorously, human beings are thought of as endowed with freedom. We know that chance works at a higher level than we do when it deceives our wishes rather than accept them. Consequently, we do not unite ourselves to some unknown cause in order to satisfy our passing caprices, but to reach higher moral perfection by rising above all that is ephemeral and personal. Only then is courage at full force, and resignation fully acceptable' (B. Constant, *De la Religion etc.*, 7, 7).

all of which stimulate us to judge that the justice-alternative is far better for us than a choice of injustice. In this way, we come to pronounce a practical judgment, composed of moral and eudaimonological elements, more favourable to good than to evil.

It is clear, therefore, that pronouncing a more effective judgment in favour of virtue is the work of the faculty of judgment and of the association of ideas and feelings. The help which these faculties are able to provide the will so that it may reach out for good and not bow before evil depends upon the state in which the faculties are found.

719. Both the judgment and the *association*, however, then depend upon the *unitive force* of the soul; in the last analysis, judgments and associations of every kind form a bond brought about between different elements by the unity of the soul. Here, too, the weakness of the will varies, this time according to the degree of defect found in the *unitive force*. To the extent of this debility the will finds itself without the means with which to enforce its choice. Such limitation is a very noticeable source of weakness in the will.

720. Degrees of moral weakness in human beings can now be clarified, therefore, if we turn our attention to defects which underlie the human *unitive force*.

Extreme defects of this kind affect the unitive force to such an extent that they produce total idiocy. Idiocy is total when human beings are so lacking in unitive force that they do not succeed in forming easily and perfectly even *intellective perceptions* of external things, that is, those operations through which the soul *unites* with ideal being the action it has received by means of sensations, and judges from its experience that a subsistent being, different from itself, exists. These extreme cases of idiocy can be seen in hospitals for the mentally afflicted amongst patients who are almost unaware of the presence of external objects despite the sensations produced by these objects. Thought has been almost entirely obliterated in these persons.[312]

721. Working upwards from this extreme defect in unitive force or from impediments to its use, we can notice continual variations which offer a solid explanation of the degrees of

[312] See the description of such cases in Dr. Pinel's work, sect. 3, 3.

weakness in moral character from individual to individual. They also serve to explain the variety in the power of will relative to the practice of virtue in individuals. Several people may have an equal desire for virtue without, however, showing equal executive responsiveness to the common decision reached by their wills.

722. We note here that the *persuasion* accompanying a *ruling* pronounced by the will in favour of the law draws its weight in the soul not from the *multitude* of elements bound and fused together in the decision, but from the *compactness* with which, bound and unified, they form a single, simple force that serves as a single brilliant light influencing the soul.

723. We have to confess, however, that this matter is still very mysterious. Variation in the *degree of persuasion* presents phenomena still unexplained despite all the reasons we have offered for it.

In certain persons the development of a very high degree of persuasion is most clear without its being able to depend either upon the *number* of elements composing the ruling in favour of virtue, or upon their *quality*, and most definitely not upon the *perfection of their mixture* and fusion. It is undeniable that all these things normally influence persuasion greatly by the efficacy they add to it. But persuasion, when it is strong and efficacious, seems to draw most of its strength from altogether different, hidden sources.

There is no doubt that the resolution present in the first, instantaneous act with which we use our freedom to *determine* our will, that is, in our choice, is usually numbered amongst these secret sources of strong persuasion. In addition, there seems to be in some ideas a hidden effectiveness which may be impossible to subject to determined laws. This effective force takes possession of and entirely dominates the soul, although its action remains inexplicable. Sometimes it disturbs the soul intensely and profoundly, like Neptune with his trident in the immense ocean, as the story tells us. If this dominant idea expresses what is just and upright, it has an incredible power to draw us to heights from which we can look down and behold the universe which seems nothing in comparison.

Divine grace, of course, provides an immediate explanation of this fact, but here we are pointing to a wonderful moral phenomenon that is not confined solely to the sphere of religious and divine matters. A high, noble, generous idea, dominating the soul, has always been the guide, the divine light and the genetrix of heroes. What resonance, and hidden analogy with the soul, does this idea possess for one person when for everyone else it is only ordinary and inoperative?

But we also need to reflect carefully that in the case of the noble persuasion which forms heroes, the opposite to what we have described frequently takes place. As we said, a thought, the ruling of a practical judgment, justice when assented to, takes a more vigorous hold of the human spirit as its eternal beauty and worth is pondered at length. But in the case of heroes, the contrary occurs. The ennobling, decisive idea strikes like lightning and immediately, without the slightest delay, prostrates them. The dawning light of that idea is not a surface brilliance, but flashes in the very depth of their spirit. Perhaps the strange power of that idea, which then serves as the beginning of all the hero's magnanimous actions, is due in great part to the speed of its operation. In fact, under careful examination all sublime feeling can be seen to arise as a result of the spirit's sudden passage from one state to another very different state. Once again, an exquisite unitive force, reaching out instantly to very distant and diverse things, would seem to be present.

724. We also said that the ruling passed by a practical judgment produces greater interior energy in so far as the spirit is nourished by multiple ideas, considerations and feelings; the more cultured and developed a person is, the greater the assistance available for intensifying the persuasion his practical judgment has over him. Once more, the opposite can be seen in the case of the hero's noble persuasion. Simplicity seems the distinctive character of heroism; a single idea dominates the spirit which is neither distracted nor divided by any other idea. Unlettered persons, peasants, ordinary workers become instant prodigies, extraordinary persons.

Take for instance, someone like Cathelineau or Hoffer. It is impossible not to weep with tender wonder at the simple sublimity of such characters. Certainly, I am in no position to judge the moral worth of the actions of these great people, in whose unclouded spirit a single spark was sufficient to start a blaze enveloping the most extraordinary undertakings. But surely we can all see that the nobility of character enabling them to take their place amongst the wonders of this world is strictly related to the simplicity of their preceding life as peasants or artisans? And it is equally obvious that heroes of this stamp are almost impossible to find at other levels: how often, for example, do we ever see persons in cultivated, refined, high society who never act for a secondary end, whose attention is always fixed on their aim without thought of anything else, without self-deception, without the distraction of temptation, and who are prepared to sacrifice themselves totally to the generous feeling that rules them? There is only one exception to this, and we find it as we ascend to a higher sphere: Catholicism alone, heavenly grace alone, propagates these heroes everywhere. Simple women and tender children have despised death which they desired far more ardently than any of the amusements of their age, as we all know. And we know, too, that the Gospel has produced saints in all conditions, and even at the highest levels of society.

B. Weakness in the command

725. So far we have considered the will's weakness relative to what is good principally from the point of view of *choice*, that is, from the point of view of simple volition. We shall now speak of it in relationship with the *command* given to the other powers.

This second kind of weakness also springs from some defect in the *unitive force* of the subject. The will's incapacity to make itself obeyed easily by the subject's powers and bodily organs points to an evident flaw in its connection with the various powers. There is some shortcoming in the relationship between the commanding principle and the subject faculties.

I have already indicated the order existing in human faculties, and shown how together they form a chain by nature. The last link of this chain connects with freedom which communicates its command from link to link down through the whole chain (cf. 644–649). I have also proved elsewhere that free human activity, moving as it were from a centre, communicates with four other spheres. The first sphere to be moved is that which includes esteem for the objects nearest to the centre. The second, moved by the first, is that of the spiritual affections which in its turn communicates movement to the sphere of bodily passions; from this sphere movement is directed to the final external sphere of bodily movements.[313]

This union between the commanding will and the powers it commands involves the communication of movement from the judgment by which we esteem things to the affections and external movements. We called this union a *dynamic link*.[314] It is clear that any shortcoming in this link diminishes the subject's perfect unity. This in its turn implies some weakness in our dominion over ourselves and our activities. Powers not ruled and corrected by this single force, which is their natural master, acquire their own independent movements and act individually as though they no longer formed part of human unity. In varying degrees this unnatural dispersion of human powers is an obvious fact in all human beings.

726. Catholic teaching, which never disregards any of the noble, profound facts presented by mankind to impartial observation, recognises the fact under discussion here, and explains it through the story of human nature's degradation by the first fault. St. Augustine has no hesitation in teaching that animal instinct, through its connection with the will, would have been continually supervised and directed by the superior power in all its movements if human nature had not suffered defilement. But human nature lost that degree of power with which it would have exercised such complete mastery over the body.[315] He illustrates his point with a delicate observation on the power still exerted by

313 *PE*, 114–181. *Storia comparativa dei Sistemi Morali*, chs. 1; 5, art. 6; 7, art 6, §3; 8, art. 3, §5.

314 The dynamic link under consideration here was well known to ancient writers whom I have quoted elsewhere. Tertullian describes it briefly and with absolute truth when he speaks of free will, and says: 'Nature follows the directions of free will' (*De Anima*, c. 21). A holy ecclesiastical author of the 5th century says with great precision that God commanded human beings first *to know*, and then, having known, *to love* and *to will*. I have with me only a translation of this Greek Father which reads: 'By nature, human beings possess that readiness of spirit which God seeks of us. He orders us, therefore, first *TO KNOW*, then, after knowing, *TO LOVE*, and *SEND FORTH* our will' (Marcus the Hermit, *De Paradiso, et lege spirituali*). Nothing could be clearer than these last words.

315 *De Civ. Dei*, 14, 21.

the soul over the body. He notes that it moves parts of the body that we think are outside the will's activity, such as the lungs, or the vocal and epidermic organs. Some people, he continues, can move both ears simultaneously, or one at a time; others can move their hair without moving their head (I think they do it by moving the skin covering the skull up and down the forehead);[316] others have such command over the stomach that they can control at will the food within and the peristaltic movement of the intestines. The sweat and tear ducts are mastered in such a way that sweat can be released at will. Finally, the whole nervous system, including the cerebral organ, can be dominated so that people can withdraw themselves from external sensations. It should not seem incredible, therefore, that in unharmed human nature the power of the will would be able to govern those members which are now withdrawn from its control.[317]

§4. The third limit, posited by the judgment

727. As human beings we make theoretical and practical judgments before acting. Only the practical judgments, however, give rise to action.

This judgment is distinguished by its deliberative, operative force from the theoretical judgment, but not separated from it. On the contrary, the theoretical judgment is related to the practical as the design of a house is related to the house.

We shall therefore consider the faculty of judgment taken in all its extension, and examine the relationship that the theoretical and practical judgments have with human freedom. In particular, we shall see if human beings can be brought necessarily to judge falsely.

728. It is clear that if this were so, the false judgment, which must have some influence on our actions, would add a new limit to freedom. It is true, of course, that human beings, if they could be led without fail to a false judgment, would be seduced by the

[316] I too had a servant who could move in an extraordinary way either all or part of the skin covering the skull. The border of his hair came down extremely low over his forehead.

[317] *De Civ. Dei*, 14, 24.

forceful attractions of instinct, of which we have already spoken. In this case, the limitation put to human freedom by the judgment would also originate in the instincts. Nevertheless, this cannot be called a straightforward limitation. The instincts work in two ways: either by determining us to act independently of the judgment, or by means of a judgment which they have falsified. We have already discussed the first kind of determining act; here we have to examine the second.

A general consideration, starting from the principle that the judgment depends in great part on the will[318] allows us to conclude without difficulty that if the will can be seduced and overcome by instinct, any judgment springing from a will already seduced and deluded must in all probability itself be false. This conjecture is not sufficient, however, to solve the problem. We have to question nature, and see if it allows us to answer the difficulty on the basis of fact.

I
Can human beings be induced necessarily to form a false theoretical judgment?

729. Observations on deranged people seem to show that a state exists in which animality can act with such pressure on the spontaneity of the will that human beings can be drawn to false reasoning and judgments. Moments of derangement all seem to be simply false judgments produced by a will that has been irresistibly moved by sensations and images, in a word, by the sensuous instinct.

Dr. Pinel, in his *Trattato sull'alienazione mentale* thus describes a deranged patient inflicted with insanity for seven years:

> He knows his state perfectly, and sums it up wisely, as though it were someone else's affliction. He would be glad to make efforts to free himself of it, but at the same time is convinced that it is incurable. We point out the difference between what he thinks and what he says, and in good faith he agrees. But he also says that this inclination dominates him with such force that he cannot avoid it. And he adds that although he is not convinced of the truth of the judgments he forms, he has no power to correct them.[319]

[318] *Certainty*, 1246–1363.

[319] Sect. 2, 5.

Pinel describes another deranged person in the following terms:

> I was in charge of his treatment. He lived in a house within sight of the dome of Val-de-Grace, but claimed that this building had to be transferred to the gardens of the Tuileries. Two men would be sufficient for the work, he said. He imagined that there was some relationship between the strength of these two men and the resistance offered by the enormous mass. It wasn't easy to convince him of the immense disproportion with practical examples, although we took an approximate weight for each of the stones of this vast building. He continued to think that the work was definitely possible, and proposed carrying it out himself.[320]

730. Must we believe that this person's imagination altered the measure of the two terms of the judgment (the strength of the two men and the weight of the blocks of stone forming the dome) so much that by increasing one and decreasing the other the patient was forced to see equality in the face of such evident disequality? In this case, the soul's *unitive force*, with which he should have formed his judgment, would have been prevented from carrying out its operation directly. Or should we suppose that the will, carried away by impetuosity, wanted to be persuaded of such equality by forming a totally arbitrary judgment even before a comparison had been made between the two forces. Whichever way we view the matter, no one could affirm that this deranged person was free when he made the judgment. On the contrary, he must have been involved in the judgment necessarily, although voluntarily because, as we said, judgment is also an act of will.

But perhaps he judged hastily? If he had examined the case better, perhaps he would have noticed his mistake? This presupposes that he could have suspended his conclusion. But it is precisely at this point that the person finds himself necessitated. He is in such a state that he cannot suspend the affirmation of his judgment. On the one hand, no one suspends his judgment when he is persuaded that he sees things clearly;[321] on the other,

320 *Ibid.*

321 There is no doubt that young people have to be accustomed from a very early age to extreme diffidence about themselves when their judgments contradict those of others. Prudence and habitual modesty of this kind, combined

there is an irresistible necessity impelling him to determine between suspension and decision, and decide in favour of the latter.

731. Pinel, whom we have quoted, is convinced of this. After long experience in looking after the insane at Bicêtre and Salpêtrière, he writes: 'False, illusory perceptions sometimes dominate the intellect of the deranged with such mastery that they are drawn by an irresistible force to judge in accordance with their internal feeling. What they feel could be the effect of a violent change taking place in their physical state.'

732. Once again, experience can prove this. Sometimes the faculty of judgment is assisted and rendered capable of normal activity by the application of a purely physical remedy.

733. Often enough our faculty of judgment is reorientated simply by the presentation of data and materials suitable for making judgments. In arousing feeling, these materials need to be sufficiently strong to draw and fix the attention in such a way that the will, when it judges, cannot ignore them, nor the imagination by-pass them. Simply by forcing the afflicted person to divert his attention and take account of these materials in his calculations, without his usual unheeding disregard for them, we find the judgment correcting itself and the mind regaining its sanity. This proves that mistakes in these lightning judgments and immediate beliefs arise when conclusions are reached without previous true comparison between the terms of the judgments. An immediate, instantaneous, forceful persuasion about matters has been generated. In other words, we are dealing with *prejudice* or pre-judgment rather than *judgment*.

734. Dr. Pinel, whom we have already quoted frequently, speaks about the healthy effects of strong, opportune restraint as an aid to the restoration of judgment:

> Sometimes energetic restraint can be used to block

with respect for common sense, can become a useful instrument for tempering the impetus of passion if it is sown sufficiently early in young souls. It is a kind of ballast helping the little boat to hold the right course on its perilous navigation through life: it would help us to avoid many errors and misdirections dependent upon over-confident judgments, and save humanity from innumerable disasters. Nevertheless, we look in vain to modern education for persons who will take care to infuse this wisdom, this habitual logic, in young souls.

outlandish judgments. For instance, a young woman becomes insane through devotional excesses. She is now very odd, and beside herself with rage. She orders people about in the most imperious tones, and calls down fire from heaven upon anyone who offers the slightest resistance to her desires. Her ferocity, threats and curses have no limit. Everything is a source of irritation and frenzy. At this point she is taken to the cell and put into a strait-jacket. Several hours later, the director of the hospital goes to visit her, and jokes with her about drawing down fire from heaven when she isn't capable even of freeing herself from the strait-jacket, which prevents any movement she may want to make. In the evening she is calmer, and from then on her return to health is unimpeded.

It is clear that this young woman took no account of her own weakness when she formed her judgments. But what she had neglected in her judgment, for the sake of the elements presented and enlarged by her imagination, was brought to the attention of her feeling through direct experience. In this way, her faculty of judgment was prompted to act more directly. At the same time, her frenzy was reined in as her judgments proved useless for attaining the satisfaction and exercise of power that she desired.

On the one hand, sensations, images, instincts and impetuous desires pressurise the faculty of judgment and impel it towards mistaken conclusions; on the other hand, more regular and more vivid sensations and images, when opposed to what has already occurred, can cure the judgment and restore the freedom needed for judging sensibly. This is because the later sensations and images have more power to draw and retain the attention, and because the hope of satisfaction from urgent desires is eliminated.

735. Hence the common observation of the best doctors who maintain that nothing is more helpful in the care of the insane than reason accompanied by irresistible force. This restraint should offer no hope of conquest or victory to the patients, but constrain them to brake the thrust both of their actions and of their ideas which they can then fix on the reasonable things suggested to them. Little by little their understanding perceives the previously neglected justice and truth of things, and habits are formed in harmony with it.[322]

322 'One of the advantages of well ordered hospitals is the opportunity they

736. Experience of this kind in treating the insane merits examination from a wider point of view. It does in fact offer a general means suitable for assisting the judgment in its operations — it is not only the insane whose judgment is faulty. Without being looked upon as insane, many are led astray in their judgments by the violence of passion, the agility of their imagination and the intensity of their feeling. And we have to admit that even crimes punished by law are not always purely and simply the result of malice. Very often they depend in great part on erroneous judgments, false opinions and the bizarre confusion of a bewildered mind. Criminal justice will reach perfection only when it takes this into consideration in afflicting punishment, and ceases to think of convicted people solely from the point of view of their misdemeanours. Those found guilty must also be seen as people tragically deceived and misled. In this way punishment will finally be thought of not only as a mere *vindication of justice*, nor simply as a way of *repressing outbreaks of crime*, but also as a *cure* for the intellectual disorder which often preys upon the condemned. It is from this human, charitable, religious point of view, which also forms part of justice in the strictest sense that the *penal system* merits careful consideration by wise governments.

737. Another important consequence of the principle under discussion relates to the education of children. Infancy is the period in which feeling is at its liveliest, imagination is without restraint, instinct is immediate, reason is without influence, and power over oneself at its weakest. The judgments we make as children need to be directed and assisted in every way possible; the impetus of physical instincts has to be opposed by physical

provide of impressing vividly upon the deranged who are adequately receptive the conviction that they are faced with overwhelming force capable of mastering their will and caprices. This idea must be put before them constantly. It arouses their intellect, brakes their insane outbursts and gradually makes them used to restraining themselves — one of the first steps towards health. Sometimes, if they are allowed home too soon, awareness of their new independence and of the freedom they have to follow their own impulses makes them act without restraint. The result is irregularities in their way of life, and the stimulation of untoward affections destined to revive their previous disability.' Pinel, *Tratt. medico-filosofico sull'alienazione mentale*, sect. 6, 1.

restraint. Thinking we can eliminate all corporal punishment in education is therefore a modern mistake. There has been abuse unfortunately, but we have gone to the opposite extreme in trying to avoid it.

We need to distinguish *anger* from *chastisement*. Abuse is found when children are chastised in anger, a brute, irrational passion that ought never to be observed on the face or in the acts of parents and teachers. What should be seen is obvious reasonableness, enlightened justice, together with benevolence and meekness, although benevolence and meekness themselves may have to appear sad and sorrowful (but never indifferent, frivolous or careless). Chastisement without anger is never excessive nor disproportionate, but the most useful and effective punishment for children. Inflicted without anger, chastisement is free from bitterness and irritation, although it is and must be painful. If we want to improve our coming generations, we need to return to belief in the Bible, which says: 'He who spares the rod hates his son, but he who loves him is diligent to discipline him.'[323]

Let us now examine the other question.

II
Can human beings be led necessarily to form a false practical-moral judgment?

738. As we said, our judgment can be irresistibly seduced. This does not mean that with truth before our minds we can be brought necessarily to disown it, but that we can fall into error either when truth is removed from our vision or our vision itself is confused. We should recall what I have said elsewhere about the intimate nature of error. I have shown that in the last analysis error is always ignorance;[324] that every error is preceded by confusion of ideas and mental activity;[325] and finally that anyone who errs does not judge (in the proper sense of the word), but acts on prejudice, that is, reaches a conclusion without

323 Prov 13: [24]

324 *Certainty*, 1361–1362.

325 *Ibid.*, 1325–1327.

having first compared the two terms of the judgment and seen their relationship.[326]

But on occasion error can arise relative to moral truth and to the practical judgment on which our actions are based. Not only the eyes of the body, but the eyes of the spirit also, can be clouded and blinded. The following considerations will help to see how this comes about.

739. All *passive* human faculties have their root in the inmost feeling or universal sense of our soul. In the same way, all our *active* faculties arise from the same root, where they are fused in that first, original faculty of inmost feeling which is called 'subject' rather than feeling because it is indeed the human being itself.

740. This substantial feeling or *myself* takes on different levels of vitality. In other words, the subject feels more or less intensely. *Myself* receives an increase of life and a higher grade of existence as it takes on greater intensity and is felt more strongly. Such a strengthened feeling of the subject's own existence and of the increase in its being also entails a higher degree of happiness. Ultimately, complete happiness is only the vital existence of *myself* taken to its final limit — all that is good in feeling brought to the ultimate term of every appetite.

741. The *myself* feeling, however, is twofold: intellective feeling and body-sense feeling. *Myself* finds its being augmented whenever one or other of these two feelings increases in force. If the body-sense feeling takes on immensely greater force while the intellective feeling remains sluggish and marginal, *myself* must necessarily lose sight of and become almost unaware of its being as an intellective feeling. This intellective mode of existence no longer holds the interest of the subject because experience of an increasing degree of life and existence is no longer given along with it. Consequently, the subject no longer has any hope or desire to increase and expand in this direction. Intellective feeling becomes a kind of dull, moribund, withdrawn existence in the depths of the soul. It cannot be destroyed, of course, but it can lie dormant and unheeding, and as such the source of a propensity to materialism, the profession of persons in whom animal existence has become intensely active, and intellective knowledge only a faint memory.

[326] *Ibid.*, 1328–1334.

742. We must also note that in every being *modes of action* correspond to *modes of being*. *Myself*, for example, is a feeling: its mode of being consists in feeling; it exists where it feels and as it feels. The *myself* which feels animality with great intensity, exists and therefore acts more as an animal than an intellective feeling; the *myself* which lives a powerful intellective and moral life acts more like an intellective and moral being. *Myself's* activity is never more than a protraction of the elementary action begun in the feeling and affections.

We should not be surprised, therefore, if truth and even moral truth becomes obscure to the eyes of the soul. Although truth is ever-present, the soul, enthralled by another kind of desire, no longer looks at truth. It allows its judgments and movements to be governed by another desire. The light of truth striking the soul obliquely, as it were, produces within it only a tenuous, ineffective impression rather like that of a coloured body acting upon a distracted gaze.

743. It is important to note, however, that while we affirm the possibility of our sometimes being led astray necessarily in our judgments, we are dealing with extraordinary, accidental cases which initially are always blameworthy. Normally, we come to such a miserable state, in which the spontaneity of the human will has been made captive, only as a result of preceding malice, and because we have not made use of means within our power to preserve the freedom of our will and judgment, or to liberate them when they have been enslaved.

744. The great teachers of the Catholic Church are right, therefore, in holding that usually we can either deceive ourselves or grasp the truth. St. Ambrose says: 'It is our free affection that draws us to error; the will which follows reason draws us away from error.'[327] Philastrius, bishop of Brescia in the 4th century, has this comment on the words of Genesis, 'You shall master your desire': with these words God commands Cain to master 'his evil thoughts which fall under his decision. Each person, through his decision and his will, can free his heart from the evil thought put there by the demon.'[328] In the same way Cyril of

[327] *De Jacob, et vita beata*, bk. 1, c. 1.

[328] 'Scripture does not say that he will rule his brother . . . but you shall rule your evil thought, which is indeed subject to your decision. Each person by

Alexandria attributes human salvation or damnation to the mastery that we exercise over our thoughts. As he says, the Creator 'gave free power to rational creatures. To each he assigned the government of his own will so that every human being might choose what had previously been *judged* as good. Those who have chosen the better part will have glory and reward in conformity with the *choice* they have made; others who have dragged themselves down with their evil *thoughts* and been brought low by their own desires will rightly be tormented in eternal punishment as wicked ingrates.'[329]

§5. The fourth limit, determined by opinions

745. Human freedom finds another bond in previously formed *opinions*, that is to say, erroneous opinions. An opinion is an affirmation 1. received by us as true; 2. no longer subject to examination; and 3. posited amongst things judged as incontestable.

746. Opinions remote from practical determination effect human actions less than other, more proximate opinions. But all opinions exercise some degree of influence from near or far upon our way of acting, and all contribute to the make-up of our moral character by moulding our inclinations and directing our steps along the path of life. Especially harmful are mistaken opinions about moral matters.

747. There is no doubt that we have to render an account to God even of our opinions. St. Justin says: 'God, when he created us, gave us understanding, and through the power of free decision enabled us to follow what was true and do good. Not a single one of us, therefore, can excuse himself before God. We were created by God as *rational* beings, apt for contemplation.'[330]

748. But I do not want to consider here the degree of human freedom present in forming mistaken opinions. Opinions are formed by judgments, and what has been said about freedom of judgment will be sufficient to cover that problem. Abstracting

his decision and will either rejects the evil thought put in his heart by the devil, or by not rejecting it falls into endless wrong' (*Haeres*, 80).

[329] *In Joann.*, bk. 9, c. 10.

[330] *Orat. ad Ant. Pium.*

therefore from possible freedom and imputability in the formation of erroneous judgments, I affirm that on occasion invincibly erroneous judgments are present in human beings, and that in general certain formed opinions determine human activity and limit our freedom as long as they remain in our mind.

749. Only God can judge such complicated, hidden and multiple activity in human nature. So many things have to be considered: the force of our illusions, the degree of attraction that education exerts in our spirit, the authority of our elders, the opinions that we have heard proclaimed with certainty from our earliest days, universal beliefs breathed in like air, as it were. And all these opinions are strengthened inevitably by the natural passions, feelings and instincts associated with them. There is no doubt that *opinions*, *passions* and *feelings* modify one another reciprocally, directing one another to various destinations. Set in motion, harmonised and jumbled together they form almost a single force to which the spirit is subject and from which it receives impulses, a certain character, and what we may call 'moral configuration'.

I am speaking not simply of physical passions and feelings, but of the most elevated feelings possible to mankind: magnanimity and greatness of spirit, patriotism, glory, love, piety, all that is splendid within the human spirit and approximates to virtue. Our *opinions* modify and develop, or retard and envelop, all these feelings, just as feelings, when very forceful, either modify, purify and ennoble our opinions or degrade and barbarise them.

Take for instance Byron's *Corsair*, a perfect example of someone with sublime gifts for good and evil, and placed in extraordinary circumstances. No merely human tribunal could ever pass judgment on such a human nature, conditioned as it was, in the midst of the internal and external moral agents that the English poet imagined for his buccaneer. If you say 'That's only a story; human nature has never been like that', then take the case of the Tartar, Kara-Aly, a real person who died last year at Zarajek under the lashes of the knout.[331] It is impossible to say how much the beliefs and opinions of this ferocious yet generous assassin influenced his life and at the same time diminished the

[331] The account of the trial of this Asiatic Russian was published in the Petersburg Gazette, and aroused considerable interest.

culpability of his misdeeds. Muslim fatalism, for example, impressed deeply in his spirit from youth, must have served to quieten his remorse, and render him simultaneously cruel and resigned to the will of God even in death.[332] His belief that he was the legitimate Sultan of Kazam deprived of his throne by his uncle,[333] combined with his harsh treatment at home and his conscription into the Russian army, must have served to accumulate immense anger in such a naturally robust, proud, and vital person whose whole enjoyment consisted in facing danger. No one can tell how another kind of upbringing, in other circumstances, with other beliefs, might not have brought him to strong, noble virtue, in which even humanity and gentleness might have played their part. That atrocious soul was endowed with elevated feeling, a glorious imagination and a wonderful instinct for language, all of which he showed in the gratitude, reverence and love he expressed towards his beautiful wife, Fazry.[334]

§6. Fifth limit, determined by virtual and habitual volitions

750. Another limit to freedom arises from virtual and habitual volitions. By *virtual* volition I mean a disposition already present in the will by which the will is inclined towards some object which it wants as soon as the object reveals itself, although previously it was unknown. The will itself may be ignorant of this inclination, or of the object to which the inclination is leading it.

By *habitual* volition, on the other hand, I mean that disposition by which the will is not only inclined towards a given object, but has already decided for it once and resolved to have it, without ever retracting this desire. These *habitual* volitions thus have their origin in an *actual*, preceding volition. What I call *virtual* volitions do not presuppose an actual volition already decided by the will, but simply an inclination which turns the will to the object as soon as the opportunity to do so presents itself.

332 When he saw he could not escape, he threw away his *yagatan* and shouted at his captor: 'God has willed it. Kill me or let me live! Do what you like! Fate has overtaken me.'

333 Noussiram-Bey.

334 The daughter of Noussiram-Bey.

751. The existence of virtual and habitual volitions in the human spirit is a mysterious fact, but nevertheless a fact.

There is a striking analogy between the existence of *abstract ideas* in our intellect and of habits in the will. A very close connection exists between these two things, which, however, we cannot discuss here. I simply wish to point out that those who deny the existence of abstract ideas are necessarily predisposed to deny habits in the human spirit. Because they do not understand these habits, they think themselves authorised to deny their existence. Many times I have shown the vanity and presumption underlying this kind of reasoning, and I do not think it necessary for me to stop now and prove the existence of virtual and habitual volitions. Prefering to appeal to the consciousness of people who know how to observe what takes place in their spirit, I am certain that volitions of this kind will be recognised as extremely real.

752. My first affirmation, therefore, is this: given the presence in human beings of unchanging *virtual* and *habitual volitions* prior to action, freedom of action is limited as long as these volitions last because they influence subjects in their decisions. Let us begin with *virtual* volitions.

There is no doubt that human beings possess an already formed state of will inclining them towards something vague but still unknown which, as soon as it reveals itself, is recognised by the will as the object it secretly desired and sought. At the moment of recognition the will knows what it previously desired so ardently, blindly and uncertainly.

This is the psychological fact which the novel about Gertrude[335] intends to portray when it shows her still a young girl in the monastery, listening for the first time to her companions' gossip about banquets, late-night parties and entertainments. Suddenly she finds herself totally changed. 'These images' — this is not a novelist writing, but a recorder of the human spirit — 'cause turmoil in Gertrude's mind; her thoughts are as busy as bees that find a great basket of fresh flowers put down in front of their hive.' Later the author describes another great change in the girl's condition. Gertrude, no longer a child, 'is moving towards that critical age when a mysterious power seems to enter the

[335] The nun of Monza.

spirit, lifting us up, embellishing and strengthening all our inclinations and ideas which it can sometimes even change and set on unforeseen paths', paths normally directed by *virtual volition*, as we have called it. This volition surfaces, grows and is strengthened through the development of instincts with which it has some affinity and analogy. Finally, when it discovers the reality corresponding to its proper object, it reaches fulfilment by bursting forth as an actual volition.

753. Sometimes, some inherent partiality is already present in the human will which undoubtedly heightens the spontaneity of desire by adding energy of will to the impression of an object. Without this addition, spontaneity would not be completely operative. The will gravitates towards the object rather like a body poised on a balance which rolls down at the least movement.

In this case of 'partiality' the total cause of movement results from the common aim shared by the impression of the object and the associated inclination of will. The two causes mingle in different proportions to produce the full effect of voluntary movement and consent in such a way that less pressure is required from the object as the disposition and inclination of the will increases, and vice-versa. As a result, even an impression which, slight in itself, would be incapable of overcoming the smallest obstacle in one person, proves of immense efficacy in another already prompted by passion.

The history of human passions and of passionate people is all here. They are sensitive in the extreme not only to everything related to their passion, but even to the shadow and distant image of the objects enthralling them. They behold the objects of their affections everywhere, even where they are least likely to be found. One man jealously nourishes hatred for another, and sees everything done by his enemy as foul and injurious to himself: the other's slight neglect becomes a crude, intolerable offence; the most innocent actions are exaggerated and interpreted evilly; even the courtesy and benevolence with which the other treats him is construed as the result of bad motivation, and used to fuel the hatred burning within. Other passions are of a similar nature. All give rise to heightened sensitivity, disastrous inclination in the will, total blindness relative to any object opposed to the passions, and mistaken sharpness of vision in relationship to anything favouring them.

754. According to Christian teaching, even the evil disposition posited in humankind by original sin consists in one of these *virtual volitions*. Cornelius à Lapide writes: 'The movements of concupiscence are not restricted to *sense-appetite*. They pertain also to the *will* which, vitiated in its origin, inclines towards good which is pleasant, honourable and satisfying to curiosity.'[336]

755. We have already dealt with sense-appetite when we saw that it produced a kind of diseased vivacity, exaggerated force, and unfulfillable promises. Nevertheless, the will would be able to withstand sense-appetite without abandoning itself blindly and hopelessly to the pleasure of sensations and the deceitful delight of primary instincts if the will itself tended towards what is good, and reason were less lazy in initiating activities relative to the attainment of justice. It is true that at first the will could still be deceived. The uncontrolled, falsified pleasure of such instincts could be thought to contain more good than they actually do. But this is very different from the mistake we are considering at the moment. Such an error would consist only in an exaggerated degree of esteem and affection given to the titillation of the senses. The exaggeration could later be corrected and emended without great difficulty. Our present case, however, is one in which the will errs easily in the *degree* and *singlemindedness* of its affection. Here, the will is accustomed to giving excessive and exclusive affection to feelable things in which it immerses itself.

The cause of this blind abandonment is to be found only in the blindness and tardiness of reason, and in its apathy relative to matters immortal. At the moment in which feeling has already opened and passed through a large breach in the human heart, reason does not provide the will with any noble object. When it does finally discover the sublime objects we call justice and virtue, they lie dormant for long periods like insignificant, immobile larvae overwhelmed by the intense reality and urgent presence of feelable things. The will, without anything to sustain it, allows its spontaneity to follow its own course almost without hindrance along the path traced by exterior, feelable matters.

[336] 'The movements of concupiscence are not restricted to sense-appetite. They pertain also to the will which, naturally vitiated in its origin from Adam, inclines towards good which is pleasant, honourable and satisfying to curiosity' (*Comm. in Ep. ad Rom. 7*).

From this moment, we are conspirators with instinct, as St. Gregory says, and 'we turn the knife upon ourselves.'[337]

Worse follows. The evil inclination of our will, and the bad, habitual affections acquired from the first moment of human existence, have an added fatality. These *excessive*, *singleminded* affections are also *final* in the sense that the will imagines it can find its complete satisfaction and supreme happiness in feelable things. This is the ultimate, greatest degree of disorder. It is shown in certain people from the very outset of the will's activity, and begins with something initially defective and false in the will. Such final disorder differs from the first, which depends upon a deterioration in *feeling*, and from the second, which springs from weakness and sloth in the *understanding*.

756. Nevertheless, anyone examining in depth the state of the human will beholds something more mysterious and wonderful than all the conditions we have listed so far. They will see that from the beginning the will has been attuned and inclined to something absolute, and that it moves towards a supreme good of which it is ignorant but from which it cannot prescind. They will see that the will experiences in itself an immensely active need, absorbing all other needs, for this unknown, but highest good. Certainty and trust in eventually finding such good never deserts the will, although the certainty is illusory and the trust presumptuous. No doubt arises about the imminent discovery of this good nor about the chance of reaching out to it immediately. Without stopping to think, the will sees and grasps it (or rather thinks it sees and grasps this final good) in any good that appears to stimulate the will. Whatever misery of privation it suffers without this hoped-for good, some glimmer of light, a mirage or illusion still shines before it. Through this disorder of innate presumption, the human will endlessly convinces itself of its power to make itself happy with any kind of good or imagined good, and to provide for its own bliss.[338]

[337] 'When evil suggests something to us, we fulfil through our will what has been suggested, and together with the will inflict injury upon ourselves' (*Moral.*, 13, 11).

[338] This credulous presumption is assisted by the sluggishness and weakness of the understandng which, although it knows that something is *good*, has to work very hard to know how good this thing is. In other words, the

This pitiful, unceasing pride of the will is evident in the whole of human history. Every step that humanity has taken, every excogitated philosophy, and every imaginary religion bears its own steady witness to this degradation. No human waywardness is inwardly bereft of the sad persuasion expressed in the proud affirmation of the letter to Leucippus: 'Any object whatsoever, however fragile it may be, can form our happiness.' Such is the briefest and most explicit formula of the inner malfunctioning with which the human will is born.[339]

757. One of these virtual volitions, although incomplete, or at least not invincible, is present in human beings, therefore, inclining them to favour evil whenever the opportunity occurs. This constitutes the basis of original sin.

This volition draws us in the direction both of false judgments and evil works. St. Prosper expresses the point well when he affirms that man's very judgment was degraded by original sin.[340] A great 8th century author uses this telling expression in his description of the same sin. He says that 'the goodness of the will was withdrawn from free decision',[341] and means that although *good* and *bad volition* were *possible* to free decision, the former was taken away and free decision itself was inclined to bad volition. Saint Augustine touches the two simultaneous wounds in understanding and will when he says: 'Approving what is false as though it were true in such a way that human beings err without wishing to do so and find themselves unable to refrain from unlawful actions, is not something natural to

understanding finds it difficult to establish the limits within which this word is restricted. Without the knowledge of these limits, however, we find that in accepting something as good we have only an indeterminate idea of its goodness. Precisely because this idea is vague, the will dreams its dreams and finds in the object it enjoys a kind of satisfying infinity.

339 Facts which prove that the human will is continually inclined to suppose itself capable of finding total happiness in every good, however limited and imaginary (a supposition and belief which helped, encouraged and directed mankind to form for itself every sort of philosophy and superstition), can be found in my *Saggio sulla Speranza*, in the 2nd volume of the *Opusculi Filosofici* (Milan, 1828) and in the *Frammenti di una storia dell'Empietà* (Milan 1834).

340 '. . . by which the will's judgment was degraded, not taken away' (*De vocat. gentium*, 1, 8).

341 Alcuin, *De Trinit*, 2, 8.

humanity, but a penalty of condemnation.'[342] According to Catholic teaching, therefore, it is grace that heals this wound of the will.[343]

758. But let us return from facts to theory. As we said, an *habitual* volition is present in us if the volition has indeed passed into act, if the object of the volition is known, and if an explicit or at least implicit propensity to desire the object remains in the spirit. *Habitual*, like *virtual* volition, remains permanently in us as one of those acts which we call 'immanent'. It serves to determine and constitute a *state* of the human spirit.

759. Normally we reflect only upon our changing acts, and find it extremely difficult to conceive of a lasting, constant act in our spirit unless it produces something new in it. It is not easy to think of anything which endures within us without growth or diminution in intensity, or without its requiring effort or tension from our spirit. Nevertheless, without facts of this kind nothing can be explained in nature: *existence* itself is one of these acts; our *powers* are simply immanent acts; our *habits* are a third kind of such acts and, considered as more developed powers, have taken another step towards their natural term and final perfection.

760. Everyone wants the highest good. This is an immanent, natural act which is, at the beginning, only virtual because the highest good is still unknown to us. We know only good as such, in which all good, and especially the greatest good, is present virtually. Anyone tending to good as such, tends *virtually* to the

342 'Approving what is false as though it were true in such a way that human beings err without wishing to do so and, despite their repugnance to carnal slavery, find themselves unable to refrain from unlawful actions, is not something natural to human beings, but a penalty of condemnation.'

343 Hence St. Gregory the Great says: 'Free will is directed towards good in the elect when through the help of grace their mind is turned away from earthly desires. The good that we do is both God's and our own: God's, through his prevenient grace; ours, through the piety of our free will' (*Moral.*, 33, 20). Cardinal Jacques de Vitry says: 'After the infusion of first grace, we ourselves must co-operate with God through our free will, after it has been liberated by grace' (*Serm. Dom. 12 post octavas Pent*). In these and other places we see that the stimulus of grace does not constitute of itself an actual volition, but is made such by the co-operation of the will. Of itself, therefore, grace is a *virtual* volition. And not only a virtual, but an *habitual* volition because God, the object of good, communicates himself, although in a hidden way, in baptism.

supreme good. When we begin to gain some knowledge of the supreme good and want it, we have an *actual* volition for it, which then becomes *habitual.*

The habitual volitions we have described may be good or blameworthy. If the habitual volition for moral good lies at the very depth of our soul, we are good. If the habitual volition for evil is present there, we are bad. Our good or evil state depends on these volitions.

761. These volitions of ours are profound and hidden, veiled to other people, and concealed even from ourselves who possess them. Hence Scripture numbers amongst God's attributes that of 'searcher of the heart'.[344] And of Christ, too, we read that 'he knew what was in man',[345] that is, he knew whether the habitual volition lying deep in the spirit was good or blameworthy.

Actions spring from our *habitual volitions* to which we liken the Gospel *tree* whose fruits are constituted by our actions. So we read that 'every sound tree bears good fruit, but the bad tree bears evil fruit. A sound tree cannot bear evil fruit, nor can a bad tree bear good fruit'[346]. It is clear that a distinction is made in this passage between two kinds of goodness, that of the tree and that of the fruit, just as there are two kinds of evil, that of the tree and that of the fruit. The goodness or evil of the tree are the virtual and habitual volitions, good or bad; the goodness or evil of the fruit, our actual good or bad actions.

762. We conclude, therefore: virtual and habitual volitions are a fetter restricting freedom as long as they endure; but freedom can to a certain point annul and destroy them.

763. We think it will be useful here (before we begin the next book which deals with the human subject as the single subject of all our passive and active powers) to offer readers a summary table of the principal human powers of which we have spoken so far. They are set out according to their natural order in the following schema:–

344 'The heart is deceitful above all things, and desperately corrupt; who can understand it? "I the Lord search the mind, and try the heart"' (Jer 17: [9, 10]).

345 Jn 2: 25.

346 Matt 8: [17, 18].

SYNOPTIC SCHEMA OF THE

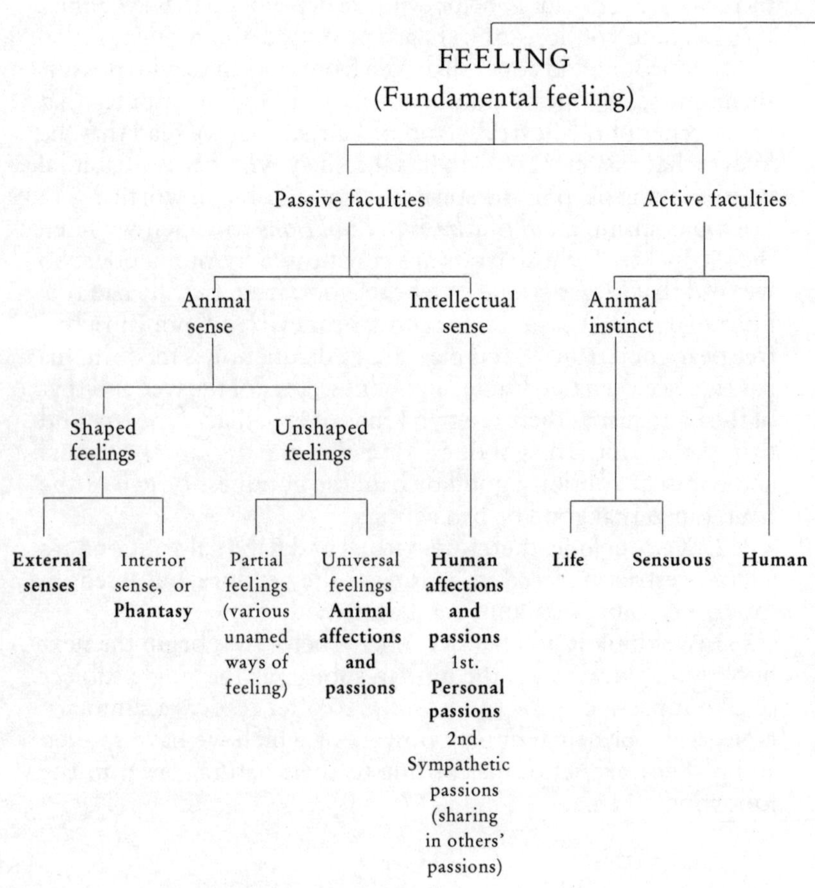

FACULTIES OF THE HUMAN SPIRIT

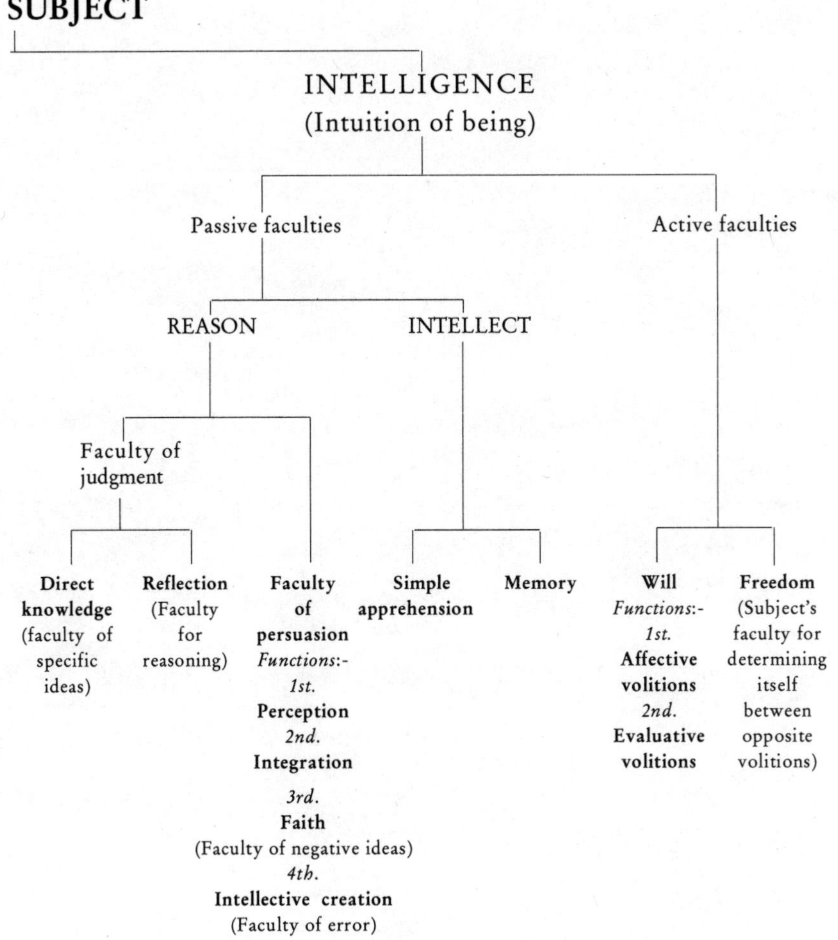
SUBJECT
INTELLIGENCE
(Intuition of being)
Passive faculties
Active faculties
REASON
INTELLECT
Faculty of judgment
Direct knowledge (faculty of specific ideas)
Reflection (Faculty for reasoning)
Faculty of persuasion
Functions:-
1st. Perception
2nd. Integration
3rd. Faith (Faculty of negative ideas)
4th. Intellective creation (Faculty of error)
Simple apprehension
Memory
Will
Functions:-
1st. Affective volitions
2nd. Evaluative volitions
Freedom (Subject's faculty for determining itself between opposite volitions)

Book 4

THE HUMAN SUBJECT

DEFINITIONS

I

764. *Essence* is 'that which the spirit intuits in an idea'.

II

765. Substance is 'that first act of being through which an essence subsists'.

III

766. A (*substantial*) *individual* is 'a substance in so far as it is indivisible, incommunicable, and has all that is necessary for its subsistence'.

IV

767. A *subject* is 'a sentient individual in so far as it contains within itself an supreme, active principle'.

V

An *intellective* subject is 'a subject that intuits ideal being'.

VI

A *human subject* is 'a subject that is simultaneously a principle of animality and of intelligence'.

VII

768. *Myself* is 'an active principle in a given nature in so far as the principle is conscious of itself'.

VIII

769. *Person* is 'an intellective subject in so far as it contains a supreme, active principle'.

770. From the beginning of this work I have defined the human being as 'an animal, intellective and volitive subject'. I

then divided the definition into its parts so that each part could be discussed separately. These parts are three: animality, intelligence and the principle common to both animality and intelligence (the subject). Till now I have dealt only with the first two, animality and intelligence; I must now consider the human *subject*, which is simultaneously an animal and intelligent principle. I will then have fulfilled, to the best of my ability, the task I gave myself of examining the definition of human being in all its parts, which is the final aim of anthropology.

I must begin by examining what is meant by *subject* in general, because this will prepare the way for discussing *human subject*.

1

SUBJECT IN GENERAL

Article 1.
Subject applied to all beings, including beings without feeling

771. The general meaning given to the word *subject* includes beings that have no feeling. In this sense, *subject* simply means *substance*, or more generally, 'the being in and through which we conceive the existence of accidents'. This meaning is found in the origin of the word itself. Etymologically it means 'that which lies beneath' (this is the way people generally conceive it), that which supports something else resting upon it. As I have said, it is a metaphorical sense, taken from what is seen or believed to happen in bodies.

Furthermore, this meaning is not restricted to the order of real things; it is also applied to purely ideal things produced by the spirit. The topic of a discourse is called a *subject* because we imagine our reasoning ranging over the topic, as it were, and working at it, as a sculptor works at marble with his chisel to sculpt and shape it. This meaning of *subject* clearly has a twofold metaphorical sense. First of all, the word *subject* is itself metaphorical, as I have said. Secondly, the matter of the discourse (the thoughts) is compared to real, corporeal matter, even though the words, which indicate the thoughts only externally, do not in any way affect or modify them. In paying attention to thoughts connected with a definite theme, the mind does not change or modify the theme itself.

772. These meanings of *subject* require us to note carefully that whenever the word is applied to a non-feeling thing, whether real or ideal, it means properly speaking no more than the way we think. Non-feeling things, which feel neither themselves nor what is different from themselves, do not enjoy any sensation; they exist not to themselves but only to the one who feels and conceives them.[347] Hence, even the intrinsic order conceived in them by the mind exists only to the mind, that is, only as *thinkable*. Such a use of *subject*, therefore, clearly expresses no more than a relationship or order which the contemplating mind notices between the quality and properties of the thing thought. The basis of this relationship and order is that one of the properties is necessary for thinking the others, and gives them their unity; indeed, this one property in which all the other properties have their origin is the first act of the thing thought. Thus, the name *subject*, given to this first act which constitutes the individuality of a thing and provides a foundation for its concept, has no value apart from the mind. We believe, therefore, that this species of being should not be called *subjects* without qualification, but *subjects of the mind*.

Article 2.
Subject, applied to beings that have feeling

773. The case of beings that feel is quite different. Feeling is an internal principle, not a mere object of the mind contemplating it. There is an immense difference between the mode of being of that which feels and of that which does not feel. The former, granted its existence, needs nothing else; it is something of itself, a form, not simply uninformed matter. The latter constitutes only an existence *relative to a feeling*, so that it is no more than the matter or term of the feeling.

[347] Cf. *PE*, 21–42 [*App.*, no. 9].

774. We can therefore justly infer that *subject*, in its correct meaning, applies solely to beings with feeling. Matter can constitute part of a subject but not the total subject. Its mode of being is to form part of a whole and not to form a whole of itself. As I said, it is conceivable only as a term of feeling, without which its whole concept vanishes.[348]

Article 3.
The word *subject* applied to simple, feeling beings

775. Modern philosophy is principally responsible for the observation in the preceding article. But philosophy as a whole also offers a more precise, correct use of the word *subject*.

The word *subject* is taken in conjunction with both the word *accident* and with the word *object*. When taken in conjunction with the word *accident*, it means 'the principle which supports the accident', that is, 'that in which and through which accidents subsist'. This is the definition of substance (cf. 765).

776. This was the more usual meaning of the word among earlier writers. Hence Boethius' statement that 'a simple form cannot be a subject'.[349] If the form is entirely simple, it does not have accidents, and the principle supporting the accidents cannot be distinguished from the accidents supported.

777. But when *subject* is taken in conjunction with *object*, it can be defined as 'that which is a principle of action, or receives action in itself'. This was the meaning invariably given by grammarians, for whom the subject is expressed in the nominative case; it is also the meaning to which modern philosophy pays greater attention. In this sense, *subject* can be a simple form without accidents, provided it is a principle that has its own mode of being within itself, without any obligation to obtain this mode from something else. In other words, it is a principle which feels.[350]

[348] I would willingly apply the word 'supposed' to what I have called 'subjects of the mind'. In this way, we would have two different words, one for so-called inanimate subjects, the other for true subjects. But the use of these words is too fixed for their meanings to be altered.

[349] *De Trinit. 2.*

[350] The struggle between aristotelian philosophy and Christian dogma at a

Article 4.
The definition of *subject*

778. To summarise what we have said. There are subjects conceived by the mind alone and these too are classed amongst non-feeling beings. There are true subjects, in the proper, absolute sense which is understood solely of feeling beings. To these the word *subject* is applied to indicate either a principle which supports the accidents, or a principle which has its own absolute mode of being and is not merely relative. According to our use of the word, the second meaning properly speaking constitutes the essential characteristic of a subject. We consider as 'subject' any simple form, devoid even of all accidents, in so far as it has its own existence, that is, has life and feeling, in which consists real, absolute existence.

779. We have therefore the following definition of subject: 'A sentient being in so far as it contains within itself a supreme, active principle' (cf. 767).

The definition contains the words *active principle* because the

time when no one wished to abandon either Aristotle's philosophy or still less the Catholic faith is a matter for wonder. A compromise had to be struck with aristotelism under which aristotelian philosophy would be allowed to maintain faithfully all its terminology, provided that the meaning of the terms could be changed in certain circumstances. In fact, if aristotelian philosophy had faithfully and constantly held to the meanings it had given to *subject* and *person* (*person* should have meant an *intelligent subject*), the two words would have had to be banished from theology. As understood by the Aristotelians, they include the concept of accidents and matter, and therefore exclude the divine nature in which there is neither matter nor distinguishable accidents of any kind. Hence, it was necessary to make a distinction by saying that 'the word *hypostasis* (that is, *person*) considered in its original sense does not apply to God, because accidents cannot be predicated of God, but does apply to him in so far as it expresses something subsistent' (St. Thomas, *S.T.*, I, q. 29, art. 3, ad 3). Christian theology therefore took the words *subject, hypostasis* and *person* to mean not 'a principle supporting accidents' but, as St. Thomas teaches, 'something subsistent', something which has no need of anything else in order to exist. In other words, theology does not take these words in meaningful conjunction with *accidents* but in meaningful conjunction with *object*, so that they come to express a subjective existence which is proper, internal and independent. The use, therefore, which modern philosophy makes of the word *subject* clearly stems from the hidden, beneficial influence exercised over philosophy by the enlightened ideas of Christianity.

subject, even if it were only a feeling being and felt merely passively relative to the agent arousing feeling, is in itself an activity which supposes an actual existence.

Secondly, according to the definition the subject may or may not have accidents. Even if only a uniform feeling were present, that is, a simple, indivisible feeling free from every kind of modification, the subject would still exist, possessing all that is necessary for its entity as subject.

At the same time, if the feeling of this sense-being received different modifications, the active, feeling principle, provided it remained identical, would be the subject of all the different feelings. Both the proper existence of the being, as a feeling principle, and the modifications experienced by the feeling would be grounded in this principle.

780. Furthermore, we see how the two meanings of 'subject' as opposite of *object* and of *accidents* unite and have as their common root the property of constituting the reason for the subsistence. The active principle constituting the subject contains its own reason for subsistence,[351] while the modifications or accidents have the reason of their subsistence in the principle. This explains again why the principle is called 'subject': in either case the principle is the source of subsistence and merits the name 'subject'. 'Subject' means having its own changeless mode of existence, that is, it is a real principle of existence within a given nature.

781. Finally, the definition says that the *active principle*, in order to be called'subject', must be supreme within the nature. If it were subordinate to some other principle, it would depend on that principle and not have within itself the basis of its own existence — it would not be the nail, so to speak, on which the entire feeling hangs.

[351] When I say that 'the subject has in itself the reason of its own subsistence', I am not referring to the ultimate cause but the reason found within the sphere of the nature in question, even if the nature itself depends and subsists through another principle different from itself.

Article 5.
The definition of some words that have affinity to *subject*

782. The use we have described of the word *subject* will be more distinctly understood if we compare it with the definitions of other entities which might be easily confused with it.

We will consider some of the ontological definitions we have already given, and add others necessary at this point.

First, *essence* is that which is understood in the idea of a thing,[352] (cf. 764).

783. Second, *substance* is the act by which the essence of a thing subsists[353] (cf. 764 [5]).

This definition shows how substance is distinguished from accidents. Accidents are not the act by which essence subsists; they are rather the term and effect of such an act.

784. Third, *individual* is any being in so far as it is unique, indivisible, incommunicable, and distinct from all other beings.[354] (cf. 766).

The Schoolmen, who debated the very important but difficult question: 'What is the principle of individuation?' affirmed with Aristotle: 'Matter is the principle of individuation.' But this answer has no place in a universal ontology. It is limited, and, like all aristotelian responses, is evidently derived from a partial, limited consideration of corporeal beings, not from a consideration of beings in general.

I have observed that matter which can individuate the feeling whose term it is, cannot individuate anything else. I now add that matter could not even individuate the feeling whose term it is, without having the principle of individuation in itself in some way. The scholastic problem, therefore, is not solved but carried a step further by the reply, because we still have to ask: 'How does the individuation of matter come about?' And we answer this difficult, subtle question as follows.

785. We distinguish the *order of ideal being* from the *order of real being*. According to us, that which is truly *individual* is

[352] *OT*, 646.

[353] *Ibid.*, 657–659.

[354] '"Individual" is that which is undivided in itself, but divided from other things' (St. Thomas, *S.T.*, I, q. 24, art. 4, corp.).

found only in the order of real being; in individuation the principle is the *reality* itself of being.[355] On the other hand, the *universal* is found only in the order of ideal being; the principle of universality is the very *ideality* of a being. This teaching is so consistently true that it brooks no exception. Consequently, any being whose concept excludes all multiplicity — such as the concept of God and the concept of 'myself' — cannot be known by means of a pure concept, but has to be really perceived. Without this, we cannot have a positive idea of it. Indeed, the pure concept of God without perception of him does not exist.

786. We must not confuse the *individual* with the *idea of the individual*. The individual is something necessarily real. The idea of an individual, as idea, is not an individual; it is a true universal, in the way that all ideas are said to be universal.

Nor must we confuse an imaginary individual, a complex unity formed mentally, with a real individual. An imaginary individual may be called a fictitious or *artificial individual*, but it is never a natural individual in the true and proper sense.

787. This supports the truth of St. Thomas' opinion that 'the individual is placed in a special way in the genus of substances'.[356] Indeed, the individual has its basis in the act by which a being first subsists. This act supports all successive and accidental acts, and has in its very self (as is clear from the definition of substance) subsistence itself.

788. Finally, the observation I made when discussing *subject* can also be applied to the *substantial individuals* under discussion: where feeling is lacking, there is only a relative not a proper mode of existence. We distinguish *individuals conceived mentally*, that is, purely mental individuals, from individuals in an absolute sense — just as we distinguished subjects. The latter are normally included in the definition of a subject, so that we could also define a subject as 'a substantial, feeling individual'.[357]

[355] This truth did not escape St. Thomas [*App.*, no. 10].

[356] *S.T.*, I, q. 29, art. 1, corp.

[357] Does the soul separated from the body constitute an individual, a subject, a person? A negative answer was given to this debated question because the soul is part, not the whole, of a human individual. The reply is correct if the question concerns the *human* individual or subject. The *human* subject is composed not of one but of two parts, soul and body. But if it is accepted that individuality, subjectivity, personality possess their own *subsistence*,

2

THE FEELING SUBJECT

789. We must now describe special subjects, and among them the human subject, the specific aim of our discussion.

We have defined the subject as 'a feeling being in so far as it contains within itself a supreme principle of feeling'. Feeling, therefore, is necessary for a subject, but not material feeling or any other special feeling whatsoever; we are dealing with feeling in the widest possible sense of the word. In this sense, feeling includes intelligence, because intelligence has for its foundation a feeling proper to the soul. This feeling exists in and through the intuition of the idea, which, on revealing itself to the soul, produces in it an intellective sense. Attributing such a feeling to the intelligent soul is confirmed by the most ancient, authoritative use of language.[358]

790. Subjects, therefore, are of two kinds: *feeling* and *intellective*.

we have to say that even the soul separated from the body is an individual substance (although not a human being); it is both subject and person, and has in itself its own subsistence without drawing it from the body. We must distinguish, therefore, the subsistence proper to the soul from its subsistence relative to the body. Relative to its proper subsistent, it is individual, subject, person; in its subsistence relative to the body, it is neither individual nor subject nor person. Lastly, we must note that if we are dealing with a purely feeling soul, it has a subsistence relative only to the body. The Schoolmen, in fact, began with the feeling soul and from it took their solution to the question under discussion. Cf. St. Thomas, *S.T.*, I, q. 29, art. 1, ad 5.

[358] St. Basil, comparing the soul's action with the action of intelligence, says: 'Let no one protest: "You, with your head in the clouds, what do you mean by coming here and philosophising about an incorporeal and totally immaterial essence?" I think it's absurd to allow the senses to make free with what concerns them and then to prevent the mind from carrying out its own activity; the mind reaches out to intelligible things just as feeling reaches out to feelable things. Furthermore, God our Creator placed natural judgments in us without the guidance of human authority. Nobody teaches the eye to see colours and shape, or hearing to perceive sounds and voices, or taste to perceive flavours, or touch to perceive hard and soft, hot and cold things. In the same way no one teaches the mind to deal with intelligible things.' *Ep.* 8, Class. 1, n. 8.

To these we have to add the *human being*, a mixed, feeling-intellective subject or, simply a *rational* subject.

791. When talking about the feeling subject, we did not consider it in general but in the form and nature it manifests in animals. In this form the subject is equipped with many accidents, and with appetitive and instinctive faculties as well as feeling. Our investigation must be limited to it because it is the only feeling subject we know.

The concept of the feeling animal subject depends principally on the concept of the animal's *individuality*. In this respect we have seen what constitutes the simplicity and unity of the feeling principle, and have distinguished the mathematical simplicity attributed to a point from spiritual, non-abstract, real unity. This unity does not consist in being term to an extension but in having a nature entirely different from extension[359]

We also said that *extension* is a mode of *sensation* or more precisely a mode of the *that which is felt*, and is itself something felt. It resides in the term of feeling (the thing felt), not in the principle (the feeling thing).

We then noted that extension measured with bodies constitutes only a relationship between one assignable part in a felt thing and the other assignable parts of the thing, that is, between one felt thing and another. Measured extension, therefore, can be conceived only by perceiving at the same time the assignable parts of the felt thing or of many continuous felt things.

On the other hand, if we compare the thing felt with the feeling principle, the relationship in which extension consists is completely removed. The only relationship left is that of a higher order of things, a relationship between feeling and felt, not between extended and extended. Consequently, although the activity of the feeling principle spreads, as it were, into the whole of the felt, extended thing, it does not take on any extension. It does not spread as an extended thing spreads and diffuses itself in extension, but in the way a feeling force enfolds its terms, that is, in an entirely simple, unextended way.

359 Aristotle said that indivisibility *relative to quantity* is not the same as indivisibility *relative to species*, although indivisibility according to aristotelian species is more a dialectical indivisibility than anything else. Cf. *De Anima*, bk. 3, less. 11 [6].

That the force and activity required for perceiving something extended is itself unextended and simple was also demonstrated by us. As we said, it is obviously absurd and contradictory to affirm that something extended feels what is extended. We will see this immediately if we consider that nothing *extended* can exist without that which is *continuous*, and that the continuous can exist only in what is unextended. Nothing continuous exists unless the parts are simultaneously united to each other without any interval. Such unity can be brought about only by an entirely simple principle different from all the parts into which the continuum can be divided. No part of the continuum is united with the others; it has an existence of its own. Hence, it cannot make a whole with the others unless a principle, alien to the parts, is added and draws all the parts into a single whole containing the relationships of continuity and co-existence.

The continuum, therefore, supposes a simple principle which feels it, just as the principle is required by all the relationships which do not exist in the individual terms of the relationship, but in their union and harmony.

792. This observation allows us to correct an ontological teaching frequently encountered in modern philosophy which asks how the substance remains unchangeable in an individual while the accidents change. The argument runs: 'The individual has two parts, one of which changes and one of which does not. The part that does not change is called substance or object; that which changes, accident.'

In my opinion, this does not sufficiently explain the relationship between *accidents* and *subject*. I accept that one of the properties of what is called 'subject' is that of being unchangeable relative to the accidents. But we must bear in mind that the subject cannot be subject of the accidents, unless it *participates* in the change of the accidents which it bears, as it were, within itself, sustaining and supporting them. We have to explain, therefore, how the subject remains unchangeable while the accidents, which subsist in and through the subject, change. This is the real difficulty, and it is not solved by simply distinguishing two parts in the individual and affirming that something unchangeable and something changeable is present. We need to demonstrate the relationship of these two parts, to reconcile them, and explain how what is unchangeable and what is changeable can constitute a single individual.

Help in doing this can be found in my earlier observation that the extended, the continuum and the multiple exist solely in what is simple and one. This relationship must be accepted for what it is, without the introduction of anything arbitrary on the part of our ever active imagination. If we keep in mind the genuine nature of this relationship, which unites what feels and what is felt, we understand how *that which is felt* can change without any necessary change in the principle of feeling (*that which feels*). When only the felt (to which extension is proper) changes, no change takes place in the nature of the relationship between *that which is felt* and *that which feels* — the relationship, as we said, is not one of extension but of sensility. The source, therefore, of the modifications and accidents in an individual is that which is felt, which we have also called 'the matter of feeling'. This is the sense, it seems to me, in which we must take St. Thomas' statement that 'an individual composed of matter and form subsists, relative to the accidents, in dependence upon matter'.[360]

The explanation, therefore, of how what is changeable exists in the unchangeable must be sought in the real relationship of what feels and what is felt. This explanation is not only similar to, but the same as, the explanation we gave when we asked how the extended existed in the unextended.

The changeable and the extended remain solely within the sphere of what is felt and do not form part of the relationship which binds that which feels and that which is felt. Similarly, that which feels is united to what is extended and changeable not because the extended and changeable have the nature of *extended* and *felt* but because they have the nature of *that which is feelable* and *that which is felt*. Extension and changeability,

[360] *S.T.*, I, q. 29, art. 2. ad 5. This statement seems at first sight to be contradicted by the following: 'Accidents proper to something are the effects of substantial forms' (*S.T.*, q. 29, art. 1, ad 3). However,, the statements are easily reconciled: the subject is the cause of the accidents in so far as it supports them and they subsist in and through it, but the matter itself exists only on condition that it is united to a substantial form. The substantial form, therefore, puts the matter in act; the matter, once activated by the substantial form can change and give rise to all the accidental changes.

therefore, do not enter into the feeling principle, which remains simple and unchangeable. Nevertheless, that which is extended and changeable is united to the principle through their property of being feelable. In other words, everything that is felt in a feeling object is changeable. But that which feels, in so far as it feels, changes neither in regard to itself nor in regard to the nature of its relationship with what is felt.

793. We now come to the second question, which we have already touched on in various places: 'Does a subject (we are still talking about a feeling animal) feel itself? It is as important as the first question for anyone wishing to penetrate more deeply the notion of a feeling subject.

It is clear that if that which feels were to feel itself, it would to this extent lose its relationship of feeling element and become part of what is felt. Its relationship as a feeling element is contrary to any relationship as felt, which can never be confused with that which feels. The reply, therefore, to the question must be: that which feels is never felt. The feeling element is a being that belongs to the order of intelligible, not feelable things;[361] it is a real *noumenon* and not a *phenomenon*. Thus, everything felt, in so far as felt, belongs to the term, not the principle of feeling.

We must take careful note of the felt element in an extended feeling. Obviously, nothing is felt beyond the extension in which the feeling is diffused. The extended-felt element is the only thing which is felt; it is a single thing, not two things. Nevertheless, in this one thing (the extended-felt) some passivity and some activity is felt. Both are felt because to feel is to act and experience simultaneously — action and experience are felt. Thus, the feeling principle feels experience and action fused as one and as contributing co-causes which continually place the extended-felt element in act. The term of the feeling principle is that in which passivity and activity appear as feelable. The feeling principle's passivity and activity, fused together in the feeling element, constitute the mode of being of the feeling element itself. Although the feeling element does not properly speaking feel itself, it feels *its mode of being* in

[361] But this does not mean it pertains to things which are *intelligible of themselves*. These constitute the *ideal* world. That which feels pertains to *intelligible* things *by means of ideas*.

theextended-felt element. We can take a rough example from a solid sphere. If we supposed that the sphere does not feel itself but only its spherical form, we could say that the sphere feels the spherical form without knowing that the form belongs to it. This is precisely what happens in purely animal feeling: the material, feeling subject feels what is extended in various ways. In the extended element, the subject feels experience and action fused together,[362] but never refers what it feels to itself (such reference is proper to human beings); the subject's feeling stops at this point and goes no further. The pronoun 'self' cannot be applied to what is merely animal.

794. Certain consequences calling for our consideration follow from these observations:

1st. If the whole of *what is felt* is included in what is extended, and feeling exists solely through what is felt, it follows that the feeling element does not, as such, feel itself. Once more, therefore, we have to repeat that the only way in which the felt element can divide into parts without destroying the feeling is for the feeling principles to multiply because the feelings are multiplied.

795. 2nd. Hence, we can infer that the unicity of the feeling, and therefore the unicity of the animal (note, I am speaking of *unicity*, not *unity* or simplicity), depends on the perfect continuity of the felt-extended element.

796. 3rd. Thirdly, we are able to deduce the correct concept of the sameness or *identity* of an animal and determine what is changeable and not changeable in an animal. It is clear that this identity cannot be founded solely on the feeling principle; the feeling principle is not felt and therefore could never disclose such identity. Furthermore, the feeling principle alone, separated from everything that is felt, cannot be conceived as something subsistent but only as a beginning of subsistence which is completed by the felt element. Finally, a feeling element without a term would be an indefinite, unlimited principle lacking any individuation. Only in the felt element, therefore, must we seek the identity or sameness of feeling. This identity resides in the identity of action limited and balanced by the experience

362 By 'fused together' I mean that the felt extended element contemporaneously unites in itself a feeling of pressure and a feeling of action.

undergone in the extended element. Thus, the extended element changes, changing the quality of the feeling diffused within it, but the active-passive mode of the feeling element (which adheres to the felt element and is itself felt) never changes. Both continuity in space and the active-passive mode itself of being in time are that which maintain the identity of an animal. *Reality* is the foundation of these elements of identity. As we said, individuality is a primitive property of *real being*, and from it come the identity of space, the identity of the mode of being in time, and incommunicability.

To clarify the matter further, we should note that passivity and activity must be considered as a single act in which are found energy and limitation, an act glimpsed under the two forms or relationships of passivity and activity. We have seen that all the *passive phenomena* to which the animal is subject are virtually included in the first passivity, that is, the fundamental feeling, and that all the active phenomena manifested in the animal are virtually included in the *primitive activity*, that is, the life instinct by which the feeling principle concurs in the production of the fundamental feeling. The explanation of everything the animal *will experience* and *do* is found in the first element. When the animal feels this first activity, which embraces all its experiences and actions, it feels a single thing, a single act. In other words, the unicity, unity and identity of the animal consist, in my opinion, in the unicity, unity and identity of that which is first felt and developed but not changed. From being implicit it becomes explicit, and, because it has initially within itself what is passive and active, it must subsequently become part of the animal's feeling.

Moreover, the single act (the root and source of so many modifications) need not be felt by the animal as its *own* (this relationship is discovered by reason alone). It is sufficient for it to be the principle of, and govern effectively, the *act* it feels, and to posit the active and passive elements which make up this act. There is no choice in this, only a physical connection provided by nature. Nor is it required that the feeling element reflect on itself, or turn back upon itself in any way in order to perceive itself as agent and receiver. Its term is outside itself; here it commands and has all its existence, without ever returning to itself. The very existence of the animal is transfused, as it were, into the outside world. Consequently, if all experience and action is removed, leaving only the feeling principle, the principle itself completely disappears and our concept of animal is destroyed [*App.*, no. 11].

3

THE PURELY INTELLECTIVE SUBJECT

797. We have no experience of a purely intellective subject. Our experience is simply of the human subject, which is simultaneously animal, intellective and rational. Abstraction, therefore, is our only way of forming the concept of a purely intellective subject. We have to strip the human subject of its animal part and, by retaining only the constitutive elements of intelligence, obtain the notion of a purely intellective subject.

Just as there are two constitutive elements of feeling, so there are two constitutive elements of intelligence. Feeling is constituted by the feeling element and the felt element, the intelligence by that which understands and by that which is understood.

There is a first felt element and a first understood element. That which is first felt places the fundamental feeling in act; that which is first understood constitutes the intellect.

798. There is, however, an immense difference between the first felt and the first understood. The former is the body, the latter is being; one is finite, the other infinite. Moreover, the way in which the felt adheres to the feeling element is very different from the way in which the understood element adheres to the intelligence. The bond between that which is felt and that which feels is one of *action*, the former acting in the latter; the bond between that which is understood and that which understands is properly speaking one of *knowledge*, not action. A bond of action is present when one being makes a force felt in another; a bond of *knowledge* when one makes itself known to another.

799. The being that acts is called real; the bond joining it to another being is called a *real bond*. The being that is revealed to

another is called ideal, and the bond revealing it is called an *ideal bond*.

Only ideal being can reveal and make itself known; it is light, and its presence constitutes the intellect. Real being can only act; it is force, and its presence constitutes feeling.

800. The principle that understands is the intellective subject, or at least constitutes the foundation of the intellective subject, just as the principle that feels constitutes sensitivity.

The feeling subject feels only its term (cf. 793), that is, the felt element; in the same way the intellective subject knows only its term, the understood element.

If the intellective subject did not communicate at all with the real world and were purely intellective, its existence would be solely in the world of ideas.

801. These ideas, or ideal beings, objects of the subject's understanding, could be limited solely to that which is the foundation of human intelligence, namely, universal, indeterminate being. If the subject's intelligence were limited in this way to one object (an object that presents nothing definite or subsistent and lacks restriction and variety of any kind) the subject's existence would also be indefinable. It would not feel itself but would feel, or rather intuit, only being. It would exist in intuited *being*, without any action, movement, or even a true passivity in the common sense of the word because being does not use *force* to make itself known; it would exist without turning back on itself. In this state, the understanding subject would be entirely absorbed by being, and forever hidden from itself and from all other things that are outside God, who is Being itself.

On the other hand, the ideal being present to the subject could be varied. It could take different determinations by means of images that are truly felt but do not elicit affirmation. In this way many ideal beings could made known to the understanding subject. However, even in this case, the subject would still remain unknown to itself; its existence would still be absorbed and hidden in the ideal beings that it intuits. These beings alone would constitute the subject's knowledge, the known element, felt by its intelligence.

For the understanding subject to begin to have some indication of itself, therefore, it must not be purely intelligent, communicating only with the ideal world. It must also have contact with the real world, and have an action of its own which gives it some feeling of its own activity in which the nature of what is real reveals itself.

802. Let us now suppose that the intelligent subject possesses a feeling capable of eliciting affirmation (the feeling need not be corporeal). In this case, if the infinite being which manifests itself under the form of *idea* communicated itself also as *substance*, the subject would possess the maximum of feeling, that is, would feel God.

803. In the same way, we must believe that every real being has its own mode of acting on other real beings and, as it were, of infusing its own energy into them (energy which is a part of itself). In this way, one being exists in other beings by exercising its action in them and arousing a feeling conformable with the action. In the physical order of nature our only experience is of material feelings, unless we grant that even souls feel each other in friendship and love and mutually exercise some mysterious action of their own — which I think is the case.

804. Here, it is sufficient for us to indicate that the existence of a purely intelligent subject is the existence of a subject without action, intense excitation or movement of any kind, a subject sunk in fixed contemplation which detains the subject outside itself in such a way that the subject can never move towards finding itself. If, however, we wish to conceive an intelligent subject enjoying consciousness, we must first posit its communication with the world of realities, and think of it as capable of receiving an external feeling from the action of real beings, and of thus becoming an active principle itself. It will then feel its own experience, its own action, and the unity of its own forces. When it has perceived unity in its feeling, the intelligent subject will be able to apply ideal being to the feeling and in ideal being see the activity as one. In the light of this being, the intelligent subject will be able to find the subject of the force on which it depends. In short, it will be able to find itself, recognising that the intelligent subject from which the unity of experience and action depends is the same subject that intuits being and discovers the necessity of a perceiving, understanding subject. In this way consciousness is born, and the understanding subject pronounces the word *I*, as we shall see in the following chapter.

4

THE HUMAN SUBJECT AND THE GENERATION OF 'MYSELF'

805. We have come to the human subject and described the generation of 'myself', which expresses the subject. Let us recapitulate.

The human subject feels materially that which is extended and its own activity. This activity, in which passive and active are mixed, is identified with the felt, extended element. The human subject also intuits being, and feels its own cognoscitive activity indivisibly in intuited being.

This, however, is not sufficient. The single, simple human subject unites what is felt with what is understood, and by means of this union sees that *what is felt* exists in *what is understood* as being. It sees that the feeling makes an equation with the idea, that the feeling is a realisation of the being intuited in the idea, and that consequently there is in the feeling a being or feeling principle. This union of feeling and idea brought about by the human being produces the perception of the *feeling principle*, without which the feeling itself would be inexplicable.

806. In a similar way the human subject discovers an intelligent principle, when, instead of applying the being to his own *material feeling*, he applies it to his own *knowledge*, that is, either to the intellective perception of the feeling, or to intuited being itself. He now sees the cognition or perception in the idea of being, equates the two terms, and acknowledges that the cognition or perception is simply being itself realised. And precisely because there is cognition, perception, intellection, he concludes there is someone who knows or perceives, that is, an intelligent principle.

807. Moreover, the human subject, in joining and equating the feeling with the idea (and we can say the same about the cognition and the idea), acknowledges that they are the same being under two forms, that is, under the ideal form and real form. In doing this, the subject exercises a new activity.

The activity which unites feeling and idea is neither the activity which feels what is extended, nor the activity which intuits ideal being. It is a third activity, unifying and reconciling the first two.

This third activity takes the felt-extended element (product of the feeling activity) and the intuited being (presented by the intelligent activity), unites these two terms of the two feeling and intelligent activities, and composes a single ideal-real being. This is the meaning of 'to perceive intellectively'.

The human subject feels this third activity, and feels it as dominating the other two. As a result it feels the two as dependent on the third and therefore possessing a common principle. The subject concludes that the feeling principle and the intelligent principle are a single, identical activity, which simultaneously feels and understands.

808. But this higher activity, in which both the intelligent and the feeling principles participate, is not only *felt* but *perceived* intellectively by the human subject. The subject can compare this activity with the ideal being it possesses and acknowledge that, like any other entity, the activity is already contained in ideal being, just as drops of water are contained in the sea. At the moment the human being sees the higher activity in ideal being, he changes it into a *being*, that is, he has acknowledged it as a being. But it is a being only on condition that it has an active, subsistent principle (through the principle of substance). In this activity, therefore, the human being discovers entity or substance, that is, the *feeling, intelligent, unifying* active principle, which, although totally one and simple, is endowed with a trine act.[363]

809. At this point the human being has found himself without knowing that he has found himself: he does not know that the being or substance he has discovered is himself; he has formed no consciousness of himself and cannot yet say 'myself'. But in order to confer this new level of existence on himself and verify

[363] This entity or substance therefore is only intelligible, not feelable. It is a true *noumenon*, not a *phenomenon*. One philosopher, when he saw that a part of the subject was feelable and another part (which is strictly speaking the foundation of the subject) intelligible, made two subjects out of one by distinguishing a *phenomenal* and a *substantial* subject. This is obviously an error, and I have shown the absurdity of the consequences of such a distinction. I refer the reader to my *Rinnovamento* etc., bk. 3, c. 13.

not only that he is alive but is beginning to know he is alive, and alive to himself, he needs to take one step only. He needs to re-examine the way in which he discovered the single principle which feels, understands and reasons.

When he contemplated the bonding or reasoning activity in being and saw it in the principle, he performed a new act with which he perceived the reasoning activity. At the moment when the human being sees that the act which perceives the reasoning activity is identical with the reasoning activity, he has perceived himself and can say 'myself'. 'Myself' expresses the identity between the reasoning principle and the principle which says 'myself'. The very pronunciation of the word indicates that the person pronouncing it is aware of the existence of an activity which, through speech, announces itself and is conscious of itself. Anyone who says 'myself' must have reflected on his own activity and been conscious that that which reflects is the same principle as the activity on which he is reflecting.

Finally, we have to explain how the human being can recognise that the *reflecting*, speaking activity is also the *perceiving*, reasoning activity.

The identity of the principle in the different reflections is indicated by the intimate feeling which the human being has of his own universal activity. All partial activities are potentially found and identified in this activity, where the human being feels that the act by which he perceives and reasons is simply an act or partial application of the first, fundamental activity. This fundamental activity is the source of reflection upon what has been perceived and reasoned, that is, upon perceptions, reasonings and reflections themselves. It is the activity which, by saying 'myself', pronounces and posits itself.[364] In this way 'myself' is generated.

[364] 'Myself' does not express simply the *subject* but also the relationship which the subject has with itself by means of the intimate feeling and the subject's various reflections. The pronouns 'you' and 'he/she' add another relationship, because they indicate the 'myself' of a subject pronounced by a different subject. One subject in conversation with another expresses his relationship with 'you'; when the other subject is absent, the relationship is expressed with 'he/she'. — In *Rinnovamento* etc., bk.3, c. 18, I demonstrated that 'myself' is not known through itself; it is not the first thing known. Here I have also shown that 'myself' is something formed only after the use of

810. Consequently, we clearly see that

1st. a purely feeling subject exists which neither understands nor feels itself;

2nd. an intellective subject exists even before it understands itself;

3rd. a human, intellective-feeling subject exists prior to consciousness of itself;

4th. when the human subject acquires consciousness of itself by means of the various functions of its faculties, it becomes 'myself'.

811. 5th. Finally, from this process of the generation of 'myself' we can deduce an important difference between the concept of 'myself' and the concept of 'subject'. The latter is a supreme, active principle in a given individual, the foundation of the subsistence and activity of an individual. The concept of 'myself', however, consists properly speaking in having consciousness of self. Thus, if an active principle, conscious of itself, were present in a given individual, it would already be 'myself', even though it were not supreme and the individual's subsistence were to depend on some other subsistent principle in the individual. Only this other principle could fittingly be called a 'subject'.

5

COMMENTS ON HUMAN GENERATION

812. We can now make a few comments on human generation. We have already described how animal propagation and multiplication very probably take place.

Human generation exhibits the same external phenomena as the generation of other animals. It seems impossible to doubt therefore that human beings as animals are subject to animal laws of propagation. But in the human being intelligence as well as

intelligence. Therefore, a previous idea is required not only in order that 'myself' may be known, but in order that 'myself' may exist and be placed in act.

animality is present. The difficulty consists in explaining the origin of the former.

Let us recall the teaching we have established relative to our present investigation:

1st. Because the human subject is a feeling-intellective principle, it necessarily exists simultaneously with the *matter* of its feeling and with the *object* of its intelligence (being), both of which are posited simultaneously by nature;[365]

2nd. If the matter of feeling and the object of intuition ceased, the human subject and all its elements would cease;

3rd. If only the matter of feeling ceased, the human subject would change into a merely intellective subject;

4th. If, on the contrary, the object ceased, leaving only the matter, the human subject would become a purely feeling or animal *subject*.

813. Before continuing, it will be helpful to observe that, although the human subject would lose its identity if the object (being) were removed, an element would still remain despite the destruction of the human subject. The proposition has two parts:

1st. 'The feeling principle remaining after the removal of the object of intelligence (being) would not retain its identity with the preceding feeling principle.'

The truth of this will be seen by anyone who considers the relationship between the animal principle and the human principle or subject. The word 'principle' properly speaking expresses the higher, intelligent principle[366] because the intellective endowment is the substantial basis of what is human. Feeling activity, therefore, does not have the true *nature of principle* in the human being while he exists. Only the intelligent, reasoning

[365] This teaching is expressly taught by St. Thomas, who writes: 'Animal signifies that which has a feeling nature; rational is that which has an intellective nature. The human being has both' (*S.T.*, I, q. 85, art. 5, ad 3).

[366] St. Thomas says: 'The human being is that which is according to reason' (*S.T.*, III, q. 19, art. 2). The fact that the *intelligent subject* considers *sensations* while the feeling principle does not consider ideas shows the intelligent principle to be the *higher* of the two. Hence, the natural order between *sensations* and *ideas*, between feeling activity and intellective activity. Intellective activity is superior to feeling activity, that is, to sensations, which it does not form but beholds as already formed, dominating them as something different from and inferior to itself.

activity, which ceases as soon as the object is removed, has this nature. The feeling activity, which is not removed but remains alone when the object is taken away, does however take on the nature of principle because 1. there is nothing superior to it, and 2. feeling originates from it.

814. 2nd. 'Although the identity of the subject is no longer present once the natural object of the intelligent spirit has been removed from the human being, an element of it does remain.'

If we compare the human being with what remains after the hypothetical removal of the object of his intelligence, we find no change in the material feeling. It is true that this feeling cannot be called a human subject, but we are not prevented from considering it as the matter of the human subject which, in order to become a subject again, needs only the restoration of its form.

815. Granted these teachings as proven or accepted, let us see if we can successfully investigate the more general laws governing human generation. Relative to the multiplication of the animal element, the investigation, as we have said, presents no difficulty. The animal element can be understood to multiply as other animals do. The difficulty consists in explaining how this animal element, this feeling principle, is raised to the level of intellective soul,[367] and consequently to the level of a soul which survives the loss of all its corporeal matter.

Note, we are not asking how the feeling principle can, of itself and without the intervention of the Creator, rise to the level of intellective soul. Such a question would be absurd: there is no doubt that the hand of the Creator is necessary for the origin of an intelligent soul. This fact is beyond discussion. We are concerned with the beginning of a new intellective soul not relative to God who creates it, but relative to the soul that is created. We are asking 'whether in the soul placed in existence by the Creator there are any laws or steps, as it were, taken by the soul towards its complete subsistence'. We want to indicate these laws and steps.

[367] Saying that 'the feeling principle is raised to the state of intellective soul' does not mean in any way that a purely feeling principle has *preceded* the intellective soul in time. We are not dividing time-wise that which feels from that which is humanly intellective (both can in fact be contemporaneous); we are indicating precedence solely in the order of concepts.

816. Keeping within the limits of the question, we first say that what is animate is already present in nature. We have indeed attempted to give some explanation of its *multiplication* and its *movement to perfection*, but never of its *origin*. We took subsistent, animate reality as a basic fact explained only by Genesis, not by philosophy. The subsistence of the human being is another fact also explained in Genesis where we read: 'The Lord God formed man of dust from the ground, and breathed into his nostrils the breath of life; and man became a living being.'[368]

Animate reality and the *human being*, therefore, are facts. Their origin is the origin of the world. And first facts, as we know, are not explained but used in the explanation of subsequent facts.

If we now compare the *human being* and the *animal* and look for the source of the human being's superiority to the animal, we find that the former is intellective as well as feeling; intelligence is the difference between the human and animal subjects. Let us therefore investigate the nature of this difference and try to discover its ultimate composition.

We have repeatedly said that a feeling subject necessarily becomes intelligent when the intuition of being is added to it. The difference therefore consists in the *intuition* of *being* given to a human, feeling subject but not to a brute-feeling subject. Consequently, the existence of the intellective subject is created by the object when this manifests itself to the subject. If we simply keep to fact and ignore hypothesis, it is certain that simultaneously with the intuition of being we must also grant an intelligent subject in such a way that intelligence is necessarily conceived and arises contemporaneously with the vision of being. No matter how mysterious the case may be, analysis of the intelligent subject gives the following result: if *being* is removed, the intelligent subject disappears; if being is made visible, the subject returns at once. We thus arrive at an extraordinary truth, that 'ideal being has the power to manifest itself, and that its manifestation is therefore one and the same as the creation of an intuiting subject'.[369] Prior to the intuition, no principle can be assigned to the subject (unless we

[368] Gen 2: [7].

[369] In manifesting itself, being suffers no change; all change is relative to the intuiting subject.

introduce gratuitous hypotheses), but simultaneously with the intuition an intuiting and therefore intelligent principle is found.

817. Consequently, when matter and idea are removed from the principle or subject, all that remains is a kind of indeterminate possibility, that is, the first matter of which earlier writers spoke. According to them this matter, although it had not yet received any form, was capable of receiving every form; it was matter in potency, and nothing more.

Such matter certainly does not exist in itself; it is nothing, and to draw things from it is truly to draw them from nothing.

818. It may be objected that the human being, in addition to feeling and intelligence, also possesses activity, or instinct, and the feeling of this activity. But what we have said demonstrates that every activity is contained like a seed in the first act by which the subject feels and intuits.

819. We must now explain how the animal, which multiplies according to the laws of physical generation, finds the object or being on which it can gaze and so obtain the light of the intellect. The feeling principle is touched, as it were, by the object, that is, being makes itself intuited by the principle. This contact and union raises to a much higher state the feeling principle that now intuits; the principle changes its nature, becoming intellective, subsistent, immortal. In short, the principle shares the sublime qualities of the object with which it is now indivisibly united.

820. The human soul therefore is 'a feeling principle which has being in general as the term of its feeling'. Being in general is eternal and simple, outside place and time, and it is clear that the soul, united immovably to being, participates in all these noble prerogatives of being.[370]

[370] If the soul were detached from its object, it would no longer conform to the definition and would cease to be soul. It would be annihilated, and we would rightly consider its annihilation opposed to the perfections of the Creator. — Earlier teaching, which is to be found principally in the books of the Platonists, agrees with what we are saying, but it needs to be stripped of its arcane, mysterious and false language. At the beginning of 'Mysteries', attributed to Jamblicus, we read: 'Our being is to know God' (here *God* should be understood as *idea of being* because the platonic gods were ideas) 'since the principal element of the soul is its intellect, in which existence and the understanding of divine things (ideas) is a single reality having an enduring

821. The whole problem therefore is reduced to indicating the law according to which a feeling subject which has *matter* as the term of its feeling also begins to have *being in general* as the term of its feeling.

We must first bear in mind that the object of intelligence, *ideal being*, is one and the same for all human beings, who are enlightened by it.[371]

Second, we must remember that the union of being with the subject is given by nature. Human nature, therefore, which is the union of being with a feeling, corporeal principle, is also given by nature. We simply want to know how this human nature, this basic union between being and the sentient, corporeal principle, is propagated in many individuals of the same nature.

Ideal being shines as one and identical before all intelligences, which it creates, and therefore does not need to be multiplied. It is enough that the individuals of human nature, to which being is bound, are propagated and multiplied; being will then shine immediately before each new individual belonging to human nature.

Taking as basic facts that 1. being is bound to human nature,

act. The powers of the soul are derived by reasoning from this principal existence.'

[371] The *identity* of the truth known by the human understanding, was the cause of the great error of the famous Arab who 'commentary made'. He falsely argued that a single intellect is common to all human beings. But intellects are many, not because the object (being) is not the one, identical being seen by all humans, but because the subjects seeing the same object are many. Thus, everyone has a different subjective intuition of the same object. St. Thomas, who agrees with this teaching, admits the identity of the object (being, truth) seen by all human beings, but rejects the unity of the intellect suggested by the Averroists. The Saint's precision when discussing Averroes' opinion is shown by the following words: 'This opinion is true in so far as the identity of the same knowledge in teacher and pupil is considered according to the unity of the thing known: the same truth is known by both teacher and pupil. But, as we said above, the opinion is false in so far it posits one possible intellect for all human beings' (*S. T.*, I, q. 117, art. 1, corp.). The unity and identity of the truth, which is intuited by all the human beings that have existed, exist now and will exist throughout the whole world, and intuited by all the intelligences of the universe, has been demonstrated by me in *Rinnovamento* etc., bk. 3, cc. 44 and 45.

and 2. being is bound according to the *law* that every individual of this nature shall see being, it is clear that the manner of multiplication of human beings will be found as soon as we find how the individual principles of animal nature multiply.

822. Now, there can be no contradiction or difficulty in admitting that God constituted such a law from the beginning. The law was necessary if human nature was to have all it needed for development.

823. Indeed, the law constituted by God that 'being in general is always visible to every new individual issuing from human nature by means of animal generation' is fully in harmony with the customary manner of divine operation which follows fixed laws.

824. This way of conceiving the multiplication of human beings is also found to be in full accord with the words of Genesis, and with the constant opinion of Church tradition that 'in creating the first human being, God not only gave origin to an individual, but in that individual instituted the whole of human nature and the human species'. This must apparently be understood to mean that 'God, in the first operation and formation of the human being, constituted the laws which govern all human nature and the human species'.

825. This way of understanding the well-known passage in Genesis where the infusion of the soul into the human being is described (translated by the Vulgate as 'breathed into his face the breath of life')[372] conforms fully to the letter of the Hebrew text, which instead of 'the breath of life', says in the plural 'the breath of lives'. Thus the spirit infused into the first human being was intended to communicate life to others without being limited to the one life alone, just as the title 'tree of lives' was given to what was intended to preserve the lives of all the human beings who ate of its fruit.

826. This interpretation conforms, as we said, to the constant expressions of the Fathers. They apply to the origin of our soul everything God did in creating the first human being. Lactantius says: '(God) formed the body and infused the soul BY WHICH WE LIVE.'[373]

[372] Gen 2: 7 [Douai].

[373] DD. 2, 2, 12.

In the same way, St Athanasius, describing the creation of the first human being, says: 'God, maker of the world, formed through his Word the human race in his own image, and gave it (the human race) understanding, and knowledge of his eternity.'[374] And a little further on: 'Hence, the maker of things wished that the *human race* which he had founded should continue as he founded it.'[375] According to these passages, God imparted the light of the intellect not only to Adam when he created him, but at the same time and with the same act to all Adam's descendants.

St. Basil also speaks of the creation of the first ancestor as the foundation constituting human nature: 'The human being is certainly a wonderful thing; he has received something of great value from his natural constitution. Amongst the things we see on earth, what else was made in the image of the Creator?'[376] Here we see that 'human being' is taken to mean human nature, not simply one individual of this nature.

Gregory Nazianzen also sees the whole of humanity in Adam: 'Because the Creator-Word wishes to demonstrate this, he makes the human being a unique animal by uniting visible and invisible nature.'[377]

Gregory of Nyssa has written a entire treatise *on the making of the human being*, in which we clearly see how little he deals with the creation of the individual. The principal object of his meditations is human nature instituted in the first individual.

St. John Chrysostom applies to all human beings the words 'Let us make man to our image and likeness': 'Just as he said *image* because of our source, he also said *likeness*, in order that we may render ourselves like God according to human forces.'[378]

Cyril of Alexandria also speaks of Adam as human nature: 'This animal, completed by God the Creator with all the conditions proper to its own nature, was immediately endowed with the divine likeness.' And a little further: 'After losing the grace of God and being despoiled of the good with which it had been

[374] *Orat. contra gentes.*

[375] *Ibid.*.

[376] *Homilia in Psal. 48.*

[377] *Orat. 42 [45]* which is *Orat. 2 de Pascha.*

[378] *Homil. 9 in Genes.*

[826]

enriched at the beginning, ***human nature*** was banished from the paradise of delights and became deformed.'[379]

St. Augustine says expressly that the human race was 'as it were radically instituted in Adam'.[380] He says that we were all in Adam, indeed we were the single Adam, because 'if the form in which we lived as individuals was not yet individually created and distributed, nevertheless the seminal nature from which we were propagated was present.'[381] Once again, Adam was certainly a human being, but this human being 'was the whole human race'[382]. Finally, all were in Adam's loins by means of the seed.[383]

827. Eadmer, a pupil of St. Anselm, sees his own nature already formed in the likeness of God at the beginning of the world. He says: 'My (some read *our*) nature was created at the beginning in the likeness of God.'[384] In another place he says: 'As

[379] *De adorat. in spir. et verit.*, bk. 1.

[380] *De Gen. ad litt.*, bk. 6, 11.

[381] 'We were all in the one human being when we all constituted that being who fell into sin through the woman who, before sin, had been made from that being. The form in which we were to live as individuals had not yet been individually created and distributed to us. But seminal nature from which we were to be propagated existed as a nature disordered because of sin, held by the bond of death, and justly condemned. This was the only natural condition in which a human being would be born from a human being (*De Civ. Dei, 13, 14*).

[382] *In Jo. Tract.*, 11, 2 [10, 11].

[383] 'By means of the seed, human beings were in the loins of Adam when he was condemned. Thus, he was not condemned without them. Just as the Israelites were in the loins of Abraham when he was chosen, so Abraham was not chosen without them.' In order to show that he drew his teaching from Scripture, he continues against Julian: 'Those who said these things knew better than you the meaning of the seed, and were careful to send letters to be read in the Church of Christ, where those born of Adam are reborn, lest they remain condemned in that line' (*Op. imperf. contra Jul.*, 5, 12). He repeats this in many other places. The following will serve as an example: 'The (children) also acted in this parent because they were in him when he acted; he and they were still one. Thus, they did not act as human beings do, but by reason of their seed. You try to hide what has been said so clearly by him who wrote: "As sin came into the world through one man and death through sin, and so death spread to all men because all men sinned". He knew that what is sometimes seen in diseases of the body had been perpetrated in that ancient, great sin of the one first parent, in that sin by which the whole of human nature was disordered' (*Op. imperf. contra Jul.*, 2, 177 [5, 12]).

[384] *De excell. Mar. Virg.*, c. 9).

we show that (human nature) must have been created in justice, so we show that those who might have been propagated without a preceding sin would necessarily receive justice simultaneously with rationality. For it is clear that he who created the first human being without parental generation, also creates all those who are to be propagated from that first parent by means of created nature.'[385]

828. Moreover, theologians generally argue to the gifts and knowledge with which God must have endowed Adam from the fact that Adam was not only an individual but also head of the human race.[386]

829. But St. Paul himself, even before the Fathers and theologians, sees human nature founded in the first human being: all descendants are in the first human being in whom, he says, all have sinned and all have died.[387]

Hence, Catholic doctrine consistently teaches that human nature itself sinned in Adam and fell in the first parent.[388] If the first

[385] *De conceptu. Vir. et orig. pecc.*, c. 10.

[386] Alexander of Hales uses this argument where he says: 'Adam had full knowledge. If it is fitting for God to carry out perfect works, how much more fitting is it to make perfect in nature him who is the origin of the whole race and, in a certain way, the end of all?' (*Summa*, part 2, q. 92). A little further on he calls Adam 'father, beginning and seedbearer of the whole human race'. St. Thomas also shows that our first parents had to be taught by God. He begins from the principle that 'the first parents were instructed by God not only as individual persons but as the beginnings of all the human nature which was passed on from them to their descendants' (*S.T.*, II-II, q. 164, art. 1, ad 3). This is the common teaching of all Catholic theologians.

[387] Rom 5: [12]; [1] Cor 15: [22].

[388] 'Life, damaged by various passions, came to a human nature initially and totally bereft of divine benefits and destined to corruptible death. Erring (human nature), having turned from following the right road that leads to him who is truly God, became subject to the lost and evil throngs. It was scarcely aware that it had gone after pestilential enemies as gods and friends' (*De Eccles. Hier.*, c. 3, p. 3 [2]). St. Justin says that 'the human race . . . fell through Adam into death and the deception and seduction of the serpent' (*Dial. cum Triph.*). But the clearest statements relative to our proposition are the many places in St. Augustine where he comments on and explains the two passages of St. Paul that we have quoted. For example, he says: 'Moreover, this clear and fully authoritative opinion is contained in the sacred canonical books. The Apostle proclaims: "Sin came into the world through one man, and death through sin, and so death spread to all men because all men sinned." Thus, it

parent sinned and human nature fell in him, that is, all human beings perished in Adam, why should we not believe that all are founded in him and begin to exist in virtue of that very act of creation by which God made and gave life to the first parent? We are not saying that all human beings existed at that time; we are saying they come into existence in virtue of that act.

I believe that the law I am discussing was established in the act (the single breath of life) mentioned by Genesis when it says God breathed the breath of life into the figure formed of earth. By this law, ideal being, the intellective light, is united to every individual of human nature. Here we have the origin of intelligence, the creation of all the intelligent souls that inform new individuals at the moment of their generation.

830. This explains why Job in his search for the origin of human intelligence turns to the first breath of life. When he says: 'There is a spirit in men, and the inspiration of the Almighty gives understanding',[389] he is obviously referring to the Genesis account of the animation of the first human being.

In the breath of life mentioned in Genesis, the Fathers also see and admit the principle of intelligence, not only of Adam but of all human beings without exception.

St Basil says: 'Human beings possess a power by which they can know and understand their Creator and Maker. The Creator *breathed into him*, that is, added to the human being a part of his own grace so that by means of this likeness formed in him the human being might know him to whom he had been made alike.'[390]

cannot be said that Adam's sin did not harm sinners, when Scripture says: "because all men sinned"' (*De peccator. merit. et remiss.*, 3, 7). 'For sin came into the world through one human being, and death through sin, and so death spread to all because all sinned. Through the evil will of one human being all sinned in him when all were that one human being. From him therefore they have each contracted original sin' (*De nupt. et concup.*, 2, 5). 'Cease to proclaim vain things. All those who were not yet born could certainly do neither good nor evil through their own wills, but they could sin in the one human being in whom they were present by reason of the seed. When he with his own will perpetrated the great sin and disorder, he changed and damaged both himself and human nature. Understand if you can, but if not, believe' (*Op. imperf. contra Jul.*, 4, 104. Cf. *De peccator. et remiss.*, 1, 10).

[389] Job 32: [8 (Douai)].

[390] *Hom. in Psal.*, 48.

St. Gregory Nazianzen also explains the breath of life as intellectual light added immovably to human nature.[391]

Gregory of Nyssa observes that, just as the *matter* of human nature was instituted when God made the figure from earth, so the *form* was given in the breath.[392] John Damascene, following the steps of the earliest authors, is careful to explain the origin of the material and spiritual parts of the human being in the same way.[393]

Let us conclude. The constant opinion of Church tradition is that when God created the first human being, he laid down the unchangeable, constituent elements of human nature. One of these constituent elements is that every individual of human nature intuits being. Thus, when the Almighty breathed the breath of life into the first human being, he simultaneously enacted the law that 'ideal being be manifested to every new individual of the human species'. He then willed that multiplication of human individuals should take place through the action of humans themselves by means of generation. Thus, the statement that after six days 'he rested from all the work he had done' is completely verified.[394]

831. Two causes, therefore, concur simultaneously in the generation of a new individual of the human race: the human being with generation, and God with the manifestation of his light. The human being posits the animal, and God creates the intelligent soul at the very moment the human animal is posited. He makes the soul intelligent by enlightening it with the splendour of his face and sharing with it part of himself, ideal being, light of all intelligent creatures.

391 'When the Maker wished to manifest the Word, therefore, he formed this single animal into a human being from visible and invisible nature. The body of the human being is formed from matter previously produced, and the Creator breathes into it the breath which Scripture calls the image of God and the intellectual soul. He places a large world, as it were, on our little earth' (*Orat. 42 [45], quae est orat. 2 de Pascha*).

392 'The MATTER of the creature is first prepared and his FORM designed to show an exemplar of outstanding beauty. Then the Creator makes a nature similar to himself and like him in its in actions (*De hominis opificio*, c. 3).

393 *De fide orthod.*, bk. 2, c. 12.

394 Gen 2: [2].

6

PERSON

832. Person can be defined as 'an intelligent subject'. A more exact definition would be: 'Person is a substantial, intelligent individual in so far as the individual contains a supreme, active and incommunicable principle.'

833. If we compare this definition with the definition we have given of subject, we see that the words 'subject' and 'person' express the intrinsic order of being in a feeling individual. They each have for their foundation a *relationship* between the intrinsic principle (on which the subsistence and all activity of the individual depend) and everything else in the individual that is supported and activated by the principle.[395]

It is true that not everything in a substantial individual constitutes properly speaking subject or person, but, as I said, subject and person are founded on the *supreme principle* within the individual. Other elements, which can indeed form part of the individual itself, pertain to subject or person only through the very close connection they have with the supreme principle, in virtue of which they subsist and together with which they form a single individual.

Hence, just as we call 'subject' that which is a supreme principle of activity in any feeling individual whatsoever, intelligent or not, so we call 'person' that which is the supreme principle in an intelligent individual. Thus, the difference between subject and person is the difference between genus and species because we take feeling in the most universal sense, which includes understanding (understanding can be reduced to a special kind of feeling). Person, therefore, is a class of the most noble of subjects, the intellective.[396]

[395] Hence, 'person' cannot mean simply either a *substance* or a *relationship*. It must mean a *substantial relationship*, that is, a relationship found in the *intrinsic order of being* of a substance.

[396] St. Thomas says that 'person means that which is most perfect in all nature, and subsists in a rational nature' (*S.T.*, I, q. 29, art. 3, corp.). He shows how the word 'person', originally meaning a mask used by actors in the theatres, came to mean human beings constituted in dignity. He says: 'Because actors

834. The definition also indicates the other properties of person. Person must be:

1st. A substance.

2nd. An individual, and therefore pertaining to real, not purely ideal things.

3rd. Intelligent.

4th. An active principle — 'activity' here should be understood in its widest sense, which in a way includes passivity. Person is the principle to which, as the ultimate source, all the individual's passivity and activity is referred.

5th. A supreme principle, such that nothing is present in the individual which is superior to this principle and changes its existence. If other principles are present, they must depend on the supreme principle and subsist in the individual through their bond with the individual.

835. Note that the personal principle is called supreme not because it must have other principles below it, but because it excludes any principle above it. The word 'supreme' could give the impression of having something below it since it seems to imply a relationship with something lower. But to call supreme that which could in fact be unique cannot be unacceptable — 'first', for example, can mean one without reference to others. However, 'supreme' could be substituted by 'independent', or something similar.

836. 6th. *Incommunicable* — this is a consequence of the preceding properties, and in a way is understood in the notion of individual. An individual cannot communicate itself without ceasing to be the individual it was. The incommunicability of subject and person must be understood in this way.

837. We see from all these facts that person is not absolutely and necessarily identical with that which is expressed by the word 'myself'. There is a marked difference, a difference of concept, between person and 'myself', just as there is a difference between 'subject' and 'myself'.

It is true that 'myself' principally expresses an intelligent

played the parts of famous people in comedies and tragedies, the word "person" was applied to those who had this dignity. — And because subsisting as a reasoning nature is a great dignity, every individual of reasoning nature is called "person"' (*S.T.*, I, q. 29, 3, ad 2).

subject, and we use the word solely to mean our own personality, of which we are conscious. For this reason 'I' is called a personal pronoun. But if we consider the matter carefully, we can without contradiction imagine in an individual an intellective principle which is conscious of itself without its being a supreme principle. The word 'I', but not 'person', could be correctly applied to this principle.

7

THE HUMAN PERSON

838. In the human being the *intellective* (rational) *subject* and *person* are therefore the same thing. The intellective principle, which does not differ from the volitive principle, is that which is supreme and most excellent in human nature.

In brute animals the feeling, instinctive principle constitutes the *subject*. There is nothing above this principle in brute animals, there is nothing on which it depends; it is truly a *principle*. The whole activity of the brute animal begins from this principle, and its subsistence is grounded in it. In the human being, however, the principle, which is the highest point of his existence, is properly speaking intellective rather than simply sensitive; feeling is added only as a kind of instrument, something which serves, a means to an end, the matter of knowledge.

We must now look more closely at the way everything in the human being adheres and is joined to the final principle, 'human person', which constitutes the summit, as it were, of human nature. We have already touched upon the topic, but here we must reconsider human unity and its order.

Article 1.
The physical bond between the human person and his powers

839. The human being, whom Cicero rightly calls a *multiple animal*, is multiple in his actions, attitudes, external

appearance, and the different forms of his nature. It is a source of unending wonder that the unity of this nature can offer such inequality, be almost infinite in its variations, and exhibit new aspects and characteristics in individuals, in societies at all times and places, in diverse races, climates, levels of development, qualities and events. This multiplicity of forms undoubtedly presupposes multiple powers which themselves manifest a multiplicity of actions, habits and conditions. However, all this multiplicity can be reduced to a few principles, and ultimately to a single principle, *person*, the pinnacle of human nature.

840. Earlier we listed the *principles of action* found in human nature. We said that, in addition to the material forces, they are five: life instinct, sensuous instinct, human instinct, will and freedom. We showed how the subordination of these principles, effected by a dynamic bond, enabled the feeling instinct to modify the life instinct, and the human instinct to modify the feeling, while the will controls the human instinct, and freedom inclines and bends the will to one of two possible contrary volitions. And because we can be conscious of all these subordinate activities, the principle of consciousness (which is consciousness of our person) informs us that they are all moved indirectly (not directly) by ourselves. Thus, when we act freely, the first activity emanating from us is free activity, which makes all the other activities obedient to it.

The fact that we cannot move our lower powers directly, and indeed are obliged to move and control them by means of their link with the neighbouring powers, reveals a related truth: the lower powers are not, properly speaking, ourselves (our person) although they are so closely bound with us that they form a single *individual*. We must therefore distinguish *powers* from *principles of action*.

841. All principles of action are powers, but not all powers are principles of action. We call *principles of action* those powers which govern a complete genus of activity and constitute the active principle of the genus. Different principles of action can be joined together in one individual, as in the case of the human being. But although joined together and subordinate to a supreme activity, they do not cease to have an activity of their own.

842. Consequently, the different principles of action united in

one individual operate in two ways: of themselves, according to the laws of their own nature, or moved by the supreme principle. If they act of themselves without the intervention of the supreme principle, their acts are simply *natural*. But if they are moved by the supreme principle, their acts are called *personal*. Hence, in the human being, acts are *natural* and *personal*.

843. We should, however, bear in mind that person can intervene in two ways in the actions of the active principles below it: either by *moving* them to act or by *permitting* them to act with its consent. In both cases, there is personal action, but in the second case personal action is merely by consent, an act chosen by the will; in the first, personal action is one of force, an act of command, involving the practical force.

844. This *physical* or (if we prefer) *dynamic* superiority of person over the other active principles is *natural*, that is, intrinsic to its nature independently of its good or evil acts. Hence, when the human will gives in to the attractions and charms of the appetite, the will does not lose its nature, which is essentially superior to the appetite. Remorse, on the other hand, arises in the human being because he was aware of degrading and subordinating himself when he should have been in command.

We can support our argument by another observation. The instinct can never move the will by command or violence. Like one who invites and begs, it can only use bland persuasion, imposing no action forcibly. Consequently, if the will, by refusing to move, did not respond to the invitation, the instinct could not move it in any way whatsoever. On the other hand, if the will moves, the instinct cannot prevent the movement unless the will consents to immobility. In the case of the instinct, however, the direct opposite is true: the will commands it imperiously, forcibly and firmly opposing the instinct's first movements, which it suppresses. Hence, even when the animal instinct manages to influence the will, it does so only in a servile way, never as a master. The will, however, is the master of the instinct, and makes it obey forcefully, not by persuasion. Early authors expressed this double aspect of command by two words, with which we can terminate our discussion. The kind of control exercised by the animal appetite on the will was called *diplomatic*; the control exercised by the will, *despotic*. We see here the natural superiority of the will over instinct.

845. Let us now attempt to determine more exactly the proper seat of person in the human individual.

When the human being first exists, the five principles of action observable in him are not as distinct from one another as we have made them. They can in fact be reduced to two: the principle of subjective action and the principle of objective action. The three instincts, life, sensuous and human, are reduced to the first; will and freedom to the second. In fact, every action either begins spontaneously from the subject, or is aroused by the object. The fundamental feeling is the basis of the innate subjective principle; the intuition of being the basis of the innate objective principle.

In the case of all the other powers, Condillac's opinion that they are not innate can be accepted as true. These powers are not distinguished in the essence of the human being, but become distinct according to the different way in which the primitive, innate principles operate.

846. With the principles of human nature reduced to two, it is clear that person as innate can exist only in the second, that is, in the *principle of objective action*, and that person itself is susceptible of the same development and modifications as the principle of objective action.

Article 2.
The moral bond

847. So far we have discussed the bond between the lower, active principles and the human person, a bond that is real, powerful and *physical.* But there is also a *moral bond*, a bond which by right entails a superiority of person over all the other powers of human nature.

848. This moral excellence and superiority by right, which elevates the human person above the whole of nature, must have the same source as all morality and right. This source is the light of reason, the source of right and of moral good and evil.

The will, therefore, is more noble than the other powers because it acts in virtue of knowledge and follows the light of reason.

849. Freedom, or the power of inclining the will to one or other of two opposites, is, considered physically, the natural master of the will. It is also more excellent than the will when considered morally, that is, considered simply as a power, not yet issuing in acts of virtue. And because the will in this state is determined neither to good nor evil, freedom is able to determine it to good. If the will receives its degree of excellence from its being ordered to follow the light of reason, freedom receives its excellence from being ordered to move the will towards the fullness of the light of reason. Hence the moral dignity of freedom as a principle of moral good and merit.

850. Moreover, it is clear that the moral superiority of freedom is independent of freedom's good or evil acts, because the excellence we are discussing comes to freedom not from good acts but from the *ability* to do good acts, from being born to do them, as their cause.

8

THE PERFECTING OF PERSON AND THE PERFECTING OF NATURE

851. All the powers forming part of an individual constitute the individual's *nature*, but the individual's person is constituted by the most noble power and highest active principle, that is, the rational power.

852. Nature, therefore, can be said to increase in perfection every time the powers it contains are perfected. But we cannot say that person is perfected unless the highest and noblest of the active principles present in the individual where person resides is increased and perfected.

853. It is this difference between the perfecting of nature and the perfecting of person that makes many err in their judgments and speculation about movement towards human perfection. People sometimes show enthusiasm for things which perfect human nature but do not improve the human person. This is an illusion which draws human beings to boast about things which are not their own.

This discussion deserves further development because it offers a key to the explanation of a great many facts about humanity, and presents true criteria for appraising the different states of the human race and the different kinds and levels of civilization. Under its guidance we ultimately come to know how morality alone perfects human beings as persons. However, such a development would take me too far out of my way. It is sufficient to have indicated a principle whose consequences and applications I will show more appropriately elsewhere.

9

THE DIFFERENCES BETWEEN WHAT IS PERSONAL AND WHAT IS MORAL

854. I shall omit discussion on the general perfectibility of human *nature* and confine myself to the question of the perfection possible to the human person. But we must first compare that which is *personal* with that which is *moral*, noting carefully the differences.

Article 1.
The close relationship between that which is *personal* and that which is *moral*

855. I have said that morality consists in a relationship of the will with the moral law (cf. 574-478). Hence, there can be no actual morality unless there is 1. an individual intelligence sufficiently developed to evaluate the objective value of things, and 2. an individual will. But an intelligent, volitive individual presupposes person. A very close bond, therefore, exists between morality and person.

Article 2.
Differences of concept between what is *moral* and what is *personal*

§1. First difference

856. We must establish a difference of concept between what is *personal* and what is *moral*. That which is *moral* concerns only the relationship of the will with the law, whereas that which is *personal* includes the concept of the supremacy of the active principle.

§2. Second difference

857. We must also distinguish *person* from the *principle* which *causes* morality. The concept of what is personal is formed in part also by *passivity*; person acts but also experiences, that which acts is itself that which experiences. On the other hand, mere experience on the part of person cannot constitute a cause of morality. Nothing moral exists in the human being as person without its being produced through co-operation from some movement or at least inclination of person, that is, without some degree of personal activity.[397]

858. The experiences of person can be called *personal experiences*, but not *personal acts*, although they can be *acts* of the nature to which person belongs. For example, if the sensuous instinct delights the will, we would have an *act on the part of human nature* and an *experience on the part of the human person*.

[397] Hence, when St. Thomas is investigating the difference between *punishment* as evil and *fault* as evil, he says that the former harms *person*, while the latter harms person in its *action*. Hence, some action is supposedly always present in fault. He says: 'The concept of punishment includes that which harms an agent in itself; the concept of fault, however, includes that which harms the agent IN ITS ACTION' (*S.T.*, I, q. 48, art. 5, ad 4). Note, what he says here about the *agent* he says expressly elsewhere about person (cf. *S.T.*, I-II, q. 21, art. 1, ad 3).

§3. Third difference

859. Furthermore, the conditions proper to *personal* acts are not always moral. To be moral they must be part of the bond between the will and the law, where alone *morality* is located (cf. 856). Certain conditions of person relate not to the law but to person simply as supreme, active principle. The following considerations will clarify my thought.

From the first moments of human existence, human personality has its seat in the objective principle of action, and develops with this principle. We have already described the important developments of the objective principle; we said that the will acts spontaneously first by co-operating with the animal instinct and then with the human instinct. Finally, when it begins to distinguish the objective value of things, its action takes on a new and much more noble form: freedom. All these phases to which the will's action is subject form part of the subjective principle and its development.

As long as the will is in the first phase, its action is certainly less noble than that of the second or third phase. Nevertheless, its action is personal, not because its operating principle is objective, but because the activity by which it acts is the most excellent of all its possible activities at the time.

We can say the same about the second phase. When the objective principle has reached this level of development, everything the will does is carried out by its noblest and highest activity, thus acquiring the characteristic of personal activity.

Finally, the third phase, more excellent than the other two, follows the same process.

860. However, this is not sufficient, because the following universal law regarding the action of person must be kept in mind: 'In any particular act whatsoever, person always uses the noblest activity it can dispose of at the time.'

For example, let us suppose that the objective principle in which person is located is fully developed and has reached the phase of freedom. If a human being has reached this state of freedom, he can only act freely; he cannot, for instance, use some kind of lower activity, nor act solely in accord with the law of spontaneity. He must act freely, and do so because freedom is his supreme activity in act. In other words, he must act freely because person, in its mode of action, is governed by this law: it must always act with its most sublime activity, granted the necessary conditions for positing its action.

861. Person, therefore, considered in its *potentiality*, is located in the objective principle. But considered in its *exercise*, it is located in the finest activity emanating from the objective principle, granted the necessary conditions for drawing this activity into act.

862. This development through different states and acts dependent on varying conditions does not render person morally better or evil. Here we have another difference between that which is merely *personal* and that which is *moral*. This difference shows that everything modifying person does not directly and essentially modify the moral state of the human being.

863. The same observations can be made about the development that the will and freedom receive from the corresponding development of the understanding, which moves from an order of lower reflections to an order of higher reflections. Now, because the will is 'the principle which acts according to knowledge', it is certain that a higher activity on the part of the will corresponds to every higher order of reflections. This, too, is an application of the law that the human being acts with whatever activity corresponds to the highest of his actual reflections. However, although acting according to an order of higher or lower reflections does in fact determine a particular state and mode of personal action, such action does not pertain directly and essentially to morality. Moral good and evil can be found at its highest level in every order of reflections and in every corresponding activity of the will.

§4. Fourth difference

864. From all I have said we can infer a fourth and last difference between that which is moral and that which is simply personal.

The personal element is innate, and accompanies the human being from the first moment of his existence until the end of his life. On the other hand, the *moral act* (we are speaking about act, not habit) does not manifest itself either in the first or second phase of the will's action, but only in the third.

In the first two forms of human action, the human being tends solely to eudaimonological good. He does not yet know moral good, because he does not know the objective value of beings. This does not mean, however, that we can deny person in first human acts; the personal principle should be sought in every single action provided it is intellective.

The supreme, intellective activity which operates in every single action has its origin in the objective principle, and is supreme in that one action. Hence, it is also the foundation of person; it is personal. It is certainly true that moral reasons have not appeared at this stage in the human mind, but as we said, although they make person moral, they do not constitute it in its being as person.

10

THE MORAL VALUE OF ACTIONS

865. The moral good or evil of an action constitutes the moral value of actions. In other words, an action has value in proportion to its moral good, and lack of value in proportion to its moral evil.

As we have said, moral good consists in the will's adhesion to the law, or in willing good according to the objective order of beings. Moral evil, on the other hand, consists in disharmony between the will and the law, or in not willing good according to the known objective order of beings.

When the will adheres to beings according to their objective order, it shares, as fully as the objective order requires, in the entity to which it adheres, and thus wonderfully ennobles itself.[398] On the other hand, the will that refuses to adhere to the

[398] St. Thomas explains this increase in good, acquired by adherence to the law, by showing precisely that such adherence makes us share more abundantly in *being*: 'The good and evil of actions is the same as the good and evil in things because each thing produces an action according to its being. Things

known objective order of beings lacks good, and so deforms itself.

866. We need to note that the beauty and dignity of a good will, and the deformity and ugliness of an evil will, can be called infinite, because being in its order, with which good will ennobles itself, is characterised by infinite good, while opposition to this being is characterised by infinite evil.[399]

867. Such great moral good or evil embellishes or disfigures the volitive, personal principle producing the good or evil, and is different from every other good and evil which may be added to the human being independently of his will. This latter kind of good and evil does not make the human will and person good or evil, although it can help or harm his nature.[400]

868. Finally, when the will makes itself good by following the objective order of beings, it raises itself to eternal things, because the order of beings is eternal. From this height it rules supreme over all temporal things. Enthroned on the object, the will rules over the subject, that is, over itself and its own nature. Adhering to the object in this way, the will now receives a new, divine power and finds in the object itself the means for attaining a more sublime activity. Thus, the personal principle raises itself to a new level, as it were, because it is the supreme activity manifested in willed actions.

have as much good as they have being, because being and good are interchanged (one is taken for the other) — Hence, an action ceases to be good and is called evil in so far as it lacks the fullness of being proper to it (such as the quantity or place assigned to it by reason)' (*S.T.*, I-II, q. 18, art. 1, corp.).

[399] St. Thomas touches upon the explanation for the supreme value of morally good actions when he says: 'The evil which is punishment removes the creature's good. — But the evil which is fault is properly speaking opposed to uncreated good. — It is clear therefore that fault is of its nature more evil than punishment' (*S.T.*, I, q. 48, art. 6, corp.).

[400] This is expressed by St. Thomas in the following terms: 'Because good consists simply in act and not in potency, and the last act is the action or use of anything whatsoever we possess, human good is to be found simply in good action or good use of things possessed. But we use everything through our will. Hence a human being is said to be good according to the good will with which he uses what he possesses. — Because fault consists in a disordered act of the will, while punishment consists in the deprivation of any of the things the will uses, fault is by nature more perfectly evil than punishment' (*S.T.*, I, q. 48, art. 6, corp.).

869. It is true that there is some kind of good in evil itself, a good worthy of the devil — a kind of wicked enjoyment, I mean, which the intelligent spirit finds in the use of its freedom, despising all *obstacles*, the nature of things, the law and the Creator.[401] Rebelling in this way against being and objective good, the intelligent spirit can experience a feeling of proud activity, a crazy, credulous confidence in challenging everything, even the infinite, and in setting itself above every power, above God himself. This miserable exercise of its freedom contains a human feeling of power, a monstrous form of greatness; the very experience of this mortal exultation is a kind of good. But it is equally true that this good does not compensate for the infinite evil accompanying it; just as this good experienced in the subject's nature does not render the person good but simply guilty.

Yet the fascination of such a good did not seduce Lucifer alone. Many facts of human history, especially the fury with which limitless freedom of every form and species is sought and pursued, can only be explained by this mad desire to experience the delight of an unbridled exercise of freedom. Such formless freedom of human nature is ultimately the most oppressive enslavement of the human person.

11

THE IMPUTABILITY OF ACTIONS

Article 1.
The difference between what is *moral* and what is *imputable*

870. Imputability, as we understand it, pertains to moral actions. To impute an action means to attribute the action to the agent who as its cause produces it.

We have seen that the moral agent is the volitive, personal principle: the will is the cause of actions conforming to or deviating from the law. We must remember, however, that the will

[401] That is, provided the Creator preserves the spirit and allows it to act.

operates in two ways: with spontaneous movement or also with free movement. In both cases moral good or evil can be present. In the preceding chapter, we saw that the conditions required for moral good are two only: 1. a moral law known by the will, and 2. a will knowing and adhering to the law — the opposite is moral evil. Only willed activity, therefore, not free activity, is required for the existence of moral good and evil.

This teaching on the essence of moral good and evil accords fully with the dogmas of Christianity which alone made it known by teaching that in the human being moral evil exists prior to the exercise of freedom, and consists in a virtual aversion from the law and from God. Christianity also teaches that in a baby regenerated by baptism, which removes original sin by infusing the Saviour's grace, moral good exists prior to and independently of the exercise of freedom .

871. Granted therefore that moral good and evil is present whenever the will is properly or evilly disposed relative to the law, is it also true that every moral good and evil is imputable to the person in whom it exists? I say 'to the person in whom it exists' because the sin transmitted from parent to child in human generation is undoubtedly *imputable* relative to the will of the first parent who was its free cause. It is also certain that the moral good of a baptised human being must be imputed to the Redeemer's merits. Our question therefore is: 'Must the moral good and evil present in a person who is not its free cause be imputed to this person?'

In attempting a reply to this difficult question, we first have to concede that the good or evil we correctly call *natural* must equally be called *personal*, because such good or evil truly affects the person, that is, the supreme, objective principle, the will. But saying that this good and evil is *personal* is quite different from saying that it is truly *imputable* to the individual person in whom it is present.

At this point, it will be helpful if we recall the definition we gave of imputability. We said that to impute a moral action means attributing it to the cause which produced it. We need to see, therefore, whether the will or person can truly be called the cause of an action which it cannot avoid. To do this, let us consider the elements which give rise to the force which necessarily produces in the will and person the good and evil under discussion. We need only recall what has already been said about the movements and laws according to which the will moves.

For the will to move and incline necessarily to moral good or evil, it must first be stimulated by some good or bad instinct. But stimulation of the instincts, no matter how powerful, is never a complete, necessitating cause of the will. The cause becomes complete when the will cedes and consents to the instinct's invitations. But this consent of the will is spontaneous, not free (which would be contrary to the hypothesis). Hence, consent comes about in virtue of the natural laws of spontaneity, which we discussed earlier. The elements of the force which necessarily inclines the will, therefore, are two: 1. the pressure of instincts; 2. the laws of spontaneity. A consideration of these two elements shows that relative to both, the will and person is passive, not active.

In the case of the first element, it is clear that the will and person is passive, because the instinct stimulating the will is foreign to the will upon which the instinct exercises its influence.

In the case of the second element, the laws of spontaneity proceed from the same nature which constitutes the will, and are therefore unchangeable. Their cause is not the will but the Author of the will and of nature. The will does not have authority over these laws; it can only be governed by them and submit to them obediently. The will, therefore, is still passive, and totally passive relative to these laws which are firmly imposed on it.[402]

The will, although passive relative to the two elements which constitute the full cause of necessary moral good and evil, is not the cause of necessary good and evil. Necessary good or evil cannot be imputed to the will and person, because, as we said, to impute an action is simply to attribute it to the cause from which the action proceeds.[403]

[402] Earlier thinkers distinguished two kinds of operation of the will, calling the first 'will as nature', and the second 'will as reason'. St. John Damascene names the first [θεληοις], and the second [βουληοις] (Bk. 2). Cf. St. Thomas, *S.T.*, III, q. 18, art 3.

[403] It should be carefully noted that the will cannot be called simply a cause of action unless it is a *first cause* not determined by a preceding cause. It must

The will and person, therefore, may not be the first cause of necessary moral good and evil (which consequently cannot be imputed to it). Nevertheless good and evil can be called and truly are *personal*. As we have seen, the will and person can be the subject of both actions and experiences; it can be in a state of passivity and activity. But in order to be the *cause* of moral good and evil, the will must be active, and in order to be sufficiently active, it must be free (cf. 857). Imputability, therefore, is a consequence of freedom. Bilateral freedom, however, does not constitute person as such, although it does constitute the truly active person by providing person with the noble qualification 'cause'.

Article 2.
The difference between a will that first chooses good and a will necessitated to good

872. Let us further clarify the concept of a will *necessitated* to good. For the will to be truly necessitated to good, we must suppose that the movements determining it are greater than the forces the will can use to oppose the movements. Thus, a necessitated will presents the concept of a will weaker than the necessitating forces. This weakness in face of the necessitating forces can be caused by different circumstances, which we have discussed elsewhere.

One of these circumstance is the limited development of the understanding. The will is always limited to the good presented to it by understanding and feeling. Thus, if only one good were presented, the will could not compare this good with another. As a result the will would necessarily be determined towards that good through one of the laws of spontaneity which naturally incline it to good. If more than one purely subjective good were presented, the will would be necessitated to the greatest of them, according to another law of spontaneity which directs the will to the greatest good.

Only when an objective good is presented in contrast with a

be the cause of determination and choice between contrary volitions.

subjective good, does the will master the laws of spontaneity and become free. But even in this state of intellectual development, another circumstance can necessitate it. If the subjective good attracting the will stimulates it so intensely that time for reflection is denied, the will's weakness then arises from this delay in reflection.

A third circumstance which renders the will comparatively weak is force of instinct and the attraction of some good which exceeds the will's strength.

In all these three cases in which the will either does not know the objective good, or is too slow to reflect on it, or is intrinsically weak when confronted with the attractions of subjective good, a defect or limitation in the human person is present.

873. Objective good, as an idea, never necessitates, but absolute good, that is, God, necessarily determines the will when he fully communicates himself, as he does to those in heaven. This necessitated determination of the will does not suppose any defect in the person so necessitated, who in fact is elevated by the communication of divine nature.

874. If we consider the question from all points of view, we can conceive the case in which God makes the actual vision of himself dependent on the will of a being. In this case, God, united continuously with the being, could be either contemplated or not by the being. Although the being which actually contemplates God must love him exceedingly, such a being would first have the power of placing itself in this state of necessity or not . Hence, no contradiction is involved in having a person who was free (or not free if it so pleased him), particularly in the first moment of his existence.

875. In this first moment of existence, the person could freely decide for good, that is, to do the will of God. And in order to do God's will he could decide to grant or not grant to himself a greater or lesser amount of the vision of God present to him. An ability of this kind would, however, be an entirely gratuitous gift of God. In this case, although the person is always determined to good in virtue of the first, absolute determination enduring in him, we could not say that he would be necessitated. In fact, everything he did would depend on an act of his wise, most powerful and completely free will.

Article 3.
Various ways in which the will and person can be the cause of the imputation of moral good and evil

876. Moral good or evil not *caused* by the will, or person, cannot be imputed to it; properly speaking it cannot cause such good or evil unless 1. it is free; 2. the action depends upon it; and 3. it is not only passive, but truly active. The will is passive, not active, if its action depends on an overpowering, superior agent and it is not the first agent on which the existence of the action's proximate cause depends.

All the other elements, therefore, that come to constitute the full, proximate cause of the action must depend on the will if the good or evil is to be imputable to to it.

877. But because this *dependence* can vary, there are various ways in which moral good and evil can be caused by the will and person, to whom, as a result, moral good and evil can be imputed.

Indeed the lower, active principles, the instincts, sometimes act in complete independence of free will, as in sleep and mental alienation. These cases cannot be imputed to the will because it is not the first constitutive element of their cause. The will and person are passive; these are events happening in us without our involvement. This extraordinary phenomenon was not considered to any great extent by ancient philosophy. It was discovered by Christianity, which called attention to a fact as profound as it is certain.

878. However, although the will plays no positive role in the actions of the instincts, it can sometimes be present like a spectator at a play. In this situation two conditions can obtain: first, the will finds itself so totally weak that all its own activity is exhausted simply by looking dazed at the action before it which it can neither accept nor reject. If this state is not of its own making, the will cannot be said to cause whatever is being carried out in its presence by sudden, overpowering instinct.

879. Second, the will can make a judgment and either reprove or approve the instinctive actions. Finding itself with a certain degree of activity, the will is obliged to disapprove what is base,

and to master all that is happening in the human individual. It cannot remain indifferent, without at least some defect.

880. The will can of course approve the instinct and consent to its disordinate act. In this case, even if the will does not contribute with its energy nor incite the instinct positively to act, it becomes guilty of consent by allowing the instinct free rein. But if the will's energies extend no further than disapproving what the instinct does, without being able to oppose the actions of instinct, it is not obliged to anything more, although it is defective.

881. However, the will can be strong enough not only to disapprove the instincts' disordinate movements but to resist them. In this case its power, which had previously extended solely to chosen acts, extends to acts of command. When the will finds within itself forces enabling it to oppose the forces of an instinct which arises independently, a struggle takes place between will and instinct. If the will makes use of all its forces, but still cannot immediately subjugate the instinct, the result must be ascribed to the instinct, not the will.

If the will is seduced by the instinct and acts according to the laws of spontaneity, the theories we have stated above should be applied. We should see whether freedom to resist was still possible for the will, or whether it had to give way, as happens apparently in certain first movements. In this case the will, which does not reflect on the law during the act, can be called a *rational*, but not a *moral power*.[404]

On the other hand, if the will is positively active, and provides the impulse for the instinct, it is clearly the cause of all the effects which proceed from this initial impulse and were understood or foreseen by the will.

882. Actions imputable to the *will* are certainly imputable to *person*.

883. Consequently, what has been said elsewhere seems true: three relationships can be distinguished between the will and the active principles subordinate to it: a relationship of 1. diversity,

[404] Not all passive movements, it must be noted, are merely *animal*; some are human or *rational*, like those caused by the knowledge or intellective apprehension of something (for example, an imminent danger or news of a disaster).

when subordinate principles act without any intervention at all from the will; 2. opposition, when a struggle takes place between the subordinate principles and the will; 3. concord, when subordinate principles act in harmony with the will.

In the first two cases a division exists between person and nature, because the actions of the lower principles, unknown or opposed to the will, cannot be called *personal*. On the other hand, when all the active principles subject to the will are in harmony, a perfect, personal unity is found in the human being, and all actions, including those directly proceeding from the lowest active principle, must rightly be called 'personal'.[405]

Article 4.
The difference between *moral* good and *praiseworthy* good

884. All that we have discussed so far indicates that we must distinguish between good which is simply *moral* and good which is *imputable*. But when moral good is imputable to the will and person that causes the good, it is also *praiseworthy* good; it is our reason for praising this person.

885. Thus, properly speaking, *praise* can be given only to a will and person, and in this sense is essentially *personal*. Moreover, in order to be praised, will and person must be the cause of some moral good. Hence, praise is essentially *moral*.

[405] Just as the actions of the lower active principles become *imputable* when the will produces or directs them as first, determinate cause, so these actions, blind and instinctive in themselves, are generally called *willed* and *rational* by earlier thinkers when the actions are considered from the point of view of their natural subordination to will and reason. This observation indicates the way we must understand certain expressions used by authors. At first sight, they seem to confuse animal *instinct* with *will* and *reason* and thus posit in brute-animals powers which are proper only to the human being. St. Thomas speaks expressly about the matter, and even defends Aristotle who sometimes gives the name 'reason' and 'will' to animal feeling and instinct: 'We know that feeling or sense-appetite, IN SO FAR AS IT EXISTS TO OBEY REASON, is called rational by participation, as we see in Aristotle, *Eth.*, I (last chapter). And because will is in reason, we can equally say that feeling is WILL BY PARTICIPATION' (*S.T.*, III, q. 18, art. 2). Again he says: 'The actions of the feeling soul in some way obey reason, and are therefore rational and human in so far as they obey reason' (*S.T.*, III, q. 19, art. 2).

All praise attributed to *things* and not to *persons* is improper. And praise given to persons by any other title than that of their being author and cause of moral good is also improper and unjust.

Article 5.
The difference between *sin* and *fault*

886. Just as moral good is imputed as *praise* to the person who is its cause, so moral evil is imputed as *reproach* to the person who causes it. This constitutes the difference between *sin* and *fault*: every moral evil is called sin; when imputed, it is called 'fault'.

'Just as the notion of *evil* is more extensive than that of *sin*,' St. Thomas says, 'so the notion of *sin* is more extensive than that of *fault*. For an act is said to be culpable or praiseworthy when imputed to the person performing it. To praise or to blame simply means to impute to someone the goodness or malice of his action. But the act is imputed to the agent when he is able to control it; this happens in every voluntary act[406] because a human being controls his actions through his will — only voluntary (*free*)[407] acts of good and evil therefore are subject to

[406] As the context shows, St. Thomas is speaking about will as free. A human being has no mastery to do or omit an action unless his will is in this state.

[407] St. Thomas habitually calls *will* or *willed acts* those alone which he understands as necessarily *free*. This way of expressing himself can cause confusion to inattentive readers, and in fact has caused serious problems for theologians. The difficulty is noticeable in the first article of the second part of his *Summa* which acts as a foundation for the whole moral treatise that follows. Sometimes, in this first article, St. Thomas says simply *will*, but at other times he says (synonymously) *deliberate will*. Thus, he says: 'Only actions under the control of the human being are properly called human. But the human being controls his actions through reason and will.' A little further on, however, he uses the following expressions for the same concept: 'Only actions proceeding from a DELIBERATE WILL are properly called human.' We must not think that he makes no clear distinction between *will* as such and *deliberate will*; he does so very well indeed, attributing to the latter a different act of its own, that is, choice, whereas the more general act of *volition* pertains to the former. St. Thomas' mind, however, is clearly indicated because wherever he uses *will* and *deliberate will* indifferently, the context determines and explains the meaning to be given to each expression in every case.

praise and blame; and in them, evil, sin and fault are the same thing.'[408]

887. Consequently St. Thomas teaches in another place that a sin cannot be imputed as a mortal fault unless in addition to the simple presence of the will, a deliberating will is also present. He says: 'Mortal sin consists in aversion from the final end, which is God. This aversion pertains to deliberating reason, whose function is to order things to their end. Sometimes, however, the soul's inclination to something contrary to the final end is not mortal sin because the *deliberating reason* had no possibility of taking action, as happens in sudden movements.'[409]

Article 6.
Imputability of habits

888. Willem van Est writes: 'Only externally good or evil actions are rewarded or punished by humankind, never good or evil habits hidden in the soul. With God, however, not only internal actions but also habits (which are, AS IT WERE, CONTINUOUS, INTERNAL ACTS) receive their recompense.'[410] We should note that the author is speaking here about habits of the will and moral habits, not about the habits of other powers.

In order that good and evil moral habits may be imputed, therefore, they must be produced by the will and person; nothing can be imputed unless the will or person is the true, first cause of what is imputed.

But the only way the will or person can produce good or evil

Elsewhere he expressly says that just as he considers the intellect and will as a single power, so he considers *will* and *freedom* as acts of the same power (*S.T.*, III, q. 18, arts. 3 and 4, corp.).

408 *S.T.*, I [II]-II, q. 21, art. 2, corp.

409 'Mortal sin, that is, sin imputed as mortal fault, consists in aversion from the final end, which is God. This aversion pertains to deliberating reason, whose function is to order things to their end. Sometimes, however, the soul's inclination to something contrary to the final end is not mortal sin because the deliberating reason had no possibility of taking action, as happens in movements to which the soul is subject' (*S.T.*, I-II, q. 77, art. 8 corp.). [*App.*, no. 12]

410 In II, distinct. 30, §8.

moral habits is by the acts it posits which leave some permanent quality in the soul inclining the soul to good or evil, and giving it a propensity for one or the other. The imputability of these habits therefore must, properly speaking, be referred to the free acts which have produced them. Hence, the moralists' principle that 'the human being neither merits nor demerits by habits.'[411]

889. This kind of habit, which consists solely in some inclination and facility to do good and evil, must be distinguished from another kind, to which, properly speaking, we should apply Willem van Est's opinion that habits somehow have the nature of 'continuous, interior acts'. This kind of habit consists in a firm intention deep in the soul to do good or evil. As long as the intention remains, it is truly a continuous act, and the human being is continually its author and cause.

Habits of this kind, therefore, are not only imputable to the will and person through the first acts by which they come into existence, but of themselves. The will, which could at any time reform them, is continuously their cause if it does not do so.

12

THE UNION OF MORAL AND EUDAIMONOLOGICAL GOOD

Article 1. The ontological law requiring the union of *moral* and *eudaimonological good*

890. An eternal law of justice shines before all intelligences. It decrees that a morally good will should be happy. This law,

[411] Hence, St. Thomas justly considers habits more as *means* of meriting than as merits themselves. He says: 'We are said to merit by something in a twofold way. First, by merit itself, in the way we are said to run by running; in this case we merit by our acts. Second, we are said to merit by something as the principle of meriting, just as we are said to run by motive power; in this case we merit by virtues and habits' (*S.T.*, I-II, q. 55, art. 1, ad. 3).

which is self-evident, is confirmed by an irresistible feeling in our consciousness.

891. But the explanation of the law, which admits of no exception, is complex, and lies hidden amongst the secrets of ontology. It springs from the depths of being, and is one of the laws constituting the *intrinsic order of being*, the first fact in the chain of all facts.

Here, I have no intention of entering these sublime regions, or investigating the deep roots of a law which no one denies or can deny. But I shall make a few observations which, I think, will be quite sufficient to justify the law.[412]

892. First, the person who conforms himself to the law by adherence to and just evaluation of being, acquires from being itself, to which he is joined, an extraordinary value and a wonderful, moral beauty springing from the reflection of virtue in the virtuous soul, and generating an infinite love in those who contemplate it. Plato was speaking of this spiritual beauty when he said that 'if virtue were made visible to our corporeal eyes, it would excite tremendous love and desire'.

893. But sublime, rational, evaluative love, founded in the beauty of virtue and of the virtuous person, implies a desire and wish for every good for this person, and the absence of all evil. This sentiment is aroused in every rational being together with love and esteem.

A virtuous person, endowed therefore with sublime beauty, is worthy of all love, and draws love from every intelligence. Such a person is therefore worthy of all good also; every intelligence desires and wishes every good for this person, and judges it fitting for such a person to be happy. This explains both the feeling of congratulation and approval which spontaneously arises in us every time we see virtue prosper, and our sorrow and painful displeasure, sometimes close to desperation, when we see the just suffer and the wicked at their proud ease amidst great pleasures.

Moral good therefore arouses *love* from intelligence, and love decrees that moral good should be accompanied by *eudaimonological* good. These three realities are united by a very close bond, founded in the essence of things.

894. This bond can be understood more easily if we consider

[412] I dealt with the bond between *moral* and *eudaimonological good* in *Storia comparative de' Sistemi morali*, c. 7, art. 3, §7, to which I refer the reader.

that all intelligent beings, that is, beings which have the nature of end (moral good orginates in and amongst such beings) are destined to be valued and loved reciprocally for what they are, and to communicate themselves mutually to each other with love and knowledge. Happiness, which consists in this intercommunication of intelligences and universal love, means simply enjoyment of the totality of being, which is rooted and consummated in the first, infinite intelligence, God himself. Being virtuous consists simply in contributing one's own part to love, that is, in loving all intelligences, all existing things, according to the intrinsic order of the things themselves. The virtuous person gives all he can of himself to the union and intimate intercommunication of beings, and to the happiness of all. It is therefore just and fitting that he himself share in the bliss and perfection of everything of which he is author, and that he be repaid by the entirety of love, communion and joy to which he adheres.

895. We should note carefully that these reasons which explain and justify the bond between *moral* and *eudaimonological* good apply not only to the moral good imputable to a will or person but to any moral good whatsoever, even if necessary and not free. The lovableness and beauty of such good together with its part in the moral happiness of all is an intrinsic, essential property independent of external considerations. It originates entirely from the will's harmony with the law, that is, from the conformity of the will and person with the eternal order of being which beautifies the soul united to it as the soul immerses itself in it.

Article 2.
Merit

896. If, in addition to moral good, we consider the will or person that causes it, that is, free will producing moral good, the question of *merit* arises.[413]

As we said, moral good is imputed to the will and person. Hence,

[413] Innocent X condemned the following proposition of Jansen (n. 3): 'Merit or demerit in the human being requires only freedom from force, not from necessity, in the state of fallen nature.'

intelligent natures, which are the aim of moral good, are not only naturally and spontaneously inclined to communicate with one another, and enjoy together intelligent being (which communicates itself to them), but to show such being true *gratitude*. This being is seen as freely just and good, something which values and loves them, ready to communicate itself and be united with them.

897. This kind of gratitude, or correspondence of love with love, is founded in *justice*. The person who loves gives of himself, since love is free and proper to the giver. It is therefore *just* that love be restored to the one who gives love, and good be restored to the one who desires and wishes good for others and that in this way the lover should acquire as much from others as he gives of himself.

898. When we discussed moral good without considering free will, the cause of moral good, we saw that the reward of *happiness* for *moral good* must come from the instinct, as it were, of beings, and from the constitutive law of intelligences. If we now consider the *freedom* that caused moral good, we find that *justice* itself decrees the happiness of the virtuous human being. This is the notion of *merit* proper to a person practising virtue.

899. Note, because esteem and love proceed directly from freedom, *merit* is not founded on purely external works but on esteem and love, which are entirely internal.

A virtuous human being can acquire merit from his virtue, therefore, even if it has given no external benefit to intelligent natures, because love is always present, and of itself alone requires love. All possible benefits are found in love, because to love another is to wish all possible good for the other, and to be ready to make every sacrifice for the other.

Consequently, even acts of love that terminate in God have the power to merit from him, in as much as he, beloved and best, does not withdraw but gives and communicates himself to the lover, on whom he bestows reciprocal love. To respond in this way is fully fitting and conformable to the intimate nature of that perfect Being, whose essence is being.

900. Relative to other limited natures, the virtuous person, because his virtue is to their advantage, can merit by bestowing external benefits as well as by showing internal esteem and love.

This is true for intelligent natures whether considered as individuals, or united in societies and bound with mutual ties.

901. It was under this aspect that St. Thomas principally considered the notion of merit:

> The words *merit* and *demerit* express the relationship between action and recompense. Recompense under the title of justice is given to the person who works for the advantage or harm of another.
>
> We must consider that the person living in a society is somehow *part* and *member* of the society itself. To work for or against another in the society is to work for or against the whole society, just as the person who injures a hand has also injured the human being. Working for the good or evil of an individual has *merit* or *demerit* for two reasons. First, because recompense is due from the person who has been helped or offended; and second, because recompense is due from the whole group. On the other hand, a person who directs his act immediately to the group must be recompensed first by the group, and then by the individual parts.
>
> When a person does something to his own advantage or harm, recompense is due to him because his act affects the common good (he himself is part of the group). But in so far as the act is the individual's own, recompense is not due because the individual is himself the agent, unless through some similarity we mean the opposite, as when we speak about justice to ourselves.[414]

Article 3. Recompense

902. Recompense is the *reward* or *punishment* received by the *merit* of virtue or vice.

903. Hence, eudaimonological good or evil, as a *natural consequence* of moral good or evil, must be distinguished from the eudaimonological good or evil required by *imputable* moral good and evil. Only the latter, which proceeds from free will, can, properly speaking, be called *reward* and *punishment*.

904. Every moral good and evil is linked with a eudaimonological

[414] *S.T.*, I-II, q. 21, art. 3, corp.

good or evil; this is a law, we said, arising from the nature of things. But that a person freely doing good be rewarded, and punished for freely doing evil, is a law of personal justice, and has its origin in the eternal norms of what is just and upright.

905. Consequently, the *very nature* of things makes the virtuous person happy in the first case, because the nature of things (considered generally) is ordered intrinsically; no *judgment* is required to decree what recompense must be given to the virtuous or evil person.

In the second case, however, we are dealing with the application of reward and punishment according to the norms of personal justice. This always requires and presupposes the intervention of a *judge*, because the general norms of what is just and upright must be applied to the will and person as the free cause of the good and evil. This application must result in an acknowledgement of merit or demerit, followed by the decree of recompense and the application of reward or punishment.

* * * * *

CONCLUSION

906. All we have said in this work shows that the many elements composing human nature together form a perfect unity. Everything in the human being is interconnected and tends to a single end. Matter is pervaded by animal feeling, which seeks to control matter completely; instinct begins and continues in feeling; the unity of instinct constitutes the individual.

But superior to animal feeling is a greater principle, intuiting ideal being and destined to govern feeling totally. This subjective principle reveals itself as reason and will. A person now exists, and expresses the primacy of all rational activities.

This person is itself governed by ideological and physical laws which have their origin in the intrinsic order of ideal and real being. The laws emanating from real being have a determined relationship with those emanating from ideal being; this gives rise to morality. Through this relationship the person becomes moral and enters the sphere of things which partake of the infinite and acquire an infinite value.

But the subject principle does not allow itself to be governed entirely by these laws, nor does it necessarily preserve their natural relationship. It either withdraws from them or freely submits to them. Hence, freedom, a new form of activity, in which is found the pinnacle of human nature as potential nature (but not its full actuation).

This activity, greatly superior to all the others, cannot be considered simply in itself; it must also be considered in its act, together with the extraordinary effects of its act. Through this act the human being *merits*, and spontaneously moves to unite himself to all beings and to the source of beings, loving them all and receiving love from them all. He gives of himself to all beings, and they give of themselves to him. He thus widens his own limits, bringing his restricted, deficient nature to completion. A tiny part of being, he enjoys not himself alone but all entities, and in the expanse of essential being finds and receives his own happiness, a moral happiness which he can no longer refuse, a good he cannot lose. Such is the end of human beings, the noblest end of *person*, and hence, the end of human nature. This communication and mutual society of beings with the being of beings and between themselves is the end of the universe.

Appendix

1. (7).

In industry experience has shown that the division of work is very helpful, because each part can stand on its own. For example, a person who works in a factory producing sewing accessories and is employed in putting the point on needles, does not need to know how to make the eye; this can be done by someone else. We become more skilled and attentive in proportion to the simplicity of the task assigned to us. Contemporary society, occupied in mind and spirit by material things, thinks that *sciences* follow the same law as *industry*, and so divides the sciences into tiny parts.

The Encyclopedia came into being under the influence of this impoverished way of thinking. A Scottish philosopher, Reid, founder of the philosophy school of Glasgow, speaks of the categories of Aristotle in this way: 'Of all methods of arrangement, the most anti-philosophical seems to be the invention of this age; I mean arranging the arts and sciences by the letters of the alphabet, in dictionaries and encyclopedias. With these authors, the categories are A, B, C, etc.' (cf. *A brief account of Aristotle's logic* by this author, published in *Sketches of the History of Man* by Lord Kames in 1773).

I do not deny that scientific dictionaries can render some service; I am indicating only the vainglory of those who pride themselves on knowledge restricted solely to dictionaries.

The harm done to science and morality by the fragmentation of knowledge is incredible. People who attend German universities can testify to the harm done to the behaviour of the young by the separation of *natural law* from *ethics* in teaching, without any regard to the intimate connection between the two. The last century, for example, was spent in discussing human *rights* but forgot human *duties*. Such presumption greatly furthered the division of law from ethics, which enabled the human being to receive from everybody and give to nobody.

A famous professor of public law (K. L. Haller) ably demonstrates the harm caused to the state by the excessive divisions introduced into *political science*. Sometimes the material and corporeal harm resulting from excessive division of the sciences has recalled us to our senses, as in the case of the separation of medicine from surgery. Outstanding people, like Stahl (*De medicinae et chirurgiae perpetuo nexu*, Regiomont, 1705), Heister (*De chirurgiae cum medicina necessitate*, Hamstel, 1732), and J. P. Frank (*De chirurgo medicis auxiliis indigente*, in t. 4 of his *Delectus opusculorum etc.*) have spoken out against the evil brought upon humanity by these divisions. But what can be said about the sciences needed by doctors of souls? The Church's pastors are responsible for considering how much harm has been caused to the education of the clergy by the divisions, limitations and restrictions forced upon *theological studies* under the pretext of piety and reforms required in seminary studies.

2. (82).

It will be helpful to point out another error resulting from the analogical use of *life*. The meaning of the word *life* (and the adjective *living* or *vital*) was not restricted to 'that which feels'; it also meant 'that which causes feeling'. *Vital* was used of colour: for example, a vital red, a vital green. *Living* was used of fire: for example, a living fire. It was also applied to what moves or seems to move of itself, as in the expressions 'living water', 'a living spring' — Politian said:

> 'Through the living, gentle crystal
> swim the silent fish together.'

The change in the meaning of *living* from 'that which feels, and feeling, moves' to 'that which causes feeling and seems to move of itself' is an ordinary example of *synecdoche*, a figure of speech originating from a failure to distinguish ideas properly. In this change of meaning, we see that: 1. life as such has been confused with what is permanently joined with life as its condition and even with the *material cause* of life; and that 2. the *sign* normally indicating life is confused with what is signified.

After these changes in the meaning of the word *life*, human intelligence was unable to withstrain itself. If the word *life* is predicated of a certain disposition of parts and of certain movements, the same word can just as easily be given to any disposition of parts and to any movement. We could call life the *force* that causes the movements of an object and arranges the parts composing it. Indeed, the phrase *living forces* and *dead forces* was a wider application of *life*. Consequently, we find ourselves saying that all forces are *living* when they cause motion. This is so true that modern naturalists are convinced they have made a great discovery, and proclaim all forces, even those thought of as merely material, as *living* forces. Ranzani explains their reasoning: for them 'life is an internal activity, but wherever a force acts, an internal activity exists. Therefore wherever a force acts, life exists. And because all the beings studied in natural history are undoubtedly endowed with active forces, they conclude that all such beings are certainly living beings'. But here, one mistake follows another. After extending the meaning of *life* so that it is equivalent to *force*, and concluding that all things live, they stretch the meaning still further by saying that all things *feel*. In this way physiologists introduce us to a new kind of *sensitivity*. But *this capacity for feeling* feels nothing; it is called 'feeling' because it moves under material stimuli.

Physiologists, having confused this new sensitivity, which does not in fact feel but gives signs of movement, with real sensitivity which does feel, now go on to claim that the two do not differ essentially (cf. 87–91). This great confusion of ideas led some materialists, after the publication of Albert Haller's well-known observations on the irritable and sensitive parts of the human body, to believe they could found their system on irritability. But scientists who understood the matter correctly, reacted against this theory. One of these, Delius, professor at Erlang (cf. *Animadversiones in doctrinam de irritabilitate, tono, sensatione, et motu corporis humani*), had to defend Haller's theory from the imputation of material feeling (cf. Tissot's *Discours préliminaire* at the beginning of his French translation of Haller's Dissertation).

3. (91).

Scarpa, in his work on the structure of bones, reports some experiments on the sensitivity of diseased bones and of the *caruncle* to which caustics have been applied. The Florentine anatomist, Felice Fontana, offered some explanations for the phenomenon in a letter of September 8th. 1801. He firmly maintained that 'only the nerves feel'. Scarpa was of the same opinion, but thought that bones could contain extremely fine nerves. Fontana rejected this, suggesting that the movement was communicated to the neighbouring nerves. He says:

> I do not deny what you have observed, but I wish to offer some observations I have frequently made, and recently confirmed after experiments on two dogs.
>
> I have often seen the cranium of animals, and even of human beings, being drilled. If the animal was calm, and felt nothing else, it showed no feeling, but at other times, it frequently showed very acute pain. If the wounds festered and were touched, or caustics applied, pain was clearly visible. This great difference, it seems to me, would be impossible if there were nerves in the bones, because nerves would give constant signs of feeling in response to the caustic, and especially to the drill.
>
> Colic once made the lower part of my stomach painfully sensitive to the lightest touch; even a movement of the hair caused pain, but the pain was in my skin, not the hair. An inflamed finger was very painful and I could not bear the nail being touched, although the nail itself was insensitive to caustic if applied gently. When nerves are struck, they can have an almost infinite sensibility: the pain in a tooth or its nerve can become unbearable; even a draught can cause toothache. A tap on an animal's bones or the vessels joined to the bones, which are more abundant and exposed in the *caruncle* you examined, can spread and be felt in nerves whose sensitivity is heightened by illness. I even believe it possible that when the fluid in the vessels stops flowing, or oscillates slightly, the adjacent nerves feel.

> Consequently, what we think is feeling in the bones attached to the tendons is only the action of the neighbouring nerve made more sensitive by illness. The same happens when something caustic restricts the flow of blood.

He suggests that according to his careful experiments the pain could be communicated to the nerves by the dispersion of the fluid which, he maintains, fills the *elementary nerve canals*. These experiments are discussed by Smit in his work 'On the digestive force of all the wounded parts of the animal body'.

I do not know if the letter has ever been published, but I possess a signed copy of it annotated by the author.

4. (149).

G. B. Venturi, who is to be the more admired because he wrote when the school of Locke held sway (1784–1801), clearly saw that a *fundamental feeling* must precede all acquired sensations. While Venturi, Araldi and other great Italians quietly pursued their investigations, their voices were drowned by those who swore 'on the words of the master'. But the Italians' writings have survived to the great credit of their authors. Let me use Venturi's authority to confirm what I have said about the existence of an animal feeling anterior to all sensations:

> Even before our vast nervous system is touched by the outside world, it apparently feels in every part an empty, vague, infinite *extension* in which all sensations arise, are divided and come to rest. *Space* seems to be the fundamental human sensation, and according to Kant, *a priori* knowledge. This sensation does not begin to exist as a result of metaphysical reflection on the order of co-existent things; it witnessed the first spark of existence in us and could perhaps have claimed innate dignity if Locke's cruel decree had not condemned innate ideas.
>
> The internal pressure of all the parts of our body on our nerves, without the action of external bodies, is alone sufficient to create the idea of the confused, indefinite and immense space our spirit experiences as we fall asleep or faint. We must not be surprised therefore if to the human imagination the most assertive and consistent of all ideas is that of *extension*. All the ideas of the physical world rest

> upon it and all the wonders of artificial memory spring from it; all philosophical dreams begin and end with it. Extension is the dark, interminable spirit and the black chaos described in all *Cosmogonies* of history. It is that pure emptiness which, once entered by the ecstatic mind of the contemplating Brahmin, leads him to believe that he is blessed and holy. For Descartes, it forms the substance of bodies; for Spinoza, it is God. It is the primitive foundation on which we have built all our ideas, the cloth woven by the contribution of each of our senses. The senses of sight and touch have delineated forms and shapes because they are appropriately equipped. But taste, smell and hearing which lack such forms place their objects in space only in a vague, imperfect way, until helped and taught by sight and touch (*Riflessioni sulla conoscenza dello spazio, che noi possiamo ricavar dall'udito*, at the end of *Indagine fisica sui colori, coronata dalla Società Italiana*, 2nd. edition, Modena, 10th year of the Republic (1801)).

The following observations are not intended to detract in any way from this admirable passage of Venturi: 1. What he says about Kant's form of external sense is inaccurate. Although the form endows acquired sensations with space, it does not suppose any preceding feeling. However, we must bear in mind that at the time Venturi was writing, Kant's teaching was almost unknown in Italy. 2. Extension, as a *mode of feeling* (*real extension*), is not to be confused with the *idea* of extension (*ideal extension*). 3. Extension is in no way the foundation of our ideas, because it is found in *feeling*, which cannot be confused with *ideas*. However it is an element in the *matter* of all the natural knowledge we have in this life.

5. (289).

Gallini says:

> I begin with the simple, incontrovertible fact that the elements composing many of the simple structures, although they gravitate to each other, are generally mobile and therefore changeable in their mutual positions and proportion. We do not need a hypothesis either to conceive the nature of the impression or action of all the agents which these structures exhibit in their own action, or to understand

how and why the impression is transmitted at different speeds along the nerves, muscle fibres and membranes to a section of cellulose material in order to set the whole of a part, and even many parts, into immediate, simultaneous action. The impression consists in the change of mutual position or proportion of the elements of living molecules as a result of any imperceptible impulse or attraction produced by stimuli. The speedy diffusion depends on the change in position or proportion of the elements of the first molecule so that it acts differently from the molecule adhering to it. And this action not only produces a similar or corresponding change in the elements of the adjacent molecule; it also changes the degree of its adherence. If, then, an interval elapses before the molecules return to their former state, an alternating contraction and dilation of volume is visible, as in the case of muscles, membranes and cellulose formations. On the other hand, if the molecules return instantaneously, the diffusion of the impression can be judged only from the corresponding sensation, or from the contraction and dilation produced in distant parts by the cause of the impression, as in the case of the nerves.

If we compare all the prominent properties of simple structures we find that just as the first three properties (hardness, elasticity and flexibility) are different gradations of a force dependent on the preponderant reciprocal gravitation of the elements, the other properties (sensibility, irritability, contractility and dilation) are different gradations of a force dependent on the preponderant mobility of the elements. In this case, however, the elements maintain their reciprocal gravitation not only by forming a solid structure but also by returning promptly to their former state.

The second force is exclusively present to living bodies for the duration of their life. The living animal fibres and molecules of an organic body differ only in the following respect from fibres and molecules that do not have, and have never had life: the first are easily impressionable and return promptly to their position after an impression, whether this is received directly from external bodies or indirectly from the impression of adjacent molecules; the others, which are forced to change the position and proportion of their elements (in which I said an impression consists) form new molecules, and do not return their elements to their former position and proportion.

All the vital phenomena, therefore, which the Padua professor accurately explains and describes, obviously result from an aggregate of molecules, and from their mutual relationship. He makes no mention of the primitive elements taken individually, which escape all observation. Hence, although he regards life as a characteristic of the first matter of bodies, his opinion accords with what we are saying if this corporeal matter of his is supposed structured and organised. For we also say that, 'although life is experienced only in an aggregate of molecules, it affects and invests basic matter, the simplest elements'. This affirmation does not exceed the limits of research supported by careful reflection. Experience gives us the first part of the proposition, because life is manifested directly only in certain structures and organs, while all its observable phenomena are presented in bodies resulting from many molecules harmoniously united. The conclusion found in the second part is obtained from a sound, attentive reflection on the fact supplied by research, namely, that life extends even to the elements because life and sensitivity would apparently be impossible if a life principle were absent from the inner recesses of the indivisible particles which compose the structures and organs (cf. *OT*, 846–870).

6. (302).

Physiologists (who have thought up some ingenious theories about life) have not kept to the core-subject of their investigations, namely, the phenomenon of feeling, which constitutes the essential difference between *animality* and *matter*. Their concept of life, as I have already shown (cf. 61 ss.), gives too much importance to *extrasubjective* phenomena and too little to *subjective*. For example, nothing could be more ingenious and novel than Forni's *Biologia*, but unfortunately the whole work is founded on the reduction of all life functions to *assimilation* and *non-assimilation*. These phenomena, although complex and important, always remain *extrasubjective*. Consequently, everything subjective, which properly constitutes animal essence, is completely excluded and forgotten. The two functions, together with all other extrasubjective phenomena, should have been considered solely in their relationship to *feeling*, which is the form of the animal and the end to which all its other functions are ordered. Forni's desire for a theory of life lacks a base, and we should not be surprised if the whole of his ingenious theory leads nowhere.

The theory supposes a universal fluid diffused by nature, and a life fluid which exists as a modification of the universal fluid. This vital fluid organises matter, and is thought to be composed of heat, oxygen and light. Life, a function of this fluid, is simply combustion.

Leaving aside the novelty of the theory, and the innumerable hypotheses contained in so few words, I simply state that, granted the existence of a life fluid, we need to know 1. 'the relationship of this fluid with FEELING', and 2. 'if this fluid is the immediate term of feeling itself'. These questions must be discussed first; only then can we decide whether the word 'life' can be applied to the life fluid. The composition and decomposition of the fluid, its properties similar or analogous to those of other weightless fluids, combustion (if this is one of its functions) and its other external functions are only findings which reveal the *extrasubjective* properties of the fluid; they cannot make known its internal properties, which alone, properly speaking, render it living.

I say this, bearing in mind the respect due to these great men for seeking to open new roads to knowledge.

7. (428).

It is undeniable that, in feeling, a succession of acts often constitutes a single, simple sensation. We have to apply to this fact what was said about the sensation we have of anything extended, that is, the sensation is felt by a simple feeling principle. The two facts — that a simple principle feels *space*, which is extended, and *time*, which is successive — although wonderful and mysterious, are nevertheless equally necessary and certain. As we have said, space, which is extended and continuous, can exist only in that which is simple. Space presupposes the simultaneous presence, unity and contiguity of all its parts, none of which, however, taken individually can explain the unity and contiguity of the whole. In the same way, the succession of facts (time), can exist only in that which in itself is one and simple. None of the facts taken separately provides sufficient explanation for the total succession. The explanation can be found only in a being to which all the facts can be simultaneously present, although it sees them as distinct by the way in which they exist antecedently to one another. The *feeling principle*, therefore, in uniting itself to *what is felt*, truly becomes the fount of space and time. We could accept Kant's affirmations if this were his sole meaning when he spoke of space as the *form of the external sense* and of time as the *form of the internal sense*, . But these forms are absurd when they are understood as proceeding from the soul alone (cf. 181), which certainly cannot possess them in itself. They arise rather from *that which is felt* when it comes in contact, as it were, with the soul.

But we must go back to the special fact indicated to us in succession itself, where several acts or facts are perceived by the feeling principle in a single, undivided feeling.

This marvellous truth offers a key to innumerable animal phenomena which would otherwise remain totally unexplained. For example, if every feeling has corresponding movements, and if several contemporaneous or successive acts can be felt with a single feeling, it follows: 1. that an animal which feels simultaneous acts in a single feeling will be able to produce with a single corresponding act many simultaneous movements; 2. that an animal which feels successive acts in a single feeling will be able to produce in a single, simple, corresponding act many successive movements.

This last corollary explains many complex acts which, although attributed to habit, depend in fact upon such a law. Let us take memory as our first example. How is it possible to repeat with such ease something that has been learned by heart, and roll it off our tongue without paying scarcely any attention to what we are saying? Learning by heart means simply uniting in *a single*, internal *feeling* a *succession* of vocal sounds. Once the union has been established, one act alone from that individual feeling is sufficient to produce the successive movements of the speech organs, and to explain the ease with which a long discourse can be repeated without need for attention to its individual words or parts. These no longer exist separately, but in the whole. This can be ascertained by noting that the same words cannot be repeated if their order is inverted. The object of the memory, therefore, is not the parts or the individual words, but their *succession*. If the order is inverted, a new succession is produced which is as yet unformed in the spirit. Although the same words are used, they are not unified in feeling.

Single words are repeated as a result of single acts, but joined words form only one act. Each arrangement of words requires new *unification* in feeling, and a different, corresponding complex act when the arrangement is repeated out loud.

It may be objected that memory belongs to the intellective, not to the feeling, order. This is true, of course, but the law that we have indicated, to which memory is subject, depends on the imagination's suggesting sounds to the memory. And the imagination is a kind of animal feeling.

Similar acts are found in a pianist or a dancer, for example. Playing the piano or dancing is simply a succession of movements carried out by the hands or the legs easily and promptly, and without reflection. The pianist or the dancer could not possibly produce an individual act for every movement of hand or foot; renewed attention to every movement would destroy all hope of uninterrupted progress. A single act of the will, therefore, orders the whole series of the varied movements by directing the series as though it were a single movement. The will is not applied to each individual movement. But the unity of this single, internal act and command embracing the whole series of movements can only be imagined on the presupposition that all the movements have already been perceived together and united in a single feeling through the *unitive force* of the animal. This single feeling produces a single act of instinct which is then permitted by the will to operate. This is the source of the explanation of innumerable complex facts which animals manifest in their way of acting.

8. (602).

This is the famous question of help 'without which' (*sine quo*) and help 'with which' (*quo*). St. Augustine says that the first human being was helped by a kind of grace *without which* he could not desire good. It was a condition necessary for making his will capable of good. He says that much more was given to human beings redeemed by the Saviour, that is, they receive a kind of grace *with which* they desire good. This help is a sufficient, full cause for producing good will in us. 'Thus the aids must be distinguished. One is a help *without which* nothing is done; the other a help *with which* something is done' (*L. de corrept. et gratia*, c. 12). The first is that given to Adam; the second, to Christians. 'The first (grace) is that by which a human being may have justice if he will. The second does more and enables him to will.' (*Ibid.*, c. 11). Note that according to Augustine the grace of the Redeemer is that 'which enables a human being to will', but he never says that its effect is such that 'a human being must will', that he 'necessarily wills'.

There is a great difference between these two ways of speaking. To say that grace is the kind of energy 'with which a human being may will' indicates only that it is a sufficient, full cause capable of moving his will; it does not indicate that the will itself is unable to resist the grace, which would be the case if we said 'so that a human being must will' or 'so that he wills necessarily'. For example, to say that the human will is that with which we move our feet when walking does not mean that moving feet and walking is such an absolutely necessary effect that our feet cannot be stopped by a cause different from our will. It means simply that our will, if it is not impeded, is the sufficient, full cause of moving our feet.

It is in fact a dogma proclaimed by the Church that the grace of Christ is sufficient for saving us, and rendering our will completely good; it is sufficient for us to be rendered capable of willing good. The Church teaches precisely this when she says that the sacraments effect salvation in us *ex opere operato*. Although the effect of sacramental grace is absolute, full, independent of, and superior to our will because sacramental grace clothes the will itself with holiness and justice, this does not mean that we cannot place an obstacle to the grace of the sacraments. The one does not destroy the other. The power of the sacrament on our spirit, therefore, remains complete although we can still obstruct its effect. This does not mean that

I deny extraordinary cases where grace has triumphed, nor that the merit of some saints has been unable to obtain for them confirmation in grace even in the present life.

Finally I think the problem of the *gift of perseverance* must be distinguished from the problem of assistance in general. Perseverance can be brought about in two ways, not in one only: either through confirmation in grace, or by the foreknowledge with which God sees that a human being will not resist the effect of divine grace which in itself is certain and full.

9. (fn. 347).

The observation I have made about brute matter, whose concept implies an essential relationship with feeling, explains many philosophical opinions and errors. As far as I know, philosophers did not clearly see that there is a concomitant, relative, conceptual mode of being. Hence the invention of false systems to explain the reality of matter. There are basically three of these systems: the first simply says that matter is inexplicable and unintelligible; the second (idealism) denies outright the existence of matter (it causes too much trouble in philosophy); the third confuses matter with feeling, giving matter the attributes of feeling or even of intelligence, that is, it makes matter itself feeling and intelligent.

The first system, that of Plato and Aristotle, contains some truth, as Plato understood it. According to him, matter is not intelligible through itself but only through the light of the mind. Aristotle on the other hand favoured dividing matter from all its forms and making it an abstraction. But this abstract being, which in reality is nothing, is therefore truly unintelligible. The question under discussion does not concern abstract matter but inanimate, real matter, lacking only the form of feeling.

The second system, idealism, did not begin with Berkeley; it has always been present wherever philosophy has been pursued. In India the Bracmans, or Brahmins as they are now called, teach that the material world is simply an illusion, a dream or magical deception. Bodies, to exist in reality, would have to cease to exist in themselves and be absorbed into that which is nothing (properly speaking, this *nothing* is the *idea*) which through its simplicity forms the perfection of all beings (cf. *Brahmins* in Naigeon's *Enciclop. Method. Philos. anc. et mod.*).

The third system has been repeated many times. It took various forms, for example, the soul of the world. Another form, similar to idealism, is the Platonists' teaching that our souls made our bodies (cf. Macrob. *Somn., Scip.*, bk. 1, c. 6, 14 and 17; bk. 2, c. 3; also Huet, *QQ Alnet.*, bk. 2, c. 8). A third form is T. Campanella's system: in his well-known book *De sensu rerum et magia* he attributes feeling to all bodies: 'We cannot give to another what we do not have in ourselves. Hence, all that is contained in an effect must also be found in the cause. Animals have feeling, but because feeling does not come from nothing, we must conclude that the elements, the constitutive principles of the animal, also have feeling. The animal therefore feels heaven and earth.' These ideas of Campanella seem to have led Leibniz to his two systems of *monads* and the *minute immortal animal.* A legitimate offspring of this is the tiny ethereal body which, according to Bonnet's presupposition, perpetually envelops souls.

All these systems are clearly exaggerated. The most we can say about matter is that 1. it has real existence, 2. its real mode of being is concomitant with the existence of feeling, 3. its conceptual mode of being (the concept we have of it) logically implies an essential relationship with feeling. To go further would be to transcend the limits of the question; it would mean that inadvertently we were speaking about the *corporeal principle* or the *cause of matter*, rather than about matter itself and its concept (in the way we actually possess it).

10. (785).

Generally speaking, St. Thomas teaches that 'every SUBSISTENT thing is only one in number'. We can see this by comparing the following places of the *Summa*: I, q. 11, arts. 3 and 4, corp; q. 44, art. 1, corp; q. 75, art. 7, corp. For us what is *subsistent* and what is real are the same. In St. Thomas, we must distinguish the places where he is restricted to using accepted aristotelian language from the places where he speaks and thinks for himself. In the latter he manifests his genius and his own sureness of touch. It is not surprising, therefore, that opposing views are sometimes to be found in St. Thomas, the philosopher of the Schools and the original thinker. For example, in one place St. Thomas makes the following statement about the individuation under discussion: 'Substance . . . is individuated of itself, but accidents are individuated by the subject, which is substance' (*S.T.*, I, q. 29, art. 1, corp). This is the original thinker speaking, and if we understand *substance* as *subsistence, reality*, the statement exactly expresses our opinion. But we cannot deny that it seems very difficult to reconcile this statement of St. Thomas with the aristotelian statement, often found in his works, that 'matter is the principle of individuation'. Matter is said to be the principle of individuation only because matter is considered as the source of the accidents, which terminate and complete the subject. Hence the statement that 'an individual composed of matter and form subsists, relative to an accident, in dependence on matter'. St. Thomas teaches this (*S.T.*, I, q. 29, art. 2, ad 5) on the authority of a famous commentator of Aristotle (Boethius, *De Trin.*, 2). But if matter is both that which permits the subject to subsist relative to the accidents, and the principle of individuation, the accidents would individuate the subject, which is contrary to the earlier statement that 'accidents are individuated by the subject'. This is at least an apparent contradiction. However, the two statements can be reconciled by limiting both of them. The *act of reality* or subsistence in all real, subsistent beings is that which individuates them. But material, corporeal feeling does not *subsist* without matter. Thus, it is matter that makes this feeling subsist, drawing it to its determining substance, as we have explained. Matter, therefore, can be called the principle of individuation in that feeling.

11. (796).

We must note a progression of errors in sensist thinkers:

1st. They began by establishing that all the objects of our thoughts can be reduced *to acquired sensations*.

2nd. Following this principle, Condillac correctly concluded that Locke had not gone far enough in affirming the non-existence of all *innate ideas*; indeed, he should have said there were no *innate faculties* either.

3rd. But Condillac's observation only took the system a step further. If sensism was to be logical, it could not limit itself to the denial of ideas and innate faculties; it should have said that not even an innate human *spirit* existed. And clearly, if all feelings are reduced to acquired sensations, human beings had to acquire the human spirit. Helvetius drew the same conclusion: 'The spirit,' he writes, 'is only the complex of our ideas. According to Locke, our ideas come from the senses, and we can conclude from this principle and from mine that the human spirit is simply an *acquisition*' (*Récapitulation de l'Homme*, Sect. 2, c. 1). This was the opinion in France. Italy, although endowed with great clarity and nobility of intelligence and called by Providence to think for itself and be a master of truth, was for a long time satisfied to regurgitate the errors of other nations. We have heard Helvetius' opinion re-echoed in Gioia, who writes in his elements of Philosophy: 'The whole of our existence is simply a continual movement of sensations' (*Elem. di Filosofia ad uso de' Giovanetti*, t. 1, p. 140, Milan edition, 1822). Foscoli also repeats the opinion, transforming the error into a basic theory of literature. Many other Italians have repeated the opinion, but less boldly.

4th. The spirit, that is, the human soul, is therefore an acquisition. But if it is only a complex of acquired sensations, what gives it unity? — We would have to say that there are as many souls as there are sensations or, as sensists call them, ideas. Such a necessary consequence did not escape Hume in his dialectic; he dissolved the human spirit into many unconnected ideas without a subject, as we can see in his writings on *Human Nature*. Such in fact is the final development of the sensist theory: the abolition of the *human subject* and the abandonment of acquired ideas, left to drift in an limitless sea! Hume's teaching, which turns the soul into ideas, is exactly the opposite of the Platonists' error, which turns ideas into souls (into a subject) (cf. Plato's *Parmenides* and Ficino's explanation of the dialogue).

Considering all these errors we note: 1. the usual partial view proper to sensism that cannot see further than the feeling or animal part of the human being; 2. the imperfection of such an observation limited even to animality — the observation concerns only multiple, *acquired sensations* without arriving at the unique *fundamental feeling*, of which the acquired sensations are only modifications. As we said from the beginning the animal feels the unity of its own feeling. In this feeling, it feels passivity and activity and that first energy which virtually includes all sensations and actions subsequent to the feeling. These sensations and experiences proceed from a single, active principle which produces and governs them with a single, harmonious authority.

12. (fn. 409).

It must be noted that here St. Thomas is speaking about a formal action, an *inclination of the soul*, not a material action. He means an *inclination of the will* because, as he teaches, it is the will that inclines the soul. Such a sin, however, is not imputable as mortal fault, although the will is certainly present. We have noted that according to St. Thomas the soul acts only with the power of the will. But freedom, the *deliberating reason*, is lacking. The imputability of actions as fault, therefore, depends on freedom, not simply on the will. Freedom, according to St. Thomas' way of expressing himself, makes *perfect* what is *willed*, or fully possesses the nature of what is willed. Hence, the Saint teaches that praise and blame are not united to any willed act whatsoever, but solely to the act which has fully the nature of that which is willed: 'Praise and blame (or fault) follow a willed act according to the full nature of what is willed' (*S.T.*, I-II, q. 6, art. 2, ad 3). These words need to be correctly understood; if they are interpreted contrary to the author's mind, they have a false, harmful sense. It will be helpful therefore if I add and explain the words that follow this last quotation. He continues by establishing the nature of the *perfect willingness* of an act. For him it exists when the principle of the act is from within and accompanied by perfect knowledge of the end: 'Perfect knowledge of the end is present not only when we know what the end is, but when we know also the reason why the thing is an end, and the proportion between the end and the action ordered to the end' (*ibid.*). Perfect knowledge of the proportion between the end and the action is possible only if the human being knows or compares both the action and omission of the action with its end. He may then see the good of doing or omitting the action in such a practical way that he has time to deliberate and choose. Purely speculative knowledge of the end and means is possessed even by those in heaven and hell, but, as the Saint says, they have no capacity to merit or demerit. Hence, we have to maintain that in order to receive praise or blame, in the strict, correct sense, the human being needs more than knowledge and will in a general sense; a *deliberating* will (as the Saint calls it) is required. 'In this way,' he says, 'the human being is master of his acts and can deliberate about them. When the deliberating reason is faced with two opposites, the will can decide *for one or the other*' (*S.T.*, I-II, q. 6, art. 2, ad 2).

Index of Biblical References

Numbers in romans indicate paragraphs; numbers in italics indicate footnotes. Bible references are from RSV (Common Bible) unless marked †. In these cases, where the author's use of Scripture is dependent solely upon the Vulgate, the Douai version is used.

Index of Persons

Numbers in romans indicate paragraphs or, where stated, the appendix (app.); numbers in italics indicate footnotes.

General Index

Numbers in romans indicate paragraphs or, where stated, the appendix (app.); numbers in italics indicate footnotes.